After the Third World?

The emergence of the 'Third World' is generally traced to the onset of the Cold War and decolonization in the 1940s and 1950s. In the 1960s and 1970s the "three worlds of development" were central to the wider dynamics of the changing international order. By the 1980s, Third Worldism had peaked entering a period of dramatic decline that paralleled the end of the Cold War. Into the 21st century, the idea of a Third World and even the pursuit of some form of Third Worldism has continued to be advocated and debated. For some it has passed into history, and may never have had as much substance as it was credited with, while others seek to retain or recuperate the Third World and give Third Worldism contemporary relevance. Beginning with a comprehensive introduction this edited volume brings together a wide range of important contributions. Collectively they offer a powerful overview from a variety of angles of the history and contemporary significance of Third Worldism in international affairs. The question remains; did the Third World exist, what was it, does it still have intellectual and political purchase or do we live in a global era that can be described as After the Third World?

This book was previously published as a special issue of *Third World Quarterly*.

Mark T. Berger has been Visiting Professor in the Department of Defense Analysis at the Naval Postgraduate School (Monterey, California) since July 2006. He has published over 70 articles in international journals and chapters in edited books. He is the author of *The Battle for Asia: From Decolonization to Globalization* (2004) and *The American Ascendancy and After: Empires, Nation-States and Changing Global Orders* (2009: forthcoming). He is also editor of *From Nation-Building to State-Building* (2007) and co-author of *Rethinking the Third World: International Development and World Politics* (2009; forthcoming).

Third World Quarterly

Edited by Shahid Qadir, *University of London*

THIRDWORLDS will focus on the political economy, development and cultures of those parts of the world that have experienced the most political, social, and economic upheaval, and which have faced the greatest challenges of the postcolonial world under globalisation: poverty, displacement and diaspora, environmental degradation, human and civil rights abuses, war, hunger, and disease.

THIRDWORLDS serves as a signifier of oppositional emerging economies and cultures ranging from Africa, Asia, Latin America, Middle East, and even those 'Souths' within a larger perceived North, such as the U.S. South and Mediterranean Europe. The study of these otherwise disparate and discontinuous areas, known collectively as the Global South, demonstrates that as globalisation pervades the planet, the south, as a synonym for subalterity, also transcends geographical and ideological frontiers.

After the Third World?

Edited by Mark T. Berger

Routledge
Taylor & Francis Group

LONDON AND NEW YORK

First published 2009 by Routledge
2 Park Square, Milton Park, Abingdon, Oxfordshire OX14 4RN

Simultaneously published in the USA and Canada
by Routledge
711 Third Avenue, New York, NY 10017, USA

First issued in paperback 2014

Routledge is an imprint of the Taylor & Francis Group, an informa business

Typeset in Times by Value Chain, India

British Library Cataloguing in Publication Data
A catalogue record for this book is available from the British Library

ISBN 13: 978-1-138-87479-4 (pbk)
ISBN 13: 978-0-415-46637-0 (hbk)

Dedicated to the memory of Edward W. Said (1935–2003)

In Memoriam

When Edward Said died on 25 September I lost a close and beloved friend, and the world lost a powerful and distinctive presence, one of a handful of public intellectuals whose words literally resonated throughout the planet. Edward was an eloquent, imaginative and highly influential voice on behalf of the Palestinian people, but he was also a most gifted interpreter of the interface between culture and politics, especially in the context of the imperial relationship between the West and the world. His 1978 book *Orientalism* is as widely read and discussed as any single book written in the past several decades, brilliantly accounting for the distorted renderings of the Arab world by Western colonial and post-colonial scholars, and indeed, depicting a whole way of misrepresenting that has lethal consequences when enacted in political action. Said's illuminating critique of how to not see 'the other' remains of acute relevance, especially during these days of US military pre-eminence and expansionist ambitions. Never has our citizenry and leadership been more in need of 'self-scrutiny', beginning with the challenge of listening closely to those others whom we seek to subjugate by force of arms.

The originality of Edward Said cannot be separated from his life and work. Perhaps, alone among world class scholars and intellectual figures, Edward as a Palestinian living in the United States was able to express both the reality of Palestinian victimisation and the dangerous reality of the US with its self-anointed mandate to rule the world. His experience and insight were deeply affected by this interplay between a dual identity as a Palestinian 'out of place' (as suggested by the title of his autobiography) and as a widely admired American professor of comparative literature at a leading university, but in fundamental respects, also out of place.

Those of us who had known Edward for a long time were deeply moved by his brave struggle against leukemia for an anguishing period of 12 years. During these years, despite many torments, Edward sustained his struggle and continued to write at a furious pace, and to travel around the world giving lectures to overflowing lecture halls. Periods of exertion alternated with periods of relapse, the disease retreating and advancing in sinister fashion. Toward the end of his life, when asked how he was doing, he would often respond, 'It is my anger that keeps me going'.

It would be a mistake to think of Edward only as an exceptional literary scholar or eloquent advocate of Palestinian rights and critic of Israeli and American wrongs. He was, above all, a complete human being, with a range of talents and appetites, and frailties. I heard him perform as a classical pianist at a wonderful concert given at Columbia University. Edward served for many years as the music critic of *The Nation*, and was especially appreciated for published commentaries on opera. He was a talented squash and tennis player as I discovered to my despair. Edward cared about all facets of life, valuing friendship, collecting fancy pens, delighting in gourmet food and indulging in playful banter. It was always hard for me to comprehend how one person could be so accomplished in so many different domains. Edward's son, Wadie, delivering the eulogy at his father's funeral noted that he never understood how his father managed to write so much because he always seemed to be talking on the phone. It was astonishing and humbling how he managed to keep in close contact with friends and colleagues, as well as a wide array of journalists from around the world, and yet be so productive even during this last period of illness.

Edward's life, scholarship and personality are inseparable from his engagement with the struggle of the Palestinian people. Ever since the Oslo years, beginning in 1993, Edward stood outside the

Palestinian mainstream by his refusal to see any hope for a just peace emerging from such a one-sided process. I recall trying to persuade him to stand within the debate, but he stubbornly refused and has been vindicated by subsequent developments. Edward resigned from the Palestinian National Council and rejected the leadership of Yasir Arafat, yet remained steadfast in his commitment to Palestinian self-determination. When all realist voices on both sides were trying to craft the contours of a two-state solution, Edward insisted that only a state that brought the two peoples together in a unified political community could bring enduring peace and justice. Again, his prophetic voice is only recently gaining adherents, as more and more observers on both sides come to realise that the Israelis have created so many 'facts on the ground' as to make it impossible at this point to imagine a workable two-state outcome. What is most impressive to me, however, is not this gift of political insight and individuality exhibited by Edward, but rather his strength of will and character, ignoring on principled grounds the pressures of 'responsible' and 'reasonable' people. I found this capacity and willingness to stand by unpopular beliefs part of what made Edward such an inspirational figure for me and for so many others.

If we ask about Edward's legacy, I think it safe to conclude that his main works such as *Orientalism* and *Culture and Imperialism* will be read within academic circles for as long as serious cultural and literary reflection persists. As well, Edward is likely to be singled out as an—possibly as *the*—exemplary public intellectual of this era, combining first-class scholarship with lucid media commentary on the great events of the day. And finally, Edward's role in articulating the Palestinian struggle, while appreciating the need to safeguard the future of the Jews in Israel, was a characteristic of his approach that was not appreciated by extremists in either camp. I was struck at the funeral that the great Israeli pianist, Daniel Barenboim, was the only person listed on the formal program who was not a member of the Said family, contributing three beautifully rendered musical works. It was a final expression of Edward's extraordinary combination of passionate engagement with his even more extraordinary insistence on reconciliation and empathy with the supposed enemy. Edward is gone, but he and his work will not be forgotten.

A line from the great Palestinian poet, Mahmoud Darwish, perhaps best summarises both Edward's life and his legacy: 'What use is our thought if not for humanity' ('The Hoopoe', *Unfortunately, It Was Paradise*). And in a more personal final note, I would endorse the spirit of another line of poetry, this from May Swenson: 'Don't mourn the beloved. Try to be like him'. Edward's last words to his children was to carry on with the struggle, and in some attenuated sense, I would like to think that we are all Edward's children!

When Words Fail

The eye sees but cannot tell
The heart knows but cannot say
The mind weeps but cannot cry
Such feelings do no more
            than announce such a death
To feel this loss
    alone in moments of shared silence
  comes closer to words than words
    as even apt and precious words
  die of grief on our tongue
    never to be born
           or possibly, stillborn
    escaping as if exhaled smoke
    escaping as birds streaking south
        as autumn vanishes
And yet this loss is far from forgetfulness
    the heartbeat of memory lives as before
  his words, his passion, his grace
    remind us daily of anguished absence
    yet equally of haunting presence
  as vital as the lives we lead.

RICHARD FALK

Contents

Notes on Contributors

Mark T. Berger has been Visiting Professor in the Department of Defense Analysis at the Naval Postgraduate School (Monterey, California) since July 2006. He has published over 70 articles in international journals and chapters in edited books. He is the author of *The Battle for Asia: From Decolonization to Globalization* (2004) and *The American Ascendancy and After: Empires, Nation-States and Changing Global Orders* (2009: forthcoming). He is also editor of *From Nation-Building to State-Building* (2007) and co-author of *Rethinking the Third World: International Development and World Politics* (2009; forthcoming).

Radhika Desai is Professor at the Department of Political Studies, University of Manitoba, Winnipeg. She is the author of *Slouching Towards Ayodhya: From Congress to Hindutva in Indian Politics* (2004) and *Intellectuals and Socialism: 'Social Democrats' and the Labour Party* (1994), a *New Statesman and Society* Book of the Month, and editor of a special Issue to *Third World Quarterly* (Vol 29. No. 3, 2008) entitled *Developmental and Cultural Nationalisms*. She has also contributed numerous articles in *Economic and Political Weekly, New Left Review, Third World Quarterly* and other journals and in edited collections on parties, political economy, culture and nationalism. She is currently working on two books: *When Was Globalization?: Origin and End of a US Strategy* and *The Making of the Indian Capitalist Class.*

Arif Dirlik is Chair Professor of Chinese Studies at the Centre for East Asian Studies, and Professor, by Courtesy, of History, and Religious and Cultural Studies, at the Chinese University of Hong Kong; Concurrent Professor, Center for Marxist Social Theory Studies, Nanjing University; and Distinguished Visiting Fellow, the Peter Wall Institute for Advanced Studies, University of British Columbia. His latest book-length publication is *Global Modernity: Modernity in the Age of Global Capitalism.*

Arturo Escobar is a Kenan Distinguished Professor in the Department of Anthropology at the University of North Carolina at Chapel Hill. His research interests are related to political ecology, the anthropology of development, social movements, Latin American development and politics. His recent publications include *World Anthropologies: Disciplinary Transformations in Contexts of Power* (2005), co-edited with Gustavo Lins Ribeiro and *Women and the Politics of Place* (2005), co-edited with Wendy Harcourt.

Richard Falk is Albert G. Milbank Professor Emeritus of International Law at Princeton University and Visiting Distinguished Professor in Global and International Studies at the University of California, Santa Barbara. His most recent book, *The Great Terror War* (2003), considers the American response to September 11, including its relationship to the patriotic duties of American Citizens.

Devleena Ghosh is an Associate Professor in the School of Social Inquiry at the University of Technology, Sydney. Her research interests are in Indian Ocean studies, postcolonial studies and the cultural history of migration. Her books include *Colonialism and Modernity, Cultures of Trade: Indian Ocean Exchanges, Women in Asia: Shadowlines* and *Fresh and Salt, Water, Borders and Sovereignty in Asia and Oceania.* She is currently involved in a project researching intercolonial networks in the Indian Ocean, specifically the movements of people, technologies, ideas and commodities between the British colonies of India and Australia.

Vedi Hadiz is an Associate Professor in the Department of Sociology, National University of Singapore. He is the author of *Workers and the State in New Order Indonesia* (1997), co-author of *Reorganising Power in Indonesia: The Politics of Oligarchy in an Age of Markets* (2004) and editor of *Empire and Neoliberalism in Asia* (2006). He has also published articles in such journals as Development and Change, Pacific Review, Journal of Contemporary Asia, Journal of Development Studies, Historical Materialism, and Democratization.

Fouad Makki is Assistant Professor in the department of Development Sociology at Cornell University. He has published and researched on questions of comparative developmental trajectories, colonialism and modernity, and contestations of nationalism.

Philip McMichael is Professor and Chair of Development Sociology, Cornell University. His current research addresses globalisation counter-movements and food security. His most recent publication is the third edition of *Development and Social Change: A Global Perspective* (2004).

David Moore is Professor of Development Studies at the University of Johannesburg in South Africa. In 2007 he edited *The World Bank: Development, Poverty, Hegemony* for the University of KwaZulu-Natal Press. He also wrote '"Intellectuals" Interpreting Zimbabwe's Primitive Accumulation: Progress to Market Civilisation?' for *Safundi's* April edition, and 'Coercion, Consent, Context: *Operation Murambatsvina* and ZANU-PF's Illusory Quest for Hegemony' which came out in 2008 in Maurice Vambe, editor, *Zimbabwe: The Hidden Dimensions of Operation Murambatsvina*, Harare: Weaver Press, 2008.

Thomas Olesen is Assistant Professor of Political Science at the University of Aarhus and author of *International Zapatismo: The Construction of Solidarity in the Age of Globalization* (2005).

Rajeev Patel is currently a postdoctoral fellow at the Centre for Civil Society, School of Development Studies, University of KwaZulu-Natal, South Africa, where he researches agrarian change. He has degrees from the Universities of Oxford and London, and Cornell University. He previously worked with the Institute for Food and Development Policy (Food First) in Oakland, California, and is currently writing a book on the global food system.

Vicky Randall is Professor of Government at the University of Essex. She is the author of *Women and Politics* and *The Politics of Child Daycare in Britain* and co-author (with Robin Theobald) of *Political Change and Underdevelopment* and (with Joni Lovenduski) of *Contemporary Feminist Politics*. She is the Editor of *Political Parties in the Third World* and *Democratization and the Media* and co-editor of *Gender, Politics and the State* and *Politics in the Developing World*. She is the author of numerous articles on women and politics, the politics of childcare and political parties in the developing world. Her current research focuses on political parties in the developing world.

John S. Saul is Professor Emeritus of Political Science at York University, Toronto. He was a long-time activist in the anti-apartheid movement and has also taught at universities in Tanzania, Mozambique and South Africa. He is the author or editor of at least a dozen books on Africa, his most recent is *The Next Liberation Struggle: Capitalism, Socialism and Democracy in Southern Africa* (2005).

Heloise Weber is Lecturer in International Relations and Development Studies at the School of Political Science and International Studies, University of Queensland. Her research interests are in the global politics of development and inequality, development theory/critical development theory, international relations theory, and the politics of international institutions in development. Her research has been published in (among others) *Review of International Political Economy*, *Review of International Studies*, *Third World Quarterly* and *Globalizations*. She is also co-author (with Mark T. Berger) of *Rethinking the Third World: International Development and World Politics* (forthcoming). She is also working on a monograph *Organizing Poverty: The Global Politics of Microfinance*.

After the Third World? History, destiny and the fate of Third Worldism

MARK T BERGER

> In its pure, unadulterated form, Third Worldism did not suffer approximation or partial results. It had chosen utopia as its standard, history as its demanding judge. It would have to live with history's hard and unappealable verdict.[1]

From the bustling Gambir Railway Station, located on the eastern side of Lapangan Merdeka (Freedom Square) in central Jakarta, one can take a train south and east through the seemingly endless slums, plazas and suburbs of Indonesia's capital. The urban sprawl of Jakarta gradually gives way to rice paddies, and eventually the train ascends into the hills. If the train is an express train, it will take about three hours to arrive at another of the largest cities in Indonesia and the capital of the province of West Java. High in the hills the provincial capital is cool compared with the sweltering humidity of the coast. Leaving the train, the traveller can make his/her way to Jalan Asia-Afrika (Asia-Africa Avenue) and Gedung Merdeka (Freedom Building) near the centre of town. Inside this building is a museum commemorating a famous meeting that involved, among others, Sukarno, Jawaharlal Nehru, Ho Chi Minh, Gamal Abdel Nasser and Zhou Enlai. The city, of course, is Bandung, and the conference, held from 17 to 24 April 1955 was the Asian–African Conference. More than any other single event, this conference in a hitherto obscure city (in an Indonesia that had only emerged as a sovereign nation-state in the 1940s) symbolised the moment of arrival for the Third World.[2]

Participants and observers subsequently conjured with the 'Bandung Spirit', while others now talk retrospectively of a 'Bandung Era' (1955–75).[3] The historic meeting in Bandung became the touchstone of a wide array of initiatives associated directly and indirectly with Third Worldism.[4] The idea of the Third World was increasingly deployed to generate unity and support among a growing number of non-aligned nation-states whose leaders sought to displace the 'East–West' (cold war) conflict and foreground the 'North–South' conflict.[5] The 1970s were the 'golden age' of Third Worldism. Some commentators point, for example, to the Declaration and Programme of Action for the Establishment of a New Economic Order, passed in April 1974 by the Sixth Special Session of the General Assembly of the United Nations, as evidence of the 'triumph of Third Worldism'.[6] While a number of governments committed to Third Worldism had appeared and/or disappeared in the 1950s and 1960s, the 1970s saw the emergence of a number of new rulers who adopted a distinctly revolutionary Third Worldist tone and outlook in Asia, Africa and Latin America. By the 1980s, however, Third Worldism as both a revolutionary and a reformist project had entered into a period of precipitous decline.

With the end of the Cold War, some movements, governments and commentators have sought to reorient and revitalise the idea of a Third World, while others have argued that it has lost its relevance. The views of the former are not homogeneous, but they all generally agree that the new circumstances of the post-cold war era and the 21st century can still be clarified via the elaboration and reconfiguration of the idea of the Third World and/or that progressive political initiatives can still be pursued under the umbrella of some sort of revised form of Third Worldism.[7] Critics of Third Worldism, however, often emphasise its profound shortcomings during the Cold War. They also emphasise that the spatial and political divisions of the cold war era between the First, Second and Third Worlds, had become so thoroughly scrambled by the dawn of the post-cold war era that the idea of the Third World now imposes a dubious homogeneity on a large and diverse area of the world at the same time as Third Worldism is grounded in political, economic and territorial distinctions that have become irrelevant.[8]

This book contains a wide range of contributions, all of which engage with the idea of the Third World and with Third Worldism. In some cases this involves 'reinventing the Third World', while in other cases the authors make a case for 'ending with the Third World'. In an effort both to establish an historical framework for the contributions that follow and to take a position in the ongoing debate about the idea of the Third World this introductory article provides a critical overview of the history of the rise and demise of Third Worldism in its classical form. I attempt to clarify both the constraints on, and the appeals of, Third Worldism in the context of its wider emergence and its eventual (and in my view at least, terminal) decline. Movements and governments directly informed by Third Worldism in the cold war era can be divided into first-generation (1950s–60s) and second-generation (1960s–70s) Bandung regimes.[9] While these generations overlapped and displayed considerable internal diversity, second-generation regimes (as already suggested) were generally more explicitly socialist in their overall approach to national liberation and economic development than first-generation regimes. As a worldhistorical movement, Third Worldism (in both its first- and second-generation modalities) emerged out of the activities and ideas of anti-colonial nationalists and their efforts to mesh often highly romanticised interpretations of pre-colonial traditions and cultures with the utopianism embodied by Marxism and socialism specifically, and 'Western' visions of modernisation and development more generally. Apart from the problems associated with combining these different cultural and politico-intellectual strands, Third Worldism eventually came crashing down because of the contradictions between its utopian vision on the one hand and the ungainly scaffolding for a rising Third World provided by the emergent new nation-states and the international political–economic order of the Cold War on the other.[10]

Third World rising: first-generation Bandung regimes, 1950s–60s

Challenging neocolonialism I: the dawn of Third Worldism

The first stirrings of Third Worldism can be traced to the complex milieux of colonialism and anti-colonial nationalism in the early 20th century.[11] At the same time, of course, the overall consolidation of Third Worldism is grounded in the post-1945 conjuncture of decolonisation, national liberation and the Cold War.[12] For example, the Bandung Conference flowed from the slow pace of decolonisation and the way in which the United Nations had become enmeshed in the rivalry between the two cold war superpowers. More specifically, the organisation of the Bandung Conference by the governments of newly independent Indonesia, Ceylon, India and Pakistan was a result of their frustration with the political logjam surrounding new membership in the United Nations. By 1953–54 no new members had been inducted into the organisation since the acceptance of Indonesia in January 1950.[13] The 1955 meeting in Bandung was attended by delegations from 29, primarily new, nation-states or nationalist movements in Asia and Africa. Also included in the proceedings were members of the African National Congress, as well as observers from Greek Cypriot and African-American organisations. The key figures at the conference, and the main leaders of the first generation of Bandung regimes, were Sukarno, President of Indonesia (1945–65), Jawaharlal Nehru, Prime Minister of India (1947–64), Gamal Abdel Nasser, President of Egypt (1954–70), Ho Chi Minh, leader of the Democratic Republic of Vietnam (1954–69), Kwame Nkrumah, the future Prime Minister of Ghana, (1957–66) and Zhou Enlai, Prime Minister (1949–76) and Foreign Minister (1949–58) of the People's Republic of China.[14]

At the Bandung meeting, these leaders and the other assembled delegates emphasised their opposition to colonialism, singling out French colonialism in North Africa for particular criticism. The French war (1954–62) to prevent Algerian independence was underway at this time and representatives of the Front de Libération Nationale (FLN), which would eventually come to power in the 1960s and occupy an important position in the Third Worldist pantheon, were in attendance in Bandung. There was also a major debate as to whether Soviet domination of Eastern Europe was equivalent to Western European colonialism in Asia and Africa. The final communiqué of the conference condemned all 'manifestations' of colonialism and was thus widely viewed as not only an attack on the formal colonialism of the Western European powers, but also on the Soviet occupation of Eastern Europe and the informal colonialism, or neocolonialism of the USA. The proceedings ended with a call for: increased technical and cultural co-operation between the governments of Asia and Africa; the establishment of an economic development fund to be operated by the United Nations; increased support for human rights and the 'self-determination of peoples and nations', singling out South Africa and Israel for their failure in this regard; and negotiations to reduce the building and stockpiling of nuclear weapons.[15]

Although the Bandung Conference failed to lead directly to any long-term organisational initiatives (a second Asian–African Conference planned for Algiers in 1965 never took place because of the politics of the Sino-Soviet split) it did, as already emphasised, provide the indirect inspiration for various Third Worldist organisations. A particularly radical example was the formation of the African–Asian Peoples' Solidarity Organisation (AAPSO) at a meeting in Cairo in 1957. In contrast to Bandung, which was primarily a meeting of government leaders, AAPSO was set up as an organisation of ruling and non-ruling political parties, including delegates from the USSR and China. Despite a number of meetings in the late 1950s and early 1960s, AAPSO soon lost its significance in the context of the Sino-Soviet split and the formation of the more moderate Movement of Non-Aligned Countries, which would become known as the Non-Aligned Movement (NAM) by the 1970s.[16] In September 1961 the First Conference of Heads of State or Government of Non-Aligned Countries was held in Belgrade, Yugoslavia. Hosted by Josip Broz Tito, President of

Yugoslavia (1953–80), it was attended by officials from 25 governments and representatives from 19 different national liberation movements.[17] A number of governments, such as Pakistan, which had been in attendance in Bandung, were excluded if they were seen to be clearly orientated towards the USA or Soviet Union. A number of former French colonies that were closely tied to Paris were also excluded, but this stipulation did not lead to the exclusion of representatives from Castro's Cuba from the meeting, even though Havana was becoming an important client–ally of Moscow. The Belgrade Conference was followed by Cairo in 1964, then Lusaka (Zambia) in 1970 and Algiers in 1973.[18]

By the time of the non-aligned meeting in Cairo in 1964, if not before, the complicated and conflicting interests of the new nations in Asia and Africa (against the backdrop of the universalisation of a system of sovereign nation-states centred on the United Nations) were increasingly preventing the creation of a strong coalition of non-aligned governments. Despite Third Worldist attempts at non-alignment, most nationalist movements and Third World regimes had diplomatic, economic and military relations with one or both of the superpowers. Also, as already noted, Third Worldism was further complicated by the Sino-Soviet split in the early 1960s. After 1949 the People's Republic of China (PRC) had initially aligned itself with Moscow, signing a Treaty of Friendship, Alliance and Mutual Assistance with the USSR in 1950.[19] This coincided with the rise and fall of the PRC's commitment to a Soviet-style development model and its increasing efforts in the 1950s to play a leadership role in the emerging Third World. From 1949–53 Mao and the Chinese leadership followed economic policies that included co-operating with or allowing the continued commercial activities of those members of the bourgeoisie who had not worked with the Japanese. At the same time in rural areas they focused on land redistribution, the execution and purging of landlords and the consolidation of the power of the Communist Party. In 1954 the Chinese leadership set up a state planning apparatus and began nationalising industry and commerce, while in 1955 they moved to collective agriculture along Soviet lines. By the second half of the 1950s, however, many members of the Chinese leadership became increasingly critical of the operation of the Soviet model in China. In particular, they were concerned about low levels of agricultural growth and excessive centralisation. This was the context for the launch of the Great Leap Forward (1958–61).[20]

The Great Leap Forward was closely connected to China's various foreign policy initiatives towards the emerging Third World generally and towards Southeast Asia more specifically. The Chinese Communist Party (CCP) leadership was seeking to increase China's economic significance and its international position dramatically. At the Bandung Conference Zhou Enlai had successfully vied with Nehru for a leading role among the non-aligned nation-states in Asia. In the wake of Bandung China's relations with Indonesia increasingly improved, while Zhou Enlai's personal relationship with U Nu of Burma led to the resolution of concerns about their shared border. China's relations with Cambodia, Laos and the Democratic Republic of Vietnam (North Vietnam) were also strengthened in the late 1950s, while only Thailand and the Philippines had joined the US-sponsored Southeast Asia Treaty Organisation (SEATO), set up in

1954 to support South Vietnam.[21] The winding back of the policies associated with the Great Leap Forward in the early 1960s coincided with the complete rupture of Beijing's relationship with Moscow, and growing friction with the USA. The USSR and USA signed a nuclear test ban treaty in 1963 which was roundly criticised by Mao. China successfully tested its own nuclear weapon in 1964. As the Chinese leadership's war of words with Moscow and Washington escalated, Beijing sought to position itself as a key nation-state in, if not the leader of, a wider Third Worldist challenge well beyond Asia. Ultimately, however, the China-led Third Worldist push had limited success—reflected in Beijing's unsuccessful effort to have the USSR excluded from the 'Second Bandung Conference' that had been scheduled to meet in Algeria in June 1965.[22] Beijing's initiative led to the cancellation of the conference when many of the governments involved, such as Egypt and India, saw continued benefits in maintaining their connections to Moscow and thus not supporting Beijing. Prime Minister Nehru's opposition to China's manoeuvres also flowed from the fact that the relatively good relations between China and India that had characterised the 1950s had been completely ruptured by the Sino-Indian war of 1962 fought along the disputed Himalayan frontier.[23]

Challenging Neocolonialism II: a tryst with destiny

India's credentials as a leading Third Worldist state were also in relative decline more generally by the mid-1960s. Gopal Krishna has characterised the Indian diplomatic trajectory in this period as a 'retreat from idealism'.[24] In the 1950s Nehru's international profile and his commitment to a combination of parliamentary democracy, economic planning and socialist principles helped to focus considerable world attention on India, while his diplomacy sought to mobilise a Pan-Asian coalition and a broader grouping of non-aligned Third World regimes.[25] For some observers in the USA, meanwhile, India was regarded as an important prize: they conjured with the political and ideological benefits for Washington that an alliance with one of the most influential non-aligned governments in Asia would bring. According to this vision, if the USA strengthened ties with Nehru's government, Washington could help ensure that India would serve as an anchor for, and model of, democratic capitalist development in the Third World to counter the explicitly anti-capitalist and state-socialist alternatives exemplified by China and the Soviet Union. However, for other US strategists Pakistan was the most important nation-state in the region for military-strategic reasons: they emphasised its proximity to the Soviet Union and its position in relation to the Middle East. By 1954 the emphasis on the relative importance of Pakistan had led to the decision to enter into a mutual security agreement between the USA and the government of Pakistan. At the same time Pakistan also became a founding member of the US-sponsored SEATO that was formally established in February 1955.[26]

In this period the government in New Delhi set about balancing its relationship with Washington by deepening its economic and military links to Moscow, while also seeking to maintain good relations with the Chinese government.[27] In part as a result of these changes, by the end of the 1950s the US approach to

South Asia had shifted away from an emphasis on Pakistan and towards an emphasis on India. Worried that the USSR, in particular, was gaining influence in Indian government circles, via its generous trade and aid arrangements, and concerned that if the Indian government failed to achieve its national development plans the strength of the country's communist movement would increase, President Eisenhower expanded his administration's economic aid programme to India in his final years in office. By the end of the 1950s the Eisenhower administration also shared the concern, voiced by Senator John F Kennedy and others, that economic decline in India could enhance the Chinese government's prestige in international affairs, undermining the US claim that the democratic-capitalist model was superior to the state-socialist model of national development.[28]

Nehruvian socialism and Nehru's commitment to Third Worldism reached their peak during the second half of the 1950s. By the time Nehru died in May 1964 the notion that a benevolent technocratic elite could successful guide India to Nehru's distinctive vision of Indian socialism and that India could both be part of a broad Third World coalition and serve as a model for other parts of the Third World was already in crisis, as were the first generation of Bandung regimes more generally.[29] Nehru's conception of state-guided national development is often seen as being shaped by the Soviet model; however, his approach was always tempered by a critique of the lack of democracy in the Soviet Union and the human cost of Soviet industrialisation. In fact, for some observers Nehru's views by the 1950s had much more in common with social democracy in post-1945 Western Europe than they did with state-socialism in the Soviet Union, despite the much publicised Soviet support for national development in India. Nehru certainly rejected key aspects of the Soviet model and his perspective bore similarities to social democratic currents in Western Europe. However, Nehru's government also drew on China's post-1949 approach to national development, especially its approach to agriculture.[30] In fact, Nehruvian socialism exemplifies the way in which Marxism was assimilated to national circumstances in the wider context of decolonisation, the Cold War and the emergence of Third Worldism.[31]

Within less than two years of Nehru's death, Sukarno, another key exponent of Third Worldism—who sought to synthesise nationalism, Islam and Marxism, a project that was embodied in his famous formulation *Nasionalis-Agama-Komunis* (NASAKOM)—was overthrown by General Suharto in a bloody and prolonged anti-communist purge in Indonesia.[32] While Nehru had earlier, and somewhat patronisingly, regarded Sukarno as one of his 'disciples' in Asia and antagonised his host in Bandung in 1955 as a result, the Indonesian leader had also attained a position in the Third Worldist pantheon that was as transcendent as, although different from, that occupied by Nehru.[33] During the 1950s parliamentary democracy in Indonesia had increasingly given way to what Sukarno called 'Guided Democracy'. By the late 1950s Indonesia had embraced an approach to economic development that involved an increasingly high level of state intervention to restructure the economy in the context of the nationalisation of Dutch owned property. The Indonesian state directed earnings from the commodity export sector into the primarily state-owned and state-operated manufacturing sector. Export earnings were also directed towards public works, health, food production, education and transportation, not to mention as payment on foreign debts. The Indonesian Army (ABRI) played an ever more important political and economic role under Sukarno, taking over direct control of large sectors of the economy in the late 1950s.[34]

Apart from the military, Sukarno's 'Guided Democracy', which involved full presidential powers and rule by decree, rested on a complex web of political alliances that revolved around the Partai Nasional Indonesia (Nationalist Party of Indonesia—PNI), the Communist Party (PKI) and a major Muslim party. He played these parties off against each other, at the same time as he pitted the mainly anti-communist military against the PKI. 'Guided Democracy', underpinned by Sukarno's strident anti-Western nationalism and its synthesis with NASAKOM, bolstered by the Third Worldist vision of which he was an important proponent, represented an explicitly state-led attempt at national development. By the early 1960s, however, stagnation and decline in the sugar and rubber sectors, combined with falling commodity prices, had resulted in a shortage of funds and a serious balance of payments problem. By the first half of the 1960s it was increasingly apparent that not only was Indonesia's economy on the brink of collapse, but the political structure centred on Sukarno was also in crisis.[35] This was taking place against the backdrop of a conflict (*Konfrontasi*) with Malaysia over the setting of their respective postcolonial borders.[36] When it came, the end of Sukarno's regime in Indonesia involved a much sharper break with first-generation Third Worldism than did the more gradual waning of Nehruvian socialism in India. Following Sukarno's overthrow in 1965–66, Suharto dramatically reorientated Indonesia's military and economic links, bringing Indonesia into close alignment with the USA and Japan, against the backdrop of the effective elimination of the large PKI, which had been an important source of support for Sukarno. Suharto presided over an increasingly conservative anti-communist and authoritarian version of national developmentalism in Indonesia, erected on the foundations of Sukarno's failed state-guided national development project.[37]

Challenging neocolonialism III: an appointment with destiny

Another pivotal first-generation Bandung regime was Egypt under Gamal Abdel Nasser. After World War II Egypt emerged at the centre of Pan-Arabism and the wider Third-Worldist push in the Middle East.[38] Of particular geostrategic importance because of the Suez Canal, Egypt effectively became a protectorate of Britain in the 1880s (a status that was formalised in 1914). After World War I the former Ottoman province emerged as a nominally independent monarchy with links to Britain that were increasingly perceived by Egyptian nationalists as neocolonial. But it was not until over 30 years later, on July 23 1952, that Egyptian nationalists ousted the British-backed King Farouk in a bloodless coup. This initiated a process that led to the departure of all British troops from Egypt and the Egyptian takeover of the Suez Canal in 1956.[39] The Suez crisis (which involved an ultimately unsuccessful Anglo-French-Israeli effort to regain control of the Canal) dramatically undermined British prestige and influence in the region at the same time as it catapulted Nasser to prominence as a major figure not only in Egyptian nationalism, but also in Pan-Arabism and Third Worldism.[40] A radical and secular nationalist, Nasser's ideas became increasingly socialist over the course of his years in office.[41] Shortly after coming to power he published *Egypt's Liberation: The Philosophy of the Revolution*, which held up the Egyptian military as the vanguard of the national struggle against 'feudalism' and 'imperialism'. He conjured with the idea of an independent Egypt as the pivot, not only of an expanding group of united and liberated Arab nation-states, but of Africa and the Islamic world as well.[42] At the same time, like Nehru in India and Sukarno in Indonesia, Nasser was presiding by the late 1950s over the dramatic deepening of the state-led national development project in Egypt. The central goal was industrialisation; however, in Nasser's grandiose vision of progress, and his vague conception of socialism, industrialisation and socialism were usually conflated. At the same time the Egyptian leader clearly linked nationalism and import-substitution industrialisation to both wider social (or populist–socialist) goals and to the broader Third Worldist agenda and the struggle against neocolonialism. In a well known speech in late 1958 (at a time when Egypt was part of the United Arab Republic (UAR) with Syria), Nasser said that 'we have an appointment with destiny to build up in the UAR a strong nation which feels independent' and in which everyone works for themselves 'not for foreigners' and 'imperialists'.[43] From the vantage point of the 1970s, however, the socialism of the first generation of Bandung regimes, such as Nasser's Egypt, seemed increasingly tepid. For example, although the coup in Libya, led by Muammar Qaddafi in 1966, had been directly influenced by Nasser's own trajectory, the regime that emerged in Tripoli was far more radical and far less secular in its approach.[44]

A key, if not always terribly effective, vehicle for Nasser's influence in the Middle East was the Arab League. Formed in the waning days of World War II at a conference in Alexandria attended by the governments of Egypt and Iraq, along with Lebanon, Syria, Saudi Arabia, Transjordan and the Yemen, the Arab League was ostensibly aimed at the promotion of economic, technical and cultural interaction between the governments and people in the Arab world. A representative of the Palestinian Arabs also attended the initial conference. Libya joined the League in 1951. Sudan joined in 1956, followed by Tunisia and Morocco in 1958, Kuwait in 1961, Algeria in 1962, South Yemen (formerly Aden) in 1968, then Bahrain, Qatar, Oman and the Trucial States in 1971. A council based in Cairo guided the operations of the League, but there was no significant central governing body and it operated as a relatively decentralised collection of nation-states. Until the mid-1960s the main foci of activity for the League were supporting the Palestinians against Israel and attempting to check the French presence in Lebanon and North Africa. While Nasser was president of Egypt he dominated the organisation. With his death in 1970 Egyptian influence on the League declined, while that of the Palestine Liberation Organisation (PLO) rose. After Anwar Sadat became president of Egypt, the headquarters of the League shifted from Cairo to Tunis.[45] At the same time, throughout the 1950s and 1960s, Nasser not only sought to link his brand of Egyptian nationalism to Pan-Arabism, going so far as to federate Egypt with Syria to form the United Arab Republic

(1958–61), but also to Pan-Islamism and Pan-Africanism. His government provided political and material assistance to national liberation movements in Africa. In the late 1950s and early 1960s Egyptian government radio repeatedly irritated London and Paris with its enthusiastic support for the Mau Mau rebellion in Kenya in the early 1950s and the FLN in Algeria during its struggle against French colonialism from 1954 to 1962.[46]

Despite Nasser's support for national liberation in Africa, the key figure in Pan-Africanism and the key African Third Worldist in the 1950s and early 1960s was, of course, Kwame Nkrumah.[47] He was the first prime minister of Ghana, which was, in turn, the first colony in southern Africa to gain independence. Formerly the British colony of the Gold Coast, it became an independent nation-state in 1957. Numerous other transitions from colony to nation-state soon followed. In 1960, for example, 16 new African nation-states, including the major new national polities of Nigeria and the Republic of the Congo (formerly the Belgian Congo), were inducted into the United Nations.[48] Meanwhile, Pan-Africanism, which had been discussed as early as the 1860s and had gained some significance in political and cultural terms in the USA between the first and second world wars against the backdrop of the Harlem Renaissance, took on an increasingly explicit socialist tone by the 1930s and 1940s, emphasising co-operative agriculture and state-guided industrialisation. However, this vision remained linked to the goal of recuperating Africa's pre-colonial cultural heritage and the building of regional unity along cultural as well as political lines. While Pan-Africanism underpinned the push by Nkrumah and others for national self-determination and some form of post-colonial socialism, attempts to deepen the political structures of Pan-Africanism in the immediate post-colonial period were relatively short-lived. For example, Nkrumah (who ruled Ghana until he was overthrown in a military coup in 1966) and Ahmed Sékou Touré of Guinea formed the Ghana–Guinea union in 1958. However, this was a relatively brief arrangement, as was the Ghana–Guinea–Mali union, not to mention the Federation of Mali (Senegal and Mali). The regional vision that informed Pan-Africanism increasingly lost momentum as more and more independent nation-states emerged.[49] Nevertheless, Pan-Africanism survived in an attenuated form with the formation of the Organisation of African Unity (OAU) in 1963.[50] Meanwhile, shortly before the Ghanaian military overthrew him in 1966, Nkrumah published *Neo-Colonialism: The Last Stage of Imperialism*, which argued that, although the erstwhile colonies of Africa had gained political independence, national liberation could not be achieved until they attained economic independence via a break with neocolonialism, something that could be more effectively carried out on a regional or transnational basis.[51] In the post-cold war era Nkrumah's concern that independent African nation-states could only progress as part of a wider economic and political grouping is now seen as more prescient than ever. At the same time Muammar Qaddafi has spearheaded a recent attempt to revitalise Pan-Africanism and the OAU, with the latter having been reorganised and renamed the African Union (AU). With the judicious use of military and economic aid Qaddafi ensured that 42 of the member governments of what would become the AU showed up for a major conference in Tripoli in 1999.[52]

Third World reorientated: second-generation Bandung regimes, 1960s–70s

The golden age of Third Worldism

Qaddafi still leads one of the few surviving one-time second-generation Bandung regimes. Apart from Qaddafi, the other main survivor from this period is Fidel Castro in Cuba, who has been in power since 1959. Qaddafi and Castro came to power against the backdrop of a wider wave of second-generation Bandung regimes that included those of Ahmed Ben Bella (1962–65) and Houari Boumédienne (1965–78) in Algeria, Tanzania under Julius Nyerere (1965–85), Chile under Salvador Allende (1970–73), Jamaica under Michael Manley (1972–80), Libya under Muammar Qaddafi after 1969, the Derg (Committee) in Ethiopia (1974–91), Guinea-Bissau from 1974 under Amilcar Cabral's successors, the People's Republic of Angola under the Popular Movement for the Liberation of Angola (MPLA) after 1975, Mozambique under Samora Moises Machel (1975–86) and Nicaragua under the Sandinistas (1979–90). This far from exhaustive list could also include the rapid rise and fall of Patrice Lumumba, the leader of the Mouvement National Congolais (MNC) who emerged as the key figure and Prime Minister in the Republic of the Congo at the time of independence in June 1960 until his assassination by the Belgian authorities (with the complicity of Washington) in January 1961.[53] Like Che Guevara after him, Lumumba's early death quickly elevated him to a position of major significance in the pantheon of Third Worldist leaders. More broadly, the second-generation Bandung regimes (framed by the Cuban Revolution at the beginning and the Nicaraguan Revolution at the end), for which figures like Lumumba and Guevara became powerful symbols, increasingly intersected with a major revolutionary wave between 1974 and 1980. If the revolutionary regimes with dubious long-term, if not short-term, progressive credentials that emerged in the second half of the 1970s are counted, the list of 'revolutionary' regimes in this period not already mentioned above includes: Vietnam, Cambodia and Laos in Southeast Asia; Iran and Afghanistan in Central Asia; and Zimbabwe, along with Sao Tomé e Príncipe and Cape Verde (which, like Angola, Guinea-Bissau and Mozambique emerged out of the collapse of the Portuguese Empire) in Africa. Meanwhile, Grenada under Maurice Bishop in the Caribbean was also part of this wave, at the same time as major, albeit unsuccessful revolutionary movements were gaining ground in El Salvador, Guatemala, the Philippines and elsewhere in the late 1970s and early 1980s.[54]

Second-generation Bandung regimes (with the exception of post-1979 Iran, which was, and sometimes still is, positioned as a revolutionary Third Worldist regime) reflected a more radical, more unambiguously socialist, Third Worldism than the first-generation Bandung regimes. (Important exceptions were the People's Republic of China and the Democratic Republic of Vietnam, which were both first-generation Bandung regimes led by Communist parties committed to Marxism–Leninism and state-socialism.) In fact, some commentators, such as E San Juan Jr, emphasise that the first-generation regimes, led by nationalists such as Sukarno, Nehru and Nasser, were exemplars of the 'bourgeois national project initiated by the Bandung Conference'. He also includes Ghana and the Philippines in the same category as Indonesia, India and Egypt, while juxtaposing these 'nationalist bourgeois struggles' with Vietnam under Ho Chi Minh and Cuba under Fidel Castro. San Juan situates the first-generation Bandung regimes led by Nasser, Nehru and Sukarno with newly independent nation-states generally, representing them all as 'postcolonial states' that were 'modernising on the basis of anticommunism and pragmatic philosophy', while relying on 'Soviet military support' and engaging in a 'cynical playing of the 'American card'.[55]

However, as outlined in the previous section of this introduction, this characterisation does not actually apply to many of the first-generation Bandung regimes. Nehru, Sukarno and even Nasser often had a more complicated relationship with 'socialism' and their own national communist parties than is conveyed by San Juan's formulation. At the same time San Juan celebrates leaders of the second generation movements such as Amilcar Cabral, who led the African Party for the Independence of Guinea and Cape Verde (PAIGC) from 1956 until his assassination in 1973.[56] San Juan acknowledges that 'we cannot of course return wholesale to the classic period of national liberation struggles'. He says he is primarily concerned with using Cabral 'to refute the argument that historical materialist thinking is useless in grasping the complexity of colonialism and its aftermath'.[57] Ironically, by making such a sharp distinction between the 'national bourgeois project' of first-generation Bandung leaders and the socialism of primarily second-generation leaders, he simplifies the 'complexity' of the 'colonialism and its aftermath' he is seeking to understand. First-generation Bandung regimes were certainly, by and large, less radical than the second-generation Bandung regimes, but to view the former as simply anti-communist national bourgeois projects not only misrepresents their intellectual and organisational relationship to Marxism, but also stereotypes the complexities of their interactions with the cold war superpowers. Furthermore, Cabral's particularly pragmatic brand of socialism makes him an exceedingly poor example of the ostensibly sharp break between the bourgeois nationalism of the first-generation of Bandung leaders and the second-generation of which Cabral was a member. While he was widely regarded as progressive, he drew on Marxism rather than positioning himself as a Marxist.[58]

While the representation of the first generation of Bandung regimes as reformist supporters of the national bourgeoisie and the second generation as revolutionary Marxists committed to state-socialism is overdrawn, the latter group was still generally more radical than the former. For example, if the Bandung conference was symbolically the most important meeting for the first generation of Bandung regimes, one of the key events for the second generation was the Tricontinental Conference of Solidarity of the Peoples of Africa, Asia and Latin America, held in Havana in January 1966. While the Bandung Conference had brought together a relatively small number of leaders from mainly recently independent nation-states in Asia in order to stake out a non-aligned position in the Cold War, the 1966 Tricontinental Conference in Havana involved delegates from throughout Asia, Africa, the Middle East and Latin America. It articulated a far more radical anti-imperial agenda that located the participants firmly in the socialist camp at the same time as they formally emphasised their independence from the USSR and Maoist China.[59] Second-generation Bandung Regimes, directly or indirectly linked to the tricontinentalism of the late 1960s and 1970s, represented the practical complement to the rise and spread of dependency theory (along with other revitalised Marxist theories of development and social and political change).[60] In this era second-generation Bandung Regimes and their supporters attempted to radicalise state-mediated national development efforts in various ways in the name of socialism and national liberation. The example of the Vietnamese revolution had influenced many of the second-generation Bandung regimes. At the same time, revolutionary regimes were also directly inspired and, in the case of Algeria, for example, supported by Castro's Cuba.

Triumph and tragedy: from exhausted colonialism to exhausted nationalism

In Algeria the escalating military struggle against French colonialism that began in 1954, in the context of the expanding Cold War, culminated in the departure of the exhausted colonial rulers and the triumphant emergence of an independent Algeria in July 1962.[61] The triumph of the FLN in Algeria marked an important turning point for the region and for Third Worldism more generally.[62] Robert Malley goes so far as to call the FLN's ascension to power in 1962 'a defining moment in the history of Third Worldism'. The Algerian Revolution was pivotal to Third Worldism because the struggle had been so lengthy and violent at the same time as the FLN was 'acutely aware' of the struggle's 'international dimension'.[63] Following the founding meeting of the OAU in Addis Abba in May 1963, the Algerian leader, Ben Bella, delivered a particularly stirring address to those in attendance as 'one of the leaders of the Third World struggle'. While attracting the attention of the USA for his radical ideas and his links with Cuba, Ben Bella was also able to garner allies in sub-Saharan Africa during what would be a relatively brief period as president of the Algerian republic.[64] In 1965 Ben Bella was ousted in a military coup led by Houari Boumédienne, his Defense Minister and also his former comrade-in-arms. The latter, a charismatic military officer who enjoyed considerable popular support in Algeria and remained more or less committed to the populist socialism and state-guided economics of his predecessor, emerged in the 1960s and 1970s as a key figure in Third Worldism. Boumédienne, as will be discussed below, played a central role in the call for a New International Economic Order (NIEO) at the United Nations in the mid-1970s.[65]

Meanwhile, the way in which the Cuban revolution overthrew a regime that had long enjoyed the support of Washington and embarked after 1959 on the creation of a radical socialist state in such close proximity to the USA was also extremely important to Marxist and Third Worldist intellectuals and revolutionaries.[66] Following the Cuban Missile Crisis in 1962, and the replacement of Nikita Khrushchev (1953–64) by Leonid Brezhnev (1964–82), Moscow increasingly urged the Communist parties in Latin America to adopt a gradual approach to social change.[67] This approach had the effect of further encouraging many revolutionaries to break completely with Moscow in the 1960s and try to emulate the Cuban revolution. While the new regime in Cuba became highly dependent on the Soviet Union, members of the Cuban leadership continued to articulate a far more revolutionary stance than their patrons in Moscow in this period—Havana gave considerable encouragement and support to insurgent groups in Nicaragua and Guatemala which had split from the traditional communist movement (or had never been linked to it in the first place). In fact, the early 1960s in particular were characterised by a concerted effort to try and spread the Cuban revolution to the rest of Latin America and beyond. This process was reflected in Ché Guevara's assertion of the need to create 'two, three, many Vietnams' and it reached its zenith with his death in 1967 in Bolivia.[68]

Che Guevara personified revolutionary idealism and Third Worldism in its second-generation form. While Fidel Castro increasingly aligned himself with the Soviet Union and sought to focus on building communism in Cuba as the 1960s progressed, Guevara was increasingly influenced by Trotskyism and by the idea that the success of Cuban communism was dependent on the spread of revolution to the rest of the Third World. However, Guevara departed from Trotsky's emphasis on a vanguard party, and found in *foco* theory the key to initiating action. With *foquismo* Guevara emphasised that a small nucleus of guerrillas could provide the leadership and revolutionary élan required to establish a successful guerrilla insurgency. In early 1965 Guevara resigned from the Cuban government and led an expedition to the Congo. This effort was a disappointment, however, and he soon shifted his focus back to Latin America, arriving with his small group of *foquistas* in Bolivia. However, his guerrilla group failed to gain the support of the indigenous inhabitants of the Bolivian highlands. His efforts to foment revolution were also regarded with suspicion by the Bolivian Communist Party. He was captured and executed in October 1967 by counter-insurgency troops of the Bolivian armed forces.[69] Following Guevara's death, and the virtual elimination of guerrilla groups in Colombia, Venezuela and Guatemala by the end of the 1960s, rural insurgency and Cuban militancy in Latin America were curtailed.[70]

As the 1970s began Cuban policy in Latin America had come more into line with that of the USSR. At the same time the Cuban government had helped to educate and influence an entire generation of revolutionaries in Latin America and beyond.[71] For example, the Frente Sandinista de Liberación Nacional (Sandinista National Liberation Front—FSLN) in Nicaragua, and its leader Carlos Fonseca (who was killed in 1976 in a battle with Somoza's national guard), was profoundly influenced by the Cuban experience.[72] And, although Cuba had curtailed its direct involvement in Latin America by the 1970s, Africa was a different matter—Cuban troops played an important, even pivotal, role in the revolution in Angola in the 1970s.[73] As has already been noted, Africa was a major arena of the revolutionary resurgence of the late 1970s. In 1974–75 the ongoing, armed struggles in Portugal's colonies, combined with the overthrow of dictatorship in Portugal itself, led to the independence of Angola, Mozambique, Guinea-Bissau and Sao Tomé e Príncipe and Cape Verde.[74] Angola and Mozambique, in particular, continued to be torn by externally funded guerrilla insurgencies seeking to topple the Marxist and Third Worldist leadership, a process that continued into the post-cold war era, only apparently winding down in the case of Angola in recent times. Angola represents a particularly stark example of the tragedy that came in the wake of national liberation and the ostensible pursuit of Third Worldist goals.[75] White-ruled Rhodesia also emerged as central to the wider dynamics of national liberation and the Cold War in southern Africa. In 1965 the white settlers of Southern Rhodesia, under the leadership of Ian Smith, launched the famous Unilateral Declaration of Independence (UDI). What followed was a protracted war of national liberation led by the Patriotic Front, an uneasy coalition of Joshua Nkomo's Zimbabwe African Political Union (ZAPU) and Robert Mugabe's Zimbabwe African National Union (ZANU).[76] In 1980 Zimbabwe achieved full independence and majority rule under the elected government of former guerrilla leader, and now President, Mugabe. His increasingly erratic and despotic rule, which is now in its third decade, has become an extreme example of the exhaustion of national liberation as a political project and of the tragedy of Third Worldism more generally.[77] For example, while millions of Zimbabweans were facing the prospect of a major famine as a result of Mugabe's government's shortcomings, Mugabe himself sought to burnish his Third Worldist and nationalist credentials at the latest meeting of the Non-Aligned Movement in Kuala Lumpur in late February 2003, joining the Iraqi delegation, General Than Shwe of Burma and Fidel Castro in their enthusiastic support for the lambasting that their host, and the incoming leader of NAM, Mahathir Mohamad, delivered to Washington and the West at the summit.[78]

The last avatar of development economics: The NIEO and the global crisis of national development

Third Worldist regimes such as Mugabe's in Zimbabwe had come to power with the intention of dramatically transforming what were still profoundly hierarchical and primarily rural societies via land reform and state-directed import-substitution industrialisation strategies. However, despite these efforts, which sometimes never went beyond the planning stage, long-standing divisions in these societies, in the context of complex colonial legacies, were reinforced and reconfigured rather than undermined, and most state-capitalist and socialist-orientated national development projects in the Third World were already in crisis before relative late-comers such as Mugabe even came to power.[79] The state-mediated national development project as it emerged in Africa and elsewhere rested on a growing range of governmental structures to manage production for domestic and export markets. These elaborate tariff systems and dual exchange rates, and a range of subsidies on food and other items, combined with the expansion of the education system, health care and other social services and led to the emergence of overburdened states that increasingly buckled under rising foreign debt and the predations of corrupt elites both civilian and military.[80] This general crisis provided the context for the UN Declaration on the Establishment of a New International Economic Order (NIEO).[81] The call for a restructuring of the world economy in favour of the nation-states of the Third World made at the special session of the General Assembly of the UN between 9 April and 2 May 1974 was reinforced by the 1973 oil crisis, but flowed from, and built on, earlier efforts to address the structural inequalities of the international political–economic order. These previous efforts included the establishment of the Group of 77 at the 1962 Economic Conference of Developing Countries in Cairo and the establishment in 1964 of the United Nations Conference on Trade and Development (UNCTAD). Raúl Prebisch, who was Director-General of the UN-sponsored Economic Commission for Latin America (Comisión Economica para América Latina—CEPAL) from 1948 to 1962, also helped to found and then went on to head UNCTAD from 1964 to 1969, using the latter as a forum to encourage preferential tariffs for exports from the late-industrialising nation-states of the Third World. The immediate impetus for the NIEO, meanwhile, was the decision by the Non-Aligned Movement, taken at its meeting in Algiers in September 1973, to ask the UN to hold a special session on 'problems relating to raw materials and development'.[82]

As noted earlier, a central figure in the promotion and planning of the NIEO Declaration was Houari Boumédienne, President of Algeria, who was responsible for the initial request to the UN that a special session on international economic development be held. The other main sponsors were the presidents of Venezuela and Mexico, Carlos Andres Pérez (1973–78) and Luís Echeverría Álvarez (1970–76) and the Shah of Iran, Mohammed Reza Pahlavi (1954–79). The changes asked for in the NIEO were, of course, never implemented. The NIEO effectively called for the extension to the international economic system of the redistributive framework that had been consolidated in the social democracies of Western Europe after World War II but was now in crisis at its point of origin. Implementing such a set of reforms would have required a new global structure of governance that went far beyond the UN-centred international system. This new global structure would have required the power to reorganise global markets and extract taxes at a global level and then redistribute them globally as well. In retrospect the NIEO was, in the words of one commentator, the 'last avatar' of post-World War II development economics, while the latter was, in turn, the intellectual anchor of state-mediated capitalist development between the 1940s and the 1970s.[83] The call for an NIEO followed on the heels of the 1973 oil crisis and the demonstration by the Organisation of Petroleum Exporting Countries (OPEC) of its ability to set the price of oil. While some commentators see OPEC's assertiveness in the 1970s as an example of the wider Third Worldist push in this period, OPEC's growing influence weakened rather than strengthened Third Worldism. The rise of conservative, anti-communist, oil-rich nation-states, particularly in the Middle East, and their often strong links to the USA, represented a major obstacle to the realisation of the NIEO and the wider Third Worldist project. Of course, in a somewhat contradictory fashion, the new 'petro-states' were also in a position by the 1980s to resist the economic liberalising thrust of the US-led globalisation project.[84]

Third World retreating: the end of the Bandung era, 1980s–2000s

The climacteric of Third Worldism

The 1980s ushered in the climacteric of Third Worldism. At the very moment when the Third World was being seen by some observers to have 'come of age', the Bandung era was already coming to a close.[85] For example, wars between the 'red brotherhood' of Vietnam, Cambodia, Laos and China in the late 1970s pointed to the obvious failure of socialist internationalism and its close relative, Third Worldism.[86] More broadly, by the beginning of the 1980s, the emphasis on restructuring the world economy to address the North–South divide was challenged with increasing effectiveness by the emergent US-led globalisation project.[87] With the world recession and the Debt Crisis at the start of the 1980s, and the subsequent spread of neoliberal economic policies and practices, the UN-sponsored idea of a New International Economic Order disappeared from view, displaced by the globalisation project. The International Monetary Fund and the World Bank, supported by the administration of Ronald Reagan (1981–88), the governments of Margaret Thatcher in Britain (1979–90) and Helmut Kohl in (West) Germany (1982–98), encouraged the governments of the Third World to liberalise trade, privatise their public sectors and deregulate their financial sectors.[88] This trend also coincided with the renewal of the Cold War and the further weakening of the Non-Aligned Movement. Despite regular meetings, NAM played an increasingly limited role in international affairs during the so-called New Cold War and after.[89]

During the New Cold War, from the end of the 1970s to the late 1980s, the Reagan administration presided over an unprecedented military build-up and a reinvigorated anti-communist crusade directed at the Soviet bloc and Third Worldist regimes such as Nicaragua.[90] Apart from Central America, a key regional focus of the New Cold War, which also highlights the vicissitudes of non-alignment specifically and Third Worldism more generally, was Southwest Asia. Once the Soviet Union entered Afghanistan to prop up the increasingly embattled state-socialist regime in Kabul in late 1979, US aid to Pakistan, which Washington had suspended because of nuclear testing by Islamabad, was restored and then significantly increased. In the 1980s the Pakistani military, and the country's powerful intelligence organisation, the Inter-Services Intelligence directorate (ISI), played an important role (along with the Saudi Arabian and the Chinese governments) in supporting the loose coalition of resistance groups (Islamic Unity of Afghan Mujahideen) fighting the Soviet occupation. The Carter administration (1977–80) also attempted to improve its relations with the Indian government, under Prime Minister Morarji Desai (1977–80), who was trying to lessen reliance on the USSR. However, once the USA resumed military and economic aid to Pakistan and increasingly tilted towards China against the backdrop of Washington and Beijing's rapprochement in the 1970s and the war in Afghanistan after 1979, Prime Minister Indira Gandhi, who replaced Desai in 1980, moved again to strengthen Indian relations with the USSR. This situation only changed when Soviet military forces withdrew from Afghanistan (between May 1988 and February 1989), and when the subsequent end of the Cold War brought about the end of all US aid to Pakistan (in the context of renewed US concern about Pakistan's clandestine nuclear weapons programme in the 1990s). The general deterioration of US relations with Pakistan was paralleled by improvements in US relations with India in the post-cold war era.[91]

While there were clear shifts in direction and geographical orientation in post-cold war USA foreign policy there were also significant continuities. On the one hand the administration of Bill Clinton (1992–2000) introduced a range of reforms that were ostensibly aimed at 'enlarging the community of democratic nations worldwide' with important implications for the erstwhile Third World.[92] For example, the four main goals of US foreign aid in the post-cold war era were identified in the 1997 US Agency for International Development (USAID) Strategic Plan as: the promotion of the 'rule of law', the promotion of 'elections and political processes', building and expanding 'civil society' and improving 'governance'. Movement towards all these objectives was regarded by USAID as 'necessary to achieve sustainable democracy'.[93] A greater emphasis was also placed on humanitarian assistance and sustainable development. However, the foreign aid bill that was passed by the US Congress in 1994 continued, not surprisingly, to reflect a commitment to often long-standing geopolitical concerns. In the year the bill was passed Israel and Egypt received over one-third of all US foreign aid. The figure for Israel was US$3 billion and for Egypt it was $2.1 billion, while the 1994 figure for sub-Saharan Africa as a whole was $800 million.[94] This was more or less the same percentage for Israel and Egypt as they had received in the 1980s. Israel's importance to US foreign policy (and to domestic US politics) goes back decades, while Egypt has been a major strategic outpost for Washington since 1977 when Nasser's successor, Anwar Sadat, ended his government's ties to the USSR and became a central player in the US-sponsored peace process in the region. From the time of this reorientation to the end of the 1990s Cairo received at least $46 billion in military and economic aid from Washington. Since the late 1970s US policy towards Egypt has viewed it as the key to making and expanding peace in the region.[95] With the end of the Cold War foreign aid was also directed increasingly at the former Second World, again for broad geopolitical reasons, related particularly to a concern to improve relations with, and enhance the political stability of, a post-communist Russia that still possesses a major capacity for nuclear warfare and is the world's second largest oil exporter after Saudi Arabia.[96]

The redirection of, but limited changes to, the basis of US foreign aid policy after the Cold War make clear the relative continuity in US strategic thinking in the 1990s. For example, planning documents and the public pronouncements that emanated from the administration of George Bush Sr (1989–92) reflected the continued preoccupation with Russia and some of the other successor states, such as the Ukraine, that had emerged from the collapse of the Soviet Union. There was also a continued focus on the Middle East, at the same time as Central America quickly dropped from view.[97] Despite the high degree of continuity in US foreign policy in the 1990s, the Clinton administration emphasised at the outset that it intended to shift from 'containment to enlargement'.[98] Clinton advised that his administration's main goal was not just to 'secure the peace won in the Cold War', but to strengthen the country's 'national security' by 'enlarging the community of market democracies'.[99] However, like the administration of his predecessor, the Clinton team understood that the immediate post-cold war world conferred clear geopolitical and economic advantages on the USA and they sought primarily to manage and maintain the status quo. Like the Bush Sr administration, Clinton remained focused on the major powers: the UK, Germany, France, Russia, Japan and China. Clinton, like Bush before him, also attempted to maintain as high a level of defence spending as possible. Throughout the 1990s rhetoric about humanitarian intervention to the contrary, the Clinton administration clearly viewed Europe, East Asia/the Asia–Pacific and the Middle East/Southwest Asia as the three most important regions in the world in terms of US strategy and security. Meanwhile, Latin America, Africa and South Asia, were perceived as regions where no vital US security or economic interests were at stake. Europe was apparently at the top of the list, while the Middle East/Southwest Asia was third. In this period East Asia/the Asia–Pacific was regarded as number two and rising. The interconnection between security and economic development was also particularly obvious in the thinking of defence planners in relation to East Asia. For example, a 1995 Department of Defense document described the US military operations in the Asia–Pacific as the 'foundation for economic growth' and the 'oxygen' of 'development'.[100] This reflected the wider approach that perceived a close connection between China's economic development and geopolitics, as the search for threats to the US position in the world shifted increasingly to East Asia in the 1990s.

It was in the Asia–Pacific, in fact, where the end of the Bandung era and the decline of Third Worldism more generally had become particularly evident well before the end of the Cold War. For a growing number of observers the economic success of the Newly Industrialising Countries of Northeast and Southeast Asia by the 1980s and 1990s had called into question many of the tenets of, and the need for, Third Worldism. For increasingly influential neoliberals the capitalist transformation of Asia had undermined the Third Worldist idea that the hierarchical character of the world economy was holding back the Third World. From this perspective, and from the perspective of proponents of state-mediated development as well, the notion of a Third World still remained relevant. But, now the developing countries of the Third World could become successful late-developers by emulating the Newly Industrialising Countries (NICs) of Asia. At the same time, by the late 1970s successful capitalist development in East Asia had displaced the socialist agenda contained in the idea of the Third World and Third Worldism.[101] This process of displacement was consummated by the turn to the market on the part of the People's Republic of China and the Democratic Republic of Vietnam (the only first-generation Bandung regimes that had pursued fully fledged state-socialism) in the 1980s and 1990s. In ideological terms, Third Worldism was increasingly marginalised in Asia by efforts to promote a distinctly post-Third Worldist Pan-Asianism grounded in state guided capitalist development.[102] Most of the key elements of this shift are reflected in the efforts of Singaporean leader, Lee Kuan Yew (whose recent autobiography was entitled *From Third World to First*). He linked an increasingly conservative nationalism to an equally conservative Pan-Asianism, while presiding over a state-guided export-orientated industrialisation project grounded in a very particular history, which he, nevertheless, represented as providing development lessons for the rest of the world.[103] Meanwhile, by the 1980s the Prime Minister of Malaysia, Mahathir Mohamad (1981–2003), was articulating a particularly strident anti-Western Pan-Asianism that was grounded in an explicitly racial conception of national and international power relations. Interestingly, however, Mahathir not only increasingly took on the mantle of the voice of Asia, but at the very moment when Third Worldism was in dramatic decline, he also positioned himself as a voice of the Third World.[104] Against this backdrop, as already noted, Mahathir assumed the chairmanship of NAM (which now has 114 member nation-states) in February 2003.

Reinventing the Third World

As demonstrated by Mahathir's Third Worldism, undergirded by Malaysia's assumption of the leadership of NAM, the idea of a Third World continues to have geopolitical, if not conceptual, significance in many quarters. In fact, in her contribution to this book Vicky Randall argues that, while the idea of a Third World has continued, albeit diminishing, relevance at the geopolitical level, there has been a dramatic decline in its conceptual relevance for comparative political analysis.[105] She concludes, however, that it still retains strategic relevance in some geopolitical circumstances. In 'The rise of neo-Third Worldism: the Indonesian trajectory and the consolidation of illiberal democracy', Vedi Hadiz suggests the Third World retains even more conceptual utility than that implied by Randall. His article examines both the older and more recent theories of modernisation and development in the Third World, with a focus on debates about democratisation in Indonesia. This provides the backdrop for a detailed examination of the intellectual sources for ideas and definitions of democracy deployed by contemporary Indonesian political actors in their efforts to rebuild the archipelago's political system in the wake of the demise of Suharto's New Order. He goes on to argue that the post-cold war world order centred on US hegemony is weakening rather than strengthening those forces that support liberal democracy in Indonesia, reinforcing the consolidation of illiberal democracy and the rise of 'neo-Third Worldism' in Indonesia and beyond. For Hadiz, neo-Third Worldism has revived the most conservative characteristics of Third Worldism without retaining any of the progressive and internationalist ideals of the early cold war era.

John Saul also looks at the significance of the deployment of Third Worldist rhetoric in the post-cold war era. He looks at what he regards as both the strengths and weaknesses of the continued use of the Third World, grounding his analysis by focusing on the African National Congress (ANC) in South Africa since its election to government and the end of apartheid in 1994. Saul is especially interested in the presidency of Nelson Mandela's successor, Thabo Mbeki. Under Mbeki, the ANC has continued to present itself as a leader of the Third World. However, there are, argues Saul, 'profound contradictions inherent in the ANC's effort both to retain its Third Worldist credentials and to present itself as a reliable client to the Bretton Woods institutions and foreign investors'. Since 1994 the ANC has followed a series of policies that Saul describes as 'deeply compromised quasi-reformism', which have worked 'to deflect consideration away from the options pressed by other, much more meaningfully radical international and South African labour organisations, environmental groups and social movements'. This has meant that, as the ANC reaches the 10-year mark as a governing party, a number of significant grassroots movements have increasingly opted to mobilise against the government's 'bankrupt policies'. This growing grassroots opposition might eventually help to steer South Africa—via the dramatic transformation of the ANC or the establishment of a new political project in South Africa with the same potential for hegemony as the ANC—away from quasi-reformism and back into the ranks of the progressive groups, movements and governments that are increasingly looking for and applying 'innovative and appropriately revolutionary approaches to challenge the geographical, racial and class-based hierarchies of global inequality'.

Taking up a set of concerns that flows from the same geographical location and the same political–economic question, David Moore examines the current crisis in development theory and development policy. Moore seeks to advance the ongoing debate about progress beyond the cold war nomenclature of three worlds of development into the increasingly global, but still highly differentiated, political–economic terrain of the 21st century. At the same time he seeks to retain and reinvent the notion of the Third World. The post-cold war era of neoliberal globalisation, says Moore, is also the 'Second Age of the Third World'. In its 'First Age', the Third World' was defined by comparisons with advanced capitalism and state socialism and by Third Worldist efforts to pursue a non-aligned path between the two superpowers and the competing models of development they represented. In its 'Second Age', argues Moore, the identity of the Third World is now framed by its re-entry into the protracted process of primitive accumulation. For Moore, 'the uneven, destructive and creative, route towards proletarianisation and private property' is both accelerated and aggravated under neoliberal globalisation. The brutality of primitive accumulation in the post-cold war era has thrown 'contemporary development theory into disarray, especially when confronted with the ever-present but usually hidden role of the increasingly internationalised state'. A key response by development theorists has been the notion of 'global public goods'. Moore, by contrast, following a detailed discussion of primitive accumulation and global public goods, proposes that a better alternative is to be found in what he calls 'public accumulation'.

Meanwhile, in her contribution, 'Re-crossing a different water: colonialism and Third Worldism in Fiji', Devleena Ghosh looks closely at the possibilities and prospects for postcolonial Fiji in the wake of a series of major political and social crises in the past 15 years. She emphasises the deterritorialisation, or transnationalisation of the Fijian conflict, looking at the ways in which indigenous Fijians and Fiji's Indian communities have sought to reconstitute national and communal identities via various strategies that involve transnational networking as well as more localised approaches. Drawing on the specificity of the postcolonial Fijian trajectory she proffers a 'non-reductive way to think about decolonisation, cultural transformation and notions of autonomy and Third World solidarity'. From a complementary perspective Arif Dirlik probes the Eurocentric dimensions of Third Worldism. In 'Spectres of the Third World: global modernity and the end of the three worlds' he emphasises that the three worlds of development 'was a product of Eurocentric mappings of the world to deal with the postcolonial situation' that unfolded in the aftermath of World War II. By 'mortgaging' their future to some form of socialism or some form of capitalism, 'which was a premise of this mapping', Third Worldist regimes embraced 'a future dominated by alternatives of European origin'. Meanwhile, the present juncture, Dirlik argues, is one of 'global modernity' by which he means 'a post-Eurocentric modernity that has scrambled notions of space and time inherited from modernity'. While the post-cold war era flows directly from 'the struggles that the idea of three worlds sought to capture … those struggles have led to unanticipated reconfigurations globally, including the reconfiguration of capitalism, which has globalised following the fall of the second world (the world of socialisms)' and produced a range of new challenges. In particular Dirlik examines the way in which the 'spectre of the Third World' continues to inform questions about globalisation and modernity regardless of whether or not we are reinventing the Third World or ending with the Third World.

Ending with the Third World

In contrast to the contributors discussed above the rest of the contributors to this book clearly seek to exorcise the spectre of the Third World and move beyond the three worlds framework rather than revise or reinvent it. In 'Transforming centre–periphery relations', Fouad Makki traces the history of the idea of development and its rise to centrality in 'understanding global hierarchies of wealth and power'. His article historicises the 'development framework' and its links to the making and unmaking of the Third World (the latter formulation was, of course, made well known by Arturo Escobar in the mid-1990s in his influential book, *Encountering Development: The Making and Unmaking of the Third World*), highlighting the way that neoliberal globalisation has emerged as a new, but still fragile, framework of global power relations grounded in the transformation of the centre–periphery dynamics that underpinned the earlier development framework. Meanwhile, in 'From national bourgeoisie to rogues, failures and bullies: 21st century imperialism and the unravelling of the Third World', Radhika Desai draws attention to the fragility of neoliberal globalisation. In fact she goes further than Makki and argues that: 'if globalisation spelled the end of development … then the launching of the war on terrorism signals the end of globalisation'. According to Desai, the 'post-globalisation phase' ushered in by the 'war on terrorism' represents a particularly 'aggressive' form of 'US imperialism'. For Desai, the US imperium is 'no longer based on primarily financial globalisation' as the means by which Washington and US-based corporations exercise and extend global power. Instead, US imperialism is 'now more openly based on the direct control of productive assets and territory'. In her view this historical turning point also signals 'the definitive end of the idea of the Third World and its associated ideology of Third Worldism, although this end has, of course, been repeatedly proclaimed and contested over the past two decades'. She argues that 'the idea of the Third World, and the associated ideas of development and non-alignment were predicated upon the core concept of the national bourgeoisie and associated notions of the inherently progressive potential of nationalism'. Furthermore, the 'idea of a united and rising Third World had a greater reality as a hope than it ever had as an objective historical possibility'.

The analysis I have offered in this introductory article, meanwhile, has also argued that the age of the Third World has passed irrevocably into history. I have also emphasised that the state-centred character of Third Worldism and its emphasis on an alliance of ostensibly sovereign territorial nation-states is a key element in the overall failure of Third Worldism generally and of the failure of a wide array of state-guided national development projects more specifically. As we have seen, the nation-state became the embodiment of the efforts of both the first- and second-generation Bandung regimes to mediate the transformative impact of colonialism and build an anti-colonial politics that combined tradition and cultural specificity with Marxism and/or 'Western' modernity more generally. Once in power, however, Bandung regimes used Third Worldism as a powerful legitimating narrative at the same time as they were unable to realise the prosperity and progress that national liberation and independence were supposed to deliver. The failure of Third Worldism—as an ideological trend centred on a wide array of anti-colonial nationalisms and national liberation movements that linked the utopian strands of Marxism and/or liberalism to romantic conceptions of the pre-colonial era—needs to be set against the wider history of decolonisation, the formation of new nation-states and the Cold War. It was the contradictions inherent in the universalisation of the nation-state system and the global economic order of the cold war era that both produced the Third Worldist challenge and eventually helped to undermine it as a serious alternative to liberal capitalism or state-socialism. At the same time, even if the mantle of Third Worldism can successfully be taken up in the post-cold war era by non-state centred movements, the now irrelevant tripartite political, economic and territorial division of the globe lingers on in the continued use of the idea of a Third World to manage diverse and complex polities in an era when the US-led globalisation project is at the centre of the reshaping of the nation-state system and the global political–economic order. I take the view that the notion of a Third World, even in a limited or reinvented form, is intellectually and conceptually bankrupt, while politically Third Worldism has already lost any relevance or legitimacy it once had. Challenging neoliberal globalisation and post-cold war capitalism means moving beyond the territorial politics of nation-states—a politics to which Third Worldism is inextricably connected. Furthermore, it can be argued that the notion of the Third World has now been most successfully appropriated by the very US-led globalisation project that proponents of a reinvented Third Worldism want to challenge.

The way in which the Third World has been appropriated as part of the managerial repertoire of the US-led globalisation project is highlighted in detail in Heloise Weber's article, 'Reconstituting the Third World? Poverty reduction and territoriality in the global politics of development'. She notes that world politics are increasingly conceptualised by development theorists and policy makers in terms of globalisation and/or fragmentation. Implicit in much of the discussion about globalisation (whether by proponents or critics) is the idea that territorially grounded notions of the political should be superseded by an approach that takes global social formations as it primary focus and views world order as socially and not territorially constituted. Significantly, however, the dominant political and policy prescriptions for alleviating inequality and immiseration are still articulated primarily, if not exclusively, via strategies of poverty reduction and development that focus explicitly on 'developing countries' and the 'Third World'. Weber argues that, against the backdrop of the globalisation project, it is not just the continued deployment of the Third World that is problematic—it is, in fact, the 'continued political significance of the territorial in strategies of neoliberal governance' that needs to be addressed and challenged. At the same time, she emphasises that the centrality of 'territorial politics' to the dominant discourse on development and world order is most readily apparent in relation to the theory and practice around the 'governance of the Third World'. By and large the 'governance of the Third World' is approached via the incorporation of the politics of development (or more specifically by focusing on the question of poverty reduction) in the so-called 'developing countries' into the overall framework of 'neoliberal governance'. Weber points in particular to the recent revision of conditional lending strategies, centred on the introduction of the 'Poverty Reduction Strategy Paper (PRSP) approach' by both the IMF and the World Bank. While the PRSP approach has been promoted as a way of strengthening democracy, Weber argues that the PRSP approach is best seen as an effort to 'constitutionalise' a particular type of 'supra-state governance of the Third World' via detailed conditions and constraints that include directly linking poverty alleviation and development objectives to the goals of the World Trade Organization (WTO). She concludes that the PRSP approach ultimately promotes a type of governance that 'reconstitutes the Third World' geographically regardless of the increasingly supra-territorial character of globalisation. For Weber the Third World is being reconstituted within the contemporary global order in a way that cuts across efforts to pursue 'social solidarity as a political project—both within and across state boundaries'. This means that the Third World serves as a key site of 'empowerment' in the global politics of development and also as a key site of 'disciplinary efforts to manage the contradictions' of neoliberal globalisation.

Arturo Escobar also sees a need to overcome the limits the idea of the Third World continues to place on the pursuit of progress. He argues that, as it becomes increasingly clear that 'there are modern problems for which there are no modern solutions', it also becomes clear that it is necessary to move 'beyond the paradigm of modernity and, hence, beyond the Third World'. Escobar points to the need for 'imagining after the Third World'. The post-cold war context for this project includes what he calls an emergent 'new US-based form of imperial globality', which he defines as 'an economic–military–ideological order that subordinates regions, peoples and economies world wide' which is in turn complemented by what he calls 'global coloniality': a process that involves 'the heightened marginalisation and suppression of the knowledge and culture of subaltern groups'. Another key characteristic of this new era is 'the emergence of self-organising social movement networks, which operate under a new logic, fostering forms of counter-hegemonic globalisation'. For Escobar 'these movements represent the best hope for reworking imperial globality and global coloniality in ways that make imagining after the Third World, and beyond modernity, a viable project'. As part of an effort to do this he looks in particular at the social movements in black communities on the Pacific Coast of Colombia.

In 'Third Worldism and the lineages of global fascism: the regrouping of the global South in the neoliberal era', Rajeev Patel and Philip McMichael also seek to move the politics of development beyond the Third World. They argue that the theory and practice of development generally has been grounded in a form of 'biopolitics, rooted in a regime of sovereign state control, and designed to mobilise citizens in ways favourable to capital'. Furthermore, Third Worldism 'embraced this form of sovereignty and its biopolitics' at the same time as Third Worldism can be also be located in direct relation to the rise of 'global fascism'. They emphasise that many 'contemporary resistances to neoliberalism' (global justice movements, or the forces of 'globalisation-from-below' or counter-globalisation), now recognise the state's complicity with capital. These 'new internationalisms', which have emerged from the wreckage of Third Worldism, increasingly articulate an approach to 'sovereignty' that runs counter to the dominant conception of state sovereignty that was universalised during the rise and decline of Third Worldism between the 1940s and the 1970s.[106]

A major exemplar of 'globalisation-from-below' has been the rise of the Zapatistas in southern Mexico in the post-cold war era. As Thomas Olesen emphasises, the rebellion launched on 1 January 1994 by the Ejército Zapatista de Liberación Nacional (EZLN), better known as the Zapatistas, captured the imagination of activists and academics in the Americas and around the world. In the second half of the 1990s the Zapatistas and their main spokesperson, Subcomandante Marcos, increasingly occupied an important international position comparable with, but also clearly distinct from, the romantic guerrilla Marxism and Third Worldism of the cold war era.[107] Virtually all observers agree that the uprising in Chiapas represented an important departure from the Marxism and Third Worldism of this era. Furthermore, the Zapatistas have had an important impact on progressive politics in Mexico and in Latin America. Olesen, meanwhile, focuses on the way that the Zapatistas quickly became an important rallying point for progressive organisations and solidarity activists in Europe and North America and beyond. In the mid-1990s they emerged as a symbol of progressive social change for those looking for new political alternatives in a post-cold war world apparently bereft of systemic alternatives to neoliberal globalisation. Olesen argues that one of the important aspects of the global solidarity efforts that surround the Zapatistas is the partial dissolution of cold war era ideas about 'solidarity with the Third World' and the 'one-way' paternalism that was often central to this type of support. Many of the post-cold war global solidarity efforts around the Zapatistas are based on what he suggests is a new, 'two-way' relationship between the Zapatistas and their international supporters. This reflects the changing character of the post-cold war global order and the notion that there are lessons flowing in both directions in a world in which the analytical salience and political purchase of the idea of the First World and the Third World have dramatically diminished or disappeared entirely.

Conclusion: history, destiny and the fate of Third Worldism

The articles in this book both reflect, and reflect on, the overall breadth and significance of the idea of the Third World and the practice of Third Worldism. As they also make clear, both the history of, and the current perspectives on, the Third World and Third Worldism are linked to a wide range of political and intellectual positions, organisations and initiatives engaged in the rethinking of the history and contemporary significance of the Third World against the backdrop of a whole range of other trends. It is hoped that by bringing together a number of approaches to the question of 'After the Third World?' this book will facilitate and stimulate engagement with the power of the idea of the Third World and the wide range of Third Worldist currents and their relationship to the changing global order of the 21st century.

Notes

[1] R Malley, *The Call From Algeria: Third Worldism, Revolution and the Turn to Islam*, Berkeley, CA: University of California Press, 1996.

[2] For example, Edward Said enthusiastically overstated the situation when he said that: 'By the time of the Bandung Conference in 1955 the entire Orient had gained its political independence from the Western empires and confronted a new configuration of imperial powers, the United States and the Soviet Union'. E Said, *Orientalism: Western Conceptions of the Orient*, London: Penguin Books, 1995, p 104.

[3] R Abdulgani, *Bandung Spirit: Moving on the Tide of History*, Djakarta: Prapantja, 1964. See also CP Romulo, *The Meaning of Bandung*, Chapel Hill, NC: University of North Carolina Press, 1956. For the notion of the 'Bandung era' (1955–75) see S Amin, *Eurocentrism*, London: Zed Press, 1989, p 143.

[4] The key elements of Third Worldism, as I am using the term here, are the assumptions that: 1) the 'popular masses' in the Third World had 'revolutionary aspirations'; 2) the fulfilment of these aspirations was an inevitable working out of history that linked pre-colonial forms of egalitarianism to the realisation of a future utopia; 3) the vehicle for the achievement of this transformation was a strong and centralised nation-state; and 4) in foreign policy terms these nation-states should form an alliance that would act collectively under the umbrella of various regional and international forms of political and economic co-operation, such as the non-alignment movement and the United Nations. This definition is similar to, but also departs in key respects from, the conception of Third Worldism provided in Malley, *The Call From Algeria*, pp 2, 72, 94–114.

[5] G Lundestad, *East, West, North, South: Major Developments in International Politics Since 1945*, New York: Oxford University Press, 1999. The notion of a Third World also became central to academic and policy-orientated work on development and underdevelopment. P Worsley, *The Third World*, London: Weidenfeld and Nicolson, 1964; IL Horowitz, *Three Worlds of Development*, New York: Oxford University Press, 1966; RA Packenham, *Liberal America and the Third World: Political Development Ideas in Foreign Aid and Social Science*, Princeton, NJ: Princeton University Press, 1973; IL Gendzier, *Managing Political Change: Social Scientists and the Third World*, Boulder, CO: Westview Press, 1985; C Ramirez-Faria, *The Origins of Economic Inequality Between Nations: A Critique of Western Theories of Development and Underdevelopment*, London: Unwin Hyman, 1991; and B Hettne, *Development Theory and the Three Worlds: Toward an International Political Economy of Development*, New York: Wiley, 1995.

[6] G Rist, *The History of Development: From Western Origins to Global Faith*, London: Zed Press, 2002, p 140.

[7] For example, see RE Bissell, 'Who killed the Third World?', *Washington Quarterly*, 13 (4), 1990; J Manor, 'Introduction', in Manor (ed), *Rethinking Third World Politics*, London: Longman, 1991; G Hawthorn, '"Waiting for a text?" Comparing Third World politics' in Manor, *Rethinking Third World Politics*; V Randall, 'Third World: rejected or rediscovered?', *Third World Quarterly*, 13 (4), 1992; M Williams, 'Re-articulating the Third World coalition: the role of the environmental agenda', *Third World Quarterly*, 14 (1), 1993; RO Slater, BM Schutz & SR Dorr, 'Introduction: toward a better understanding of global transformation and the Third World', in Slater, Schutz & Dorr (eds), *Global Transformation and the Third World*, Boulder, CO: Lynne Rienner, 1993; Slater, Schutz & Dorr, 'Global transformation and the Third World: challenges and prospects', in Slater *et al*, *Global Transformation and the Third World*; M Williams, *International Economic Organisations and the Third World*, New York: Harverster Wheatsheaf, 1994; M Kamrava, 'Political culture and a new definition of the Third World', *Third World Quarterly*, 16 (4), 1995; A Dirlik, *The Postcolonial Aura: Third World Criticism in the Age of Global*

Capitalism, Boulder, CO: Westview Press, 1997; V Randall & R Theobald, *Political Change and Underdevelopment: A Critical Introduction to Third World Politics*, London: Macmillan, 1998; P Darby, *The Fiction of Imperialism: Reading Between International Relations and Postcolonialism*, London: Cassell, 1998; M Kamrava, *Cultural Politics in the Third World*, London: University College London Press, 1999; AN Roy, *The Third World in the Age of Globalisation: Requiem or New Agenda?*, London: Zed Press, 2000; and R Pinkney, *Democracy in the Third World*, Boulder, CO: Lynne Reinner, 2003.

8 For example, see J-F Bayart, 'Finishing with the idea of the Third World: the concept of political trajectory', in Manor, *Rethinking Third World Politics*; A Loomba, 'Overworking the "Third World"', *Oxford Literary Review*, 12, 1991; MT Berger, 'The end of the "Third World"?', *Third World Quarterly*, 15 (2), 1994; F Buell, *National Culture and the New Global System*, Baltimore, MD: Johns Hopkins University Press, 1994, pp 101–37; A Escobar, *Encountering Development: The Making and Unmaking of the Third World*, Princeton, NJ: Princeton University Press, 1995; R Kiely, 'Third Worldist relativism: a new form of imperialism', *Journal of Contemporary Asia*, 25 (2), 1995; G Crow, *Comparative Sociology and Social Theory: Beyond the Three Worlds*, London: Macmillan, 1997; MW Lewis & KE Wigen, *The Myth of Continents: A Critique of Metageography*, Berkeley, CA: University of California Press, 1997; MW Lewis, 'Is there a Third World?', *Current History*, 98 (631), 1999; R Malley, 'The Third Worldist moment', *Current History*, 98 (631), 1999; C Thomas, 'Where is the Third World now?', *Review of International Studies*, 25 (4), 1999; M Hardt & A Negri, *Empire*, Cambridge, MA: Harvard University Press, 2000; A Payne, 'The global politics of development: towards a new research agenda', *Progress in Development Studies*, 1 (1), 2001; A Hoogvelt, *Globalization and the Postcolonial World: The New Political Economy of Development*, Basingstoke: Palgrave, 2001; and M Hardt, 'Today's Bandung?', *New Left Review II*, 14, 2002.

9 I am following on, but departing, from David Scott's notion of three Bandung generations. See D Scott, *Refashioning Futures: Criticism after Postcoloniality*, Princeton, NJ: Princeton University Press, 1999, pp 197–198, 221–222. Other writers, by contrast, talk in terms of a single Bandung generation. See, for example, P Gilroy, *Between Camps: Race, Identity and Nationalism at the End of the Colour Line*, London: Allen Lane, 2000, pp 288, 345.

10 MT Berger, 'The rise and demise of national development and the origins of post-cold war capitalism', *Millennium: Journal of International Studies*, 30 (2), 2001.

11 For a good discussion of the origins of Third Worldism, see Malley, *The Call From Algeria*, pp 17–33. Although Robert Young does not use the term 'Third Worldism', his encyclopaedic history of post-colonialism is also a detailed history of Third Worldism. Young restates the importance of Marxism to anti-colonial nationalism and also reinstates Marxism in the wider history of postcolonial theory. See RJC Young, *Postcolonialism: An Historical Introduction*, Oxford: Blackwell, 2001. The one region not well covered by Young is Southeast Asia. This gap is nicely filled by CJ Christie, *Ideology and Revolution in Southeast Asia 1900–1980: Political Ideas of the Anti-Colonial Era*, Richmond: Curzon Press, 2001.

12 The notion of the Third World is often traced to the writing in the early 1950s of the French economist, Alfred Sauvy. See Sauvy, 'Trois Mondes, Une Planete', *L'Observateur*, 14 Aout 1952, no. 118, p. 14. See also TC Lewellen, *Dependency and Development: An Introduction to the Third World*, London: Bergin & Garvey, 1995, p 3; L Wolf-Phillips, 'Why "Third World"? Origin, definition and usage', *Third World Quarterly*, 9 (4), 1987. Other observers have suggested that its origins also lie in the somewhat earlier promotion of a 'Third Force' in international politics by Labour Party MPs in Britain following the onset of the Cold War in 1947. Furthermore, this coincided with the call for a 'Third Force' on the part of Fenner Brockway (a British socialist) to unite people and movements in Africa, Asia and Europe in the pursuit of peace, democracy and socialism. JE Goldthorpe, *The Sociology of Post-Colonial Societies: Economic Disparity, Cultural Diversity and Development*, Cambridge: Cambridge University Press, 1996, pp 15–16. Stephen Howe, *Anticolonialism in British Politics: The Left and the End of Empire*, Oxford: Clarendon Press, 1993, pp 168–179.

13 P Lyon, 'The emergence of the Third World', in H Bull & A Watson (eds), *The Expansion of International Society*, Oxford: Oxford University Press, 1984, pp 229–230; HW Brands, *The Specter of Neutralism: The United States and the Emergence of the Third World, 1947–1960*, New York: Columbia University Press, 1990.

14 For first hand accounts of the conference see A Appadorai, *The Bandung Conference*, New Delhi: Indian Council of World Affairs, 1955; G McTurnan Kahin, *The Asian–African Conference, Bandung, Indonesia, April 1955*, Ithaca, NY: Cornell University Press, 1956.

15 Young, *Postcolonialism*, pp. 191–192. Christie, *Ideology and Revolution in Southeast Asia 1900–1980*, pp 131–132.

16 Malley, *The Call From Algeria*, p 90.

17 RF Betts, *Decolonization*, London: Routledge, 1998, p 43.

18 P Willetts, *The Non-Aligned Movement: The Origins of a Third World Alliance*, London: Macmillan, 1978; and RA Mortimer, *The Third World Coalition in World Politics*, Boulder, CO: Westview Press, 1984.

19 OA Westad, 'Introduction', in Westad (ed), *Brothers in Arms: The Rise and Fall of the Sino-Soviet*

Alliance, Stanford, CA: Stanford University Press, 1998, pp 7–29. see also C Jian, *Mao's China and the Cold War*, Chapel Hill, NC: University of North Carolina Press, 2001.

[20] Although the Great Leap Forward departed from the Soviet model, it not only retained links to Stalinist conceptions of economic development, but it also resonated with Stalinist approaches to agriculture in the 1930s in its human costs. The Great Leap Forward affected the peasantry badly as the diversion of resources to industry led to starvation in the countryside. The loss of life from famine between 1958 and 1961 is now calculated to run to upwards of 30 million people. M Goldman & AJ Nathan, 'Searching for the appropriate model for the People's Republic of China', in M Goldman & A Gordon (eds), *Historical Perspectives on Contemporary East Asia*, Cambridge, MA: Harvard University Press, 2000, pp 298–299, 302–303. In the 1960s the PRC increasingly pursued a rural-orientated communism based on mass mobilisation culminating in the social and economic upheaval of the Cultural Revolution in the late 1960s and early 1970s. Despite this shift, both the Chinese leadership and most outside observers took the view that, up to the second half of the 1970s, China's economy remained grounded in the Soviet model. Only with Mao's death were many basic Stalinist economic concepts challenged even if the Soviet model had been domesticated to and reorientated by Chinese practice at least two decades earlier. NP Halpern, 'Creating socialist economies: Stalinist political economy and the impact of ideas', in J Goldstein & R O Keohane (eds), *Ideas and Foreign Policy: Beliefs, Institutions and Political Change*, Ithaca, NY: Cornell University Press, 1993, pp 101–102; and FC Teiwes, 'The Chinese state during the Maoist era', in D Shambaugh (ed), *The Modern Chinese State*, Cambridge: Cambridge University Press, 2000, pp 139–148.

[21] M Stuart-Fox, *A Short History of China and Southeast Asia: Tribute, Trade and Influence*, Sydney: Allen and Unwin, 2003, pp 169–176.

[22] See A Hutchison, *China's Africa Revolution*, London: Hutchinson, 1975, pp72–79.

[23] JW Garver, *Protracted Conflict: Sino-Indian Rivalry in the Twentieth Century*, Seattle, WA: University of Washington Press, 2002.

[24] G Krishna, 'India and the international order: retreat from idealism', in H Bull & A Watson (eds), *The Expansion of International Society*, Oxford: Oxford University Press, 1984, pp 269–271, 282–286.

[25] S Wolpert, *Nehru: A Tryst With Destiny*, New York: Oxford University Press, 1996, pp 466–467.

[26] RJ McMahon, *The Cold War on the Periphery: The United States, India and Pakistan*, New York: Columbia University Press, 1994, pp 7, 337–338.

[27] Wolpert, *Nehru*, p 460.

[28] D Merrill, *Bread and the Ballot: The United States and India's Economic Development, 1947–1963*, Chapel Hill, NC: University of North Carolina Press, 1990; and D Engerman, 'West meets East: the Center for International Studies and Indian economic development', in D Engerman, N Gilman, M Haefele & M Latham (eds), *Staging Growth: Modernization, Development and the Global Cold War*, Amherst, MA: University of Massachusetts Press, 2002.

[29] S Khilnani, *The Idea of India*, New York: Farrar Straus Giroux, 1997, pp 81–86.

[30] F Frankel, *The Gradual Revolution: India's Political Economy, 1947–1977*, Princeton, NJ: Princeton University Press, 1978, pp 124–125.

[31] S Seth, *Marxist Theory and Nationalist Politics: The Case of Colonial India*, New Delhi: Sage Publications, 1995, pp 215–218, 221–222, 232–236.

[32] Christie, *Ideology and Revolution in Southeast Asia*, pp 159–174.

[33] Wolpert, *Nehru*, pp 460–461; G McTurnan Kahin, *Southeast Asia: A Testament*, London: Routledge-Curzon, 2002, pp 145–146; JD Legge, *Sukarno: A Political Biography*, Sydney: Allen and Unwin, 1990.

[34] N Schulte Nordholt, 'The Janus face of the Indonesian armed forces', in K Koonings & D Kruijt (eds), *Political Armies: The Military and Nation Building in the Age of Democracy*, London: Zed Press, 2002, pp 137–141.

[35] MT Berger, 'Post-cold war Indonesia and the revenge of history: the colonial legacy, nationalist visions, and global capitalism', in MT Berger & DA Borer (eds), *The Rise of East Asia: Critical Visions of the Pacific Century*, London: Routledge, 1997, pp 174–175.

[36] M Jones, *Conflict and Confrontation in Southeast Asia, 1961–1965: Britain, the United States, Indonesia and the Creation of Malaysia*, Cambridge: Cambridge University Press, 2002.

[37] MT Berger, 'Old state and new empire in Indonesia: debating the rise and decline of Suharto's New Order', *Third World Quarterly*, 18 (2), 1997.

[38] M Doran, *Pan-Arabism Before Nasser: Egyptian Power Politics and the Palestine Question*, New York: Oxford University Press, 1999; and A Dawisha, *Arab Nationalism in the Twentieth Century: From Triumph to Despair*, Princeton, NJ: Princeton University Press, 2002.

[39] K Kyle, *Suez: Britain's End of Empire in the Middle East*, London: IB Tauris, 2003. 1991.

[40] As observers, such as Edward Said, have emphasised, Nasser 'was never popular in the West', but for many this was 'a true index of how successfully he stood up to imperialism, despite his disastrous military campaigns, his suppression of democracy at home, his over rhetorical performances as maximum leader'. Ultimately, he was 'the first modern Egyptian leader … to transform Egypt into the major Arab and third

world country'. EW Said, 'Egyptian rites', in Said, *Reflections on Exile and Other Literary and Cultural Essays*, London: Granta, 2001, p 161.

[41] Young, *Postcolonialism*, pp 189–190.

[42] GA Nasser, *Egypt's Liberation: The Philosophy of the Revolution*, Washington, DC: Public Affairs Press, 1955.

[43] MM Wahba, *The Role of the State in the Egyptian Economy, 1945–1981*, Reading: Garnet Publishing, 1994, pp 70, 75–80, 86–87.

[44] Young, *Postcolonialism*, p 190.

[45] By the 1980s there were major divisions within the Arab League. Out of a membership of 20 governments, 12 supported the UN-sponsored and US-led 'Gulf war' against Iraq in February 1991 after the latter's invasion of Kuwait. R Schulze, *A Modern History of the Islamic World*, London: I. B. Tauris, 2000, pp 123–135, 260–267.

[46] Young, *Postcolonialism*, pp 190–191.

[47] For a good critical overview, see D Rooney, *Kwame Nkrumah: The Political Kingdom in the Third World*, London: IB Tauris, 1988.

[48] HS Wilson, *African Decolonisation*, London: Edward Arnold, 1994, pp 92–110, 177.

[49] F Cooper, *Africa Since 1940: The Past of the Present*, Cambridge: Cambridge University Press, 2002, pp 58–59, 81

[50] Young, *Postcolonialism*, pp 236, 240–241.

[51] K Nkrumah, *Neo-Colonialism: The Last Stage of Imperialism*, London: Heinemann, 1968.

[52] D Farah, 'Gadhafi seen as root of instability in Africa', *Guardian Weekly*, August 21 2003, p 28.

[53] L De Witte, *The Assassination of Lumumba*, London: Verso, 2002.

[54] F Halliday, *Cold War, Third World: An Essay on Soivet–American Relations*, London: Hutchinson Radius, 1989, pp 29–31; and Malley, *The Call From Algeria*, p 111.

[55] E San Juan Jr, 'Postcolonialism and the problematic of uneven development' in C Bartolovich & N Lazarus (eds), *Marxism, Modernity and Postcolonial Studies*, Cambridge: Cambridge University Press, 2002, pp 221–222, 238. For a similar perspective see A Ahmad, *In Theory: Classes, Nations, Literatures*, London: Verso, 1992, pp 291–304, or S Amin, *Empire of Chaos*, New York: Monthly Review, 1992, pp 8–9.

[56] The year after Cabral's death Guinea-Bissau emerged as an independent state under President Luis de Almeida Cabral, while Cape Verde was inducted into the United Nations in 1975.

[57] For San Juan, Cabral's 'originality' and significance lay in 'his recognising that the nation-in-itself immanent in the daily lives of African peoples can be transformed into a nation-for-itself, this latter concept denoting the peoples' exercise of their historical right of self-determination through the mediation of the national liberation movement, with the PAIGC as an educational organising force that seeks to articulate the national-popular will'. San Juan, 'Postcolonialism and the problematic of uneven development', pp 233–237.

[58] P Gleijeses, *Conflicting Missions: Havana, Washington, and Africa, 1959–1976*, Chapel Hill, NC: University of North Carolina Press, 2002, pp 185–186; P Chabal, *Amílcar Cabral: Revolutionary Leadership and People's War*, Cambridge: Cambridge University Press, 1983; and R Chilcote, *Amilcar Cabral's Revolutionary Theory and Practice: A Critical Guide*, Boulder, CO: Lynne Rienner, 1991.

[59] Young, *Postcolonialism*, p 213.

[60] AG Frank, *Capitalism and Underdevelopment in Latin America: Historical Studies of Chile and Brazil*, New York: Monthly Review Press, 1967; Frank, *Latin America: Underdevelopment or Revolution: Essays on the Development of Underdevelopment and the Immediate Enemy*, New York: Monthly Review Press, 1969; Frank, *Lumpen-Bourgeoisie, Lumpen-Development: Dependence, Class and Politics in Latin America*, New York: Monthly Review Press, 1972; W Rodney, *How Europe Underdeveloped Africa*, London: Bogle-L'Ouverture Publications, 1972; S Amin, *Accumulation on a World Scale: A Critique of the Theory of Underdevelopment*, Sussex: Harvester Press, 1974; Amin, *Unequal Development: An Essay on the Social Formations of Peripheral Capitalism*, New York: Monthly Review Press, 1976; and Amin, *Imperialism and Unequal Development*, New York: Monthly Review Press, 1977.

[61] IM Wall, *France, the United States and the Algerian War*, Berkeley, CA: University of California Press, 2001.

[62] M Connelly, *A Diplomatic Revolution: Algeria's Fight for Independence and the Origins of the Post-Cold War Era*, New York: Oxford University Press, 2002.

[63] Malley, *The Call From Algeria*, p 81. The particularly dark side of both the FLN's eventual triumph and the tactics of the French colonial authorities in their effort to avert defeat are now well known and the subject of considerable debate. For a good overview of the recent literature on this issue see A Shatz, 'The torture of Algiers', *New York Review of Books*, 49 (18), 2002, pp 53–57.

[64] Gleijeses, *Conflicting Missions*, pp 38–39.

[65] L Addi, 'Army, state and nation in Algeria', in K Koonings & D Kruijt (eds), *Political Armies: The Military and Nation Building in the Age of Democracy*, London: Zed Press, 2002, pp 182–184.

[66] SB Liss, *Marxist Thought in Latin America*, Berkeley, CA: University of California Press, 1984, pp 238–239.

[67] N Miller, *Soviet Relations with Latin America 1959–1987*, Cambridge: Cambridge University Press, 1989.

[68] R Munck, *Politics and Dependency in the Third World: The Case of Latin America*, London: Zed Press, 1984, p 328.

[69] PJ Dosal, *Comandante Che: Guerrilla, Soldier, Commander and Strategist, 1956–1967*, University Park, PA: Penn State Press, 2003. See also RL Harris, *Death of A Revolutionary: Che Guevara's Last Mission*, New York: WW Norton, 2000; J Castañeda, *Compañero: The Life and Death of Che Guevara*, London: Bloomsbury, 1997.

[70] TP Wickham-Crowley, *Guerrillas and Revolution in Latin America A Comparative Study of Insurgents and Regimes Since 1956*, Princeton, NJ: Princeton University Press, 1992, pp 209–213.

[71] Munck, *Politics and Dependency in the Third World*, pp 328–239.

[72] M Zimmermann, *Sandinista: Carlos Fonseca and the Nicaraguan Revolution*, Durham, SC: Duke University Press, 2000.

[73] Gleijeses, *Conflicting Missions*.

[74] N MacQueen, *The Decolonization of Portuguese Africa: Metropolitan Revolution and the Dissolution of Empire*,London: Longman, 1997; P Chabal *et al*, *A History of Postcolonial Lusophone Africa*, London: Hurst and Company, 2002.

[75] T Hodges, *Angola: From Afro-Stalinism to Petro-Diamond Capitalism*, Bloomington, IN: Indiana University Press, 2001.

[76] MT Berger, 'The Cold War and national liberation in Southern Africa: the United States and the emergence of Zimbabwe', *Intelligence and National Security: An Inter-Disciplinary Journal*, 18 (1), 2003. Meanwhile the control of South West Africa (Namibia) by the white minority government in South Africa and the apartheid system in South Africa itself generated powerful, armed resistance movements throughout much of the cold war era. Namibia eventually emerged as an independent nation-state in 1990, while the apartheid regime in South Africa finally gave way to black majority rule under the African National Congress in 1994.

[77] P Bond & M Manyanya, *Zimbabwe's Plunge: Exhausted Nationalism, Neoliberalism and the Search for Social Justice*, Pietermaritzburg: University of Natal Press, 2002; and M Meredith. *Our Votes, Our Guns: Robert Mugabe and the Tragedy of Zimbabwe*, New York: Basic Books, 2002.

[78] M Baker, 'West bent on domination, says Mahathir', *Sydney Morning Herald*, 25 February 2003, p 9.

[79] DA Low, *The Egalitarian Moment: Asia and Africa 1950–1980*, Cambridge: Cambridge University Press, 1996, pp 1–2; and M Mamdani, *Citizen and Subject: Contemporary Africa and the Legacy of Late Colonialism*, Princeton, NJ: Princeton University Press, 1996.

[80] Hoogvelt, *Globalization and the Postcolonial World*, pp 176–178.

[81] Third World governments had gained significant numerical influence at the UN by the 1970s. The UN's membership rose from 51 in 1945 to 156 in 1980. The vast majority of the new members were from Asia and Africa.

[82] R Gilpin, *The Political Economy of International Relations*, Princeton, NJ: Princeton University Press, 1987, pp 275, 298–301.

[83] Rist, *The History of Development*, pp 143–144, 153–154.

[84] TL Karl, *The Paradox of Plenty: Oil Booms and Petro-States*, Berkeley, CA: University of California Press, 1997; CM Henry & R Springborg, *Globalization and the Politics of Development in the Middle East*, Cambridge: Cambridge University Press, 2001.

[85] LS Stavrianos, *Global Rift: The Third World Comes of Age*, New York: William Morrow, 1981.

[86] G Evans & K Rowley, *Red Brotherhood At War: Vietnam, Cambodia and Laos Since 1975*, London: Verso, 1990.

[87] P McMichael, *Development and Social Change: A Global Perspective*, Thousand Oaks, CA: Pine Forge Press, 2000, pp 147–237.

[88] SD Krasner, *Structural Conflict: The Third World Against Global Liberalism*, Berkeley, CA: University of California Press, 1985.

[89] Between the 1961 conference in Belgrade and the end of the 1990s there was a total of 12 non-aligned conferences. Following Cairo (Egypt) in 1964, Lusaka (Zambia) in 1970 and Algiers (Algeria) in 1973, there was a conference in Colombo (Sri Lanka) in 1976. The venue in 1979 was Havana (Cuba), followed by New Delhi (India) in 1983, Harare (Zimbabwe) in 1986, with a return to Belgrade in 1989. A meeting in Jakarta (Indonesia) in 1992 was followed by Cartagena (Colombia) in 1995 and Durban (South Africa) in 1998, with 113 different national governments represented at the last two meeting in the 1990s. Lundestad, *East, West, North, South*, pp 296–298. For good overviews and relatively hopeful assessments of the non-aligned movement, see S Morphet, 'The non-aligned in "the New World Order": the Jakarta Summit, September 1992', *International Relations*, 11 (4), 1993; Morphet, 'Three non-aligned summits— Harare 1986; Belgrade 1989 and Jakarta 1992', in DH Dunn (ed), *Diplomacy at the Highest Level: The Evolution of International Summitry*, London: Macmillan, 1996.

[90] F Halliday, *The Making of the Second Cold War*, London: Verso, 1986.

[91] SR Tahir-Kheli, *India, Pakistan, and the United States: Breaking With the Past*, New York: Council on Foreign Relations Press; 1997.

[92] WI Robinson, *Promoting Polyarchy: Globalization, US Intervention and Hegemony*, Cambridge: Cambridge University Press, 1996. see also T Carothers, *Aiding Democracy Abroad: The Learning Curve*, Washington, DC: Brookings Institution, 1999.

[93] USAID, 'Agency objectives', at http://www.usaid.gov/democracy/dgso.html.

[94] F Adams *Dollar Diplomacy: United States Economic Assistance to Latin America*, Aldershot: Ashgate, 2000, pp 110–111.

[95] This has resulted in the emergence in Cairo of the 'biggest USAID program in the world' and the 'largest US diplomatic complex in the world'. R Owen, 'Egypt', in R Chase, E Hill & P Kennedy (eds), *The Pivotal States: A New Framework for US Policy in the Developing World*, New York: WW Norton, 1999, pp 120–121, 133.

[96] In fact, by the beginning of the 21st century there was a steady and significant increase in oil output in Russia. EL Morse & J Richard, 'The battle for energy dominance', *Foreign Affairs*, 81 (2), 2002, pp 16–17. Between 1992 and 1997 more than US$2.2 billion of foreign aid was disbursed to Russia by Washington under the Freedom Support Act (FSA). Over the same period over $2.6 billion was also disbursed to Russia via programmes not covered by the FSA. The figures for the Ukraine were over $1 billion FSA funds and $652 million worth of non-FSA funds, while the former Soviet republics in the Caucasus and Central Asia together received over $1.9 billion in FSA funds and $2.4 billion in non-FSA funds between 1992 and 1997 inclusive. See JR Wedel, *Collision and Collusion: The Strange Case of Western Aid to Eastern Europe 1989–1998*, New York: St Martin's Press, 1998, pp 199–203.

[97] DCF Daniel & AL Ross, 'US strategic planning and the pivotal states', in Chase *et al*, *The Pivotal States*, pp 385–387.

[98] A Lake, 'From containment to enlargement', *US Department of State Dispatch*, 4 (39), 27 September 1993.

[99] Office of the President of the United States, *A National Security Strategy of Engagement and Enlargement*, Washington, DC: US Government Printing Office, 1996, at http://www.fas.org/spp/military/docops/national/1996stra.htm, p 2.

[100] Daniel & Ross, 'US strategic planning and the pivotal states', pp 388–392, 402; US Department of Defense, Office of International Security Affairs, *United States Security Strategy for the East Asia and Pacific Region*, Washington, DC: US Department of Defense, February 1995, pp 1–2.

[101] N Harris, *The End of the Third World: Newly Industrializing Countries and the Decline of an Ideology*, London: IB Tauris, 1986.

[102] MT Berger, 'The new Asian renaissance and its discontents: national narratives, Pan-Asian visions and the changing post-cold war order', *International Politics: A Journal of Transnational Issues and Global Problems*, 40 (2), 2003.

[103] KY Lee, *From Third World To First: The Singapore Story, 1965–2000*, New York: Harper Collins, 2000.

[104] BT Khoo, *Paradoxes of Mahathirism: An Intellectual Biography of Mahathir Mohamad*, Kuala Lumpur: Oxford University Press, 1995, p 332; MT Berger, 'APEC and its enemies: the failure of the new regionalism in the Asia–Pacific', *Third World Quarterly*, 20 (5), 1999; and I Stewart, *The Mahathir Legacy: A Nation Divided, A Region At Risk*, Sydney: Allen and Unwin, 2003.

[105] For implicit, if not explicit, defence of the continued relevance of the idea of the Third World for comparative politics, see J Haynes, *Third World Politics*, London: Blackwell, 1996; BC Smith, *Understanding Third World Politics: Theories of Political Change and Development*, Bloomington, IN: Indiana University Press, 1996; P Calvert & S Calvert, *Politics and Society in the Third World*, London: Longman, 2001; and December Green & Laura Luehrmann, *Comparative Politics of the Third World: Linking Concepts and Cases*, Boulder, CO: Lynne Rienner, 2003.

[106] R O'Brien, AM Goetz, JA Scholte & M Williams, *Contesting Global Governance: Multilateral Economic Institutions and Global Social Movements*, Cambridge: Cambridge University Press, 2000; A Starr, *Naming the Enemy: Anti-Corporate Movements Confront Globalization*, London: Zed Press, 2000; WK Tabb, *The Amoral Elephant: Globalization and the Struggle for Social Justice in the Twenty-First Century*, New York: Monthly Review Press, 2001; S Gill, *Power and Resistance in the New World Order*, Basingstoke: Palgrave, 2003; N Harris, *The Return of Cosmopolitan Capital: Globalization, the State and War*, London: IB Tauris, 2003.

[107] MT Berger, 'Romancing the Zapatistas: international intellectuals and the Chiapas rebellion', *Latin American Perspectives*, 28 (2), 2001.

31

Using and abusing the concept of the Third World: Geopolitics and the comparative political study of development and underdevelopment

VICKY RANDALL

The concept of a 'Third World' has clearly proved useful in a range of political contexts over the years. But its ideological significance was always ambiguous. As deployed in the West it tended to carry pejorative connotations of otherness and backwardness, although there was an alternative, more radical construction, reflected in the rise and fall of Third Worldism between the 1950s and the 1980s. Persuasive arguments remain for retaining some version of the notion for purposes of geopolitical analysis. However, in the field of comparative politics, it is more than time that we moved beyond Third World-type generalisations to consider the (former) Third World's constituent regions and countries in their own right. This article begins by looking at the old rationales for using the term and the reasons why these have been undermined. It then considers whether there are still any arguments for retaining the concept—or something like it—for political analysis in general. Turning more specifically to the field of comparative politics, it first revisits previous justifications offered for combining such a great number of political systems or states into a single category and then considers how far these justifications are still valid.

The undermining of the old rationales

The etymology and history of the concept of a Third World have been much discussed and are reviewed again elsewhere in this special issue.[1] It would be tedious to relate them at length here. However, it is necessary briefly to indicate what I see as having been the principal and most persuasive arguments for this conceptualisation in the past in order to consider why and to what extent they no longer hold.

Successive rationales for marking out a distinct Third World have associated it with nonalignment, with the experience and consequences of colonisation, with economic dependence, and with poverty and economic 'backwardness'. The nonalignment argument, in the context of which by some accounts the term Third World originated, was never very convincing even in the early Bandung days and was undermined by the collapse of the Soviet bloc, since this removed one of the two camps between which a non-aligned position could be adopted. The so-called Nonalignment Movement itself has persisted and still meets roughly every three years; at its meeting in February 2003 in Kuala Lumpur representatives from 114 member states were expected, but the actual meeting received minimal press coverage.[2]

There were always problems with the argument about shared postcolonial status. The nature of the colonial experience varied widely. A few of the countries conventionally included in the Third World were never directly colonised, while most countries of Latin America had gained formal independence from Spain or Portugal by the 1830s, leading Cammack *et al* to suggest that their relationship with the USA had long since become much more important than any Iberian connection.[3] Certainly by the 1990s it was far from clear that, for most countries, the impact of colonisation continued to play a major determining role.

Arguments seeking to extend or replace the significance attributed to colonisation by reference to neocolonialism or economic dependency have also become increasingly difficult to sustain. Empirically they have been challenged by examples of countries seemingly breaking free of dependency's iron logic— the oil-exporting countries, the Newly Industrialising Countries (NICs)—and theoretically they have been challenged by the new paradigm, or paradigms, of 'globalisation'. By the same token, the various statistical indicators that have been used to produce world league tables of poverty and development reveal by now that the countries of the former Third World are scattered right across the categories from misery to affluence.

Geopolitics: uses of 'the Third World'

So has the time come to abandon 'the Third World' as an organising concept? That is the central question posed in this special issue but, for me, the answer is far from straightforward. It depends on the context. Although I shall be arguing that the category is problematic as a basis for understanding and comparing the politics of different countries, it remains both relevant and illuminating when the focus is on geopolitical processes and relationships.

In the first place, we should not be too preoccupied with semantics. Obviously the specific phrase 'Third World' is largely anachronistic in the wake of the collapse of what, in the original schema, was held to be the Second World, that is the Soviet Union and its satellites, although a case could possibly be made for continuing to distinguish for the moment between the (former) Second and First Worlds because of the enduring consequences of their very different histories. As Thérien notes with the end of the Cold War, the tendency has been to replace the First–Second–Third World categories with a simple North–South dichotomy, or some variant thereof.[4]

Nor does the fact that some former Third World countries no longer seem to fit its defining criteria fatally undermine its coherence. It is possible to draw the belt tighter, to exclude in particular the wealthy oil-exporting countries and the NICs, although there will always be disagreements about which specific countries should be in and which out. To the extent that the old category of a Second World has been dissolved, some of its former members should probably also be brought into the Third World fold. The old category, as far as it was specified, spanned both 'developed' and industrialised countries of Eastern Europe and 'developing', predominantly agricultural countries such as Vietnam, Cuba and of course China. These latter countries would need to be included in a revamped Third World, together with the five Central Asian former Soviet Republics— Kazakhstan, Kyrgyzstan, Tajikistan, Turkmenistan and Uzbekistan.

A Third World-type category, first, draws attention to what continues to be a major axis of economic and political inequality. It is an understatement to say that access to the benefits and opportunities of globalisation have been unevenly distributed between nations. And while it may be true, as Berger, Weber and other globalisation theorists have argued in this special issue and elsewhere, that increasingly the Third World or the South, is becoming a world-wide social category rather than a geographically defined one, this is only a trend; it is not a completed process. In 1995, as reported in Thomas, the 23% of the world's population living in the North still enjoyed 85% of its income, while the 77% in the South made do with 15 %.[5] In 1996 UNDP reported that between 1960 and 1993 the gap in annual per capita income between developing and developed countries had increased from $5700 to $15 400.[6] Such stark material differences do have substantial social and political consequences. For instance, Collier's recent study for the World Bank of the factors giving rise to civil war, reported in the *Economist*, finds that 'the most striking common factor among war-prone countries is their poverty ... the poorest one-sixth of humanity endures four-fifths of the world's civil wars'.[7]

Second, and given this continuing political and economic inequality among nations, Third Worldist 'discourse' potentially provides a powerful rhetoric and rallying-point. Just as the signifiers, 'woman', and more obviously 'black', have been political constructs obscuring or transcending the actual complexities of experience and identity formation, but nonetheless with a strategic usefulness in particular political contexts, so the terms South or Third World can help to create as much as to reflect political alignments and solidarities. How far this happens in practice is less clear. Although media reports on the World Summit on Environment and Development held in Johannesburg in August 2002 referred to the differing interests and perceptions of the developing and developed worlds, or the richer and poorer countries, it does not appear that the national delegations adopted this language themselves in any sustained way, still less that it provided the basis for a co-ordinated strategy.[8]

A third possible argument is still more contingent or tactical than the previous two and is actually a consequence or response to recent developments in Western analysis of global politics. Beginning with his article in *Foreign Affairs* in 1993 and then in his book *The Clash of Civilisations and the Making of World Order*, Samuel Huntington has played a leading intellectual role in articulating the 'clash of civilisations' thesis. In his book Huntington draws on an extensive scholarly literature to develop his theme, providing a more complex and open-ended account than in his original 'call to arms'.[9] Some of the issues he raises are serious ones to which I return in presenting my own reservations concerning the utility of Third World-type generalisations for comparative politics purposes. Nonetheless there are manifest dangers, made clearer in the wake of 11 September, in this kind of perspective, or its cruder versions, which give a sort of intellectual respectability to cultural determinism and the politics of mutual deafness and intransigence that goes with it.

Faced with this culturally polarising discourse and most pressingly with the opposition drawn between a Judao-Christian and a Muslim 'civilisation', it becomes important to (re)introduce an alternative, political-economy, viewpoint that emphasises both the historic impact of Western imperialism and contemporary dimensions of economic inequality. A Third World perspective provides a vital corrective, cutting across a civilisation-based mapping of world regions and bringing back into the picture the context of global economic relations and local economic conditions from which apparently culturally driven politics has emerged.

So far then I have been suggesting that, despite all the difficulties in deciding exactly where boundaries should be drawn and in establishing some kind of scientifically respectable, underlying or structural logic, for the distinction, a division—if only a rhetorical division—of the world into first and third worlds remains useful, even essential in some global political contexts. Indeed, I have become more convinced of this in the process of writing this article.

Comparative politics: the uses of the Third World

What about the Third World's value for comparative politics? First, I need to justify a focus on comparative politics at this point. Nowadays, more than ever, we should beware of too rigid a separation between the field of international relations and the study of politics within individual countries. The two spheres are increasingly interdependent and our scholarly perspectives should reflect this. It has also been argued that the same globalising trends that underpin this growing interdependence call into question the traditional focus, in political studies, on the country, or nation-state, as the unit of analysis. While this is not the place to pursue these debates, I am much less persuaded by this second argument: for a host of reasons including its symbolic, historic, geo-juridical and institutional resources and importance, it seems at best premature to write off the nation-state as a key determining level of political interaction. The point of these observations is to explain why the sub-field of comparative politics, centred on, though not confined to, understanding and comparing internal political processes of the world's different countries, remains a necessary and valuable part of political studies. Is the category of 'Third World' useful for purposes of this kind of comparative political analysis?

As someone who has written textbooks and taught courses whose intellectual coherence to an extent relies on making such a distinction, it seems to me that in the past there have been two main justifications, one pragmatic and the other more substantive, for doing so. The pragmatic consideration was that political science, and even comparative politics, as they developed from the 1950s remained decidedly provincial for a long time. In the UK comparison—or parallel description—was typically restricted to the USA and one or two Western European countries. The field did open up over time, of course, with the cold war-driven focus on the Soviet Union leading the way. But even then, if you wanted to get beyond a continuing parochialism that largely ignored three-quarters of the world's population, the best, sometimes the only, way to get this huge swathe of countries onto the syllabus was to bring them in under some plausible unifying rubric, such as that offered by the concept of a Third World.

It is doubtful whether such a rationalisation still holds. Even if the notion of a Third World supplied a useful vehicle, or legitimating device, through which to broaden the scope of comparative politics, this Trojan horse kind of argument could only be justified in the short to medium term. In the longer run the inclusion of an undifferentiated Third World should help to give rise to a more substantive and systematic interest in a whole range of regions or countries beyond the Western fringe. In practice, certainly in the UK, the traditional provincialism of comparative politics has not entirely disappeared—in fact my impression is that over the past 10 or so years, in a climate of educational funding constraints, it has been reasserting itself. Nonetheless (and as discussed further below) there has been growing interest and specialisation in the politics of particular regions—notably Latin America, South Asia, China and East Asia, and the Middle East.

But in addition to this pragmatic justification, it was also possible to argue that countries in the Third World, with some partial exceptions, the most noted being India, had many important political features in common. In the first place they shared what Robin Theobald and I have described elsewhere as a 'predicament of economic dependency and backwardness' that constrained politics even while it strongly shaped its imperatives.[10] Hawthorne similarly talks about the two problems, the political problem of building legitimate authority based on a sense of nationhood and the economic problem of development, facing all Third World (and also some Second World) countries.[11] But beyond this, there was, one could argue, a common pattern or 'syndrome' of Third World politics which included instability and conflict, authoritarianism and military intervention, pervasive clientelism and corruption, and which was evident whether you focused on

Africa, the Middle East, Latin America or Asia. While such features were not unknown in the First World, their extent, convergence and degree in the Third World offered a stark apparent contrast, helping to justify studying the politics of Third World countries together as a separate group.

The question is how far this still remains the case. I don't want to suggest that the situation has been transformed, that the countries of the (former or restyled) Third World no longer have enough in common politically and in contrast with those of the First World to warrant seeking to generalise about them as a category in some comparative contexts. But changes over the past two or more decades, both in the nature of politics in these countries and, just as importantly, in *what we know* about it, make this kind of approach appear increasingly crude and arrogant.

Political diversity in the Third World

There was always something disquieting about lumping together such a vast range of societies—covering around 75% (by the turn of the century more like 80%) of the world's population and 70% of its landmass—for purposes of comparative political analysis. It meant subsuming what were recognised to be very different cultural traditions, pre-colonial and also colonial histories. But arguably the expansion and development of relevant scholarship in the 'First World' and in those countries themselves has made such differences increasingly difficult to avoid.

Even if we simply focus on broad analytical approaches to Third World politics and how they have changed over time, we can see that the political 'development' or modernisation paradigm that was influential from the late 1950s was soon under attack from a social anthropology perspective for its cavalier generalisations about 'tradition', and that the 'modernisation revisionism' which succeeded it was much more sensitive to and indeed interested in the interaction of political processes like elections with the particularities of local culture and social structure.[12] There was to some extent a parallel move subsequently in the Marxist camp to modify dependency theory's sweeping generalisations about the impact of metropolitan capital on satellite economies and their societies by much more careful examination of capital's 'articulation' with specific local 'modes of production'.[13] So, from early on, attempts to impose general theories or analytic frameworks through which to understand Third World politics or political economy came up against arguments from 'reality' as mediated in particular by experts working in the 'field' and employing a more anthropological or ethnographic perspective.

At the same time, and presumably reinforcing this scepticism, there was a marked expansion in specialised 'area studies' focused on different regions of the Third World. In the UK, while there had been isolated centres such as the School of Oriental and African Studies founded in 1912, this expansion really originated in postwar government policy concerns about the country's future. Two reports to the Universities Grants Committee played a key role, that of the 1961 'Hayter' Committee on Area Studies (covering Africa and the 'Orient') and the 1962 Parry Committee on Latin American Studies.[14] Following their recommendations a series of centres were set up or enlarged for African studies, Southeast Asian studies, Middle Eastern and Islamic studies and Latin American studies. The field of Caribbean studies seems to have taken longer to separate out from Latin American studies: its first Centre was established at Warwick University in 1984.

Along with these university centres went the creation of area-studies-based professional associations such as the Society of Latin American Studies (SLAS) founded in 1964, the British Association of South Asian Studies (BASAS) founded in 1986 and the African Studies Association. To the ranks of existing area-based journals like *African Affairs*, founded in 1901, and the *Middle Eastern Journal*, founded in 1946, were added new publications such as *China Quarterly*, founded in 1959, the *Journal of Modern African Studies*, founded in 1962, and the *Bulletin of Latin American Research* (linked to SLAS) founded in 1981.

And these processes were of course mirrored by the growth of area studies in other 'developed' countries including France, the Netherlands, Australia (with a particular interest in the Pacific), Canada and above all the USA. There has been an African Studies Association in North America since 1957, which, despite internal rows and recent funding constraints, continues to draw well over 1000 participants to its annual conferences, while the US-based Latin American Studies Association (LASA) presently claims over 5000 members.[15] If there have been localised phases of contraction, there has been expansion elsewhere; for example, the African Studies Association of Ireland was established in 2000. Finally, to admittedly quite varying degrees, within the countries of the former Third World there has been increasingly systematic study and analysis by indigenous scholars of their own society and politics. India, for instance, has a large and highly respected community of social scientists who play a leading role in interpreting Indian political developments, much of the time in Indian English-language journals, including the esteemed (Bombay) *Economic and Political Weekly*.

The point I may risk labouring here is that collectively at least we now know so much more about the process and ingredients of politics in different Third World countries than in the 1950s. And with this enhanced knowledge has come confirmation of an earlier more intuitive sense that Third World thinking, the kinds of analytic containers it employed, might be obscuring key differences, whether regional or even country by country, in what politics meant, what determined it and how it worked. This is not to condone the romantic or historicist claim that each country—or indeed province—is unique, 'exceptional' and not to be bracketed with any other. Rather the contention here is that all along there have been such major differences within the Third World as to seriously limit the scope for meaningful political generalisation.

What kinds of differences are being referred to here and what has given rise to them? One answer might be to point to longstanding cultural differences among Third World countries, or regions, to some degree rooted in wider divisions between 'civilisations'. Huntington, we have seen, has recently taken up this approach. He follows the historian Fernand Braudel and others in understanding civilisations to be totalities: 'none of their constituent units can be fully understood without reference to the encompassing civilization'.[16] At the same time he emphasises their cultural dimensions—their 'values, beliefs, institutions and social structures'—and especially their historic foundations in the world's great religions. The civilisation constitutes the broadest cultural unit within which are grouped culturally differentiated regions, nationalities and so on. Civilisations are not eternal or immutable but evolve and decline; nonetheless by definition they are long lasting and far-reaching. Huntington identifies five definite contemporary civilisations: Sinic, Japanese, Hindu, Islamic, and Western, the latter having significantly outgrown its historical roots in 'Christendom'. Then there is Latin America, which may merit its own civilisation, and Russia and Israel as further possible candidates. Africa is confined to a 'possibly'. Huntington sees these civilisational differences as having always been there, although they were to some extent muffled or obscured by ideological divisions of the Cold War; subsequently, they have acquired new visibility and resonance, especially in a global political context, and as anchors of identity.[17]

As already noted, there are serious problems with this kind of thinking not just because of the political ends it can be made to serve but because of the element of arbitrariness in the selection of categories and because of cultural determinism. It tends to present culture as consisting of a single block of meaning rather than as 'polysemic', subject to reinvention, contestation and so on. It can be deployed in a highly—sometimes ridiculously—judgemental way; for instance in the edited volume *Culture Matters*, many of the contributors more or less explicitly rate the cultures under review according to how far they promote human progress—for which read capitalist entrepreneurship.[18] And Huntington's relegation of Africa to little more than a footnote is scarcely helpful.

Even so this perspective does draw attention to major cultural traditions, beyond any simple First/Third World dichotomy. With the inclusion of Japanese civilisation in the First World it cannot be said that any of these civilisations actually straddles the First/Third World divide but the deep-seated cultural heterogeneity of the Third World is underlined. Just to cite one context in which the relevance of such traditions has been asserted, consider the debate about 'Asian values', particularly as they explain, even justify, distinctive attitudes to human rights. There are arguments about whether, logically, such values need to clash with conceptions of human rights; there is also awareness that the Asian values argument has been articulated by and provided useful political ammunition for autocratic leaders such as Singapore's Lee Kuan Yew and Malaysia's Mahathir.[19] Even so Michael Barr has recently concluded that it is possible to discern Asian values, or at least East and Southeast Asian values, 'that are basically communitarian, consensual and hierarchical', whether associated with Islam, Buddhism or Confucianism, and that each of these worldviews has 'fundamental difficulties in establishing an interface with the liberal and Christian human rights agenda'.[20]

Even if we are reluctant to accept the degree of cultural determinism implied in these kinds of arguments, the notion of an extended political trajectory, in which cultural elements play a part, is more difficult to resist. This idea has been developed in particular by Bayart, an eloquent advocate of the need to recognise the political diversity of the Third World.[21] He focuses in the first instance on 'the historical irreducibility' of the Third World state. In order to analyse modern Third World states, he argues that we should view them through the perspective of the extended political trajectory or, in Braudel's phrase, the *longue durée*, going back as far as pre-colonial times. It is not just that a great number of future Third World states had their own developed and distinctive political systems, especially in Asia—India, China, Korea, Japan, Vietnam, Siam/Thailand and Cambodia—but elsewhere, notably Ethiopia and Egypt. Even where such political systems were absent, when the colonial powers 'effectively created' states, like Iraq and Jordan or most of those in tropical Africa, they did not create them out of nothing and these 'colonial creations were also subject to multiple acts of reappropriation by indigenous social groups'. And while these Third World countries faced common or similar 'ruptures' and challenges, in the form of colonisation and subsequent exogenously derived developments, their responses were markedly different and set off in consequence chains of further differentiation.

This leaves open to some degree the question of what it is that provides identity or continuity—what endures over the *longue durée*? We could conceive of it in terms of culture, even civilisation, of systems of economic production and the social power relations associated with them, or of discourses, or what Bayart calls the 'cultural constructions of politics'.

The point being made here is that there have always been important political differences between Third World countries. These differences can be understood in terms of the varying political trajectories traced by different Third World societies from pre-colonial times, however we understand the distinctive elements that have shaped these trajectories. Such differences have become clearer with the passage of time and growth of specialist knowledge.

Increasing diversity?

Not only have we become more aware of diversity; that diversity has itself increased over time. There have been many and changing meanings or rationales of the idea of a Third World. Its brief association with 'nonalignment' suggested that Third World countries would find their own paths forward rather than emulating the capitalist or socialist West. But in other conceptions the opposition has been between the Third World and a more advanced, powerful First (and even Second) World, which, in some sense, represented what Third World countries should want to become. To that extent there has been an assumption if not that Third World countries had in common their gradual approximation to the West, then—in more left-wing accounts—that the West provided a common unifying measure of what it was they could not become. Either way one could suggest that contributing to the readiness to group so many countries together for analytical purposes in a single Third World category was a belief either that as they developed they would converge towards a Western model or that they were effectively frozen in their inability to do so. Perhaps what was less anticipated was that different regions and in many cases countries would develop or modernise—or possibly regress—in different directions.

The paradigm of globalisation which has come to the fore from the late 1980s takes many different ideological forms and has many dimensions, but to the extent that globalisation itself is understood as a process of progressive global economic integration, it could be seen as a common externally derived pressure and/or opportunity all Third World (and all other) states must respond to. But globalisation does not present the same pressures and opportunities to each state. While some, most notably those of East Asia, have been able to harness it and adapt their economies to make the most of it, for much of tropical Africa opportunities for increased trade and Foreign Direct Investment have been severely limited and globalisation has meant rather the imposition of neoliberal structural adjustment regimes by debt-regulating International Financial Institutions (IFIs).

Even when we focus more specifically on patterns of politics, it is now much more difficult to demonstrate a shared 'political syndrome'. Common political features are still observed, most obviously, and in different forms, the politics of clientelism and corruption, not confined to the former Third World but seemingly particularly concentrated and endemic there with very few exceptions, including perhaps Singapore, Botswana, Chile and Costa Rica. In Africa there is little suggestion that patrimonial or neo-patrimonial politics are in decline; rather, according to Chabal and Daloz, what all states in Africa share is:

> a generalized system of patrimonialism and acute degree of apparent disorder, as evidenced by a high level of governmental and administrative inefficiency, a lack of institutionalization, a general disregard for the rules of the formal political and economic sectors and a universal resort to personal(ized) and vertical solutions to societal problems.[22]

But in Latin America too, O'Donnell suggests that the by now widespread institutionalisation of elections and a relatively free press coexist with a second extremely important institution which is 'informal, pervasive and permanent', that of particularism or clientelism, meaning:

> nonuniversalistic relationships, ranging from hierarchical particularistic exchanges, patronage, nepotism and favours to actions that, under the formal rules of the institutional package of polyarchy, would be considered corrupt.[23]

Even in many, perhaps most, of the economically dynamic countries of East and Southeast Asia, personalistic ties, based on family-type relationships and linking business and government, have featured prominently. While the factors underlying the financial crisis of 1997 have been much debated, according to Perkins, there is by now a consensus that the nature of government–business relations, sometimes referred to pejoratively as 'cronyism', played a significant contributory role in Thailand, South Korea and even more so in Malaysia and Indonesia.[24]

However, these few examples already suggest variations in the forms that these 'nonuniversalistic' relationships take and in their implications for the political and economic system. Why, asks O'Donnell, who is interested in democratic transition, have they not proved an insuperable obstacle to consolidation in India (or Italy or Japan)? Instead of being explored, he says, this anomaly has been shunted off into a 'theoretical limbo'. Rather than talking about such relationships under broad and homogenising labels like neo-patrimonialism then, we now need to produce more discriminating taxonomies that distinguish between their forms and consider how these interact with the wider political context.

The 'third wave' of democratisation could be seen, along with, or even as part of, globalisation, as another commonly experienced and at least partially externally driven pressure or influence on Third World states but its effect has been to further disrupt the old 'syndrome' of Third World politics and to accentuate and make clearer the political differences within the Third World. At a superficial level the wave's spread has been rapid and dramatic; already by the early 1990s there were no remaining military regimes in South America—as distinct from central America—and there were strong pressures on Mexico to democratise its one-party system. In tropical Africa by 1995 a plurality of the 40-odd regimes had multiparty systems and in 13 of these there had been a change of government through the ballot box. But some governments, including the substantial case of China, have barely made any concessions to democratic norms, in other countries such as Pakistan fragile multiparty regimes have succumbed to military coups (1999), while in the search for the holy grail of 'democratic consolidation' the relevant literature has coined any number of terms to describe regimes falling short—'delegative', 'illiberal', 'low intensity', 'facade', and so forth. While there are inter-regional variations, there are also regional contrasts, most strikingly between Latin America, where democracy in some shape or form, and despite wobbly moments in Peru and most recently Venezuela, prevails everywhere, and the Middle East where only the most tentative steps have been taken.

The Islamic Revolution in Iran in 1979 brought home to many Western observers the growing salience of religion in Third World politics.[25] Political conflict based on or articulated through religious differences has been on the increase in South Asia, the Middle East and North Africa and Nigeria. The events of 11 September 2001 have made Islamic 'fundamentalism' almost the number one issue associated with Third World politics, eclipsing debt and democratisation. The (re)politicisation of religious difference has been associated with the end of the Cold War and with responses to economic and cultural globalisation on the one hand and with mobilisation strategies of those engaged in domestic power struggles on the other. Yet, leaving aside problems about how and why religion emerges as a political issue, one basic requirement, as Nikki Keddie has emphasised, is that there exists a mainspring of deep religious sentiment and identification to tap into.[26] It is clear that this kind of politics really does not figure to any significant degree in large parts of the Third World. In Latin America, 'liberation theology' played an interesting, if debated, role in nourishing popular social movements, (re)building civil society and contributing to pressures for democratic reforms through the 1970s and 1980s, but this was not about religious conflict, it was about bringing greater social and political awareness into what was then overwhelmingly the dominant form of Christianity, Roman Catholicism. Observers may argue about the role Confucianism— more a moral outlook than a religion anyway—has played in shaping the political culture of East Asian states but no one would claim that religion is a major political issue in these societies.

Ethnic conflict and ethno-nationalism have likewise been on the rise in the former Third (and Second) World and, indeed, religiously identified political movements, such as that for *hindutva* in India, are often best understood as a kind of religious nationalism. But similarly the salience of ethnic conflict, and indeed of ethnicity as a basis of political identities, varies greatly within the Third World. While the character of ethnic politics has changed from its more 'primitive' tribal form in the 1960s, 'ethnicity is more central than ever to the politics of many Africa countries'.[27] In different forms it features prominently in a range of Middle Eastern and Asian contexts, but notwithstanding ethnic dimensions of guerrilla movements in Peru or the Chiapas movement in Mexico, much less so in Latin America. This may be partly because ethnic differences are 'ranked' to use Horowitz's term, corresponding to rather than cross-cutting social stratification, so that ethnic conflict is subsumed in broader class-based conflict, and it may also be that the future will see ethnicity featuring more explicitly. For the moment this marks one further important respect in which meaningful generalisation across the former Third World is constrained.[28]

Conclusion: using and abusing the concept of the Third World

There are still compelling arguments for retaining the notion of the Third World in the context of geopolitical analysis. The actual term used doesn't really matter—South would probably be better than Third World, or possibly some other term such as developing countries/world or 'emerging areas'.[29] The boundaries of the Third World can also be re-specified to exclude some old members and include some new ones. The term is needed to denote the continuing imbalance of economic and political power between (and not only within) the world's nations. Given this axis of inequality, it also provides an important rallying point as a focus of symbolic identification. In addition it may be desirable to hold onto the idea of a North and South as a corrective to current clash of civilisation arguments.

But in the field of comparative politics, Third World-type generalisations are no longer helpful. It must be recognised that there is a basic tension in the idea of a Third World. It can be understood as a response to global inequality but it is also a symptom of First World thinking, a category imposed as part of a specific First World way of seeing things. In the past the readiness to generalise about a Third World type of political system was at least partly the result both of the need to get the Third World onto the syllabus at all and of the degree of ignorance about the substantial historically shaped differences in the political trajectories of the countries that composed it. The growth of specialist area studies has generated increasingly systematic knowledge of these differences while the passage of time has revealed them more fully and reinforced their extent. We no longer have excuses for failing to do justice to the political diversity of the (former) Third World.

43

Notes

[1] See for instance V Randall & R Theobald, *Political Change and Underdevelopment*, Basingstoke: Macmillan, 1998; MT Berger, 'The end of the "Third World"?', *Third World Quarterly*, 15 (2), 1994, pp 257–275; and B Smith, *Understanding Third World Politics*, London: Macmillan, 1996.

[2] Details provided at http.//www.namkl.org.my.

[3] P Cammack, D Pool & W Tordoff, *Third World Politics: A Comparative Introduction*, Basingstoke: Macmillan, 1993.

[4] J-P Thérien, 'Beyond the North–South divide: the two tales of world poverty,' *Third World Quarterly*, 20 (4), 1999, pp 723–742.

[5] C Thomas, 'Globalization and the South' in C Thomas & P Wilkin (eds), *Globalization and the South*, London: Macmillan, 1997.

[6] Thérien, 'Beyond the North–South divide'.

[7] See *The Economist*, Special Report—Civil Wars, 24 May 2003, pp 23–25.

[8] See reports in the *Guardian* during August 2002.

[9] S Huntington, 'The clash of civilizations?', *Foreign Affairs*, 72 (3), 1993, pp 22–49; and S Huntington, *The Clash of Civilizations and the Remaking of World Order*, New York: Simon and Schuster, 1996.

[10] Randall & Theobald, *Political Change and Underdevelopment*, p 11.

[11] G Hawthorne, '"Waiting for a text?" Comparing Third World politics', in James Manor (ed), *Rethinking Third World Politics*, London: Longman, 1991.

[12] As described in Randall & Theobald, *Political Change and Underdevelopment*, ch 2. The classic example of this revisionist approach is the Rudolphs' analysis of the interaction of the caste system and modern forms of political participation in India. L Rudolph & S Rudolph, *The Modernity of Tradition: Political Development in India*, Chicago, IL: Chicago University Press, 1967.

[13] For an overview, see A Foster-Carter, 'The modes of production controversy', *New Left Review*, 107, 1978, pp 47–77.

[14] For a valuable account of the development of African studies in the UK, see the collection of essays edited by D Rimmer & A Kirk-Greene, *The British Intellectual Engagement with Africa in the Twentieth Century*, London: Macmillan, 2000, especially the essays by Kirk-Greene. I am grateful to Chris Clapham for bringing this to my attention. For a shorter but useful review of the development of Latin American studies in the UK, see L Bethell, 'The British contribution to the study of Brazil', Centre for Brazilian Studies, Working paper no. 37, 2003, at www.brazil.ox.ac.uk/papers.html.

[15] On Latin American studies in the USA see MT Berger, *Under Northern Eyes: Latin American Studies and US Hegemony in the Americas, 1898–1990*, Bloomington, IN: Indiana University Press, 1995.

[16] Huntington, *The Clash of Civilizations*, p 42.

[17] *Ibid*, pp 40–48.

[18] LE Harrison & SP Huntington (eds), *Culture Matters*, New York: Basic Books, 2000.

[19] MT Berger, 'The new Asian renaissance and its discontents: national narratives, pan-Asian visions and the changing post-cold war order', *International Politics*, 40 (2), 2003, pp 195–221.

[20] MD Barr, *Cultural Politics and Asian Values: The Tepid War*, London: Routledge, 2002.

[21] J-F Bayart, 'Finishing with the idea of the Third World: the concept of the political trajectory', in Manor, *Rethinking Third World Politics*.

[22] P Chabal & J-P Daloz, *Africa Works*, London: James Currey, 1999, p xix.

[23] G O'Donnell, 'Illusions about consolidation', *Journal of Democracy*, 7 (2), 1996, pp 151–159.

[24] DH Perkins, 'Law, family ties and the East Asian way of business', in Harrison & Huntington, *Culture Matters*.

[25] J Haynes, *Religion in Third World Politics*, Milton Keynes: Open University Press, 1993.

[26] N Keddie, 'The new religious politics: where, when and why do fundamentalisms appear?', *Comparative Studies in Society and History*, October 1998, pp 696–723.

[27] M Ottaway, 'Ethnic politics in Africa: change and continuity', in R Joseph (ed), *State, Conflict and Democracy in Africa*, Boulder, CO: Lynne Rienner, 1999, p 300.

[28] D Horowitz, *Ethnic Groups in Conflict*, Berkeley, CA: University of California Press, 1985.

[29] 'Emerging areas' has been part of the sub-title of this journal—*Third World Quarterly: Journal of Emerging Areas*—since it was first launched in 1978.

The rise of neo-Third Worldism? The Indonesian trajectory and the consolidation of illiberal democracy

VEDI R HADIZ

'Democracy' has had a precarious existence in most of the one-time Third World. In large parts of Latin America, Asia and Africa, authoritarian regimes held sway for much of the post-1945 period, and today, even after the 'Third Wave' of democratisation that culminated with the end of the Cold War, there remain powerful constraints on the advance of democracy.[1] In Indonesia, for example, the site of the Bandung Conference in 1955, the early postcolonial period saw an experiment with liberal, parliamentary-style democracy that was discontinued by Sukarno's Guided Democracy (1959–66), and which paved the way for the emergence of a highly centralised authoritarian–corporatist regime— Suharto's 'New Order'. Since Suharto's ouster in May 1998, Indonesia is now commonly assumed to be either already a democracy or in a transition towards democracy.[2] Indeed, there have been momentous changes since the end of 32 years of iron-fisted rule by the predatory Suharto regime. The character and significance of these changes have, however, been misinterpreted by most analysts, and this has significance for broader understandings of democratisation in the former Third World.

I wish to achieve several goals in this article. First, I want to link understandings of the contest over democracy in Indonesia—the world's fourth most populous nation—with more general theoretical debates about democratisation in the 'Third World', debates that have undergone numerous permutations over the past several decades. Second, I want to show how these theoretical debates on democracy/democratisation and authoritarianism have intertwined in some notable instances with domestic political debates in Indonesia, and in ways that may not be completely expected. Third, I would like to suggest that the contemporary world order based on the hegemony of the USA weakens, rather than strengthens, the forces of democratic liberalism in Indonesian society. This directly contradicts the stated altruistic aims of American empire to make the world 'safe' for democracy.[3] The present US-led global order is characterised not only by unrivalled US economic, political and military power, but also by the increasingly free use of force to mould the processes and contours of economic globalisation to suit the needs, primarily, of US-based and transnational capital.[4]

Finally, I would like to suggest that the projection of US power in the post-11 September world will strengthen the impulse towards an emerging 'neo-Third Worldism' in Indonesia and elsewhere. If the Third Worldism of Sukarno, Tito, Nehru and the like—whatever its faults, internal contradictions and deeply ambiguous relationship with democratic ideals—was driven by a vision of a postcolonial future of egalitarianism and internationalism, contemporary neo-Third Worldism is characterised by indigenism, reactionary populism and a strong inclination towards cultural insularism. Although all these elements were also strongly present in the original Third Worldism of the 1950s and 1960s, they were balanced by a progressive vision of a future world order, born out of concrete anti-imperialist struggles over several decades.

By contrast, today's more inward-looking version of Third Worldism is the knee-jerk reaction of ruling elites from Latin America to Southeast Asia to the swagger of US empire. Thus, the nascent neo-Third Worldism of Southeast Asian leaders like Mahathir Mohammad in Malaysia, Thaksin Shinawatra in Thailand and Megawati Sukarnoputri in Indonesia, or that of the Islamic fundamentalists in parts of the Middle East, South and Southeast Asia, merely reasserts the most conservative elements of the old Third Worldism depleted of its internationalist vision of the future. Indeed neo-Third Worldism has no vision. It rests, instead, on nostalgia for a romanticised, indigenous, pre-capitalist past—a sorry riposte to the triumphalism of unbridled US power, with which most of the above states have little choice but to engage, notwithstanding any apparent reluctance. This is how Third Worldism is in the process of being resurrected: as a tragicomic caricature of its predecessor.

In many respects this is not surprising. By the 1970s Third Worldism had already been drained of its revolutionary postcolonial ideals and rhetoric. In many countries a new generation of leaders had emerged whose main project was that of a centralised state developmentalism that found ready allies among the major protagonists of the Cold War. Thus, Indonesia's Suharto was eventually to lead the 'Non-aligned Movement' that had come out of the original Third Worldism of the 1950s, although his regime was clearly allied to the USA, the world power that had much to thank him for in his brutal and effective crushing of Indonesian communism in the 1960s.

Some could still hope that a new, progressive and rejuvenated version of Third Worldism might yet emanate from the civil societies of Asia, Africa and Latin America. Indeed, some might take solace in the participation of Third World-based organisations in such events as the anti-WTO protests in Seattle in 1999. Or they might take encouragement from the recent world-wide anti-war protests in reaction to the US-led invasion of Iraq, many of which occurred outside of the metropolitan capitalist nation-states. But there is at least an equal chance that the civil society-based movements involved may instead be drawn into the conservative and reactionary agendas of ruling elites who may seek to bolster their position by adopting, selectively and to varying degrees, anti-American or anti-globalisation stances as they compete for support through the employment of neo-Third Worldist rhetoric. Such competing elites in Indonesia, for example, have effectively manipulated nationalist (and religious) sentiment in relation to the US 'war on terror' to legitimise their claims to power. In Malaysia the Third World Network, which takes a vocal anti-globalisation stance, enjoys close relations with the autocratic Mahathir government, despite the Penang-based organisation's previously critical view of the prime minister and his policies. Thaksin, the Thai premier and telecom tycoon, had earlier gained much political mileage by portraying himself as a populist who would not bend easily to the neoliberal economic agenda; at least initially he had the support of NGOs and grassroots movements in Thailand. The main casualties of developments such as these are likely to be the ideals of social justice, democracy, equality and human rights that might have underpinned any notion of a rejuvenated Third Worldism premised on progressive civil society-based movements.

If Third Worldism was a product of nationalist, anti-colonial movements and the Cold War, contemporary, emerging neo-Third Worldism is a product of a post-cold war world centred on US hegemony, and in which no Second World representing a socialist alternative exists any longer. While the relationship of the old Third Worldism with democratic ideals was at best ambivalent—given the experiences with Sukarno, Nasser, Tito and the like—the emergence of neo-Third Worldism strongly suggests that economic globalisation under the aegis of US hegemony can have highly illiberal political consequences. This is not just because the American hegemon has resumed the cold war-era practice of bolstering corrupt and ruthless regimes[5] as long as they remain friendly to US corporate interests. It is also because the neo-conservative ascendancy in the USA[6] essentially promotes an illiberal form of democracy that strives for the establishment of state institutions in the 'Third World', able to protect international investors from social coalitions that pose a challenge to the power and wealth inequalities produced by the free market.[7]

Theoretical perspectives: from modernisation to illiberal imperium

This section examines the intersection between theoretical explanations for democratisation and/or authoritarianism in the Third World and domestic political contests over democracy in Indonesia.[8] Many aspects of the various theoretical explanations that have emerged over the years to explain authoritarianism and democracy have been freely deployed in Indonesia by contending forces in support of particular social and political agendas—perhaps most clearly during the formative period of Suharto's New Order. This period coincided with some of the most intense years of the Cold War, at least in relation to Southeast Asia.

Classical modernisation theory—which is still influential in the social science curricula of most major Indonesian universities—viewed the postcolonial, Third World state as an essentially benign agent of development and modernisation. That the postcolonial state would be conceived as the main agent of modernisation and development was more or less ensured by the absence of solid entrepreneurial classes in virtually all of early postcolonial Asia and Africa. More specifically, however, early modernisation theorists envisaged a particularly positive role for technocratic elites—especially those who had benefited from Western-style education and were immersed in 'Western', modern values—given the broader social and cultural conditions of the postcolonial era that were characterised as being patrimonial or pre-modern. It was the technocratic elite, more than any other historical agent—and in lieu of any 'real' middle or capital-owning classes—that was envisaged as having a crucial role to play in the growth of a modern 'civic culture', conducive to the nurturing of Western liberal democratic norms.[9] It is significant that these same elites were simultaneously imagined to be the main bastions against the spread of communism in the Third World in the context of the Cold War.[10]

Thus it was US policy in Indonesia from as early as the 1950s to nurture and sustain pro-American intellectuals, bureaucrats and military leaders through aid and training programmes. The Ford Foundation, for example, helped to develop the infrastructure for the training of 'modernising' Indonesian elites at US universities such as MIT and Cornell. It was also instrumental in developing the Economics Faculty of the University of Indonesia, which later provided the Suharto bureaucracy and his various cabinets with a steady stream of individuals with technocratic expertise.[11] It was clearly assumed that these technocrats would lead Indonesia to the world of democracy and free markets—an important project given the context of the escalating Vietnam War. However, it was to be convincingly shown, certainly in the case of Indonesia, that anti-communism and democracy and free markets did not all go together: although Suharto remained virulently anti-communist and stayed firmly committed to the US camp as far as cold war politics were concerned, he rode roughshod over economic policy and guided Indonesia towards an exceptionally predatory form of capitalism, underpinned in the 1970s and 1980s by windfall oil revenues, as well as crafting a profoundly authoritarian political system. In the process, Western-trained technocrats were often marginalised, as they had no independent base of social power. It must be understood that the projection of the image of technocratic governance was only part and parcel of the regime's strategy of containing internal as well as external criticism of its essentially authoritarian and predatory character. Of course, the case of Indonesia is in no way unique in this respect. Not that US policy makers would necessarily have had serious objections: US-based companies like the oil concern Caltex, and the mining giant Freeport profited enormously from the situation.

It is notable that Indonesian state elites found the lexicon of modernisation theory particularly attractive. The late General Ali Moertopo, once Suharto's closest aide and political henchman, borrowed freely from Rostowian 'stages of growth' theory in his own 'magnum opus', grandiosely entitled in English *Basic Thoughts on the Acceleration and Modernisation of 25-Year Development*.[12] Marrying the developmentalist orientation of modernisation theory with his strongly authoritarian–statist inclinations, Moertopo declared that:

> As a developing country, Indonesia is still always confronted with the problem of having to decide how to shape its future development. The appropriate policy is what is generally called modernisation. In order to achieve our goals as efficiently as possible, modernisation is nothing more than the process of using all available material, ethical, scientific and technical means to organise, structure and implement development based on one way of thinking.[13]

On the other hand, US 'Indonesianists' like Karl Jackson were at the forefront of studies that applied many of the assumptions of modernisation theory to the Indonesian case.[14] Within the framework of modernisation theory Indonesian development problems were typically posed in terms of producing the values conducive to modernisation. Not surprisingly, the 'heroes' of the Indonesian development process have invariably been economic technocrats (and other intellectuals) mostly schooled in the neoclassical tradition who struggled to enforce 'rational' policy in the face of an intrusive patrimonial style of politics.[15] But this suited Moertopo's vision quite well, for these heroic nation-building experts still required insulation from 'self-interested' societal pressure.

Over time, however, the technocrats came to be subjected to considerable scrutiny. John MacDougall was only one academic who began to carefully appraise the role of the technocrats in Suharto's Indonesia by the 1970s.[16] In a controversial article David Ransom spoke of the existence of a 'Berkeley Mafia'—a reference to US-trained economists in the Suharto cabinets—who, he suggested, played a comprador role by actively protecting the interests of their US patrons.[17] But, like the supporters of the technocrats, detractors such as Ransom and others who would follow exaggerated their importance. The focus on the technocrats steered some attention away from the fact that Suharto, his family and cronies—the main elements of a burgeoning capitalist oligarchy that had been incubated within the New Order—came to exercise increasingly direct, instrumental control over state power and its institutions.[18]

In any case New Order figures like Moertopo arguably would have found classical modernisation theory to be less attractive than the revisionism represented primarily in the work of the US political scientist, Samuel Huntington. By the late 1960s Huntington's work had already signalled a new emphasis in modernisation theory that effectively defined the condition of modernity in terms of the successful maintenance of political stability.[19] According to Huntington— the future proponent, paradoxically, of both a thesis on a global 'third wave' of democratisation in the 1980s and of a 'clash of civilisations' (within which democracy is essentially a Western cultural construct) in the 1990s[20]—state 'modernity' was measured on the basis of institutionalisation. Within the conceptual scheme of this revisionist modernisation theory, the institutionalisation of the structures of political power was required to avert a descent into chaos or anarchy.

Such ideas were clearly useful to the ideologues of authoritarian capitalist regimes like the New Order,[21] especially in terms of providing intellectual justification for state policies that sternly domesticated political opposition in the name of providing the stability required for economic growth. In other words, the revisionist modernisation theory of Huntington fitted quite nicely with the New Order's oft-repeated claim that the institutional framework of the regime was geared to ensuring the stability required for economic progress, and that liberal democracy—with its potentially destabilising effect—was not in accordance with economic development aims.

It would be misleading to suggest, however, that these variants of modernisation theory went completely unchallenged in Indonesia, because a discourse on democracy and a more just development process did in fact emerge in the 1970s and through to the 1990s. Theoretical explanations produced mainly in Western academe have also fed into this alternative discourse in Indonesia. For example, Indonesia, was scrutinised from a variety of neo-Marxist perspectives: Rex Mortimer, an Australian radical scholar, was one of the earlier proponents of the view that the Indonesian state was basically acting out a comprador role in relation to international capital.[22] In Mortimer's view, the Indonesian state's main function was to establish the conditions for the transfer of economic surplus to the metropolitan countries. Clearly such notions are rooted in the Latin American-inspired dependency theory which was influential among radical scholars of development in the 1960s and 1970s.

In Indonesia it was Sritua Arief and Adi Sasono who produced the most well known dependency study, arguing that persistent poverty and 'underdevelopment' was rooted in the global unequal exchange mechanisms imposed on Indonesia since its colonisation by the Dutch.[23] Such prominent thinkers on unequal development as Samir Amin, in turn, heavily influenced these writers. Significantly, authors like Sritua Arief and Adi Sasono played an important role in the emergence of Southeast Asia-based networks of NGO activists and academics in the 1980s who advanced a Third Worldist-orientated and dependency theory-influenced framework to understand the development of capitalism in the region, as well as the salience of authoritarian regimes in many countries.

But the successful excision of Marxism in general and 'class conflict' in particular from Indonesian political and intellectual discourse by the New Order showed that the Marxist-influenced critique of development policy in Indonesia had no real social or political base. The Indonesian Communist Party—the PKI—was decimated at the onset of the New Order in 1965–66. Arief and Sasono, rather than representing what may have remained of a radical Left ideological stream, actually came out of the Islamic-orientated petty-bourgeois tradition in Indonesian social and political thinking. Its social base was that of the long-declining group of indigenous, small merchants and traders who had a history of enmity towards the ethnic Chinese and the foreign bourgeoisie. The Third Worldism implied in dependency theory was attractive to them because the 'enemy' was identified as being 'foreign' in one way or another, and thus external to the Indonesian body politic proper. In other words, dependency theory was useful for petty-bourgeois populists whose main grievance was the lack of opportunities to benefit from the fruits of economic development, but who were fearful of any left-wing revival in Indonesia. In fact the political genealogy of Adi Sasono, in particular, is traceable to the Islamic youth and student organisations that were so instrumental in the New Order's violent crushing of the Left, and in this sense he is fairly typical of the leaders of mainstream contemporary organised Islam in Indonesia. It is perhaps not too surprising that he eventually became a major New Order figure himself in the 1990s, once Suharto had opened the corridors of power to Muslim intellectuals in an effort to widen his own base of support.[24]

In the meantime some liberal pluralists—emerging primarily from the urban middle class and intelligentsia—who had supported the early New Order against the communists—came to be attracted to a brand of Marxism that was particularly notable for its lack of class conflict. In articles influential among many Indonesian liberal intellectuals in the 1980s, Hamza Alavi had argued that postcolonial states enjoyed relative autonomy from social classes because of the underdeveloped class structure that had been inherited. Postcolonial states, according to Alavi, were 'overdeveloped' in relation to an underdeveloped class structure.[25] Showing the traces of a dependency perspective, the interests of metropolitan capital remained more powerful in Alavi's theoretical construct because of the weakness and underdevelopment of its local counterpart. Thus, while the postcolonial state had a dominant presence, it was structurally beholden to the interests of international capital. Alavi's work on Pakistan and Bangladesh was adapted to the Indonesian case by the late Farchan Bulkin[26]— and a host of Indonesian student and NGO activists—who argued that the underdevelopment of the bourgeoisie and middle classes was the basis for state dominance over civil society. This kind of state dominance, it was surmised, was responsible for hindering the development of democracy.

Such intellectual developments were reflective of the new penchant among liberals and pluralists in Indonesia to view the (authoritarian) state as the main enemy. This was partly attributable to their declining influence within the regime, and partly to the fact that any hope that the New Order would develop into a democracy had been crushed by the mid-1970s when it forcefully put down student demonstrations and gaoled leading liberal activists. Perhaps the most identifiable representative of this sort of development was Arief Budiman, a sociologist, political activist and public intellectual who had been an early supporter of the New Order but who had turned to dependency theory and neo-Marxism to criticise the regime. But again the emphasis on the state and, to varying degrees, the role of metropolitan capital meant little acknowledgement of internal class conflicts and dynamics, except to lament the absence of a vigorous middle class. It also allowed the adoption of Marxist-inspired ideas by individuals with political genealogies traceable to former opponents of the PKI, with little acknowledgement of the political legacy of their long-vanquished former enemies.

Other variants of state-centred approached to politics and society became influential as well. For example, in the context of the deepening of authoritarianism in Indonesia and elsewhere in the 1970s, scholars like Mochtar Mas'oed,[27] as well as representatives of NGO and student movements, began to borrow freely from the expanding literature on bureaucratic authoritarian regimes epitomised by the work of the Latin American specialist Guillermo O'Donnell.[28] More than ever the rise of civil society—especially conceived as a middle class resurgence—was put forward in the Indonesian political discourse as the antithesis to an overbearing and stifling state. It will be remembered that theorists like Theda Skocpol, influenced both by the Marxian and Weberian traditions, were also increasingly challenging Marxist theories of the state by the 1980s .[29] This kind of theoretical position, which brought 'the state back in' as a self-interested, autonomous actor, had considerable appeal in Indonesia, where state power appeared to be so pervasive. Although his framework was very different from that of Skocpol (and her colleagues), Benedict Anderson emerged as the main proponent of the state-for-itself thesis for Indonesia. His argument was that the ascendance of the New Order in 1966 represented the victory of the 'state'—which was traceable to the colonial period—over 'society'.[30]

Meanwhile, by the 1980s Richard Robison, was the scholar who was most closely identified with the sustained analysis of the state's role in Indonesia's capitalist transformation. While agreeing with Anderson that the preservation of their institutional base of power is important to the holders of state power, Robison also pointed out that state power could only be understood in relation to a wider system of class relationships.[31] Borrowing from Marx, he later suggested that 'Bonapartism' emerged in Indonesia insofar as a weak bourgeoisie forfeited power in favour of an authoritarian state in order to contain potential revolutionary impulses from below.[32] In reality a vigorous urban middle class and bourgeoisie was developing under the aegis of the New Order, as suggested in Robison's now classic work, *Indonesia: The Rise of Capital*. But, unlike the imaginings of their ideological champions, especially within the Indonesian middle class intelligentsia, these social forces were deeply conservative and inclined towards acceptance of the political status quo. Benefiting materially from Indonesia's economic growth under the New Order, they feared instability and the threat to social order and property that might accompany regime change. However, the broad issues addressed within this kind of perspective were only taken up by a handful of Indonesian scholars.[33]

Indeed, the 1980s and 1990s mostly saw a slew of writings by Indonesian intellectuals on the 'naturally' progressive nature of the middle class and/or bourgeoisie. The economist Sjahrir, for example, argued that economic liberalisation and deregulation would strengthen the middle class, and therefore the democratic impulse in Indonesian society, because the power of the state would be compromised.[34] Not surprisingly, this kind of development in Indonesia coincided with the global resurgence of modernisation theory in the form of neo-institutionalism and rational choice theory. Premised on the analytical tools of neoclassical economics, such as 'game theory', neo-institutionalism and rational choice have become increasingly pervasive across the various disciplines of the social sciences.[35] In the process, the old assumptions of modernisation theory—earlier criticised by dependency theorists and neo-Marxists—are clearly reproduced in Douglass North's influential suggestion that culturally rooted belief systems may undermine the solving of the increasingly complex problems of development.[36] Moreover, Sanjaya Lal's assertion that a powerful state is often required to constrain emerging competing interest groups is strongly reminiscent of Huntington's revisionism.[37]

Significantly, contemporary liberal theories of modernisation and development regularly emphasise the need for technocratic 'modern' elites who are capable of making rational choices. Crucially as well, the concept of democracy that is advanced is implicitly one in which technocratic experts can preside over policies in the 'general interest' without the intervention of social coalitions that may pose a challenge to inequalities in power and wealth. Thus this is essentially a form of democracy that incorporates strong regulatory and anti-liberal political aspects,[38] even as it notionally eschews state domination for fear of stifling private entrepreneurship. This is precisely the view of democracy that is being professed by American empire, with its concern to mould political conditions globally that would be conducive to free markets and international investment. Civil society is, interestingly, invoked as well, but mainly insofar as the middle class and the bourgeoisie are assumed to grow stronger with deeper capitalist development and closer integration with global markets.[39] But Rodan has argued that it is a mistake to view civil society as a single, politically progressive and homogeneous entity.[40] Interestingly, Indonesian social scientists, increasingly enamoured with the concept of civil society, tend to replicate the civil-society-as-progressive middle class thesis.[41]

It is interesting to note in this connection that a prominent feature of the literature on good governance, as produced by the World Bank and the US Agency for International Development (USAID), is the notion that technocratic expertise—rather than political contestation—is the key element in the success-ful crafting of market-friendly and democratic political institutions. Implicitly, societal pressure for a range of liberties and rights is potentially obtrusive to the exercise of an insulated, objective technocratic rationality.[42] These views are reflected in the Indonesian domestic debates today—scholar and television personality Rizal Mallarangeng, for example, is an outspoken champion in Indonesia of the rationality of the market, safeguarded by the wisdom of liberal technocracy.[43]

In this regard it is clear that the democracy being promoted in the US-dominated post-cold war world has more in common with Huntington's revision-ism of the 1960s than the classical version of modernisation theory that postulated a direct link between economic development and democracy. Further-more, although neo-Third Worldism is a conservative populist reaction to US hegemony, the illiberal kind of democracy promoted by a prodigious array of intellectuals connected directly and indirectly to US power is not completely disagreeable to aspiring neo-Third Worldists. Thaksin in Thailand, or Mahathir in Malaysia, would be quite happy with a regulated democratic system in which a fundamental challenge to the existing social order is not possible for the sake of ensuring the social stability needed to ensure investment conditions. The problem—and a source of tension with Washington—is that their efforts to position themselves against domestic challenges to their authoritarian political practices involves the selective adoption of anti-American and anti-globalisation rhetoric. Mahathir, for example, bolstered his domestic popularity by his tren-chant and repeated rejection of IMF policy advice at the height of the Asian financial crisis (1997–98). Meanwhile, since the start of the US-led 'war on terror', leaders like Mahathir and Megawati in Indonesia have needed to match the populist appeal of various Islamic-based adversaries—whose social justice rhetoric is sometimes virulently anti-American—while simultaneously ensuring continued engagement with US-led global economic and security processes.

The rise, fall, and re-emergence of Indonesian democracy: a Third World lesson?

Contrary to a great deal of contemporary analysis, Indonesia, at this juncture, is no longer in a state of transition to a liberal form of democratic rule. Instead an illiberal form of democracy is already entrenched, grounded in the logic of money politics and political violence, similar to post-Soviet Russia, Thailand or the Philippines.[44] Among its main beneficiaries have been the lower-level apparatchik, political operators and entrepreneurs, as well as henchmen and thugs of the old regime, who have now reinvented themselves as 'democrats' and 'reformers', nationally and locally. Many of these constitute predatory interests, formerly nurtured by the authoritarian Suharto regime, which have now realigned and reconstituted within a new political framework. While the institutional trappings of democracy, the rise of parties and parliaments have served them well, they have an interest in ensuring that the predatory power relations that defined the New Order, based on the accumulation of private wealth through the appropriation of public institutions and resources, remain intact. Lurking ominously in the background is a widely feared military, which is still licking its wounds after the advent of *reformasi*. At this juncture the Indonesia military is bent on ensuring that its institutional and material interests, if not its outright political and economic power and influence, are safeguarded within this newly democratised terrain.

This dimension of the problem was lost on early observers of post-Suharto Indonesia, who borrowed freely from the democratic transitions literature pioneered by O'Donnell, Schmitter and their colleagues, and which centres on elite negotiations and pacts and the crafting of new political arrangements.[45] In trying to make sense of fast-occurring developments in Indonesia, such observers were attracted to an overly linear conception of democratic change that is said to begin from authoritarian decay, then proceed through the stages of 'transition', 'consolidation' and 'maturation'.[46] Some were also attracted to the idea that the transition to democracy is primarily a question of crafting the right kinds of institutions, those which, in World Bank parlance, can produce 'good governance'. In this case 'playing by the rules' became exceedingly important,[47] although it implied no real action to halt the reconstitution and domination of old elites in new political vehicles. This was, in fact, the essential problem of the transition in the late 1990s: that they were not brushed aside by *reformasi* meant that New Order stalwarts and local operators have had ample time to hijack the democratisation process in their own interests.

There are those within Indonesia—like a number of NGO and student activists—who continue to hope that the 'good things' they associate with democracy, like accountability, transparency, human rights and the like, will still transpire in the near future. Certainly they will find solace in the reports of a number of international development organisations, like USAID, which have continued to suggest—with a certain naiveté—that what is taking place is nothing less than a 'transition to a prospering and democratic Indonesia'.[48] Indeed, there is much in common between the neo-institutionalist literature, which relies on technocratic expertise in the rational crafting of viable institutions, and the 'democratic transitions' literature, which ultimately relies on the right kind of pacts by the right kinds of elites making rational choices,[49] and pays little attention to the factor of concrete political and social struggles. But if hopes that 'all good things can go together' should finally be dashed, it wouldn't be the first time that this has happened in the recent history of Indonesia .[50] Following the attainment of formal independence from the Dutch in 1949, a parliamentary democracy system was in place characterised by intense competition among a range of parties. A milestone of the period were the 1955 elections—still regarded as the fairest that Indonesia has ever held.[51] But parliamentary democracy's hold was always tenuous and the seeds of Indonesia's long descent into authoritarianism were soon to be planted.

The turning point came as a response to regional separatist rebellions in the late 1950s, after which Sukarno gave the central military command wide powers and control over the administrative apparatus of the state. In 1957 the increasingly powerful military also took over managerial control of newly nationalised foreign companies that had originally been seized by militant labour unions, especially those associated with the communists. Sukarno—who, like the military, was relatively marginalised under the liberal democratic system—went on to disband parliament altogether and to set up the system of 'Guided Democracy'. This gave the presidency wide-ranging powers and transformed parliament into a body consisting of relatively pliant 'functional group' representatives. Under Guided Democracy, Sukarno would be the 'Great Leader', who stood above petty interests—and, indeed, was the very personification of the national interest. But Sukarno was unwittingly paving the way for Suharto's New Order.

Significantly, the PKI was the only party able to increase its power and influence during Guided Democracy by supporting Sukarno's simultaneously nationalist and Third Worldist foreign policy agenda. Indeed, the PKI grew to be the third largest communist party in the world.[52] However, the military, with increasing US support in the context of the Cold War, began to develop an alliance with a range of anti-communist forces—including Islamic, right-wing, socialist and Christian political parties. Its cause was helped by the fact that Sukarno was beginning to alienate large sections of the propertied and urban salaried classes, as his autarchic, anti-imperialist and Third Worldist economic policies resulted in disaster. By 1965, for example, inflation stood at no less than 600%. These conditions allowed for a right-wing coup under the leadership of General Suharto, accompanied by the massacre of hundreds of thousands of real and imagined communists.[53] Thus, in a relative blink of the eye, the PKI and its mass organisations were completely eliminated from the scene. Suharto then gradually usurped powers—sidelining Sukarno himself—and forged a far more centralised state corporatist system than his charismatic predecessor was capable of imagining or implementing. In the process he realigned Indonesia with the world capitalist powers. It should be recalled at this time that Indonesian liberal intellectuals, as well as Western governments and international organisations, expected the New Order to be a democratic regime.[54]

But of course the New Order turned out to be ruthlessly authoritarian. Indeed, Suharto's legacy was to further marginalise parties and parliament in Indonesia—for example he fused all the Sukarno-era parties into just two entities and privileged a single, state-controlled electoral vehicle, Golkar. He also institutionalised a corporatist system of representation that basically pre-empted independent civil society-based organisations. Workers, for example, were forced to follow a single state-dominated labour organisation, as were the peasantry, youth, women, and so on.[55] Ideologically the idea of *Pancasila* democracy was advanced ever further—as an anti-liberal, anti-communist and uniquely Indonesian system suited to the nation's culture and history.[56]

It was only in the wake of the Asian financial crisis that Suharto's New Order finally unravelled. That the New Order came tumbling down at this time reflected the fact that the ruling coalition of interests cemented by Suharto—based upon politico-business families and large corporate conglomerates emerging from the apparatus of the state itself—had earlier taken possession of the state to an astonishingly instrumental degree. This was conducive to the creation of an economic system that eventually became over-borrowed, over-invested and unconstrained, and which finally collapsed as a result of a 'fatal embrace' with the same global markets that had helped to nurture it.[57] Nevertheless, as mentioned earlier, this did not stop elements of the old ruling coalition—though now highly decentralised and diffuse—from reconstituting and seeking to appropriate Indonesia's new institutions of market and political governance. This is seen in the feverish competition in Indonesia today, nationally and locally, to achieve predatory and instrumental control over state institutions, offices and resources. But if predatory relations of power can survive the unravelling of an authoritarian regime, what could break them apart? Is the answer ultimately to surrender to the forces of the market and globalisation? If so, will economic liberalisation lead to liberal democracy in the erstwhile Third World after all, and as predicted by both the modernisation theorists of the early cold war-era and the contemporary advocates of globalisation? This remains exceedingly unlikely.

Indonesia, empire and terror

The development of Indonesia's democracy is increasingly intertwined with such phenomena as deepening economic globalisation, the US-led 'war on terror' and, ultimately, the prowess of the US hegemon itself. Indeed, Indonesia is now more structurally entangled than ever in both the global financial markets and the brave new world of a resurgent US militarism and global security-state. Not surprisingly, the proponents of US hegemony in the post-cold war era tend to claim a connection between democracy and the free market.[58] Indeed, democracy and the free market are often presented as one package. But there is a paradox in the conception of democracy. In their view, democracy is on the one hand something that liberates the individual from the state but, on the other hand, an arrangement of power within which the interests of private investors must be safeguarded. The solution can only be to have states that will functionally secure the inviolability and sanctity of property rights. In the case of Indonesia, this is shown most clearly in the unease of Western governments and international investors with the social instability that has ensued after the fall of Suharto. They have been extremely worried by the emergence of a less predictable, even volatile, set of political arrangements. The labour movement, for example, has repeatedly been singled out as a threat to economic reform. More generally, IMF officials in Indonesia expressed concern at the end of the 1990s that 'too much' democracy could be a potential threat to liberal economic reform.[59]

Anxiety about instability in Indonesia was heightened dramatically in the wake of the attack on the World Trade Center and the Pentagon and then the Bali bombings of 12 October 2002, after which it was alleged that a newly discovered militant Islamic group—the Jemaah Islamiyah—was waging a covert war against US interests in alliance with Osama bin Laden. Thus the order and security aspect of the US agenda were henceforth to be more clearly expressed than ever. Meanwhile, little is said in US policy-making circles today about the role of American companies like Exxon and Freeport in bankrolling the free-wheeling brutality of the Indonesian military in Aceh and Papua—sites of important separatist movements.[60] (In fact, these movements emerged as a direct response to the brutality of the Suharto regime.[61]) The indifference in a Washington preoccupied with order and security was apparent in the lack of response to the assassination of a Papuan political leader and the fact that the killing was publicly lauded by one of Indonesia's top generals.[62]

The overwhelming concern with order and security, at the centre of the emergent new US imperialism, has been expressed with particular forcefulness by authors such as Sebastian Mallaby, a columnist for the *Washington Post*. Writing in the influential journal, *Foreign Affairs*, he argued that the USA must take on the role of an imperial power, however reluctantly, as the failure to do so will result in world chaos and grave threats to the USA itself. According to Mallaby, modern and civil institutions are never going to develop in a distressingly high number of 'failed states'—no matter how much foreign aid is poured in—and as a result they are all potential sources of world disorder. He emphasises that international institutions, such as the UN, have also failed and it is now the duty and burden of the USA to make the world safe for civilisation.[63]

In this context governments like those in Indonesia, China and elsewhere will enjoy much latitude in defining domestic opponents as security threats and dealing with them harshly. Following the example of recent US practice, the Indonesian government intends to have the Acehnese separatist movement internationally branded as a terrorist organisation.[64] Significantly, the US government (and military) itself has been accused of systematic mishandling and even torture of suspected terrorists. Moreover, the invasion of Iraq would seem to have taken away what little moral authority the USA had left in Indonesia to preach the language of justice and human rights. This means that the sometimes ultra-nationalistic rhetoric of Megawati, or the anti-liberal populism of her opponent, Islamic politician Amien Rais, do not seem out of place in the brave new world being forged through US hegemony.

At the same time US military links with the Indonesian military have been resumed—despite the latter's long anti-democratic history and well earned reputation for abuse of human rights—after previously being cut following developments in formerly colonised East Timor. Significantly, the USA has gifted the Indonesian military with financial assistance for counter-terrorism.[65] Indeed, the Indonesian military has been praised by top US officials like Paul Wolfowitz[66]—as well as by Australian and Singaporean ones—as the main bulwark of stability in Indonesia, or essentially as the only institution that works properly in the country. This represented a remarkable change in fortunes for an institution that only a few years ago was clearly on the defensive as the tide of *reformasi* threatened to overwhelm it, if only for an instant. Ironically, some observers have suggested that sections of the Indonesian military are in fact working together with, and manipulating, militant Islamic groups in Indonesia in order to raise their own domestic political bargaining position.[67] In this situation it is particularly odd that the Indonesian military should be considered a bastion against political instability caused by Islamic militancy or international terrorism. Another (historical) irony is that it was the Indonesian military as well that had benefited most from US policies during the cold war struggle against communism.

Conclusion: the rise of neo-Third Worldism?

The situation is far from ideal. From Washington's point of the view a more predictable, technocratic Indonesian regime—certainly with the backing of a strong military—would be more useful and dependable for US and transnational corporate interests. In many ways, the illiberal democracy of Singapore—'rational' and regularised, but efficiently brutal towards potential challenges against capital—might be a more preferred model. But the choice is really only between different types of illiberal democracy. This state of affairs is reflected not only in US policy but also in the permutations in the theories of democracy and democratisation discussed earlier. In effect, liberal democracy, as an institutional mode of arranging and distributing power (and certainly anything to the left of it), is today being attacked by both the illiberalism of nascent neo-Third Worldism *and* by that of the new US imperialism, despite all the continued talk about global democratisation.

Neo-Third Worldism may be on the rise in Indonesia and elsewhere, whether expressed as a particularly virulent form of secular nationalism or, increasingly, in a brand of populism infused with heavily moralistic, religious or anti-Western overtones. This is clearly a reaction to US global hegemony. Yet beneath this there is a strange process of mutual reinforcement taking place: the fledgling neo-Third Worldists of Indonesia and many other countries need the spectre of US domination to denigrate such notions as universal human rights as an imperialist sham, while, conversely, the (no less moralistic) US hegemon requires belligerent Third Wordlists to help justify its increasing militarism and security-orientated stance. Thus, in this post-communist world, the real main enemies of neo-Third Worldism and of US empire are strikingly similar: the ideals of liberal and social democracies, and those of a world order based on equality and peace.

Notes

1 SP Huntington, *The Third Wave: Democratization in the Late Twentieth Century*, Norman, OK: Oklahoma University Press, 1991.
2 See, for example, RW Liddle, 'Indonesia's democratic transition: playing by the rules', in A Reynolds (ed), *The Architecture of Democracy*, Oxford: Oxford University Press, 2001, pp 373–399; and D Kingsbury & A Budiman (eds), *Indonesia: the Uncertain Transition*, Adelaide: Crawford House Publishing, 2001.
3 PJ Dobriansky, 'Democracy promotion: explaining the Bush administration's position', *Foreign Affairs*, 82 (3), 2003.
4 There has been a number of recent publications on American empire. One of the best known is C Johnson, *Blowback: the Costs and Consequences of American Empire*, New York: Metropolitan Books, 2000.
5 T Carothers, 'Promoting democracy and fighting terror', *Foreign Affairs*, 82 (1), 2003, pp 84–97.
6 Although neo-conservatives have played a key role in setting the current Bush presidency's foreign policy agenda, the idea of a democratic *Pax Americana* is usually viewed as a product of an alliance of conservatives of various stripes. see, for example, R Bleecher, 'Free people will set the course of history', *Middle East Report Online*, March 2003.
7 On this kind of democracy, see R Robison 'What sort of democracy? Predatory and neoliberal agendas in Indonesia', in C Kinnvall K Jonsson (eds), *Globalization and Democratization in Asia: the Construction of Identity*, New York: Routledge, 2002, pp 92–113.
8 For a good critical overview of the debates see MT Berger, 'Old state and new empire in Indonesia: debating the rise and decline of Suharto's New Order', *Third World Quarterly*, 18 (2), 1997, pp 321–361.
9 The classic work was G Almond & S Verba, *The Civic Culture: Political Attitudes and Democracy in Five Nations*, Princeton, NJ: Princeton University Press, 1963.
10 For example, see MT Berger, 'Decolonization, modernization and nation-building: political development theory and the appeal of communism in Southeast Asia, 1945–1975', *Journal of Southeast Asian Studies*, 34 (3), 2003, pp 421–428.
11 The details of this programme are elaborated in RW Dye, 'The Jakarta Faculty of Economics', *Ford Foundation Report*, 1965.
12 The book was published in 1973 by the think-tank he created in Jakarta, the Centre for Strategic and International Studies.
13 See A Moertopo, 'Our national development strategy', in I Chalmers & VR Hadiz, *The Politics of Economic Development in Indonesia: Contending Perspectives*, London: Routledge, 1997. This piece is taken from Chapter 4 of his 'magnum opus'.
14 See, for example, K Jackson & L Pye (eds), *Political Power and Communications in Indonesia*, Berkeley, CA: University of California Press, 1978.
15 See Sjahrir, 'The struggle for deregulation in Indonesia', reproduced in Chalmers & Hadiz, *The Politics of Economic Development in Indonesia*, p 156.
16 See J MacDougall, 'Technocrats as modernizers: the economists of Indonesia's New Order', PhD thesis, University of Michigan, 1975.
17 D Ransom, 'Ford country: building an elite for Indonesia', in S Weissman (ed), *The Trojan Horse: A Radical Look at Foreign Aid*, Paolo Alto, CA: Ramparts Press, 1975, pp 93–116. This is a revised version of an article that originally appeared in *Ramparts* Magazine in 1970.
18 R Robison & VR Hadiz, *Reorganising Power in Indonesia: The Politics of Oligarchy in an Age of Markets*, London: RoutledgeCurzon, 2004.
19 See, in particular, S Huntington, *Political Order in Changing Societies*, New Haven, CT: Yale University Press, 1968. For the 'democratic' ideals of modernisation theory see G Almond & B Powell, Jr, *Comparative Politics: A Developmental Approach*, Boston, MA: Little, Brown, 1966.
20 SP Huntington, *The Third Wave: Democratization in the Late Twentieth Century*, Norman, OK: Oklahoma University Press, 1991; and Huntington, 'The clash of civilisations', *Foreign Affairs*, Summer 1993, pp 22–49.
21 See JM Boileau, *Golkar: Functional Group Politics in Indonesia*, Jakarta: Centre for Strategic and International Studies, 1983, p 68.
22 See R Mortimer 'Indonesia: growth or development', in Mortimer, *Stubborn Survivors*, Clayton: Centre of Southeast Asian Studies, Monash University, 1984.

[23] S Arief & A Sasono, *Indonesia: Ketergantungan dan Keterbelakangan*, Jakarta: Lembaga Studi Pembangunan, 1981.

[24] See, for example, RW Hefner, *Civil Islam: Muslims and Democratization in Indonesia*, Princeton, NJ: Princeton University Press, 2000.

[25] See H Alavi, 'The state in post-colonial societies: Pakistan and Bangladesh', *New Left Review*, 74, 1972, pp 59–81; and Alavi, 'State and class under peripheral capitalism', in H Alavi & T Shanin (eds), *Introduction to the Sociology of Developing Societies*, London: Basingstoke, 1982.

[26] See F Bulkin, 'Golongan Menengah dan Negara', *Prisma*, 2, 1984; and 'Negara, Masyarakat dan Ekonomi', *Prisma*, 8, 1984.

[27] M Mas'oed, Ekonomi dan Struktur Politik Orde Baru, 1966–71, Jakarta: LP3ES.

[28] G O'Donnell, Modernization and Bureaucratic Authoritarianism: Studies in South American Politics, Berkeley, CA: Institute of International Studies, 1973.

[29] PB Evans, D Rueschemeyer & T Skocpol (eds), *Bringing the State Back In*, Cambridge: Cambridge University Press, 1985.

[30] B Anderson, 'Old state, new society: Indonesia's New Order in comparative historical perspective', in Anderson, *Language and Power: Exploring Political Cultures in Indonesia*, Ithaca, NY: Cornell University Press, 1990.

[31] R Robison, *Indonesia: the Rise of Capital*, Sydney: Allen and Unwin, 1986, pp 117–118.

[32] R. Robison, 'Indonesia: tensions in state and regime', in K Hewison, R Robison & G Rodan (eds), *Southeast Asia in the 1990s: Authoritarianism, Democracy, and Capitalism*', St Leonards: Allen and Unwin, 1993, p 41.

[33] One example is D Dhakidae, 'The state, the rise of capital and the fall of political journalism: political economy of the Indonesian news industry', PhD dissertation, Cornell University, 1991.

[34] Sjahrir, 'Indonesian financial and trade deregulation: government policies and society responses', paper presented at a Workshop on Dynamics of Economic Policy Reform in Southeast Asia and Australia, Centre for the Study of Australia–Asia Relations, Griffith University, Queensland, 7–9 October 1989.

[35] See C Leys, The Rise and Fall of Development Theory, Bloomington, IN: Indiana University Press, 1996, ch 4 for a survey. See also B Fine, Social Capital versus Social Theory: Political Economy and Social Science at the Turn of the Millennium, London: Routledge, 2001; and J Harriss, Depoliticizing Development: The World Bank and Social Capital, London: Anthem Press, 2002.

[36] D North, 'Economic performance through time', *American Economic Review*, 84 (3), 1994, pp 359–368.

[37] Discussed in H Shapiro & L Taylor, 'The state and industrial strategy', *World Development*, 18 (6), 1990, pp 861–878.

[38] K Jayasuriya, 'Authoritarian liberalism, governance, and the emergence of the regulatory state in post-crisis East Asia', in R Robison, M Beeson, K Jayasuriya & H-R Kim (eds), *Politics and Markets in the Wake of the Asian Crisis*, London: Routledge, 2000.

[39] Robison, 'What sort of democracy?', pp 92–113.

[40] G Rodan, 'Theorising political opposition in East and Southeast Asia', in Rodan (ed), *Political Oppositions in Industrialising Asia*, London: Routledge, 1996.

[41] Eg MAS Hikam, *Demokrasi dan Civil Society*, Jakarta: LP3ES, 1996.

[42] See the World Bank's simplistic treatment of civil society's role in development in World Bank, *Working Together: The World Bank's Partnership with Civil Society*, Washington, DC: World Bank, 2000.

[43] See his *Mendobrak Sentralisme Ekonomi*, Jakarta: Gramedia, 2002.

[44] R Robison & VR Hadiz, *Reorganising Power in the Age of Markets: Regime Change and the Ascendance of Oligarchy in Indonesia*, London: RoutledgeCurzon, forthcoming; VR Hadiz, 'Reorganising political power in Indonesia: a reconsideration of so-called "democratic transitions" ', *Pacific Review*, 16 (4), 2003, pp 591–611; and Hadiz, 'Power and politics in North Sumatra: the uncompleted *Reformasi*', in E Aspinall & G Fealy (eds), *Local Power and Politics in Indonesia: Democratisation and Decentralisation*, Singapore: Institute of Southeast Asian Studies, 2003, pp 119–131.

[45] G O'Donnell & PC Schmitter, *Transitions from Authoritarian Rule: Tentative Conclusions about Uncertain Democracies*, Baltimore, MD: Johns Hopkins University Press, 1986.

[46] G Van Klinken , 'How a democratic deal might be struck', in A Budiman, B Hatley & D Kingsbury (eds), *Reformasi: Crisis and Change in Indonesia*, Melbourne: Monash Asia Institute, Monash University, 1999, pp 59–67.

[47] RW Liddle, 'Indonesia's democratic transition: playing by the rules', in A Reynolds (ed), *The Architecture of Democracy*, Oxford: Oxford University Press, 2001, pp 373–399.

[48] US Agency for International Development, 'Transition to a prospering and democratic Indonesia', at http://www.usaid.gov/id/docs-csp2k04.html.

[49] L Rudebeck & O Tornquist, 'Introduction', in L Rudebeck, O Tornquist & V Rojas (eds), *Democratisation in the Third World: Concrete Cases in Comparative and Theoretical Perspective*, Uppsala: Seminar for Development Studies, Uppsala University, 1996, pp 3–4.

[50] RW Liddle, 'Can all good things go together? Democracy, growth, and unity in post-Soeharto Indonesia',

in D Bourchier & J Legge (eds), *Democracy in Indonesia: 1950s and 1990s*, Clayton: Monash University Centre of Southeast Asian Studies, 1994, pp 286–301.

[51] Among the major ones were the secular nationalist Indonesian Nationalist Party (PNI), which was the unofficial party of Sukarno and which was traditionally supported by the bureaucracy; the Masjumi, which was a 'modernist' Islamic party with a support base lying in the small-town petty bourgeoisie; the Nahdlatul Ulama (NU), the 'traditionalist' Muslim party, which was both largely Java-based and predominantly rural; and the Indonesian Communist Party (PKI), which had survived periods of repression under Dutch rule and then conflict with the Indonesian military. Another major party was the Indonesian Socialist Party (PSI), which was the vehicle of the urban intelligentsia—and which appealed to Western traditions of liberalism and social democracy. The 1955 general election resulted in roughly equal support for the Masjumi, NU, PNI and PKI; however, the PSI was almost shut out.

[52] R Mortimer, Indonesian Communism Under Sukarno: Ideology and Politics, 1959–1965, Ithaca, NY: Cornell University Press, 1974.

[53] WF Wertheim, 'Whose plot? New light on the 1965 events', *Journal of Contemporary Asia*, IX (2), 1979, pp 197–215; and R Cribb (ed), *The Indonesian Killings of 1965–66: Studies from Java and Bali*, Monash Papers on Asia no 21, Melbourne, Monash University Centre of Southeast Asian Studies, 1990.

[54] For the views of Indonesian liberal pluralists at the time, see D Bourchier & VR Hadiz (eds), *Indonesian Politics and Society: A Reader*, London, RoutledgeCurzon, 2003, ch 2.

[55] VR Hadiz, *Workers and the State in New Order Indonesia*, London: Routledge, 1997.

[56] See D Bourchier & VR Hadiz, 'Introduction', in Bourchier Hadiz, *Indonesian Politics and Society*, pp 1–24.

[57] R Robison & VR Hadiz, 'Oligarchy and capitalism: the case of Indonesia', in L Tomba (ed), *East Asian Capitalism: Conflicts, Growth, and Crisis*, Milan: Fondazione Giangiacomo Feltrinelli, 2002, pp 37–74.

[58] Eg Paul Wolfowitz interview by Tony Snow, Fox News Sunday, 6 April 2003. Transcribed in Defense Link, US Department of Defense, at http://dod.gov/news/Apr2003/t04072003_t0406dsdfns.html. See also 'Remarks by Deputy Secretary of Defense Paul Wolfowitz before the Turkish Economic and Social Studies Foundation, Conrad Hotel, Istanbul, Turkey, July 14, 2002', at http://www.kurdistan.org/Current-Updates/remarksbydeputysecretary.html.

[59] D Murphy, 'The mod squad', *Far Eastern Economic Review*, 19 August, 1999, pp 10–11.

[60] K Harry, 'Small budget does not justify TNI mercenary activities', *Jakarta Post*, 18 March 2003.

[61] E Aspinall & MT Berger, 'The break-up of Indonesia? Nationalisms after decolonisation and the limits of the nation-state in post-cold war Southeast Asia', *Third World Quarterly*, 22 (6), 2001, pp 1003–1024.

[62] 'Jenderal Ryamizard: Pembunuh Theys Hiyo Eluay Adalah Pahlawan', *Tempo Interaktif*, 23 April 2003.

[63] S Mallaby, 'The reluctant imperialist: terrorism, failed states, and the case for American empire', *Foreign Affairs*, 81 (2), 2002, pp 2–7. Meanwhile, Max Boot, an editor of the *Wall Street Journal*, has produced a book-length study of US involvement in 'small wars' in previous centuries, concluding that the contemporary USA should embrace the small wars of the 21st century in an effort to expand 'the empire of liberty'. M Boot, *The Savage Wars of Peace: Small Wars and the Rise of American Power*, New York: Basic Books, 2002. In a similar vein, Niall Ferguson has asked rhetorically whether 'the leaders of the one state with the economic resources to make the world a better place have the guts to do it?', concluding that 'we shall soon see'. N Ferguson, 'Clashing civilizations or mad mullahs: the United States between informal and formal empire', in S Talbott & N Chanda (eds), *The Age of Terror: America and the World After September 11*, Oxford: Perseus Press, 2001, p 141. See also N Ferguson, *Empire: The Rise and Demise of the British World Order and the Lessons for Global Power*, New York: Basic Books, 2003.

[64] *Jakarta Post*, 3 June 2003.

[65] T Carothers, 'Promoting democracy and fighting terror', *Foreign Affairs*, 82 (1), 2003, pp 84–97.

[66] Agence France Press, 16 October 2002.

[67] 'Who's driving Islamic militant groups', Laksamana.net, 24 May 2002.

The hares, the hounds and the African National Congress: on joining the Third World in post-apartheid South Africa

JOHN S SAUL

Analytically, the value of conceptualisations that cast the issue of global inequality in terms of geographically defined hierarchies (First World versus Third World, developed countries versus underdeveloped or developing countries, North versus South) have come into some disrepute in recent years—even if, in political circles, these dichotomies continue to retain considerable resonance. In an effort to address this discrepancy this article first explores the paradoxes, at once linguistic and substantive, that stalk this contested analytical-cum-political terrain before seeking, in a second section, to locate the manner in which the post-apartheid African National Congress (ANC) government in South Africa has itself come to address issues of global inequality. For the fact is that the South African government, particularly under the stewardship of now-President Thabo Mbeki, has presented itself as having an especially important leadership role to play in mediating and reconciling the gaps and tensions that such binaries evoke. We will also see, however, that there are severe and quite revealing contradictions inherent in the ANC 's attempt to articulate such a role for itself. Indeed, the peculiar difficulties of a government that has, simultaneously, professed to run with the hares of the Third World poor while also aspiring to hunt with the hounds of global capitalist power wielders will be shown to be particularly revealing for defining alternative strategies for overcoming world-wide poverty; strategies that might prove more effective than those chosen by the ANC.

What is the Third World?

What, first, of 'geographically defined hierarchies'?[1] As we mark the 25th anniversary of *Third World Quarterly* it is tempting to note the irony that Mark Berger seemed to have already laid to rest the very notion of 'the Third World' almost a decade ago—and in these very pages. 'The idea of a "Third World" ', Berger wrote, 'now serves primarily to generate both a dubious homogeneity within its shifting boundaries and an irrelevant distinction between the "Third World" (developing) and the "First World" (developed).'[2] In thus critiquing the commonsensical understanding of the existence of a straightforward causal connection between the coexistence of a wealthy North and an impoverished South that once structured many analyses in both left and liberal development circles, he and others have sought to bury both Third Worldist conceptualisations and the rest of those binaries mentioned above, which continue to be deployed by economists and policy makers. Such formulations, it is stated, have lost much of whatever usefulness they might originally have had both for analysing the (increasingly diverse) fates of the economies of the formerly colonised countries of the global South and for focusing the struggle against grinding poverty and the existing manifestations of extreme material inequality in an ever more globalised socioeconomic environment.

Of course, the idea of a Third World has seemed especially questionable to such writers, not least when considered with reference to the once rather more convincing logic of its original coinage: the disappearance—with the crumbling of the Eastern so-called socialist states—of anything that might once have been considered a Second World has underscored the most self-evident difficulties in this regard. More important is the problem (also thought to bedevil the other parallel binaries) of the increasing lack of a clear referent for the concept even on its own terms. After all, South Africa is not the only country said to have both First World and Third World conditions (ie extremes of wealth and poverty) within its borders: this is true within the most advanced capitalist societies as well. Small wonder that, more recently, a writer such as Ankie Hoogvelt can suggest global inequality to be now much more 'social' than 'geographical' in its co-ordinates: 'The familiar pyramid of the core–periphery hierarchy is no longer a geographical but a social division of the world economy'.[3] For her, a global division of labour, more centrally than ever defined along lines of class and (often) socioeconomic exclusion that cut across national frontiers, has created both a dominant transnational capitalist class and vast outer circles of less privileged people, in both the North and the South. Such a model helps, she suggests, to comprehend growing inequalities *within* countries. But it also helps us to incorporate into our approach a much clearer acknowledgement of the dramatic diversity to be found *among* the countries of the so-called Third World itself: a spectrum that stretches all the way from the material accomplishment of the Newly Industrialising Countries (NICs) to the desperate situation to be found in the countries of the most impoverished zones of Africa.

But, if the truth value of such tropes is so limited, what is to account for the fact that their continued deployment 'has legs', surfacing regularly as political and journalistic shorthand, but also in more scholarly publications (like the present journal) and debates? A number of negative reasons has been adduced as to why this has occurred. Thus Berger approvingly cited Escobar to the effect that 'to represent the Third World as "underdeveloped" is less a statement about "facts" than the setting up of a regime of truth through which the Third World is inevitably known, intervened on and managed'. Berger's own conclusion? This is a crucial means by which key Western players can 'homogenise' the experience of the very particularity of social formations on the so-called periphery, the better to control them in the name of a universalising 'modernis-ation theory'.[4] In addition, the attendant emphasis on the 'original' nature of the 'backwardness' of such social formations serves to shift attention away from a focus on the less than benign workings of 'international market relations' and of global capitalist power that explain more adequately the problems they confront. As he specifies this point, 'Economic development in the "Third World" is seen primarily as a technical or policy problem...that can be overcome by the right mix of advice, investment, aid and liberal reforms...rather than a historico-political problem'.[5]

There is also the fact that tropes, which emphasise the continued centrality of geographical hierarchy to the reality of global poverty, have been subject to the most self-interested kind of manipulation by Southern leaders of often highly dubious provenance. Once again Berger makes the pertinent point: 'Third World' elites have emerged in the international arena claiming to speak for the 'Third World' at the same time as they are deeply implicated in the prevailing international discourses and structures which work to manage the 'Third World'.[6] As Smith adds:

There is thus the risk that the expression 'Third World' might obscure the heterogeneity of social classes, each with its own political objective. The concept of the Third World has consequently been denounced...as mystification designed to conceal dependency and exploitation, as well as a device allowing rulers of Third World countries to present a common interest between themselves and the masses to disguise their own alliance with metropolitan interests.[7]

Here such points have general implications. We will see, however, that there could scarcely be better short-hand descriptions of the role chosen for itself—albeit rather against the hopes and expectations that had arisen for it during the anti-apartheid struggle—by the ANC leadership in post-apartheid South Africa.

This said, it must also be emphasised that there are several more positive reasons why conceptualisations of the 'Third World/First World' and 'developed/underdeveloped' type continue to have considerable resonance. To begin with it is not actually quite so easy to ignore the geographical co-ordinates of inequality as Hoogvelt and others imply. For, as Giovanni Arrighi and others have continued to document tirelessly over many years, there is still a great deal about the global hierarchy that remains spatially defined, and along lines that are also 'largely a legacy of Western territorial and industrial expansion since about 1800'. Thus, in a 1992 article on 'the increasing inequality of the global distribution of incomes', he demonstrated 'a major widening of the already large income gap that fifty years ago separated the peoples of the South from the peoples of the organic core of the capitalist world-economy'. His conclusion was that 'the nations of the world...are differentially situated in a rigid hierarchy of wealth in which the occasional ascent of a nation or two leaves all the others more firmly entrenched than ever they were before',[8] this exemplifying for him a 'seemingly "iron law" of a global hierarchy that stays in place no matter what governments on the lower rungs of the hierarchy do or do not do'. For, in the absence of self-conscious correctives, the 'oligarchic wealth' achieved by the West always tends to draw the bulk of capitalist activity towards it, hence widening the gap. Arrighi, updating his argument in 2003,[9] also emphasises the extent to which aggressive Northern 'neoliberal' policies deliberately reinforced this hierarchy when, in the 1970s, things seemed set to shift slightly in the South's favour. He thus comes to precisely the same conclusion he had a decade earlier as to the persistence of a North/South hierarchy of income—and this despite (even because of) the fact that some degree of industrial convergence has indeed occurred.[10]

There is, then, something important about the nature of the geographically defined, material realities of the global hierarchy that must be kept on the table.[11] As people in the Third World seek to improve their lot they actually do confront a global system of power, in economic and political terms (think the militarised US state and its complex interface with global capital), which—whatever else it may be—is also asymmetrical in spatial terms. Moreover, if a global movement to overcome inequality is to be built, one that seeks to unite struggles in both North and South, it cannot ignore the extent to which many in the North, and well beyond the ranks of the most wealthy, have come to share in one way or another in the North's 'oligarchic wealth'. In consequence, if the legitimate claims of Southern peoples to global income redistribution, equitable environmental controls, rights of migration, and freedom from high-handed military incursions are to be grasped and supported by potential allies of the South in the North, the latter will have to understand more clearly the facts regarding both the creation and the persistence of the presently existing global hierarchy.

Note, as well, that there is also a cultural dimension to the latter challenge—and to a reconsideration of the potentially positive charge of the binaries under discussion. For the imperialist history that has spawned global economic and political hierarchy has also had a strongly racist dimension, one that helps to lock into place complacency in the North regarding the legitimacy both of its enjoyment of 'oligarchic wealth' and of its often unilateral actions, economic and military, to ensure it. Small wonder that the present global hierarchy could recently be defined as a kind of 'global apartheid',[12] or that Robert Biel could write of 'the racial capitalism that exists between the North and the South' and the need to confront the racist premises of the system's functioning head-on and in their own right.[13] Small wonder, too, that Southern intellectuals have sought to complement concrete struggles for material equality carried out by the poorest of the poor with cultural assertions that claim, *vis-à-vis* Western cultural hegemony, the right to be heard in their own voice. Most recently this has taken the form, in the academy, of a preoccupation with 'postcolonialism', producing a postcolonial school of thought that claims not merely to expose Eurocentric biases within the global centres of cultural production, but also to listen afresh to those diverse voices of the South which otherwise would be squeezed out of the canon and out of global public discourse.

While suggestive, this kind of preoccupation with 'identity' and voice can also, its critics suggest, be misleading. As Arif Dirlik argues, 'postcolonial critics have been largely silent on the relationship of the idea of postcolonialism to its context in contemporary capitalism; indeed, they have suppressed the necessity of considering such a possible relationship by repudiating a possible "foundational" role to capitalism in history'.[14] It need come as no surprise, therefore, that Ella Shohat can cap her own critique of the postcolonial approach in a manner germane to the development of the argument of the present article:

> The circulation of 'post-colonial' as a theoretical framework tends to suggest a supercession of neo-colonialism and the Third World and Fourth World as unfashionable, even irrelevant categories. Yet, with all its problems, the term 'Third World' does still retain heuristic value...At this point in time, replacing the term 'Third World' with the 'post-colonial' is a liability. Despite differences and contradictions among and within Third World countries, the term 'Third World' contains a common project of (linked) resistances to neo-colonialisms [and] implies a belief that the shared history of neo/colonialism and internal racism form sufficient common ground for alliances among such diverse peoples.[15]

Note, too, that this formulation provides an additional reason for validating, up to a point, Third Worldist, left–developmentalist and Southern-focused problematics: the potential they retain for both enlivening and focusing radical projects of redress of grievances by the poorest of the global poor.[16] Shohat herself is circumspect here: 'The term "Third World" is most meaningful in broad political–economic terms, and becomes blurred when one addresses the differently modulated politics in the realm of culture, the overlapping spaces of inter-mingling identities'. For this reason, she writes, the concept of 'Third World', while 'schematically productive', must itself be 'placed under erasure, as it were, seen as provisional and ultimately inadequate'.[17] Nonetheless, the thrust of her argument links to that of others who have sought to validate such notions as part of a language in terms of which global claims are staked *vis-à-vis* global capitalism and progressive mobilisation is advanced both in the South and in the North. 'Third Worldism is in part about reminding people that poverty is still a problem, and that in general there are widening gaps between the developed and the developing countries'.[18] Indeed, what Cooper and Packard write of the 'marvelous ambiguity' of the concept 'development' might also be said of the concept 'Third World': 'What at one level seemed like a discourse of control is at another a discourse of entitlement, a way of capturing the imagination of a cross-national public around demands for decency and equity'.[19] Not 'After the Third World' then (as the title of this special issue of *Third World Quarterly* would have it). Better put, what is at issue are the ways in which notions of 'the Third World', 'the developing world', 'the global South', 'global apartheid', and even 'the post-colonial' are linked to a simultaneous consideration of the realities of the global class structure and the imperatives of the global class struggle. This is what determines, in context, both their accuracy and their efficacy.

Where is South Africa?

The ANC government in South Africa came to power with the strongest of Third Worldist credentials, the battle against apartheid having been among the most salient of 20th century liberation struggles. And while it is true that ANC spokespersons once in power have not tended to use the term 'Third World' very often, they have, nonetheless, sought in many of their pronouncements to build on their struggle credentials in order present themselves, both domestically and internationally, as key representatives, interpreters and defenders of the countries of the Southern poor. The litany is impressive, up to a point. Consider, for example, Mandela's own statement at the 1999 Davos forum that brought together heads of state and of multinational corporations to discuss the question 'Is global capitalism delivering the goods?'. Mandela was prepared to ask some questions of his own: 'is globalization only to benefit the powerful and the speculators? Does it offer nothing to men, women and children who are ravaged by poverty?'.[20] But it is Mandela's successor, Thabo Mbeki, who has taken the initiative most vigorously in a number of his speeches both before and after his ascending to the presidency. Consider his 1998 pronouncement to the effect that South Africans 'must be in the forefront in challenging the notion of "the market" as a modern God, a supernatural phenomenon to whose dictates everything human must bow in a spirit of helplessness'.[21] Consider, too, his important speech to the 12th heads of state meeting of the Non-Aligned Movement, including the statement that 'the "free market" path of development...has failed to live up to the expectations of the people of the South'.[22] As Rok Ajalu epitomised the occasion:

What then is President Mbeki's solution to the problem of market fundamentalism? He concluded his speech by urging the Non-Aligned Movement to go back to basics, to demand a new world order—'to turn itself into an effective organ for the creation of the new political, economic and security world order which will succeed actually to assist in the life and death matter that the aspirations of the weak and the poor become an integral part of the actual agenda of the entirety of our world'.[23]

It is statements like these, and Mbeki's attendant evocation of the fact of 'global apartheid' (explicitly so named), that can lead so astute a commentator on developments in Africa as Rok Ajalu to embrace their author's progressive credentials with unbridled enthusiasm—this being true, in particular, of Mbeki's much-trumpeted presentation of the need for what he calls an 'African Renaissance'. This is said by Ajalu to represent a potential rebirth of African self-respect, sense of efficacy and 'rebellion'—even to the point of 'seem[ing] to imply a subtle and sophisticated challenge to globalisation'.[24] In fact, so agog is Ajalu at Mbeki's various rhetorical flourishes, that he comes to a most startling conclusion:

> It would seem, therefore, that those who have assumed the pinnacle of Mbeki's African renaissance to be the drive for the virtues and dictates of the free market, making Africa safe for the overseas multi-national investments and private capital, are grossly mistaken. Mbeki's African renaissance represents a much more nuanced and a subtler critique of the contemporary world order than such interpretations allow. It is indeed a call to take up an anti-imperialist stance![25]

Yet one is left to wonder at the precise provenance of such a bizarre and overstated testimonial. It is not merely the fact that Mbeki tends to switch the tenor of his rhetoric markedly from one audience to another that might have been expected to give Ajalu some pause here. More important is the fact that the bulk of the evidence regarding Mbeki and company's actual practice ('Talk left, act right', as domestic critics of the ANC have come to describe such flights of Mbekian fancy-talk) suggests a quite opposite conclusion. For the ANC in action has dedicated itself to a version of neoliberalism that is, in fact, baldly market-driven and premised on a kind of 'one-worldist' celebration of the more-or-less unqualified hegemony of capital, world-wide and local. This is most evident, as is widely acknowledged by most commentators both of the left and the right, in its domestic policies but, as we shall see, it also underpins the initiatives that post-apartheid South Africa has actually taken on the world stage—as distinct from what it is given to saying that it is doing.

The deeply conservative domestic policies of post-apartheid South Africa thus provide the strongest case against Ajalu's argument. I have documented elsewhere the process by which the ANC came to embrace a starkly neoliberal domestic project, capped dramatically by then Vice-President Thabo Mbeki's pugnacious comment, 'Just call me a Thatcherite', made when he announced the government's Growth, Employment and Redistribution (GEAR) document which consolidated its move to the right in 1996.[26] True, some would argue that the choosing of this option merely confirmed the fact that 'There is No Alternative' on a world stage set by the untrammelled hegemony of global capitalism. Others are more inclined to see in the ANC's post-apartheid project a confirmation of the self-interested petty-bourgeois ambitions that were said always to have charac-terised that movement's leadership: after all, Mbeki himself had argued strenu-ously from quite early on that 'the ANC is not a socialist party. It never pretended to be one, it has never said it was, and it is not trying to be. It will not become one by decree or for purposes of pleasing its "left" critics.'[27] But, whatever the reasons for this outcome, surely few could dispute its essentially neoliberal character.

True, many of the ANC's pre-liberation formulations had emphasised the need to impose a much stronger measure of social control over the workings of the market and a capitalist economy that was very much more developed in South Africa than elsewhere on the continent. Much was heard of the prospects for nationalisations and, of special interest, of economic strategies designed to facilitate 'growth through redistribution'. Linked implicitly to a radical notion of 'structural reform' that seemed to have as a goal a progressive closing in on the prerogatives of capital by movement and state, such strategies would have sought to press capital to slowly but surely gear an increasingly high proportion of its productive energies to meeting popular needs (rather than permitting capital freely to pursue the logic of its own global ambitions). And yet, as stated, the transition would instead produce a development project premised primarily on 'global competitiveness', the centrality of foreign investment, the rule of the market and, more specifically, accelerated privatisation, an apparent indifference to rising structural unemployment and the marketisation of service delivery that makes such services unattainable to so many.[28] The esteemed Indian writer Arundhati Roy has written, both poignantly and accurately, of this sad dénoue-ment to the anti-apartheid struggle as follows:

> And what of Mandela's South Africa? Otherwise known as the Small Miracle, the Rainbow Nation of God? South Africans say that the only miracle they know of is how quickly the rainbow has been privatised, sectioned off and auctioned to the highest bidders. Within two years of taking office in 1994, the African National Congress genuflected with hardly a caveat to the Market God. In its rush to replace Argentina as neo-liberalism's poster boy, it has instituted a massive programme of privatisation and structural adjustment. The government's promise to re-distribute agricultural land to 26 million landless people has remained in the realm of dark humour. While 60 per cent of the population remains landless, almost all agricul-tural land is owned by 60 000 white farmers. Post-apartheid, the income of 40 per cent of the poorest black families has diminished by about 20 per cent. Two million have been evicted from their homes. Six hundred die of AIDS every day. Forty per cent of the population is unemployed and that number is rising sharply. The corporatisation of basic services has meant that millions have been disconnected from water and electricity.[29]

And so, for the mass of the population, doomed in practice to increasingly high levels of unemployment during the period of 'rationalisation' of the South African economy in line with global 'imperatives', their jobs as well as their welfare needs were to be provided for—mostly in the much longer run!—by the trickle-down effects that a beneficent and expansive market-driven capitalism is said to be poised to deliver. Unfortunately, the fact that this aggressively capitalist project has so far proven to be such a dismal failure at home does not seem to have dampened the ANC leadership's enthusiasm for it.

Nor has it dissuaded the ANC from pushing such 'solutions' upon others: the ANC's global and continental strategies have become, in practice (if not always in the terms of the rhetoric that accompanies them), merely an extension of its domestic approach. Thus, even while advancing a case for some measure of 'reform' (debt relief, increased aid, the lowering of Northern trade barriers and, not least, increased investment) within such bastions of global power as the International Financial Institutions (IFIS) and the WTO, South Africa's moderate approach has (in the words of senior government minister Alec Erwin) been premised on 'attempting to break with a conception of contestation by stressing partnership' and on avoiding (in the words of a core ANC document) the temptation 'to elaborate solutions that are in discord with the rest of the world' or that represent 'a voluntarist South African experiment of a special type'.[30] Yet how relevant can a 'non-discordant' practice of global reformism—a projected 'partnership' between hares and hounds—really be when global capitalism offers so little by way of positive promise for the kind of reformist strategies that the ANC says it is striving to achieve. The case for Africa is clear, at least. As Colin Leys and I have argued, the current plight:

> is relegation to the margins of the global economy, with no visible prospect of continental development along capitalist lines...Which does not mean that nothing is happening, let alone that no alternative is possible. It simply means that Africa's development, and the dynamics of global capitalism, are no longer convergent, if they ever were...Insofar as these economies remain unlikely to generate investment of a more productive and transformative variety—whether from (still extremely weak) domestic bourgeoisies, from international capital, or from complementary state initiatives—investment of the hit-and-run variety is likely to remain the commonest kind, with predictable lack of developmental results continentally, regionally and nationally. In sum, the dream of a transformative capitalism in Africa remains just that: a dream.[31]

The meagre returns to Africa from the reformist entreaties of South African and other continental leaders at sites where Northern powers meet to consider the present and future—most notably at G8 Summits at Kananaskis in 2001 and Evian in 2003—might give additional pause here. For the fact is that Africans who seek meaningful development for their continent will have to become participants in global and continental initiatives that proceed on the basis of a much more profoundly anti-capitalist perspective than the ANC leadership is currently prepared to countenance.

Moreover, the situation as regards the ANC's global programme may actually represent something rather more negative than merely the almost inevitably failed practice of a naive reformism. For recent analyses of the ANC's record in international negotiations suggest more sinister possibilities. Thus Dot Keet, in a scrupulous analysis of South Africa's role (and particularly that played by Minister of Trade Erwin) within the WTO, notes the claim (made by Erwin) that South Africa, as a 'major player' on the global stage, acts 'a bridge between the developed and the developing countries'.[32] However, a close tracking of Erwin's actual role in WTO assemblies both in Seattle (1999) and Doha (2001) provides a very different picture. When not denouncing the demonstrators in the streets in Seattle, Erwin was found to be eschewing any close contact with other African delegations and, much to the consternation of the latter, concentrating instead on the opportunity given him to enter the 'inner circle' of 'Green Room' discussions by the global heavy hitters (the EU, USA, Canada and Japan) and their occasional invitees.

As Keet documents in even more telling detail for Doha, Erwin and his delegation were once again deemed to have run principally with the hounds of global capital in seeking to push African (and other Third World) delegations towards making, in the name of 'realism' and their own 'broad agenda', various 'trade-offs' that would have compromised those delegations' demands on a wide range of fronts. Not surprisingly Keet found 'many developing countries, especially in Africa, [noting] with wry comments that, while South Africa keeps its distance from the more active and effective developing countries in the WTO, there is a contrasting readiness of South Africa to engage actively with the governments of the more powerful countries, separately and together'. Hence Keet's hard-edged but entirely convincing conclusion as to 'the South African government's highly questionable role' in such a context:

> Following the logic inherent in its own strategic choices, and independently of Pretoria's self-defined 'good intentions' and declared 'tactical' aims, South Africa played and plays an increasingly questionable WTO role within Africa and internationally. As events unfolded, in the past three years, Pretoria's strategic positioning in the WTO and tactical interventions in international negotiations have led to the widely held conclusion that South Africa is playing a role not so much as a bridge between the developed and developing countries but rather as a bridge for the transmission of influences from the developed countries for the promotion of their economic interests and global aims throughout the world.[33]

Moreover, as Patrick Bond and others have tirelessly demonstrated in their voluminous writings on related themes, much the same could be said of the role that the South African Minister of Finance, Manuel, and other South African representatives have played from the lofty positions to which they have ascended within the halls of the World Bank and the IMF.[34]

As for the much heralded African Renaissance, it seems to have been narrowed in its terms of reference to the horizons encompassed by the New Partnership for African Development (NEPAD) proposals. These were drafted, it would seem, primarily by Mbeki and his advisors and then shepherded through various pan-African bodies by the troika of Mbeki and Presidents Obasanjo and Bouteflika of Nigeria and Algeria, respectively. These leaders pushed hard to see that NEPAD was on the agenda of the G8 Summit to be held in Kananaskis, Canada, in 1999 and also that it was central to the premises that underpinned the recasting of the Organisation of African Unity into the African Union. It is, of course, tempting to hail an initiative that has sought to bring Africa and its plight to the attention of the globally powerful. Moreover, NEPAD does have some useful things to say about the extent to which trade in African products is blocked by the protectionist economic policies of Northern countries, while also including a measure of self-criticism regarding the undemocratic practices of the African regimes themselves.

Nonetheless, at core, NEPAD seems a sad, defeated document, demonstrating the ever-deepening subservience of the African leaders that authored it to the 'common-sense' of a neoliberalising, structural-adjusting global capitalism. While written by African leaders, it reads as if it could just as easily have been framed in the offices of the World Bank and the IMF.[35] Absolutely central to it, certainly, is a familiar (and very damaging) premise: that African countries must continue to 'adjust' their economies in order to provide the enabling conditions for their ever deeper penetration by global capital—with increased foreign investment presented as being the primary key to progress. Not just at Seattle and at Doha, but also on the African continent itself, South Africa emerges ever more clearly as point man for global capital. And not only for global capital. For there is also a growing suspicion in some continental quarters that the kind of further freeing up of African markets that NEPAD envisions may also serve the desire of ANC free-marketeers to batter down barriers to South African-based capital's own ambitious plans for the further penetration of the rest of Africa. Not South Africa as 'anti-imperialist', then, but as 'sub-imperialist'.

Patrick Bond has traced such policies, at least in part, to their grounding in a 'defeatist—and highly questionable—attitude' towards globalisation that he suggests is held by Mbeki and his closest colleagues in South Africa. (Trevor Manuel, his Minister of Finance, and Alec Erwin, his Minister of Trade, are among the most prominent of them.) In Mbeki's own words, 'the process of globalization is an objective outcome of the development of the productive forces that create wealth, including their continuous improvement through the impact on them of advances in science, technology and engineering'. Hence Bond's conclusion that 'the driving force of globalization boils down, in Mbeki's neutral story, to little more than technological determinism'.[36] True, the likes of Rok Ajalu can attempt to put a bold face on this, praising Mbeki for realistically urging his fellow African heads of state not to react to globalisation like 'King Canute striving to wish the waves away'.[37] And yet the mild reformism that Mbeki's approach gives rise to is far removed from a necessary understanding that the existing market-dominated global order—driven by 'a minority class that draws its wealth and power from a historically specific form of production' —is, in Greg Albo's words, 'contingent, imbalanced, exploitative and replaceable'.[38] Far indeed, that is, from the kind of genuinely 'anti-imperialist stance' that we have seen Ajalu erroneously take it to be. Yet it is such a stance—real not rhetorical—that alone can guarantee progress for the poorest of the poor in today's global economy.

Conclusion: the hares, the hounds and the African National Congress

South Africa: running, however ineffectively, with the hares or, as one increasingly suspects to be the case, hunting, however guardedly, with the hounds? Either way, the fact remains that the ANC's brand of deeply compromised quasi-reformism serves primarily to deflect consideration of other, much more meaningful, radical alternatives, both globally and locally. As Bond writes, the exercise of a more meaningful 'Third Worldism' by the South African government would involve something quite different from an approach that 'excludes (indeed most often rejects) alliances with increasingly radical local and international social, labour and environmental movements who in reality are the main agents of progressive global change'.[39] Moreover, the ANC government has also chosen, in its own country, to turn its back coldly on those forces that might begin to provide the social and political base for any more meaningful 'anti-imperialist' project. I have identified elsewhere a range of increasingly well organised grassroots initiatives surfacing in South Africa that find they have no choice but to mobilise people in active resistance to their own government's bankrupt policies.[40] Included on the list would be, among other initiatives, the Anti-Privatization Forum, the Soweto Electricity Crisis Committee, the Treatment Action Campaign, the Western Cape Anti-Eviction Campaign, the Concerned Citizens' Forum in Durban, the Landless People's Movement, as well as some unions, some churches, some women's organisations.[41] It is the further growth of such initiatives that could eventually produce the political will necessary to draw South Africa back into the ranks of those who challenge in meaningful ways the geographical, racial and class-based hierarchies of global inequality.

Notes

[1] For more detailed versions of some of the general arguments advanced here, see JS Saul, 'Globalization, imperialism, development: false binaries and radical resolutions', in L Panitch & C Leys (eds), *The Socialist Register 2004*, London: Merlin Press, 2003; and JS Saul, 'Identifying class, classifying difference', in L Panitch & C Leys (eds), *The Socialist Register 2003*, London: Merlin Press, 2002.

[2] MT Berger, 'The end of the "Third World"?', *Third World Quarterly*, 15 (2), 1994, p 258.

[3] A Hoogvelt, *Globalization and the Post-Colonial World: The New Political Economy of Development*, London: Palgrave, 2001, p xiv. See also BJ Silver & G Arrighi, 'Workers North and South,' in L Panitch & C Leys (eds), *Socialist Register 2001: Working Classes, Global Realities*, London: Merlin Press, 2000, pp 56–57). Hoogvelt's use of the term 'social' is misleading: the geographical hierarchy of nations that they themselves continue to emphasise is, of course, also a social relationship. Nonetheless, what Hoogvelt is here seeking to underscore is important.

[4] Berger, 'The end of the "Third World"?', p 260. This is also true of some of the variants of neoliberalism, that now ubiquitous 'ultra-modernist' take on development (as Fred Cooper and Randall Packer term it in their edited volume, *International Development and the Social Scientists*, Berkeley, CA: University of California Press, 1997, p 2). But note that some of the crustier architects of the neoliberal counter-revolution in development studies (like Peter Bauer) have turned this argument inside out: they also professed to see 'the Third World' as being a Western artifact, but this time as the artifact of '"Western guilt" and the politics of foreign aid'—which holds, erroneously in their view, that 'the West is responsible for the poverty of most of Asia, Africa and Latin America'! See the summary of this position in J Toye, *Dilemmas of Development: Reflections on the Counter-Revolution in Development Economics*, Oxford: Blackwell, 1993, pp 25–26.

[5] Berger, 'The end of the "Third World"?', p 270.

[6] *Ibid*, p 258.

[7] BS Smith, *Understanding Third World Politics*, Bloomington, IN: Indiana University Press, 1996, p 29.

[8] G Arrighi, 'World income inequalities and the future of socialism', *New Left Review*, 189, 1991.

[9] G Arrighi, BJ Silver & BD Brewer, 'Industrial convergence, globalization and the persistence of the North–South divide', *Studies in Comparative International Development*, 38 (1), 2003.

[10] In the same issue of *Studies in Comparative International Development* (38 (1), 2003) that carries the Arrighi *et al* article, there is also a critique of their position by Alice Amsden entitled 'Good-bye dependency theory, hello dependency theory', as well as a response to her by the original authors. This stimulating exchange merely serves to reinforce the latter's case, in my opinion.

11 As Toye has written, 'The Third World is not...a figment of our imagination ready to vanish when we blink'! Toye, *Dilemmas of Development*, p 31.

12 S Booker & W Minter, 'Global apartheid', *The Nation*, 9 July 2001.

13 R Biel, *The New Imperialism: Crisis and Contradiction in North/South Relations*, London: Zed Books, 2000, pp 131–132.

14 A Dirlik, 'The postcolonial aura: Third World criticism in the age of global capitalism', in A McClintock, A Mufti & E Shohat (eds), *Dangerous Liaisons: Gender, Nation and Postcolonial Perspectives*, Minneapolis, MN: University of Minnesota Press, 1997, p 502. In sharp contrast Robert Young (in his *Postcolonialism: An Historical Introduction*, Oxford: Blackwell, 2001) has attempted more recently to defend postcolonial theory from these kinds of criticisms by asserting that 'many of the problems raised can be resolved if the postcolonial is defined as coming after colonialism and imperialism, in their original meaning of direct-rule domination, but still positioned within imperialism in its later sense of the global system of hegemonic economic power' (p 57). This may be somewhat disingenuous. For even Young professes his own unease with the term, suggesting his actual preference for the notion of 'tricontinentalism' as capturing even more directly 'a theoretical and political position which embodies an active concept of intervention within such oppressive circumstances'. Nonetheless, he claims that 'postcolonialism' as he defines it can still serve the purposes he has in mind, capturing the 'tricontinental' character of Southern resistance to imperialism while remaining sensitive to the sheer diversity of the settings in which such resistance occurs.

15 E Shohat, 'Notes on the "post-colonial" ', *Social Text*, 31–32, 1992, p 111. As she adds, 'the "neo-colonial," like the "post-colonial" also suggests continuities and discontinuities, but its emphasis is on the new modes of and forms of old colonialist practices, not on a "beyond" ' (p 106). See also, in the same issue of *Social Text*, A McClintock, 'The angel of progress: pitfalls of the term "post-colonial" '.'

16 Berger, it should be noted, cites several related arguments in his own article. Berger, 'The end of the "Third World"?', p 258.

17 Shohat, 'Notes on the "post-colonial" ', p 110. As she further suggest, 'a celebration of syncretism and hybridity per se, if not articulated in conjunction with questions of hegemony and neo-colonial power relations, runs the risk of appearing to sanctify the *fait accompli* of colonial violence' (p 109).

18 Smith, *Understanding Third World Politics*, p 24.

19 F Cooper & R Packer, 'Introduction', in Cooper & Packer (eds), *International Development and the Social Scientists*, Berkeley, CA: University of California Press, 1997, p 4.

20 As quoted in an article entitled 'Mandela poses hard questions about reach of globalization', in *The Globe and Mail* (Toronto), 30 January 1999, p A19. Of course, this statement must be compared with his 1994 affirmation to the US Joint Houses of Congress that the free market was a 'magic elixir' that would produce freedom and equality for all. Cited in A Nash, 'Mandela's democracy', *Monthly Review*, 50 (11), 1999, p 26.

21 This is from a speech by Mbeki at the opening of the ministerial meeting of the Non-Aligned Movement, Durban, August, 1998.

22 Thabo Mbeki speaking at the 12th heads of state meeting of the Non-Aligned Movement in South Africa, 3 September 1998, quoted in R Wade & F Venerosa, 'The gathering world slump and the battle over capital controls', *New Left Review*, 231, 1998, p 20.

23 R Ajalu, 'Thabo Mbeki's African Renaissance in a globalising world economy: the struggle for the soul of a continent', *Review of African Political Economy*, 87, 2001, p 36.

24 *Ibid*, p 35. In an alternative reading I have described the domestic collapse of the notion of an 'African Renaissance' into a rationale for the self-aggrandisement of a black petty bourgeoisie. JS Saul, 'Cry for the beloved country: the post-apartheid denouement', *Monthly Review*, 52 (8), 2001. For its degeneration continentally into the New Partnership for African Development (NEPAD) project, see below.

25 Ajalu is also referencing an Mbeki speech to the Non-Aligned Summit when he cites him as stating that the process of globalisation 'ineluctably results in the reduction of the sovereignty of states, with the weakest, being ourselves, being the biggest losers—those who are already the worst off, suffer losses of the first order as a result of a marginal adjustment by another'. Ajalu, 'Thabo Mbeki's African Renaissance', pp 35, 37.

26 See Saul 'Cry for the beloved country', but also, *inter alia*, H Marais, *South Africa: Limits to Change: The Political Economy of Transformation*, London and Cape Town: Zed Books and University of Cape Town Press, 1998; and P Bond, *Elite Transition: From Apartheid to Neoliberalism in South Africa*, London: Pluto Press, 2000.

27 T Mbeki, 'The Fatton thesis: a rejoinder', *Canadian Journal of African Studies*, 18 (3), 1984, p 609.

28 See, among others of his numerous writings on these matters, P Bond, *Against Global Apartheid: South Africa meets the World Bank, IMF and International Finance*, London: Zed Press, 2003.

29 A Roy, 'When the saints go marching out', ZNet (www.zmag.org), 2 September 2003.

30 These quotes are cited in P Bond, 'South Africa's agenda in 21st century global governance', *Review of African Political Economy*, 89, 2001, p 416.

[31] C Leys & JS Saul, 'Sub-Saharan Africa within global capitalism', *Monthly Review*, 51 (3), 1999, pp 17, 25.

[32] As cited in D Keet, *South Africa's Official Position and Role in Promoting the World Trade*, Cape Town: Alternative Information and Development Centre (AIDC), 2002.

[33] *Ibid*, p 4. See also P Bond's chapter on 'The Doha trade "agenda": splitting Africa to launch a new round' in his newest book, tentatively entitled *Sustaining Global Apartheid: South Africa's Frustrated International Reforms* (in manuscript, forthcoming).

[34] Here, too, one of Bond's chapters, entitled 'Washington renamed: a "Monterrey Consensus" on finance' in his *Sustaining Global Apartheid* is particularly useful; more generally, in this book and its predecessor (*Against Global Apartheid*) Bond provides much the richest and broadest analysis of South Africa's deeply compromised post-apartheid global positioning.

[35] For a critique, detailed and powerful, of NEPAD along these lines see P Bond (ed), *Fanon's Warning: A Civil Society Reader on the New Partnership for Africa's Development*, Trenton, Ontario and Cape Town: Africa World Press and AIDC, 2002. As Bond documents, a wide range of organisations drawn from South African civil society, as well as from elsewhere in Africa, has been among the most articulate and assertive critics of NEPAD. See also, in this regard, T Ngwane, 'Should African social movements be part of the New Partnership for Africa's Development (NEPAD)?', notes from a speech given by Trevor Ngwane to the African Social Forum's African Seminar at the World Social Forum, Porto Alegre, Brazil, 2 February 2002.

[36] For Bond's argument, with several useful citations from Mbeki, see, once again, his *Against Global Apartheid*, p 139.

[37] T Mbeki, 'Statement at the 35th Ordinary Session of the OAU Assembly of Heads of State and Government', Algiers, 13 August 1999, cited in Ajalu, 'Thabo Mbeki's African Renaissance'.

[38] As Albo continues, more positive outcomes 'can only be realized through re-embedding financial capital and production relations in democratically organized national and local economic spaces sustained through international solidarity and fora of democratic co-operation'. G Albo, 'A world market of opportunities? Capitalist obstacles and left economic policies', in L Panitch (ed), *Socialist Register 1997: Ruthless Criticism of All that Exists*, London: Merlin Press, 1997, p 30.

[39] Bond, 'South Africa's agenda', p 416.

[40] JS Saul, 'Starting from scratch? A reply to Jeremy Cronin', *Monthly Review*, 54 (7), 2002.

[41] Much of the spirit and thrust of such initiatives are captured in A Desai's recent *We are the Poor: Community Struggles in Post-Apartheid South Africa*, New York: Monthly Review Press, 2002. See also the important contributions of N Alexander, *Issues in the Transition from Apartheid to Democracy in South Africa*, Pietermaritzburg: University of Natal Press, 2002; and G Hart, *Disabling Globalization: Places of Power in Post-Apartheid South Africa*, Pietermaritzburg and Berkeley, CA: University of Natal Press and University of California Press, 2002.

The Second Age of the Third World: from primitive accumulation to global public goods?

DAVID MOORE

Can primitive accumulation complete its task in the 'Third World'? This question lies at the root of the development debate. Dependency theory says no. Modernisation and classical Marxism say yes. Neither side of the debate can be reliably tested, because production relations in most of the Third World have not been fully transformed through primitive accumulation's trials.[1] During the cold war heyday of Third Worldism, outlined in the introduction to this special issue, theories and practices of development were framed by 'third way' utopias, while benefiting from the politics of non-alignment, nationalist muscle flexing, and variations of Keynesian and Stalinist planning models. Third World ideologies of difference and autonomy, combined with the politics of negotiating between two powerful global blocs, meant that the task of primitive accumulation was never acknowledged by name—except, misleadingly, by those casting doubt on state actors pursuing more primitive consumption than primitive accumulation. Nevertheless, the process was in motion. States were heavily involved.[2] Gains were made.[3]

Such state activity meant that Third Worldist development projects directly addressed a second question central in the development debate. To what extent can 'intentional development'[4] in the Third World hasten the process of primitive accumulation and simultaneously soften its devastating effects? In this era of so-called globalisation, that question is now: can 'development'—in both its accumulative and welfarist guises—be labelled a 'global public good' deserving the transfer of material resources from richer segments of the global political economy to poorer ones and the construction of public institutions to further its end?

The conjuncture that marked development's golden age wound down with the end of the West's (or First World's) equally gilded age of capitalism and the demise of the East's (or Second World's) state-led 'primitive socialist accumulation'. Neoliberalism's apostles—victors in the battle against socialism, Keynesianism and Third World amalgams thereof—proclaimed that development could emerge in the Third World only with the removal of what they called state impediments. Deliberately or not, they ignored primitive accumulation's history of state assistance and argued that it would 'take-off' if the prices were right, the state stayed in the backseat, and foreign trade and investment were encouraged more than ever.

Yet now there are tensions within the dominant development discourse about the role of the state in primitive accumulation processes, even though neither dare reveal their name, as either analytical constructs or empirical referents.[5] For over a quarter of a century, neoliberalism has delegitimised Third World states as agents of primitive accumulation, deriding them as repositories of 'rent-seekers'—protective cabals for ruling classes capable only of conspicuous consumption.[6] However, now the promise of the immediate post-cold war era has not materialised and the problems of this inherently conflict-ridden process have become increasingly evident. Nevertheless, those crafting the contours of development debates are reluctant to reintroduce the Third World state into the discourse. Thus a transnational state looms in its place.[7] Its legitimising language is that of global public goods. Its contradictions are similar to those constituting theories and justifications for the role of the state in any process of primitive accumulation. Be it 'local or global' the contemporary developmental state must simultaneously promote the bloody process and ameliorate its many devastating consequences. Advocates of global public goods believe that their global state can perform both tasks.

As well as discussing the concept of primitive accumulation and its relevance in the Third World today, this article assesses the idea of the re-emergence of an increasingly transnationalised or globalised state pursuing capitalist development under the new rubric of 'international' or 'global public goods'. It may also serve as warning that unless the stark realities of contemporary primitive accumulation on a global scale are accounted for, the global public goods panaceas will be less productive than those of their predecessors decades ago. Indeed, given that the problems they address are more likely to be better resolved by state structures with a modicum of subsidiarity than by global structures attending footloose financial capital, development specialists might better return to real questions of 'intentional' development and its legitimacy raised by the problems of primitive accumulation in their classical and Third World manifestations.

Past and present problems of primitive accumulation in the three worlds of development

Development is no more and no less than the always 'original'—and always bloody—but structurally similar process of primitive accumulation. With the end of the Cold War and the simultaneous passing of the First Age of the Third World, the Second Age of the Third World finds the globe divided as follows. The First World now consists of those geopolitical spaces, or state–society complexes, that have gone through the historic process of primitive accumulation.[8] In the First World—where most of the global rulers live—proletarians are fully separated from the means of production and power and make up the majority. Many have organised themselves well enough to influence those at the peaks of economic and political power to concede political and socioeconomic rights to them. Some of these 'rights' are also the ideological expression of the 'freedom' that comes from shaking off feudal and other pre-capitalist obligations,[9] and others have come from working class and other subaltern struggles. They have produced democracy. Serendipitously, many of these victories have forced capital to become more and more productive and expansionary—even imperial.[10] It is often redistributive enough to make many proletarians think they are 'middle class', many to think that they might be rich but for the demands of the poor,[11] and many to work for the state.[12] Meanwhile, the societies that endured 'primitive socialist accumulation' under Soviet development strategies continue to constitute the Second World.[13] The post-communist nation-states are becoming capitalist again, but under different conditions from those in the First and Third Worlds.

There are at least three reasons—aside from the sheer poverty and huge inequality between 'South' and 'North'[14]—for retaining the category 'Third World' for the part of the world so labelled during the Cold War. First, it is composed of social formations still locked in primitive accumulation's embrace, but in an altered phase, partially accelerated and more devastating than before. Its statist political economy during the Cold War simultaneously pushed and muted primitive accumulation: now it is doing more of David Harvey's 'dispossession'[15] and less of Scott MacWilliam's 'attaching'.[16] It is also re-entering world history in ways oddly reminiscent of the pre-colonial period. The (shaky) mantle of global hegemony has now passed from an imperial Britain of the late 19th century to the post-cold war imperium of the USA as if the Bolshevik experiment and its offshoots had never existed. Second, the global hinterlands are still the Third World because they are rejoining the world economy from a different platform than the former Second World. Finally, they share a history of subjugation to global capital's first *belle époque* and other conditions of 'post-coloniality', not least their state structures.[17]

Unfortunately, admitting the continuing possibility of a Third World does not mean a 'third way' can accomplish history's most unpleasant task, be it generated in global development institutions or 'national' planning departments. Although it takes place in many forms—and there are no guarantees of its completion—the process of primitive, 'primary' or original accumulation cannot be avoided. The creation of new capitalist classes and the transformation of property and production relations—including all accompanying political and cultural–ideological changes—are long and protracted in the best global contexts. In the worst—wherein dominant classes and states are not in favour of primitive accumulation processes threatening competition—it may even be permanent. However, the issue of 'stagnation or transformation' cannot be resolved until private property rights are universalised and full proletarianisation is achieved. Neoliberal globalisation may be quickening this process, but it is also exaggerating its unevenness.[18] The contradictions of primitive accumulation—exacerbated by the problems inherent in all the booms, busts, cycles and crises of profitability in full-blown capitalism—are bound to structure the current era's political struggles (including wars). Those hoping to ease the process by expanding global public goods must grasp primitive accumulation's nettle. They must recognise that only states (or suitable international substitutes) can both push the process to its limits and ameliorate some of its dislocations. They must realise that the world's most powerful states and classes—not only 'anti-globalisation' activists—will resist.

So what is primitive accumulation? It consists of three closely related elements. First are the methods by which an emerging bourgeoisie accumulates its first stock of capital in the midst of a disappearing mode of production. Second are the means by which a 'free' proletariat is created, tearing people from their ties to pre-capitalist tenure, their work relations and modes of authority. The 'stock' gained by the new bourgeoisie, partly from the old modes of production it is replacing and from parts of the world other than its 'home', enables the construction of the means of production with which the new proletariat labours to produce surplus value for its new—sometimes reinvented—rulers. In return for this labour the members of the new working class are paid money wages. Some of the commodities made for capitalists thus assist its reproduction through consumption. For example, increasing proportions of food and shelter, previously produced solely within a non-capitalist mode and for subsistence or barter, are now alienated from this partially transformed class and have to be purchased from the capitalists who 'stole' them.

The third component of this process allocates members of society the 'right' to buy their independent means of subsistence. The 'collective'—and poorly documented—rights to land in previous modes of production, largely taken by force by the emerging bourgeoisie, are transformed into 'private' rights 'freely' transferred by monetary exchange. This opportunity only benefits a minority of the displaced peoples at the same time as ideologies accompanying primitive accumulation deceptively celebrate small yeoman-type farmers replacing feudal landowners[19] and the gaining of these individual liberties, including the right to enter and exit employment. With land and labour's commodification comes the 'freedom' for their purchase and sale, celebrated by those bemoaning the coercion inherent in these relations in previous systems of production. Those less enamoured with removing the 'dead weight of previous generations', as Marx put it, are more prone to remember the communal rights and privileges of the ties to the land and the guarantees of work therein.

In fact, the vast majority of the new dominated classes cannot afford to buy land. They are forced to work for a wage to subsist. This is so even when new forms of work are slow in arriving as the new means of production take time to develop—as the emerging bourgeoisie is sluggish in investing its wealth in these new means, or turning it into 'real' capital. Thus much labour is unemployed and more sells below its reproduction rate. The alienated classes are often forced into what are now called 'informal' income gaining activities including theft and vagabondage.[20] For most people in the world's 'periphery' this process is much longer and bloodier than it was for the relatively small number of people in the core who started the global process and now benefit from developed capitalist forms.

The destruction of old modes of production and the emergence of new ones is by definition disruptive. It is also creative. Class forces within these mixtures of social relations create new collective organisations, augmenting beneficial processes, resisting harmful ones, and reinventing 'traditional' ones. These struggles transform states. Sometimes states are used as instruments of war and plunder against other countries.[21] Under pressure from subaltern social forces and their allies within new strata of 'organic intellectuals',[22] states will sometimes produce variants on 'poor laws'[23]—but ameliorative forms of 'intentional' development will be pulled away with 'liberal' capitalism's emergence. Whether these changes are dominated by the emerging bourgeoisie or moderated by a relatively strong proletariat—or 'disappearing' classes—they will be justified in the name of the public, often under the rubric of 'development'.[24] 'Public goods' are the resources and conditions constructed through these struggles and utilised by enough people so they benefit more than 'special interests'—from sanitation facilities to rules on banking, and from colonial states hastening 'civilisation's' progress to environmental legislation. 'Public bads' are the negative effects of primitive accumulation, from crime to pollution and international war—even dictators. Sometimes they call forth the creation of public goods; at others they are ignored.[25]

The main difference between historical and current epochs of primitive accumulation is that the world's ruling classes are now more 'globalised',[26] and they work with (and sometimes against, albeit less than before) states ranging from the municipal to the global level.[27] These classes are still made up of people who own actual means of production and are compelled by the exigencies of competition to innovate and expand them—and to cheapen labour and commodity supplies. Their political intellectuals change local and global state structures with varying degrees of co-ordination and conflict. Their property is exchanged on 'the market', ie their capital, including land, is bought and sold for money. These transactions are legally recognised and recorded by states and their international adjuncts. They usually—still—try to make the parts of the world that are not 'property' just that: they try to privatise and commodify them.

This essential part of the primitive accumulation process is often termed the 'enclosure of the commons'.[28] It is not easy to turn these parts of the world into easily bought and sold chunks, so various fractions of the bourgeoisie often exploit and simultaneously transform modes of production in which 'the commons' produce goods and reproduce labour power and nature: they often appear to subsidise the capital's costs. Some writers classify this process as 'permanent primitive accumulation' as if it is a 'conscious' strategy of capital, part of a well planned world division of labour.[29] Yet the contradictions of these transformations are more severe than this perspective allows, and there are simultaneous processes of 'pre-capitalist preservation' *and* transformation wherever capital meets its predecessors or cohabitants. Where these processes conflate with 'nation building' and its micro-processes—often shaping war—to talk of 'control' stretches the concept. Nevertheless, the apparent permanence of the process in the Third World separates it from the First.

Privatisation or commodification, and transformation or dispossession, *can* make proletarians and small farmers out of serfs and subsistence producers, as well as capitalists out of feudal lords, village chiefs, and perhaps members of former 'state-socialist' ruling parties. The hurdles of primitive accumulation *can* be mastered: capitalist development *can* take off. Capitalists and states may synergistically produce industrialisation—to meet the by no means spontaneous demands of local and global markets—and landless urbanised proletarians may become unionised working classes that democratise states and force capital to raise wages.[30] However, if the processes stall, permanent primitive accumulation ensues. Unwieldy articulations create stagnating social formations with small enclaves of compradorial activities feeding into the global accumulation process. Workers may be 'semi-proletarian', casually employed for a pittance a few months every year and eking out an existence from the soil or familial networks for the rest of the time, while petty entrepreneurs can only fit into 'informal' categories.

Undoubtedly peripheral processes of primitive accumulation leading to capitalist development co-exist with other modes of production around the world. Those past the formative stages of capitalist development augment their endogenous accumulation strategies with debt, diamonds and oil[31] and—not least—labour from their hinterlands. Thus they benefit from the form of primitive accumulation that does not necessarily change into capitalist relations of production. Wealth is garnered from this 'permanent' or stalled form 'outside' the loops of profit and productivity engendered solely by the augmentation of relative surplus value based on the struggles within the capital—labour nexus: the former adds to the latter but does change into it. Old modes of production incorporated into capitalism sometimes undergo the full extent of primitive accumulation; at others they are only incompletely subsumed. The nature of the process depends on factors ranging from the resources in various regions through to the nature of local ruling classes and the tempo of global capital flows.

Most of the Third World can be situated somewhere between the process of permanent primitive accumulation on the one hand or accelerating primitive accumulation on the other hand. *How* it fits is conditioned by the ways in which global capital is expanding or contracting, how 'nationalist bourgeoisies' are emerging (or contracting) out of the transitions, and how global and local variations of states manage the contradictions arising therefrom. Much of the process is shaped by how both the good and the bad sides of primitive accumulation are made public.

The foundation of the difference between Third World and First World state–society complexes rests in this incompleteness of capitalism and in the flows of huge amounts of wealth—including money[32] as well as pure labour, its products and other resources—from periphery to core. Most of the Third World is on the cusp of various 'local' permutations of primitive accumulation: its many ruling classes are becoming more and more capitalist, its property relations are becoming more and more private, while the subaltern classes are losing their modalities of sustenance rooted in non-capitalist land tenure and work relations and becoming more and more proletarianised. If they are not becoming 'industrialised' they are, as Bryceson puts it, certainly undergoing 'de-agrarianisation'.[33] The ideological and political aspects of these processes—including religion, nationalism, racism and ethnocentrism—accentuate their inherent violence within their territorial spaces and increasingly into the heart of capital (as 11 September 2001 exemplified).[34]

As at the end of the 19th century, when capital reached unprecedented global heights and depths, so now does it span the world at the threshold of a new *belle époque*. Now, as then, the intense flows of capital and its simultaneous subsumption and extension of other modes create unprecedented catastrophe in the hinterlands. As observers such as Karl Polanyi put it during colonial times, neither the peoples in the periphery nor the colonial states could protect their societies against the 'ravaging international trade and imperialism' that 'destroys precapitalist communities of kinship, neighbourhood, profession and creed … all forms of indigenous, organic society'.[35] Can they do so now? Perhaps, during the short interregnum of the development decades (roughly from 1950 to 1980) their states at least were beginning to manage what both Marx and Schumpeter might have called 'creative destruction': but that was when one could utter the word 'state' in polite company.

Only after global depression and wars did the myriad sovereignties of the Third World replace colonial rule with 'passive revolutions'.[36] For a few decades thereafter, Keynesian compromises promised to bring states, their subsidised national bourgeoisies, and civil societies to developmental heights. Primitive accumulation was helped along by states and what by Silver and Arrighi call 'developmentalist and labor–capital social contracts' promoted by the USA to meet anti-imperialist and cold war challenges.[37] By the end of the 1970s, however, neoliberalism broke that fragile consensus as global capital escaped its fetters once again. By then, the Third World challenge had almost disappeared with the coup against Allende in Chile, the stillbirth of the New International Economic Order and the coercion and compromise of the southern African liberation wars. A decade later, state socialism's collapse meant the end of another bulwark for those fearing the destabilising effects of state-less peripheral development. Now the notion of 'global public goods' has made a tentative appearance while the designers of post-cold war development worry about Asian-style financial crises, and Seattle-style demonstrators and Puerto Alegre-style social forums.[38] The Third Worldist and statist experiments in managing the contradictions of primitive accumulation seem to have failed, so softer organic intellectuals of global capital search for solutions with enough scope to link charitable humanitarian agendas to those more concerned with the extraction of absolute and relative surplus value.[39]

The essential questions about Third World development, however, have not changed. They still revolve around whether the 'global' processes of primitive accumulation hinder the 'local' ones or not? Does the 'global bourgeoisie' and its widespread practice of wealth extraction halt the creation of a landless proletariat and peripheral capitalists' accumulating practices? Does it distort the dynamic and developmental dialectics of the latter groups' relations with emerging workers and intermediate classes as pre-capitalist social formations merge with local and global variations of capitalism? Do local ruling groups freeze the development of subaltern classes in favour of alliances with global forces promoting extractive over expansionary processes? These have been the problems of 'development and underdevelopment' ever since dependency theory—or its Leninist precursors[40]—challenged the comparative optimism of both modernisation theory and orthodox Marxism. On them hinge the issue of whether or not 'real' capitalist development on the periphery is possible. The question of whether the Third World still exists (or for how long) must be resolved within this nexus: 'postcolonial identity' issues or chimerical third ways will not answer it. History has not settled it. Its sheer magnitude—brought back into focus after the pitfalls of premature and voluntarist socialism and their Cold Wars have been forgotten—still constitutes the cornerstone of the Third World's condition and of ways of improving it. Attempts to deny primitive accumulation's centrality, in its local and global manifestations, will founder on utopia's shoals or the shifting sands of piecemeal social engineering, leaving the social stagnation festering in peripheral capitalism's bottom layers. So will shying from the role of the *state*—in its global and local manifestations—in this process.

To contend that the current epoch of world history is characterised by a renewed phase of primitive accumulation is far from arguing that this is a purely 'economic' process. One must maintain that it involves much state 'intervention', congruent with Marx's conceptualisation. The newly materialising bourgeoisies forming at 'local' and 'global' levels need both force and legitimacy for their transformational accumulation projects. They must coerce and/or persuade millions of people off their various 'commons' provided by their multitudinous modes of production. They must offer a modicum of material and ideological recompense to incorporate old ruling classes and accommodate subaltern resistance. They must provide the means of production to which freely floating labour power must be attached: primitive accumulation cannot proceed without this last half.[41] When 'nations' are not emerging from colonial boundaries local and global bourgeoisies attempt to change them. There are no guarantees new ones will gel. In these cases states and their armies, amid warlords and their militias, are the accumulating actors.[42] Different sections of these classes—or their upper caste servants and idealistic young NGO workers—often come to repair war's damage: this branch of 'international public goods' is what is quaintly referred to as 'peacekeeping' and 'humanitarianism'. These actors have generated a global public goods discourse. Before discussing it, however, a comparison of old and new conceptions of primitive accumulation is in order.

Classical to postmodern modes of primitive accumulation and development's three worlds: from Marx and Engels to Hardt and Negri and ... the World Bank

Some of the confusion surrounding the meaning of primitive accumulation may lie with Karl Marx's words about capitalism's homelands. Although he was fairly certain 'progress' depended on the bourgeoisie fulfilling an historic mission to eliminate pre-capitalist social formations, he never really decided whether the capital propelling the bourgeoisie to global dominance was 'internally' or 'externally' generated.[43] If the former, as Brenner suggests,[44] agrarian revolution and proto-industrialisation were the prime generators of the 'original capital'—including, in its guilds, many aspects of the 'training' of a skilled and disciplined working class[45]—carrying Western European capitalism forward. Strong proletarians and competition pushed capitalist industrialisers towards innovations and productivity increases. Profit came from relative surplus value— that is, gains from technological invention and better divisions of labour, Taylorism, Fordism and the practices of post-Fordism such as 'lean' and 'just in time' production—rather than from the absolute surplus value gained by forcing people to work faster for longer hours, or from cheap labour in Third Worlds of permanent primitive accumulation.

However, if that original stock of capital could not have been garnered without Britain increasingly taking over the oceanic commercial and extractive networks built up by Genoese, Portuguese, Spanish and Dutch hegemony, nor without the slave trade, the Opium Wars, and India's industrial obliteration, then perhaps capitalism in the world's core was dependent on wealth taken from other modes of production in other parts of the world—and still is. It relies on the destruction of the Third World, not its development, on monopoly rather than competition, on dictators not democrats, on war instead of peace. All the West's developmental co-operation shibboleths are empty excuses for the continuing subjection of the Third World's people to classes who only want the extraction of their natural resources and their forms of labour that have not advanced far beyond slavery. In this view, primitive accumulation processes are permanently stalled because capitalists need other modes of production. When they are completed in some parts of the world they are reinvented in others. Yes, public commons and mutual solidarities (or repressive obligations) are destroyed, but rational capitalists, vigorous proletarians and productive yeoman do not arise in their place. They are denuded and supplanted by capricious compradors dominating a paralysed populace with no bourgeois freedoms superseding the rights and compulsions of 'communal' social formations. Rhetoric of growth and expansion aside, the game of capitalism remains 'zero-sum'.

A latter-day Marxist might be able to get away with this type of 'neo-Marxism', but would be confronted with variations of locally and globally initiated primitive accumulation: proletarians working in real industries, peasants as well as plantations growing and selling agricultural commodities, capitalists combating and collaborating with their metropolitan peers. Empirical patterns of primitive accumulation would be uneven, not uniform, conditioned as much by indigenous modes of pre-capitalism (or by forms of 'state socialism', as in China) as by currents emanating from the centre. Can classical Marxists argue coherently on these issues?

Contemporary theory further confuses the empirical mayhem. The writers of what has been dubbed this century's *Communist Manifesto* seem as perplexed as their progenitors. Is it coincidental that Hardt and Negri's *Empire* is the first work to raise the issue of primitive accumulation in years? Is it serendipitous that the new apostles of global revolution are even more puzzling on primitive accumulation than Marx and Engels? To both questions the answer is 'no'. First, the issue is raised again while the 21st century ushers in a new phase of global primitive accumulation, sometimes called 'globalisation'. The second 'no' is different. Hardt and Negri's mystification magnifies Marx and Engels' because the Third World has reached an ideological plane in which its various modes of production, which are articulated into the global political economy, are considered *equivalent* to any other social formation.

Hardt and Negri also have a political reason to reduce the theory of primitive accumulation to ashes: their notion of the 'multitude' as the source of global revolution includes *all* groups of people in any relation of subordination to capital and states, so they cannot privilege workers who have gone through the fire of a protracted process of classical primitive accumulation. If they did, they might have to wait forever. Instead, they have posited a new universal class. All members contribute equally to the global gathering of value—but some of them are subjected to 'post-modern primitive accumulation'.[46] Others may be NGO mendicants or computer nerds. The result of their wishing away primitive accumulation's travails is their proposal for the ultimate and utopian global good: a global social wage, a 'guaranteed income for all'.[47]

Marx and Engels, as steeped in the project of capitalist development as any captain of industry, did not hesitate to say that the non-capitalist world was 'backward'—and that it would soon disappear. Hardt and Negri are not as eager to pass civilisational judgement. They censure 'postcolonial' thought for uncritically celebrating 'non-Western' cultural modalities, they criticise forms of 'localism' attempting to ward off the tempests of global informational capitalism, and they nearly authorise Marx's notes on colonial India.[48] This may signal an advance for Third World ideologies of equivalence and representational efficacy, but by placing all modes of production around the globe within the 'highest levels of productivity' just because they are linked through a process of 'informational accumulation' that 'destroys or at least destructures ... [and] immediately integrates [them] in its own networks'[49] Hardt and Negri just about negate the fact that they have brought the concept of primitive accumulation— along with nation-state formation and democratisation—to prominence again.[50] To clarify this problem, Marx's and his heirs' notion of primitive accumulation will have to be further investigated, along with its modernist reincarnations.

As noted, Marx's perception of capitalism's blood-soaked birth is dualistic. Some of the blood is from the slaves who crossed the Atlantic, where their labour augmented the capital of plantation owners and textile, tobacco and sugar manufacturers, amid scores of other forms of mercantile plunder around the world. The rest of the spilled bodily fluids and lopped-off limbs were from those in capital's core who lost their land and feudal rights as they gained their 'freedom' to enter labour contracts with those who owned the means of production, or who were shipped off to capital's outposts in the 'new worlds' of North America and Australasia to undertake more forms of primitive accumulation (often resulting in genocide). Yet, in spite of this dualism, Marx spent more time analysing the conditions for capitalism's emergence and development in Europe than in capital's global appendages. Thus his emphasis was on the process's internal rather than external components. His analysis of 'the pre-history of the bourgeois economy' points to an intrinsic relation between the 'internally' generated transformation of a specific form of feudalism and the emergence of industrial capitalism. For example, he discusses how money became a 'highly energetic solvent' as feudalism was dissolving, how urban artisans' guilds and rural outputting were transformed into 'objectified labour' during the 14th and 15th centuries, how trading networks contributed to the dominance of exchange value over use value, and how the governments of 'Henry VII, VIII, etc' removed 'begging, vagabondage and robbery' off the list of alternatives to waged labour,[51] while those of the Reformation gave the ecclesiastical domains of the Roman Catholic church to 'rapacious royal favourites ... [and] speculative farmers and townsmen' and William of Orange's 'glorious revolution' sold crown land at 'knock-down prices' to the new large scale agricultural bourgeoisie.[52] These factors, combined with the expropriation of most people from their land rights—the essential condition, lest we forget—were the unsavoury precedents to what Amartya Sen calls the economic system allowing 'free seeking of employment'.[53] They were performed 'previous to' capitalism, often by a strong state; they cost 'capitalism' nothing and benefited its new leading members. Perhaps one could even think of them as a 'public good' for this new mode of production.

When one reads of the internal preconditions for capitalism's original phase, it is hard to accept the statement by Hardt and Negri that 'the *central* motor for the creation of capitalists ... came from outside England, from commerce—or really from conquest, the slave trade and the colonial system'.[54] Here Hardt and Negri confuse the wealth from trade and plunder with the social aspects of the creation of the *relationship* between labour and capital, without which there can be no capitalists. Hardt and Negri appear to accept this notion when they state that primitive accumulation is a '*social* accumulation'[55] (their emphasis) primarily based on the separation of the subaltern classes from their means of subsistence and production. However, their enthusiasm to give equal weight to the Third World's contribution to capital's origins forces them to write that the formation of capitalists *contrasts* with that of proletarians because the former are constituted by '"the treasures captured outside Europe by undisguised looting, enslavement and murder" '.[56] They quote Marx as if this proves their point. They fail to emphasise, even though they quote some of the phrase, that this wealth could only be '"turned into capital"' in Europe if the social conditions were propitious. Instead, they write that 'the enormous inflow of wealth overflowed the capacity of the old feudal relations of production'.[57] This almost quantitative phrasing of the process ignores the many changes within European feudalism that paved the way for this wealth to be turned into the capital relation. It also allows them to state that even now 'the productive relationship with the "dark continents" serves as the economic foundation of the European nation-states'.[58]

This formulation allows them to proceed to the assertion that the whole planet is subject to forms of 'post-modern primitive accumulation' even if it has not *quite* gone through the process of primitive accumulation and all its labourers are not exactly proletarianised. All are 'integrated in some way into the networks of informational production' so are 'immediately' rather than 'sequentially' incorporated into a mode of production newer even than capitalism.[59] A centuries-long process of primitive accumulation is leapfrogged and all of the world's producing peoples who are subordinated to global capital in any way are equal before the universalising dictates of the 'information mode of production'.

Hardt and Negri stumble over the problems of discerning whether state–society complexes with a majority of producers only partially subjected to the discipline of full proletarianisation and the wage—that is, who are not 'really' but only 'formally' subsumed by capitalist production relations—have passed through the crucible of primitive accumulation. In an elliptical and complex passage Hardt and Negri write that the 'globalisation of markets' comes from 'the desires and demands of ... disciplined labour power across the world'. As the global core's 'desiring subjectivities forced the development to go forward' they also generated 'conditions of liberation and struggle' controllable only by the forces of 'real subsumption', that is, all the disciplines and satiations of advanced capitalism, hastened by the information revolution. These modes of control have flipped back to discipline core proletarians, too. Thus the spread of their desires may have dug their own graves with a global surveillance state. However, this fusion of formal and real subsumption—or primitive and disciplinary accumulation—also fuses the world's workers into one class and, with the global state, gives them an instrument for further liberation.[60] With full subsumption, global labourers are uncontrollable. A new apparatus of global power fusing economic and political control is created. Indeed, with the material reality of the protracted processes of primitive accumulation overcome (they are *dissolved* into a 'virtual reality'[61]) we are propelled on to the stage of pure politics. That purity allows Hardt and Negri to create a new class—the multitude—and posit a global social wage as its goal. Little problems such as the relationship of the multitude's poorer elements to the land are left to World Bank technocrats, hurrying to catch up with internet capitalism.

Hardt and Negri's predilections for proletarian desires and cyberspace collectives conjure the Third World away. However, more pedestrian analyses such as the World Bank's 2003 Deininger Report on *Land Policies for Growth and Poverty Reduction*, prescribe 'private property' as the 'answer' to the 'land question' in what they still identify as the Third World.[62] Meanwhile, the populist Peruvian philosopher Hernando de Soto proffers related strategies to establish secure private property rights in urban and rural settings alike.[63] De Soto claims poverty could be eliminated if states in the Third World (undoubtedly helped by World Bank experts) would codify the 'extralegal' social contracts for property recognised by billions of more-or-less informal shanty-dwellers and agriculturalists. Then the capital embodied in their physical wealth could be invested again and again: credit based on the collateral of property could resurrect dead capital. De Soto implicitly recognises that many Third World residents have lost their rural land rights through primitive accumulation. They are proletarians (although he says Marx would be surprised to discover that the Third World's 'teeming mass does not consist of oppressed legal proletarians but of oppressed extralegal small entrepreneurs with a sizeable amount of assets'[64]) but are not sufficiently 'attached' to industrial means of production. Rather than wait for the factories or public works programmes he suggests that the *de facto* private properties of huge informal urban settlements be legally recognised so their residents can become capitalists, investing in means of production with the money they borrow based on their titled property.

De Soto ignores the initial process of primitive accumulation that forced people into the cities, thus sidestepping questions about who owns capital now, and what they are doing with it. He also masks the problems of proletarianisation with his fantasy of millions of small businesspeople. Nevertheless, he inadvertently draws attention to the fact that questions concerning the permanence of primitive accumulation cannot be 'tested' unless property rights are universalised. Capital will never be fully rooted in the social formations of the world unless a landless proletariat has emerged and has 'formal' rights to purchase the land it has lost.

De Soto's populism also avoids the ideological issues linked to the universalization of private property rights by attempting to incorporate 'tradition' with modernity. He advises state or NGO workers to research grassroots institutions and 'folk conventions' around property rights.[65] These conventions can then be incorporated into a state-system of property law, enabling the land-holding masses to be represented in a system of credit. It sounds simple, and fits with the influential notions of 'good governance', community development, popular participation, 'market empowerment', and other obfuscating buzzwords. However, if de Soto is correct, his ignorance of the primitive accumulation process is not problematic. (One wonders though: can we take seriously someone whose generous recognition of Marx's rendition of primitive accumulation describes the people thus usurped as 'small proprietors'?[66]) However, the informal property titling processes he charts happen *after* the initial stage of the subalterns' separation from the 'commons' and other pre-capitalist forms of land rights and labour obligations, and after they have moved into cities. He has prematurely bid 'farewell to the peasantry'[67] and predicted their welcome to Braudel's capitalist bell jar.[68]

Furthermore, de Soto's reliance on the roughshod settling of the American frontier as a guide to wealth creation is wrong. There one observes the concurrence of land settlement with the settling of land titling problems. The frontier of the American west was opened up through genocide, gold rushes and the contradictory relationship between cheap land and the need of industrialists for cheap labour.[69] Are those frontiers of land and industrialisation there in the Third World? Can the relations of production left behind by de Soto's very modern (he says) urban citizens fuel an agricultural revolution accompanying the freeing of 'dead capital' stored in informal/extralegal forms of property recognition? Can it be true, as de Soto asserts without equivocation, that:

> Former communist nations and the Third World are exactly where Europe, Japan and the United States were a couple of hundred years ago. Like the West, they must identify and gather up the existing property representations scattered throughout their nations and bring them into one integrated system to give the assets the fungibility, bureaucratic machinery and networks required to produce capital.[70]

While also promoting this urban vision, the World Bank offers encouragement to 'small proprietors' in rural areas where primitive accumulation's first stage has yet to gestate, places where, as the Bank notes in rural Africa, over 90% of the land has no state-recognised (or formal) tenure, be it 'customary' or capitalist, as well as in the 'second-stage' peri-urban areas in Africa and Asia wherein between 40% and 50% of residents have only informal land rights.[71] Maybe the assumption is that, if de Soto's work is done in the cities, when rural residents are bought out of their access to the land they can carry their property rights—transformed into cash—into urban areas so larger and 'more efficient' capitalists can have their rural ways. Undoubtedly the Bank's renewed emphasis on land is inspired by primitive accumulation's requirements, in spite of populist language favouring the smallholder. As the 2003 World Bank–Deininger report notes, mechanisation and the 'scope to collateral ... to overcome imperfections ... inherent to the credit market ... will favour farmers who own larger amounts of land'.[72] Furthermore, formalisation of land tenure just might lead to a 50% increase in the supply of labour to the market, as in Peru.[73] This can only indicate a desire to create a large land-owning bourgeoisie—with lots of room to rent to a yeoman class and to sharecrop to tenants with even fewer rights[74]—and a landless proletariat.

The Bank recognises that this task is far-reaching; it knows that 'changes in land relations have generally been confined to major historical transitions' and that transformations from collective to individual forms of tenure are 'not automatic ... [but] will be affected by political and economic factors, and thus will often coincide with major conflicts, upheavals, or power struggles'. The latter can 'challenge traditional authorities and institutions that previously had unquestioned authority over land allocation', they may 'coincide with land claims by outsiders and ... race and ethnicity issues', and they can 'lead to serious crises of governance, including civil war'.[75] The report even acknowledges a less than productive 'ruling class'.[76] It also knows land tenure reform is a public good for *states* to provide—although avoiding the word 'state' whenever possible. It advises that land rights need 'public provision, or [hesitating to invoke straightforward provision for the notion of a 'public'] at least regulation' because:

1. the process is expensive; its benefits are largely 'nonrival';
2. it 'facilitate[s] abstract representation and impersonal exchange of rights' thereby providing a 'necessary, though by no means sufficient, condition for participation in a modern economy through mechanisms such as mortgaging';
3. tenure rights need standardisation and clear boundaries; and without a state's monopoly on force people will waste resources protecting their claims or fighting for redress in cases of deprivation.[77]

Deininger acknowledges that 'all economically and politically advanced societies [have] ... state-managed systems for regulating land ownership and land transfers'.[78] Furthermore, although the Bank is clear that 'individual title' is by far the preferred route, such titles can never be unrestricted: they must be 'limited by the need to have rights holders contribute to the broader public good'.[79] In cases where 'customary' forms of tenure are to be formalised, or to be changed to more capitalist forms, it is necessary to have an 'authoritative interpretation of past norms'.[80]

It is thus clear that careful consideration of the process of primitive accumulation involves the development of adequate public goods. Marx's marauding bourgeoisie made full use of the state, while Hardt and Negri's multitude must establish systems of governance to implement its global wage. De Soto and Deininger's catalogues of collateral must be started and maintained by states. It is necessary, then, to investigate the discourse of global public goods before summarising the connections between them and the seemingly disparate realm of primitive accumulation.

Global public goods: the saviour of the Third World?

The need for a variety of local and global state-like activities in the post-cold war interregnum has called forth the 'global public goods' discourse. Sometimes this language refers to the collective activities needed to pave the way for original accumulation. This could be the universal legalisation of property rights, ie private property,[81] creating 'freedom' for yeoman capitalists as well as their well established global peers/competitors—and forcing the majority to 'freely' sell their labour to the highest bidder. Given the absence of the guilds and rural proto-industries in the latter stages of feudalism that created a 'certain level of skill'—ready for picking by emerging capitalists—within an embryonic proletariat in the early days of classical capitalism,[82] perhaps the 'international community' must also provide the 'public good' of education. Indeed, where 'feudal' preconditions for capitalist development do not exist in the Third World, would the establishment of their functional equivalent—something like an 'absolutist state'[83]—be a 'public good'?

If, as many theorists of public goods suggest, 'the market' is a global public good—a carefully constructed ensemble of institutions rather than a spontaneous eruption—should global managers create it with what are effectively states of their own? Perhaps the notion—already acronymed IPG or GPG—reflects the admission that there is no longer a chance for a 'national bourgeoisie' in the Third World to pull off Smith's, Marx's and Weber's grand historical mission, even in tandem with its state. Maybe this class can only carry out 'primitive consumption', not 'original accumulation'. The 'accumulation' goes elsewhere while a few international soldiers and NGO cenobites—IPGs incarnate amidst IDPs (internally displaced persons) and the other flotsam of primitive accumulation—maintain a modicum of security and mop up the mess around the enclaves of wealth extraction. Frantz Fanon's pessimism about the pitfalls of the 'national middle class' thus merges with radical civil society's scepticism, and perhaps even with those espousing a dose of 'liberal imperialism' through reinvented colonial trusteeship or plain and simple invasions of places like Iraq.[84] The chorus chants: better us than the unruly behaviour of nasty national capitalists. Better us than a concept of a state delegitimised and distorted by the short but triumphant hegemony of neoliberalism and a slightly longer chronicle of kleptocrats, human rights abusers and fundamentalist fanatics. Let us construct the collective preconditions for capitalist development. We can do primitive accumulation the modern way.

In the absence of such overt declarations, global public goods are said to involve everything from 'research' and vaccine provision to 'global coordination mechanisms', such as the Heavily Indebted Poor Countries (HIPC) initiative.[85] They include 'good governance' and sometimes even the whole gamut of development itself. The GPGs are gaining credence as a soft alternative (or accompaniment) to classic neoliberal 'development'. It is embodied by the *Gestalt* of the UN Development Programme (UNDP) rather than the World Bank and the IMF, and could represent a stronger version of the 'post-Washington consensus'.[86] Still in an early phase, its 'real' meaning is unclear: like the earlier rise of the notion of 'sustainable development', GPG is ideologically unmoored and will continue to be until one or the other forces of global hegemony bring it into their ambit.[87]

Nevertheless, one can still attempt to strip its meaning to a core. What is a public good, and what makes one global? We are led to believe that public goods and conditions are 'nonrival and non-excludable'—if one person consumes or enjoys them, others can too, and it is difficult to stop people from sharing their benefits. The definition of the concept has never been precise, changing over time with political and ideological shifts. As Meghnad Desai puts it, the historic development of public goods has had less to do with technocrats 'gauging the preferences of consumers' and more to do with politicians 'guessing what was needed to keep them from revolting—an elite response to democratic but extra-parliamentary pressure'.[88] The notion's inclusiveness could be considered a barometer of hegemony. If accepted discourse contends that public goods are the 'key to prosperity and social wellbeing', extending from health and housing to a pristine environment, and from education to 'relatively balanced distribu-tions of wealth'—and that governments, by taxing the rich, or through First World to Third World transfers, are primarily responsible for their expenses[89]—one might conclude that the world is on its way to a form of global social democracy.

On the other hand, if one is exposed to constant reiterations that the private sector or 'public–private partnerships' can supply public goods, or that public provision of public goods should be restricted to the establishment of 'efficient markets' (possibly with strong defence added on), one would be warranted in assuming that neoliberalism holds sway. That the language of public goods is taking up more and more space within development discourse at least indicates there is uncertainty within this realm's hegemonic arbiters.

Thus the ideological disputes over the extension of public goods will impinge on what has often been taken as their defining factor—their 'nonrival' and 'nonexcludable' status. Education, for example, is mostly defined in this dis-course as a 'nonrival' good. One person getting educated does not stop someone else from gaining knowledge. It is also seen as 'nonexcludable', because it is difficult to stop people from sharing it. Closer examination reveals more conflict behind such definitions. If a state subsidises universities more than primary schools, probably fewer young students will enter the system: it will be subject to both rivalry and exclusion. Market or NGO provision will exclude students without financial resources or who live far from the global nomads' fleeting location. Indeed, as the global tendency towards the privatisation of water illustrates, what were once almost universally considered state provided public goods could soon be taken under capitalist wings.[90]

The controversies and conflicts involved in identifying and provisioning public goods are multiplied at the global level. There is no central state to mediate hegemonic conflicts over the nature of these resources and conditions. Yet, with issues ranging from the environment to cross-border health concerns like HIV/AIDS,[91] and from war and crime to the contagion of financial crises, 'globalisation' brings the public goods debates to the world stage.[92] That the early 2002 Monterrey Consensus meetings were slated to discuss global public goods, but did not, suggests ideological tension around their conceptualisation. French, Swedish and UNDP responsibility for a GPG task force indicates a 'European' flavour to the notion and little enthusiasm by the Anglo-Saxon unilateralist and its junior partner.

While global politicians prevaricate, academic architects scribble, hoping their ideas will see power. Thus reformist development discourse displays the harsh symptoms of uneven development (its reports are a litany of everything wrong with the world), but hesitates to confront their causes. GPG discourse may be a new attempt to disguise the necessity of confronting the foundations of Third World primitive accumulation and how current processes and policies aggravate it. As usual with the varieties of dominant development discourses at the edges of 'reform', when the main model malfunctions, GPG discourse can be dismissed as wallowing uncomfortably between poles of romantic and technocratic wishful thinking. It may just be the window dressing allowing the Third World to continue on paths of primitive accumulation leading to the dead ends of crony consumption at best, or war modes of production at worst, while the already well ensconced cores of capital continue their relatively virtuous cycles of wealth generation and expansion.

On the other hand, the idea of global public goods may signal that a segment of transnational capital's 'organic intellectuals' installed in global bureaucracies, universities, think-tanks and world civil society organisations are aware that the post-1970s ways of dealing with the contradictions of the international political economy are deepening rather than ameliorating them. The tentative emergence of GPG discourse—in such popular–academic texts as Amartya Sen's *Development as Freedom* and the UN-speak of the Commission on Human Security (a phrase stretching a concept well beyond its original meaning, a process seemingly inherent in such a field) he co-led[93]—may imply a slow turn from global structural adjustment programmes to global 'public goods'. The timidity of the public goods alternative, however, suggests otherwise. Even the most philosophical expression of the 'true interests' hinted at by a concept of global public goods retreats from the consequences of its potentially radical democracy: as Lawrence Hamilton observes, Sen sidesteps the logical extension of his capabilities approach when it threatens to challenge the 'rights' embedded in his much stronger liberalism.[94] In the face of such a contest Sen retreats to ethics. He hints that 'democracy' be considered a public good, but hesitates to say it will take a highly robust form of democracy to ensure a modicum of more material public goods. Rather than that—and the state that might arrive in its wake – a notion of ethics is called on.

> For efficient provision of public goods, not only do we have to consider the possibility of state actions and social provisioning, we also have to examine the part that can be played by the development of social values and a sense of responsibility that may reduce the need for forceful state action. For example, the development of environmental ethics can do some of the job that [often] ... is done through compelling regulation.[95]

One wants to ask, 'from where do environmental ethics come?' and 'will those whose profits environmental protection curtail have the same ethics as those for whom relying on oil company owners' ethics is risky?' Will not the poor in heavily polluted areas have an 'ethic' including states implementing their needs? Will they not need an 'ethic' of direct action to display their needs and their power to ensure the state pays them attention? Sen's slipperiness within such realms suggests the intellectual promiscuity allowing the World Bank to invent myriad meanings for such phrases as 'social capital'.[96] If we all had an 'ethic' of public goods there would be enough 'social capital' so we could all trust one another's generosity and ensure that the elimination of poverty would be a 'public good' of such importance that states would no longer exist. There would be no need for social protest to remind capitalists of their 'ethics' and to pressurise states to regulate them when they are less than 'ethical'. Rather than rely on ethics to encourage the supply of public goods, it would be wise to remember that:

> because it is difficult or impossible to exclude people from enjoying the benefits of public goods it is difficult to make money from them. This means there is little incentive for the private sector to produce them. As a result governments generally have to play a role in securing the production of public goods.[97]

The 'freedoms' envisioned at the end of primitive accumulation, but often denied by its pursuit and its realisation, stall the promulgators of public goods from stemming its brutality or hastening its progress—if either involves concerted state action. Unless such worldly philosophers genuinely share Hayek's fear that social welfarism and other state activity leads to Stalinism, these cul de sacs either expose their own (true) interests or their display of fealty to their overlords. Even the concept of 'mutual vulnerability'—showing that 'human security' benefits rich as well as poor, so global welfare issues are a 'public good' more than a drain on the former's resources[98] (validated by '9/11')—fails to move the latter's neoliberal steamroller from its path. Instead, a pernicious mix of an inherently statist, militarist neo-conservatism with a pretence of a 'non-statist' economic philosophy (that only stems welfare costs in the core and stops the subsidised emergence of Third World bourgeoisies and industrialisation) has taken root in empire's heart. In the midst of this ideological meltdown, the sages and technocrats of global public goods muse about a watered down version of an already drastically diluted New International Economic Order, to be implemented when the world experiences another depression like the 1930s.

Conclusion: from primitive accumulation to public accumulation?

Perhaps development on the periphery during the cold war period was not much better than it is in the post-cold war period, but the Third World's First Age, unlike the Second Age that it has now entered, did see economic and political 'development'. Third Worldism's utopian nationalism and global Keynesianism, inspired by the catastrophes of the first and second world wars, the depression and the threat of state socialisms, combined to create capitalism's golden age and hide the problems of primitive accumulation.[99] In the wake of the depression, wars and decolonisation, a few 'development decades' allowed their Marxist celebrator, Bill Warren, to chronicle Third World capitalism's successes.[100] Could a particularly devastating historical path have been averted if the management of 'primitive accumulation' had been considered a public good at an earlier conjuncture?

Today, if the USA does not manage its hegemonic decline gracefully, much of the world will go down with it.[101] Liberian and Congolese warlords will demonstrate how accumulation takes place in the 'hinterland'. China illustrates the brighter but not very libertarian lights of state capitalism following 'primitive socialist accumulation'. Americans will invade more Iraqs. Yet those articulating notions of 'global public goods' beyond the merely technocratic to restart distorted primitive accumulation processes (alongside nation-state formation and democratisation) just might be able to steer a fragile trajectory to a different path. The idea of full employment as a public good, justifying sophisticated industrial strategies to absorb primitive accumulation's new proletarians, and involving new capitalist classes in productive instead of wasteful pursuits, could take root.

As this article illustrates, history's lessons and the theoretical impasse concerning primitive accumulation's permanence lead one to believe that the first stages of capitalist development cannot be accomplished without significant state involvement. At the height of globalisation, and with the threat of unilateralism when it falls, the apparatuses of a nascent 'global state' must make primitive accumulation 'public'. The ideology and practice of public accumulation must catch on. In the interregnum, breath should not be held. Even global meltdown will probably just see slightly reformed institutions crafted in Bretton Woods-like resorts. The process of primitive accumulation and the provision of (some) global public goods will circle around each other in perpetuity, only sometimes joining to dance the dialectic of democratic development on the world stage.

Notes

[1] This very abstract article has its empirical base primarily in Africa, where primitive accumulation is more protracted than in other parts of the Third World. D Moore, 'Neoliberal globalisation and the triple crisis of "modernisation" in Africa: Zimbabwe, The Democratic Republic of the Congo and South Africa', *Third World Quarterly*, 22 (6), 2001, pp 909–929; Moore, 'Zimbabwe: twists on the tale of primitive accumulation', in M Smith (ed), *Globalizing Africa*, Trenton, NJ: Africa World Press, 2003. Nevertheless,

there are many other Third World, socioeconomic spaces where the tasks of primitive accumulation are not yet complete.

[2] For a reminder that classical methods of primitive accumulation required much state activity, and that it was kept secret, see M Perelman, *The Invention of Capitalism: Classical Political Economy and the Secret History of Primitive Accumulation*, Durham, SC: Duke University Press, 2000.

[3] For example, Arrighi notes that until 1975 African growth was impressive. G Arrighi, 'The African crisis: world systemic and regional effects', *New Left* Review, 2 (15), 2002, pp 1–32.

[4] M Cowan & R Shenton, *Doctrines of Development*, London: Routledge, 1996.

[5] Mainstream development theory seldom mentions 'states' and never mentions 'primitive accumulation'.

[6] The 'primitive' forms of accumulation demonstrated by Third World elites, including corruption, are frequently not productive because the wealth gained in these processes is not attachable to 'freed' labour, or employable labour, or available means of production. For Marx, 'what enables moneywealth to become capital is the encounter, on one side, with free workers; and on the other side, with the necessaries and materials, etc, which previously were in one way or another the *property* of the masses who have now become object-less, and are also *free* and purchasable'. K Marx, 'The *Grundrisse*', in R Tucker (ed), *The Marx–Engels Reader*, New York: Norton, 1978, p 269.

[7] W Robinson, 'Social theory and globalization: the rise of a transnational state', *Theory and Society*, 30 (2), 2001, pp 157–200.

[8] On state–society complexes, see RW Cox, 'Social forces, states, and world orders: beyond international relations theory', in RW Cox with T Sinclair, *Approaches to World Order*, Cambridge: Cambridge University Press, 1996, pp 85–123.

[9] J Townsend, *CB Macpherson and the Problem of Liberal Democracy*, Edinburgh: University of Edinburgh Press, 2000.

[10] For Hardt and Negri capital's innovations—even global expansion—are forced on it from below. M Hardt & A Negri, *Empire*, Cambridge, MA: Harvard University Press, 2000.

[11] JK Galbraith, *The Culture of Contentment*, Boston, MA: Houghton Mifflin, 1992.

[12] In the USA government employees exceed those in manufacturing by 5 129 000. 'Harper's Index', *Harper's*, July 2003, p 11.

[13] Some former Second World countries—especially Central European—were mainly capitalist before becoming part of the 'Soviet bloc'. They should not be considered part of today's Second World. Perhaps China should, in spite of its split with the USSR and later attempts to lead/join the Third World.

[14] JS Saul, 'Globalization, imperialism, development: false binaries and radical resolutions', in L Panitch & C Leys (eds), *Socialist Register 2004: Imperialism*, London: Merlin Press, 2003.

[15] D Harvey, 'The new imperialism', in Panitch & Leys, *Socialist Register 2004*.

[16] S MacWilliam, 'Plenty of poverty: the development of the World Bank', in D Moore (ed), *Banking for Hegemony: Critical Essays on the World Bank*, Pietermaritzburg: University of Natal Press, forthcoming.

[17] BJ Silver & G Arrighi, 'Polanyi's "double movement": the *belles époques* of British and US hegemony compared', *Politics and Society*, 31 (2), 2003, pp 325–355.

[18] P Bond, 'Potentials for African anti-capitalism: uneven development and popular resistance', *Rosa Luxemburg Stiftung Policy Paper*, Johannesburg, 1, 2003.

[19] Dominant development discourse confuses the 'yeoman' stage of transition with 'full' capitalism. Marx's primitive accumulation account allows 'free peasant proprietors' to exist under many forms of feudal title. His teleology suggests, however, that eventually they will disappear under the pressure of agrarian capitalists. K Marx, *Capital*, Vol 2, London: JM Dent, 1930, p 794.

[20] Brett Bowden notes in correspondence that armies soak up many 'new entrants' to the labour market, as in the classical age of primitive accumulation. Think, also, of child soldiers in many Third World wars.

[21] B Teschke, 'Theorizing the Westphalian system of states: international relations from absolutism to capitalism', *European Journal of International Relations*, 8 (1), pp 5–48. Teschke's analysis of changing modes of production in Europe and war has applicability to contemporary Zimbabwean international primitive accumulation. See M Nest, 'Ambitions, profits and loss: Zimbabwean economic involvement in the Democratic Republic of the Congo,' *African Affairs*, 100 (400), 2001, pp 469–490.

[22] A Gramsci, *Selections from the Prison Notebooks,* New York: International Publishers, 1971.

[23] F Block & M Somers, 'In the shadow of Speenhamland: social policy and the old poor law', *Politics and Society*, 31 (2), 2003, pp 283–322.

[24] To exercise hegemony, 'the leading group should make sacrifices of an economic–corporate kind ... in the decisive nucleus of economic activity ... the development and expansion of the particular [ruling] group [must be] conceived of, and presented, as being the motor force of a universal expansion, of a development of all the "national" energies'. Gramsci, *Selections from the Prison Notebooks,* pp 161, 182. Hegemony is not made through culture and ideology alone.

[25] I Kaul, I Grundberg & M Stern (eds), *Providing Global Public Goods: Managing Globalisation*, Oxford: Oxford University Press, 1999, pp 3, 8 on public goods, conditions and bads.

[26] L Sklair, 'Social movements for global capitalism: the transnational capitalist class in action', *Review of International Political Economy*, 4 (3), 1997, pp 514–538.

[27] See D Moore, 'The World Bank and global hegemony: the Gramsci effect', in Moore, *Banking for Hegemony*, on the World Bank as part of an emerging global state.

[28] Midnight Notes Collective, 'The new enclosures', *The Commoner*, September 2001, pp 1–15.

[29] W Bonefeld, 'History and social constitution: primitive accumulation is not primitive', *The Commoner*, March 2002, pp 1–8; Bonefeld, 'The permanence of primitive accumulation: notes on social constitution', 2001, at www.rcci.net/globalizacion/2001/fg176.htm; and C von Werlhof, 'Globalization and the "permanent" process of primitive accumulation: the example of the MAI, the Multilateral Agreement on Investment', *Journal of World Systems Research*, 7 (3), 2000, pp 728–747. Cf P Zarembka, 'Primitive accumulation in marxism: historical or trans-historical separation from the means of production?', *The Commoner*, March 2002, pp 1–9.

[30] D Rueschemeyer, E Stephens & J Stephens, *Capitalist Development and Democracy*, Chicago, IL: University of Chicago Press, 1992.

[31] See J Bell & T Sekine, 'The disintegration of capitalism: a phase of ex-capitalist transition', in R Albritton, M Itoh, R Westra & A Zuege (eds), *Phases of Capitalist Development: Booms, Crises and Globalizations*, London: Palgrave, 2001, pp 44–46 for the specificities added to 'capitalism in general' by petroleum since the 1920s—and consider one of the reasons the USA invaded Iraq.

[32] JK Boyce & L Ndikumana, 'Is Africa a net creditor? New estimates of capital flight from severely indebted Sub-Saharan African countries', *Journal of Development Studies*, 38 (2), 2001, pp 27–56.

[33] DF Bryceson & V Jamal, *Farewell to Farms: De-agarianisation and Employment in Africa*, Aldershot: Avebury, 1997.

[34] D Moore, 'Hardt and Negri's *Empire*, real empire, and the "Third World" after 9/11', *Acme*, 2003, forthcoming.

[35] M Burawoy, 'For a sociological marxism: the complementary convergence of Antonio Gramsci and Karl Polanyi', *Politics and Society*, 31 (2), 2003, p 219, quoting K Polanyi, *The Great Transformation: The Political and Economic Origins of Our Time*, Boston, MA: Beacon, 1957, pp 163, 182–183; and Silver & Arrighi, 'Polanyi's "double movement" ', p 328, quoting Polanyi, *The Great Transformation*, pp 182–183, 207–208.

[36] J-F Bayart, *The State in Africa: The Politics of the Belly*, London: Longman, 1993.

[37] Silver & Arrighi, 'Polanyi's "double movement" ', p 329. American and other 'free-world' support for such processes was often condemned as imperialistic and supportive of dictators. Later, Foucauldians criticised the development industry in totality as but an apparatus of power. One cannot disagree with either perspective, but an empirical look at rates of growth, industrialisation and welfare before and after the age of neoliberalism can ascertain whether the age of Keynesianism or Hayekianism has been more beneficial for the material lives of most people in the Third World, and thus more conducive to the construction of critical human capabilities—presumably a basis for postmodern sensibilities.

[38] M Hardt, 'Today's Bandung?', *New Left Review*, 2 (14), pp 112–118.

[39] M Duffield, *Global Governance and the New Wars: The Merging of Development and Security*, London: Zed, 2001; and J Macrae, *Aiding Recovery: The Crisis of Aid in Chronic Political Emergencies*, London: Zed, 2001.

[40] B Warren, *Imperialism: The Pioneer of Capitalism*, London: Verso, 1980.

[41] S MacWilliam, 'Plenty of poverty'.

[42] United Nations, *Report of the Panel of Experts on the Illegal Exploitation of Natural Resources and other forms of Wealth of the Democratic Republic of the Congo*, UN Security Council, S/2001/357, 12 April 2001.

[43] He indicated that capitalism's benefits would never reach all the way into the Third World until its 'productive powers' were appropriated 'by the people'. In India this would not be until the 'Hindoos themselves shall have grown strong enough to throw off the English yoke altogether'. Is this populist or nationalist support for productive Third World bourgeoisies? Marx, 'The future results of British rule in India', in Tucker, *The Marx–Engels Reader*, p 662.

[44] R Brenner, 'The origins of capitalist development: a critique', *New Left Review*, 1 (104), 1977, pp 45–92.

[45] Marx, '*Grundrisse*,' p 269.

[46] Hardt & Negri, *Empire*, p 258.

[47] *Ibid*, p 403.

[48] Hardt & Negri, *Empire*, pp 137–146, and 118–120, agree with Marx that 'capitalism can ... be a force of enlightenment' but they criticise his failure to note alternatives and forms of resistance within pre-colonial Indian society. They fail to specify what he has missed. On the local and the global, see pp 44–46, 362, where the former is seen as being potentially 'regressive and even fascistic' when isolated and 'pure'.

[49] Hardt & Negri, *Empire*, pp 258–259.

[50] D Moore, 'Africa: the black hole at the middle of empire?', *Rethinking Marxism*, 13 (3–4), 2001, pp 100–118.

[51] Marx, '*Grundrisse*', pp 271–274.

[52] See Marx, *Capital*, Vol 2, pp 799, 801–802, 804–813 for details of expropriation from communal lands in England, Scotland, Ireland and Germany; and pp 813–822 for laws against vagrancy and crime because 'it was impossible that those who had been thus hunted off the land could be absorbed by the rising system of manufacture as quickly as they were "set free". Nor could [they] ... be expected, all in a moment, to submit themselves to the discipline of their new condition'.

[53] A Sen. *Development as Freedom*, Oxford: Oxford University Press, 1999, pp 7, 113.

[54] Hardt & Negri, *Empire*, pp 115, 257.

[55] *Ibid*, p 256.

[56] *Ibid*, p 257.

[57] *Ibid*, p 257, quoting Marx, *Capital*, Vol 1, London: Vintage, 1976, p 918.

[58] *Ibid*, p 115.

[59] *Ibid*, pp 258–259.

[60] *Ibid*, pp 255–256.

[61] Hardt and Negri contend an 'international or multinational proletariat' moved towards unity in 'one common attack against the capitalist disciplinary regime' during the 1960s and 1970s, which 'decreed the end of the division between First and Third Worlds and the potential political integration of the entire global proletariat ... Third Worldist perspectives ... were now completely useless ... blind to the real convergence of struggles across the world'. *Ibid*, pp 262–264.

[62] For the Bank, 'private property' now includes renting. K Deininger, *Land Policies for Growth and Poverty Reduction*, Oxford: World Bank and Oxford University Press, 2003, pp xxx–xxxvi, xlv.

[63] H de Soto, *The Mystery of Capital: Why Capitalism Triumphs in the West and Fails Everywhere Else*, London: Bantam, 2000; and Deininger, *Land Policies for Growth and Poverty Reduction*.

[64] De Soto, *The Mystery of Capital*, p 168.

[65] *Ibid*, p 163.

[66] *Ibid*, p 198.

[67] H Bernstein, 'The "peasantry" in global capitalism: who, where and why?', in C Leys & L Panitch (eds), *Socialist Register 2001: Working Classes, Global Realities*, London: 2001.

[68] De Soto, *The Mystery of Capital*, pp 1, 58, quoting F Braudel, *The Wheels of Commerce*, New York: Harper and Row, 1982, p 248.

[69] See Perelman, *The Invention of Capitalism*, for extracts from Wakefield and Rae on the USA and Canada, pp 326–329, 340, 349–351.

[70] De Soto, *The Mystery of Capital*, p 165.

[71] Deininger, *Land Policies for Growth and Poverty Reduction*, pp xxi, xxiii, xxv.

[72] *Ibid*, p xxx.

[73] *Ibid*, p xxvi.

[74] *Ibid*, pp xxx, xxxi. Many references to the integration of 'traditional' forms of tenure (eg pp 62–65) suggest a desire to preserve aspects of pre-capitalism compatible with either permanent or accelerated primitive accumulation. For an indication of problems raised by these issues in South Africa, see B Cousins, 'Labour pains plague land reform's *laatlammetjie*', *Mail and Guardian*, 13–19 June 2003, pp 28–29; and L Ntsebeza, 'Traditional authorities and rural development', in JK Coetzee, J Graaff, F Hendricks & G Wood (eds), *Development: Theory, Policy, and Practice*, Cape Town: Oxford University Press, 2001, pp 317–329. More generally, see J W Bruce, 'African tenure models at the turn of the century', *Land Reform*, 1, 2000, pp 17–27.

[75] Deininger, *Land Policies for Growth and Poverty Reduction*, pp xviii, xxiv. Perhaps the Bank wishes such predictions into self-fulfilment: its 1997 *World Development Report*, while 'bringing the state back in', advises technocrats to implement reforms during times of external threat or economic crisis—'when the normal rules of the game are in flux'—or during a new regime's honeymoon. World Bank, *World Development Report 1997: The State in a Changing World*, New York: Oxford University Press, 1997, p 144, quoted in D Moore, '"Sail on, O ship of state": neoliberalism, globalisation and the governance of Africa', *Journal of Peasant Studies*, 27 (1), 1999, pp 61–96.

[76] Deininger, p 15. He also notes that often only large asset holders get credit for their titles, p 50.

[77] The term 'nonrival' means 'one person's enjoyment will not reduce others' ability to benefit from the system'. Deininger does note that establishment of property rights 'exclude[s] some individuals or groups from access to these benefits'. Deininger, *Land Policies for Growth and Poverty Reduction*, pp 23, 24.

[78] *Ibid*, pp xxii, 22–25.

[79] *Ibid*, p 28.

[80] *Ibid*, p 35.

[81] De Soto, *The Mystery of Capital*, is this religion's bible, preached fervently and cited profusely by those who mean 'good governance' to be the construction of private property rights.

[82] Marx, 'Grundisse', p 269.

[83] P Anderson, *Lineages of the Absolute State*, London: Verso, 1974.

[84] P Bond (ed), *Fanon's Warning: A Civil Society Reader on the New Partnership for African Development*, Trenton, NJ: Africa World Press, 2002; and B Bowden, 'Reinventing imperialism in the wake of September 11', *Alternatives: Turkish Journal of International Relations*, 1 (2), 202, pp 28–46.

[85] R Kanbur, 'IFI's and IPG's: Operational implications for the World Bank,' paper presented at the G24 Technical Group Meeting, Beirut, 1–2 March 2002.

[86] See B Fine, C Lapavitsas & J Pincus (eds), *Development Policy in the Twenty-First Century: Beyond the post-Washington Consensus*, London: Routledge, 2003, for critical analyses.

[87] See D Moore 'Development discourse as hegemony: towards an ideological history, 1945–1995', in D Moore & G Schmitz (eds), *Debating Development Discourse: Institutional and Popular Perspectives*, London: Macmillan, 1995, pp 1–53 for an effort inspired by the co-option of sustainable development discourse. See also T Wanner, 'The power of *greenspeak* and the power of knowledge: the World Bank and s*ustaindevelopment*', in Moore, *Banking for Hegemony*.

[88] M Desai, 'Public goods: a historical perspective', in Kaul, Grundberg & Stern, *Providing Global Public Goods*, p 68.

[89] T Homer-Dixon, *The Ingenuity Gap: How Can We Solve the Problems of the Future?*, New York: Knopf, 2000, pp 244–246, 326, 358.

[90] L Mehta, 'Problems of publicness and access rights: perspectives from the water domain', in Kaul, Grundberg & Stern, *Providing Global Public Goods*, pp 556–575; and F Lumsden & A Loftus, 'Inanda's struggle for water through pipes and tunnels: exploring state–civil society relations in a post-apartheid informal settlement', Centre for Civil Society Research Report, Durban: University of Natal, 2003. On the essential notion of basic needs decommodification, see P Bond, *Against Global Apartheid: South Africa Meets the World Bank*, IMF *and International Finance*, Cape Town: University of Cape Town Press, 2001.

[91] A de Waal, 'How will HIV/AIDS transform African governance?', *African Affairs*, 102 (402), pp 1–23.

[92] The International Commission on Intervention and Sovereignty, *The Responsibility to Protect: International Commission on Intervention and Sovereignty*, Ottawa, 2001, expands on security, the classic GPG.

[93] A Sen, *Development as Freedom: Human Security Now*, New York: Commission on Human Security, 2003. Sadako Ogata is the commission's co-chair. Her former post as UN High Commissioner for Refugees indicates the 'band-aid' roots of human security discourse. South Africa's Speaker of Parliament, Frene Ginwala, is another commissioner. The Deputy Director and project co-ordinator for the report's 'development' half ('conflict' was the other) was Viviene Taylor, chair of South Africa's Taylor Report on the Basic Income Grant (BIG). The South African government's hesitation to implement a 100 Rand monthly BIG, fearing the creation of 'dependency', illustrates the contradictions of human security discourse.

[94] L Hamilton, 'A theory of true interests in the work of Amartya Sen', *Government and Opposition*, 14 (4), 1999, pp 516–546.

[95] Sen, *Development as Freedom*, 1999, p 269.

[96] B Fine, 'The developmental state is dead–long live social capital?', *Development and Change*, 30 (1), pp 1–21.

[97] South African Poverty Network, 'What good are global public goods?', *Poverty Briefing 3*, October 2002, p 3.

[98] J Nef, *Human Security and Mutual Vulnerability: The Political Economy of Development and Underdevelopment*, Ottawa: International Development Research Centre, 1999.

[99] MT Berger, 'The rise and demise of national development and the origins of post-cold war capitalism', *Millennium: Journal of International Studies*, 30 (2), 2001, pp 211–234.

[100] B Warren, *Imperialism: Pioneer of Capitalism*. 'Imperialism and capitalist industrialisation', *New Left Review*, 81, 1973, pp 3–45, on which the book was based, was published just before OPEC's and neoliberalism's effects were felt. For reconsidered optimism on Kenyan capitalism triggered by recent global trends, see C Leys, 'Learning from the Kenya debate', *The Rise and Fall of Development Theory*, London: James Currey, 1996, pp 143–163; and JS Saul, 'Afro-pessimism/optimism: the antinomies of Colin Leys', in AB Bakan & E Macdonald (eds), *Critical Political Studies: Debates and Dialogues from the Left*, Montreal and Kingston: McGill–Queen's University Press, 2002, pp 94–112. For Sender, Warren's Marxism is not 'Chicago Marxism', ie supporting neoclassical policies and condemning state intervention. J Sender, 'Reassessing the role of the World Bank in sub-Saharan Africa', in JR Pincus & JA Winters (eds), *Reinventing the World Bank*, Ithaca, NY: Cornell University Press, 2002, pp 185–202.

[101] I Wallerstein, 'America and the world: the twin towers as metaphor', *After September 11*, New York: Social Science Research Council, 2001, at www.scrc.org/sept11/essays; and R Greenhill & A Pettifor, *The United States as a* HIPC—*How the Poor are Financing the Rich*, London: Jubilee Research and the New Economics Foundation, 2002.

Re-crossing a different water: colonialism and Third Worldism in Fiji

DEVLEENA GHOSH

After the Second World War, Third Worldism provided a powerful legitimating narrative for newly independent nation-states at their moment of arrival. In Fiji, however, the internal tensions of the term have enmeshed themselves with the plurality of ways in which Fijian society must reconstitute itself after decolonisation and the coups of 1987 and 2000. The ethnic issues in Fiji have led to the employment of a number of strategies by both the indigenous and the Indian communities. Some consist of networking within transnational spaces and negotiation with external political and cultural flows, while others are more inward in their everyday strategies, offering a non-reductive way to think about decolonisation, cultural transformation and notions of autonomy and solidarity.

In a workshop on Subaltern and Indigenous Histories, Dipesh Chakrabarty asked: 'Can postcolonial histories and indigenous histories engage in a dialogue?'.[1] This question is particularly relevant for cultural studies in the Pacific because it encapsulates the intellectual and political problems that scholars of that area face. In Fiji, the task of 'provincialising' Europe means interrogating the models imported from Europe—democracy, a belief in progress and modernity, ideas of state and nation, and the powerful notions of development and economic transformation associated with the rise and fall of Third Worldism (the latter are outlined in the introduction to this special issue).

This has a particularly empowering effect because it puts the process of making history in the picture. Chakrabarty, in another context, has pointed out that non-Western histories are themselves subaltern because they exist in the shadow of Europe. This is not solely because of colonisation's powerful intrusion into other continents but because Europe's self-perceived movement towards state-building, capitalist development and modernity marked and still marks a vision of historical progress against which African, Asian, Pacific or Latin American history appears as failure of the nation to come into its own.[2]

Also, since cultural forms will always be made, unmade and remade, communities can and must reconfigure themselves, drawing selectively on remembered pasts. The relevant question is whether, and how, they convince and coerce insiders and outsiders, often in power-charged, unequal situations; for example, the issues of indigenous versus migrant rights to land and franchise in Fiji. Thus what is lost and rediscovered in new situations becomes part of the realm of normal political or cultural activity. For example, Kaplan and Kelly argue in their recent book that 'community' is not a 'universally adopted modern imaginary' but has a 'sinister political life', which, in Fiji 'clearly emerged as a new name for race'.[3] And as Peter Van der Veer points out, the contingent and contextual nature of community derives from displacement, disjuncture and diaspora and the from contradictions between the notion of discrete territoriality in the discourse of nationalism and the transgressive fact of migration.[4] Thus the concept of 'homeland' becomes a site constantly disrupted and negotiated by migration and translocation. The case of Fiji is an instance of a failure of regional integration and of concepts of Third World solidarity that has its roots in the shared colonial experiences of both indigenous and Indo-Fijians.

Shared and contested histories

The specific case of Fiji dramatises some fascinating conflicts over the conceptualisation of land, identity and nation. As the political philosopher Joseph Carens remarked in a 1992 article, 'Democracy and respect for difference: the case of Fiji', published in the *University of Michigan Journal of Law Reform*, 'What makes the case of Fiji particularly rich and rewarding for purposes of reflection is its moral complexities and ambiguities. There are two groups in conflict here and both arouse our moral sympathies.'[5] In this article Carens defends policies designed to maintain indigenous land ownership or to preserve chiefly authority in Fijian society and politics as essential to help preserve traditional Fijian culture, even though these arrangements impose some costs on the Indo-Fijian population. Carens claims that these illiberal practices have been good for native Fijians. 'It seems plausible to suppose that policies more in keeping with liberal individualism—for example an insistence on individual, alienable title to land as opposed to the collective, inalienable form of ownership adopted in Fiji—might have had disastrous consequences for native Fijians as such policies did elsewhere.'[6] Although the practices involve restrictions of individual rights, native Fijians have, on the whole, genuinely benefited from them.

Carens also has a connected negative argument. He claims that these arrangements to preserve traditional Fijian culture do not involve serious violations of moral requirements and are not 'dependent on the subordination of any other group'.[7] Thus, for example, although native Fijians have secured their continued ownership of the vast majority of land, 'Fijian dominance in this area is balanced by the dominance Indians have achieved in other areas of economic life'.[8] Carens is therefore suggesting that policies designed to preserve cultural differences may be legitimate as long as they do not violate what he calls 'minimal moral standards'.[9] He is therefore critical of the 1987 military coups because their 'goal was ... the firm establishment of native Fijian political hegemony'.[10] By contrast, Fiji's political system before the coup, including the arrangements designed to protect traditional Fijian culture, was not 'dependent on the subordination of any other group' and so did not, Carens argues, deny Indians equal citizenship.

At the end of the article, I will return to this idea of 'moral ambiguity', the counterposing of two different sets of 'rights' crucial to the debate around land and citizenship in the Pacific. However, the current political and social paradoxes in Fiji are directly related to 19th century British colonialism. The paternalistic interventions of the British governor-general, Arthur Gordon, aimed to protect the rights and way of life of indigenous Fijians after cession. At the same time the economic imperatives of colonialism necessitated the import of indentured Indians to Fiji to extract profit from the sugar plantations.

Peter France has pointed out that the efforts to establish and codify customary land tenure in Fiji began very early in the colonial period.[11] Rights of the indigenous inhabitants were initially guaranteed against the claims of European settlers and later Indian immigrants. Land assumed a different place in the ethnic relations and the political field of colonial and independent Fiji. Henry Rutz, in his article 'Capitalizing on custom', terms this the 'moral irony' in Fijian history:

> The founding of an orthodoxy pertaining to Fijian traditions in general, and to land rights in particular, had as its underlying motivation the preservation of a Fijian way of life. In the event a way of life was constructed on the foundations of village life and buttressed by bureaucratic administrative regulations and procedures. Europeans contributed to an ideology of traditionalism and to a 'Fijian world view' in which the form of the moral economy was opposed against an emergent capitalist society ... [Later] the founding of a capitalist land corporation inside the structure of invented tradition is perhaps the greatest irony of Fijian history. The case is only slightly overstated by saying that, whereas Fijian tradition was in large part invented by Europeans as a bulwark against the most harmful aspects of their capitalist system, Fijian modernism is being constructed by Fijian capitalists in a modern chiefly state.[12]

Peter France documents how this new orthodoxy of inalienability meant that Fijian land practices were now inflexibly codified in ways that proscribed such Fijian customs as diverse forms of land-gift and tribute. Social units such as lineage, clan and tribe, as well as custom, were constructed as immemorial and unchanging, 'tradition was removed from and placed above the historical events that led to its creation'.[13] However, since agricultural production and trade had to be facilitated, the Native Land Trust Board (NLTB) was created in the 1940s to leased this inalienable land to Indian sugar-cane farmers and was seen by indigenous Fijians as protective of their interests. In fact, as Rutz argues above, it caused further contradictions in the structure of land control by closing off the capaciousness and flexibility of previous land practices. It turned chiefs into effective landowners, an inversion of Fijian culture that places ownership in the hands of commoners. In fact, the protracted negotiations between the NLTB and the *mataqali* (chiefly elite) served to mask the potential conflict inherent in this system.

These complexities and conflicts are intensified because of the lived experiences of Fijians in both the past and the present. Margaret Jolly, among others, believes that for indigenous Fijians the past exists in the present; the past and the present are seen as continuous and enmeshed, rather than discrete entities. Therefore, the way of money (associated sometimes with Europeans but mainly with Indians),[14] which is seen as existing solely in and for the present, is contrasted with the way of the land (the Fijian way) that existed immutably in the constructed past of indigenous Fijians as well as in the lived present. Ironically, both communities now appear to desire a 'true' present—indigenous Fijians by 'forgetting' the history of land codification and indenture and Indo-Fijians by re-emphasising it.

Martha Kaplan also demonstrates how this contrast between the communal traditionalism of the Fijians and the individual commercialism of the Indo-Fijians derives from British codifications of their respective racial identities. Colonial relations with Fijians were posited as relations with communities, mediated through chiefs and land codifications, and kinship collectivities attached indissolubly to the land. Individual entrepreneurial spirit, pursuing the 'path of money' was constituted as a rejection of communal living.[15] Thus Fijians were discouraged from engaging in business or cash farming. In contrast and in opposition to colonial policies in India itself, the British treated Indo-Fijians as isolated individuals. As indentured labour they were conceived of as 'labour units' defined by individual agreements with their employers. Later, they were perceived as disorderly and threatening, amplified by the fact that Indians were reluctant to support the war effort during the Second World War, demanded equal pay with British soldiers and organised strikes in this period.[16] While British colonial policy emphasised the civilising mission towards indigenous Fijians, the racial identity of immigrant Indians was established as a threat to Fijian dominance. Indo-Fijian leaders such as AD Patel, from 1946 onwards, appropriated this colonial identity by claiming a place in the nation on the basis of their labour and economic contribution.[17]

One of the major consequences of British colonial policies is the fact that, at the current time, Fiji has 82.38% of its land under native title, 9.45% state land and 8.17% freehold.[18] Most Indians and Europeans farm or conduct business on leasehold of native title land. Under the 1966 Agricultural Landlords and Tenants Ordinance, many Indo-Fijian farmers secured 30-year leases at relatively low rents for sugar-cane cultivation. These leases started expiring in 1997 and an NLTB survey suggested that many landowners either wanted to reclaim their lands or alter leasing terms and rentals.

In *Fiji in Transition*, JN Kamikamica writes:

> The land question is one of the most divisive and potent political issues in Fiji. It underlies and permeates the economic, social and political fabric of Fiji society ... The Fijian indigenous community regard their land as a symbol of identification of their place and traditional role in society. To them, the land is basically a heritage to be protected and safeguarded. It maintains their links with the past and offers security to them, now and in the future.[19]

Still, the major grievance held by indigenous Fijians against the Mahendra Chaudhry government, elected in 1999, was around the issue of land. An Agricultural Landlords and Tenants Act (ALTA) task force looking into the future of the substantial numbers of land leases that were up for renewal recommended against continuing with ALTA, claiming that Fijian landowners had been denied active participation in the sugar industry and use of their land. It accused the NLTB and the government of failing to protect landowner interests and promote opportunities for Fijians. It recommended that no compensation be paid to tenants whose leases were not renewed for 'unauthorised improvements' to land (despite farmers' claims that landowners were aware of and did not object to improvements). Through consultation with the Council of Chiefs, the Chaudhry government developed proposals for a Land Use Commission and reform of the powerful NLTB. It also proposed a one-off payment of F$28 000 to farmers whose leases were not to be renewed. This engendered suspicions that Chaudhry had used land reform to divide Chiefs from commoners and throw money at his Indian constituency.

After the 2000 coup some Fijians tried to highlight the numerous pro-indigenous policies then current. Josetaki Waqanisau pointed out that the native land controlled by indigenous Fijians included more than 80 hotel or tourism leases administered by the NLTB, which is responsible for leasing Fijian-owned land on behalf of the owners. These leases include Sheraton, Warwick, Naviti, Treasure Island, Castaway and Mana Island Resorts among others. Native landowners currently receive substantial annual incomes from tourism leases.[20]

Indigenous Fijians also have scholarships available through the Fijians Affairs Board, programmes encouraging Fijians in business, such as incentives for share holdings with foreign- and Fijian-owned businesses, and easy access to credit from the Fiji Development Bank. Academics from the University of the South Pacific also pointed out that wealthy Indo-Fijians were a relatively small percentage of the Indian population and poverty in the Indo-Fijian community was comparable to that in the indigenous Fijian community.

However, a clear perception continues among indigenous Fijians that indigenous land rights, well-being and cultures are under threat. The resurgence of debates on indigenous rights in various colonies has strengthened the tropes of indigenous Fijian dispossession and oppression. During the coups of 1987 the indigenous communities in Australia, for example, were divided on whether the coups should be supported because they upheld indigenous rights or reviled as instituting a form of apartheid.

Following the coup of May 2000 a letter about Fiji's constitutional dilemma was circulated by a group of indigenous Fijians. This letter attempted to reconcile the problematic of a democratic civil society in Fiji with indigenous paramountcy and labelled the prospect of a non-Fijian prime minister as 'dangerous' since 'the Indian community remains so out of touch with Fijian interests, needs, aspirations and constraints'. It continued,

> However, it is very problematic, nonetheless, to specify in any decree or constitution that only Fijians are eligible for certain positions or offices. To the international community this is like a red rag to a bull; such a provision may also be used by the more aggressive and less understanding of our neighbours to justify sanctions or to pressure more tolerant nations into statements or actions of condemnation. It is also unnecessary. The same outcome—the reservation of certain key political positions for Fijians—can be achieved in an internationally acceptable form by requiring that the holders of the office meet the criteria of fluency in the language, customs, practices, traditions etc of the country. The criteria of cultural competency can be set to ensure that it is virtually impossible for a non-Fijian to pass the required tests. Moreover, if there is any question relating to an individual's cultural competency, the Great Council of Chiefs will be the final arbiter. Moreover, the Council can readily be restricted to Fijians in that it is an exclusively indigenous organisation in which chiefs, and chiefs alone, are authorised to sit. Non-Fijians may be invited to address the Council, but no one other than chiefly Fijians would have a right of membership.[21]

Robbie Robertson reported that, after the coups of May 1987, many indigenous Fijians termed 'democracy', 'demon-crazy'.[22] Laisenia Qarase, the Prime Minister of the interim government of Fiji installed by the military in September 2000, voiced similar sentiments when he addressed the United Nations:

> It would seem that a new form of imperialism has emerged. As if the corrosive influence and impact of their mass culture of consumerism and materialism are not enough, this new form of domination is being propagated by the 'purists' of the liberal democracies, in the name of good governance, human rights, accountability and transparency. But what is of concern is that we are being told to apply these standards and values of liberal democracy strictly according to their standards, without regard for the particular or complex circumstances in each country.[23]

Qarase expressed concern that some of the fundamental principles on which the United Nations was formed, 'respect for national sovereignty and of non-interference in the internal affairs' of a member state, 'are being eroded and violated'. While the world is 'a closely-linked global community', it does not give a country 'the right to impose on another its own standards of democratic governance and what it perceives or considers to be right and acceptable,' he concluded.[24]

Shared and contested memories

My reflections here are based on interviews conducted with Indo-Fijian women in the liminal space between two major events in their history, the coups of May 1987 and May 2000. For these women, the 'naming' of places as home determined the links between the idea of home with an entire range of personal, national, social and cultural issues.

The coups highlighted another complicating factor: that of imagining a nation in Fiji. Kaplan and Kelly have criticised Benedict Anderson's argument about imagined communities by privileging a Bakhtinian dialogic anthropology that represents global history as 'a series of planned and lived responses to specific circumstances that were also irreducibly constituted by human subjects, creating ... a dense complex network of individual and collective subjects continually responsive to one another'.[25] However, since national belonging is not singular, exclusionary or a function of direct or unmediated experience, my purpose in this part of the discussion is to elaborate how memory informs everyday life and disrupts the concept of 'Indian-ness' through ordinary narratives of dislocation and renewal.

For my interlocutors, recollections of the past serve as the 'active ideological terrain on which people represent themselves to themselves'[26] and to each other. For Indo-Fijian migrants, the past is invested with an intense significance precisely because the present has been made unstable or unpredictable as a consequence of the coups. The present acquires its meaning with reference to 'a disjointed and conflicted story of the past in which references to official narratives about colonisation and a historical memory are tangled up with personal memories and private recollections of past experiences'.[27] The past is a vital element in the construction of Indo-Fijian identity but 'it comprises a "renovated" and selectively appropriated set of memories and discourses'.[28] For this community, recollections take on a special import because they represent discourses, which are stable and can be presented as authentic. Present disruptions, predicaments and uncertainties are more bearable if the past remains unambiguous.

In this context, after 1987 and before the May 2000 coup, Indo-Fijians appeared to foreground their Indian-ness; they were interested in ways of being Indian and debates on authenticity, legitimacy, multicultural–bicultural rights were considered important. There were specific messages that people wanted to convey to those perceived as 'like' themselves as well as to 'others'. After the May 2000 coup, however, the discourses changed substantially. Indo-Fijians began to negotiate their identity in relation to indigenous Fijians and indigenous settler narratives. What emerged from my questions about the past was a confused re-narrating of memory, experience and identity that was played out in the interstices of Australian-ness, Fijian-ness and Indian-ness, meshing, adapting and recreating these concepts.

But in spite of the performative nature of their Indian identities, memories of Fiji were powerful—the plentifulness of the food in the small towns, the ease of daily life, the availability of domestic help. Abha, who came from a very poor family where she used to add to the family income by selling vegetables after school, spoke nostalgically of her idyllic childhood and mentioned in passing the many *roti* and *dalo* curries shared with her indigenous Fijian neighbours. When the first coup happened in 1987, she was visiting friends in New Zealand.

I believe had I been in Fiji there would have been pressure on me to choose sides [because she was a well known businesswoman] whether that be with the coup instigators or the other people basically the rest of the Indian people. Now when I got back to Fiji, which was about two weeks after the coup, there was a certain undercurrent in the country and I knew one or two of the coup leaders. My immediate impression was that the Fiji that I had left would not come back. Two weeks ago it was a different Fiji and after the coup the situation was quite different.

When asked to elucidate the difference, she said:

It had changed in the sense that suddenly walking on the street you could feel a certain amount of aggression and pride coming from the Fijian people. They seemed a little bit bolder. The Fijian people are very meek and mild really when you come to consider that they have such good soldiers, that warrior mentality only came out in them when they were at war but walking along the street previous to the coup they were very polite. They had just become a little bit more aggressive. At the time I was concerned I had to make a decision and the decision simply was this. If we decided to stay in Fiji, if we decided to remain here we would have to adapt to the new conditions because I knew that the old Fiji was gone, that there would be new conditions and if I wanted to remain with my family we would have to accept the new parameters that were going to be set. If I didn't want to accept those new parameters, then it would be better for me to leave. Did I feel personally insecure, no I did not. I guess this is because I had so many and I still had so many Fijian friends with whom I mixed that I could see where they were coming from and just quietly I probably had a little bit of sympathy for the way they felt.

Abha and her family moved to Australia and, even though she misses the 'idyllic life' in Fiji, she admitted that emigration had liberated her. She then mentioned the fact that her parents-in-law, who had remained behind, were now in a parlous state since their indigenous landowners had refused to renew their leases. Abha's musings revealed 'a set of submerged meanings' where, according to Ganguly, 'nostalgia becomes the symptomatic locus of repressed fantasies of identity and belongingness. Fragmented and marginalised narratives of past attachments reappear as wishful thinking, sentimentality and misremembering' at the same time as the present brings on pragmatism.[29] When I asked Abha whether she had problems travelling with her Fijian passport (as I had with my Indian one), proving her visa or citizenship status, presenting reasons for travelling whenever she crossed borders, she replied that she was determined to get a 'black' (Australian) passport as soon as possible. She also said that she was resigned to the discrimination she experienced in Australia and overseas because of her race because the position of Indians had always been contingent. 'I can cope with it. I grew up in Fiji, didn't I?'. For her, thinking about the past was also a way of affirming how much better she was in the present.

Abha, like most Indo-Fijian families I worked with, while nostalgic about the past, found their present circumstances rewarding. Their reminiscences about their wonderful lives in Fiji were constantly undercut by the imperatives of migration. For example, Ravi, who was a journalist in Fiji before she moved to Sydney, says:

I think I was very well placed, where I was, I would really, even now, I would have done really well, in my profession and would have made good money. And I would have at least had a permanent job and everything else. I mean, like, I think I was very well placed in terms of living in the city (Suva). I had my own house, and we had some of the basic luxuries and we have done a fair bit of travelling as well. I was very content and very happy, I couldn't ask for any more from life, you know, but ah, but we decided to move. We had achieved everything that we had set ourselves towards working, like, we had set goals and we had met all our goals, and we were very happy and content. But we decided to move.

When I asked why she had moved to Australia when she had been so successful in Fiji, the explicit reason she gave was the securing of her children's future; yet even this was fraught with uncertainty. The coups made her see herself as more Indian yet she was never sure whether her children would adopt this intensified Indian identity.

> But when the coup happened, that is when I was taken aback and I was basically shocked and I said, 'oh, because I am Indian this has happened and because my people are Indian this has happened. So how do I take myself from here? Now that this identity issue has become a crisis in my own life?'. But I thought, like, oh no, I'll have to send my daughter to a school where she can learn the Indian way of life, the Indian culture, tradition and then the religion as well as learn the language. And um, perhaps the coup was one of the reasons I did that. I said 'look, I can't let go of this identity'. I felt that my Indian identity was being threatened. All this other time I was taking it for granted. Look, I have this identity and I am an Indian and it will continue without asking too many questions. But when the coup happened I realised all of a sudden, look I am Indian and I felt that my identity was being threatened.

Amina, who migrated to Sydney after the 2000 coup, said that one of the major reasons for her move was the issue of race:

> Yes, I think the um, the effect, after the coup, race has become a major issue in this country. So we are like, we feel sort of, more Indian because really the Fijians are coming from the other side and we have been kind of ostracised by Fijian community. So then we have realised that race is a very big issue in the country now. We Indians are, well this is my view, we are treated, we are sort of treated as second-rate citizens. You have to walk a tightrope. Not to be seen as anti-Fiji and pro-India or whatever. But I've got at the back of my mind that this country is now a racial, it's turned racial.

After the May 2000 coup, the discourses of belonging and remembering began to veer towards different referents; the same Indo-Fijians that I spoke to recalled being Fijian rather than Indian. They began to construct renovated and nostalgic relationships to their Fijian homeland. Some came out as having Fijian ancestry, which they admitted would once have been seen as a source of shame in the Indo-Fijian community, but was now looked on as a source of legitimation. Another iterated a list of her indigenous friends and said:

> My husband was so touched, once when we went to a party—Indians and Fijians you know on a boat. When the time came to leave, the Fijians were still drinking yaqona[30] and the Indians were leaving. We got up to leave but one of our Fijian friends said, oh don't go now, let's wait for the vulagi to leave.

This speaker interpreted this statement as a crucial sign of inclusiveness because vulagi is the Fijian term for foreigner and is often used to denote pejoratively the

Indo-Fijian community. Another woman emphasised that her grandfather, unlike the stories of other indentured labour, actually wanted to leave India because of colonial oppression.

> When the ship sailed from Calcutta, he stood on the deck and said, good-bye my motherland, I hope never to see you again. In Fiji, he found the liberty to be himself.

A staunchly Hindu woman, whose husband was a member of the *Kisan Sangh* (the organisation of sugar-cane farmers in Fiji), told me a story (probably apocryphal). An Indian holy man who was deported for organising strikes among the sugar-cane workers in Fiji in the 1920s had warned the Indian community: 'What you lack is land and women. To fulfil both these lacks, you must marry the *Kaiviti* [indigenous Fijians]'. It seemed that, for these Indo-Fijians, the May 2000 coups had finalised most poignantly their rupture with Fiji. They realised once and for all the impossibility of return and this closure, paradoxically, made it safe for a therapeutic retrieval of their Fijian identity.

Shared and contested spaces: work and marriage

Most of my interlocutors had been active in the workforce in Fiji. According to Jacqueline Leckie, women's labour was necessary for the food and service sectors, especially during the initial stages of the globalisation of Fiji's economy. Historically, British regulations had stipulated that 40% of plantation labour be female. But, when sugar production shifted to small family farms at the end of indenture in 1920, these were usually too small to support extended families. Consequently men often worked in off-farm agricultural work while women and children provided the cheap labour essential for on-farm production. Recent structural adjustment programmes also affected women's formal employment opportunities, which were mainly in the public, retailing, financial, manufacturing and tourism sectors, since these were the first to be subject to downsizing and cost cutting.[31]

The gender stereotypes in the Indo-Fijian communities are also particularly conservative. Brij Lal, in his account of his time at the University of the South Pacific, recounts how young men in steady relationships would expect their girlfriends to take care of all their domestic chores. If some of these women rebelled, the men broke off the relationships, sometimes violently, leaving the girls in a terrible position because they were now damaged goods, *phuta pataka* or an exploded firecracker.[32] He recalls envying the indigenous students whose attitudes to relationships with the opposite sex were far more relaxed.

It is not surprising, therefore, that the identities of my interlocutors appeared fractured in the context of the disruptions of the past decade. Most of them found it challenging to function effectively in Australian society because the gender expectations of the two cultures were so different. Several said that their husbands had to be constantly reassured in their roles of protector of and provider for their families and this was particularly hard on their daughters. These recollections also disrupted the earlier narratives of 'idyllic life' in Fiji. Women recalled being forced into arranged marriages, of not being allowed to attend university, while brothers who had obtained worse marks at school did so. One woman recalled, with deeply felt resentment, that although her family depended on her income, she was still abused if she came home even five minutes late. Limits over women's occupational and spatial mobility were reinforced through personal ties of love and loyalty, fear of non-acceptance in the local community and bringing shame on the family.[33] Imrana Jalal and Wadan Narsey have labelled this a 'culture of silence' that condemns women's assertiveness as disrespectful to those with traditional power.[34] Many women also commented that in post-coup Fiji many Indo-Fijian families tightened controls on women's mobility for fear of ethnic violence.

It is in these contexts that 'bureau marriages' were mentioned. Initially migration to the USA, Canada or Australia was through technical qualifications but now it is increasingly through marriage and family sponsorship. All my interlocutors mentioned the great demand for overseas resident Indo-Fijians as marriage partners. A significant minority of them migrated to Australia through arranged marriages with Indo-Fijian men resident in Australia. However, there were also arranged marriages to Europeans through commercial marriage bureaux or pen pal clubs. One of the women showed me an advertisement from the *Fiji Times*:

> Canadian of European origin, single, medium height, 55 years, secure income, own property, marriage to Indian lady (slim, up to 40 years), sincere, friendly and willing to relocate. Please correspond with photograph.

There were also cases of marriages of convenience carried out to secure permanent residence in countries like Australia, New Zealand or Canada. All my interlocutors knew some cases and Amina described a particularly harrowing one:

> This man, he divorced his wife in Fiji, and married someone in Australia—a marriage of convenience—he brought his children over with them and after a few years divorced this Australian woman. And the children grew up and when they were about 21 or so, they sponsored their mother to join them. And for like 10 or 15 years this husband was away from his wife and it's a torturing experience, I mean just imagine, all these years you are away from your wife, and you live with this other woman, and you are bound to get closer to her, get involved and get emotional.

On a research trip to Fiji I had a particularly poignant interview with a young Indo-Fijian woman who was trying to migrate 'anywhere' out of Fiji. Her situation was compounded by the fact that she was a single mother who had borne a daughter out of wedlock and thus had difficulty functioning in her own community.

> I want to migrate, but it's just that I'm not qualified. Otherwise I would have left Fiji four years ago, five years ago. Because I don't have any technical qualifications. But if I could get a permanent residency I would be out of this country, tomorrow. Within weeks maybe. Just because, well, I have a daughter and I would like to send her to high school in Australia or New Zealand. I would do anything to be able to migrate.

This woman had considered bureau marriages and even contacted a few prospective 'husbands' but could not bring herself to take the final step.

In the story 'Kismet' Brij Lal recounts the experience of his protagonist Mumtaz who marries an Australian man 'who sent her the sponsorship papers and a one-way ticket'.

> Mumtaz was nothing if not enterprising. She got her Australian passport at the earliest opportunity and ... sponsored her mother. Later other members of the family arrived through sham marriages to Mumtaz's Australian friends whose fares she paid to go to Fiji: they got their paid holiday, and her brothers got their visas.[35]

While Indo-Fijians hardly ever marry indigenous Fijians or Indians of other religions, Europeans appear to be exempt from this cultural endogamy. The predicament of Indo-Fijians is now so intense that the under-supply of overseas resident Indo-Fijian marriage partners has made this type of relationship more common. My interlocutors all claimed to have heard of such marriages and many said they knew of at least one person who had come to Australia through a 'bureau marriage'. From discussions with these women it appeared that the issue of marriage was secondary, even irrelevant, compared with the opportunities offered by migration: betterment of economic status and life chances. Marriages were their passports to better lives. But details of bureau marriages, especially to Europeans, were less forthcoming, particularly in regard to their success. However, the women all agreed that they would have undertaken almost any degree of hardship to escape Fiji after the 1987 coups since 'there was no future for us there'. One woman recalls that on a visit to Fiji after the 2000 coup, numerous women approached her for help in getting to Australia:

> They are waiting for this Prince with a black [Australian] passport and even working women who've got really good jobs. One woman who used to work with me in the newspaper industry and she always was turning away all the local men, just because she wanted to move overseas. She has lost her parents and she is living with her brother and his family and she feels that she is like a burden on the family, although she is working. So she is just waiting. When I was returning to Australia, she said, 'make sure, don't forget, please arrange a boy for me from Australia'. As if it's that easy.

Shared and contested narratives

Are there possibilities of common memories and shared narratives between the indigenous and Indo-Fijian communities? Or is Fiji an example of Lyotard's 'differend': discourses so mutually exclusive, because they begin from such radically different first positions that there can be no consensus?[36] Vijay Mishra has commented that there are few theoretical studies of Fijian politics and culture or of the creation of the Fijian nation-state that could open up the national repressed or remind us of Walter Benjamin's observation in another context, that the documents of civilisation are simultaneously documents of barbarism. Mishra asks whether it is possible to frame a moment (the coup of May 2000) that signifies a compulsion to return to some lost nirvanic past, when that moment is simultaneously one of redemption (for the Fijian) and betrayal (for the Indian)?[37]

According to Mishra, for the 60 000 indentured labourers who arrived from 1879 to 1917 land ownership was not a mystique but a commodity, a 'point of entry into the psyche of a feudal system from which, in India, they had been excluded',[38] although members of the Indo-Fijian community have pointed out that emotional and spiritual bonds can co-exist with other ties. Indo-Fijian leaders such as AD Patel, from 1946 onwards, claimed a place in the nation on the basis of their labour and economic contribution.[39] The Indian indentured labourer's lament, according to poet Raymond C Pillai, went thus:

> We came in answer to your plea,
> We came to build your land.
> But now that you are strong and free,
> You turn our hopes to sand.[40]

Indian petitions to the Constitution Review Commission counteracted Fijian ethnocentrism with statements such as:

> The Indians brought Fiji out of savagery to the present brilliant, progressive and prosperous status.

> Fijians want ready made money, ready made *kana* [food], ready made clothing and housing. Fairy tale life style won't work. One thing was good, that we Indo-Fijians were in Fiji, otherwise the Fijian population would have been only good enough to suit Museums and Zoos and the highland as happened in New Zealand, Australia and America with the natives.[41]

During my stay in Fiji in September 1999 about eight months before the coup, I spoke to a number of sugar-cane farmers whose leases were about to expire. One old man said:

> What the *Kaiviti* [indigenous Fijians] don't realise is that if we hadn't been used as cannon fodder on the sugar-cane plantations, they would have had to do it. They would have worked and died and their culture would have been destroyed. Why do they want to destroy us? You should have seen this land when our family got it. It was a jungle. We've made it beautiful, made it pay. It is our mother too.

Conclusion: colonialism and Third Worldism in Fiji

In a 1997 article Ian Boxill claims that Indo-Fijians, by virtue of their history, are more disposed to dealing with the world capitalist economy than Fijians, because many more Fijians than Indians live in isolated rural communal settings—on the periphery of the periphery. Despite its semi-feudal nature, indentureship carried with it aspects of capitalism, including waged labour, rational calculation and individualism.[42] Nii-K Plange agrees that, under the colonial state, 'Fijian access to, and effective participation in, the newly introduced economy ... were discouraged' via various politico-administrative arrangements.[43]

The way in which the two communities construct their relationships to land, the 'way of the land' opposed to the 'way of money' also informs their conceptions of nation. Henry Rutz writes that, since independence in 1970, leaders of both communities exhorted their constituencies to imagine a multi-racial and harmonious nation. Indians wanted to be newly created citizens with full political rights, including a one person/one vote system in a civil society that subordinated the status of religion, race and particularist culture. In contrast, the Fijian rhetoric of accommodation presumed that the nation would be imagined as 'mutual respect' between different racial communities, reinforced by a narrative of 'multiracial' harmony and voting by racial communities for persons of the same race. As Rutz percipiently says, the coup of 1987 halted the experiment of transplanting an 18th century nation-state in the time–space of Fiji. It took away the 'other' against which the Fijian identity had been dialectically shaped by racial politics during the colonial and independence periods.[44] Henceforth, the contest over 'the nation' would be de-centred, resurfacing within the Fijian community itself.

After the coup in May 2000 Teresia Teaiwa also commented that the problem with Fijian nationalism was that there is no Fijian nation.[45] Fiji's problem, she said, was Fijian, not Indian. Teaiwa highlighted the fact that 'part-Europeans' form the largest and most influential group of general voters and, in the post-coup era, they shifted from their historical identification with colonial European privilege towards a reclamation of their 'part-Fijian' roots, reflecting a recognition of the contemporary realities of political power in Fiji: indigenous Fijians rule. George Speight's father, a 'part-European' and former general elector named Sam Speight, became a 'born-again Fijian' in the post-coup era. She continued, 'George Speight claims to represent indigenous Fijian interests. Sporting his European name, speaking exclusively in English, drawing on his Australian and American degrees in business for *mana*, and wearing his designer clothes, Speight does indeed represent indigenous Fijian interests. But Speight's indigenous Fijian interests are clearly neither the indigenous Fijian interests of Ratu Mara nor those of the late Dr Bavadra.'

One of the rhetorical strategies linking tradition to the nation, the strategy of the betrayal of the land, is discussed in Rutz's 1995 article. The leader of the Fijian Nationalist Party (formed in 1980), Sakeasi Butradoka, argued that independence for Fijians lay in the future, not the past because Fijians had to free themselves from the democracy that had linked their destiny to the Indians. Democracy and equality, he said, were Western constructs that were major obstacles to the true independence of Fiji.[46]

> The Fijian Nationalist cannot accept the equality of all the races … Equality of rights … has to involve a recognized and accepted inequality of rights due to history.[47]

In Butradoka's vision, the indigenous Fijian and the Indian Fijian could not both be equal citizens of some future Fijian nation. The propositions of both liberalism and Marxism that assume that one is born to certain particular identities and/or struggles to acquire general or universal identities of a class, of the citizen of a nation, or even of the human were anathema to him because they were incapable of describing the politics of identity in contemporary democracies. European political theory assumes that democracy is about development—

of the individual into a citizen with legal and political rights, equal to all other citizens, of the nation into a secular set of communities living harmoniously with each other. In the past few decades, however, postcolonial democracy has also had to incorporate concepts of multiculturalism and diversity. In the politics of diversity, identities are not so much given and then transcended in the interest of an overarching unity; they are acquired and performed in contexts in which unities are seen as always contingent and shifting.[48] Indo-Fijian writer Subramani agrees:

> We can move all move towards being Fijian, which ... is an identity that we have yet to imagine fully ... The political logic of accepting difference is inventing and supporting institutions that help difference to be maintained. It is not necessary to create one people and one nation; rather, we should learn to view a system of difference as our unity.[49]

Thus Butradoka was not saying that Indo-Fijians had to have unequal rights because they were racially inferior; indeed, some Fijians claimed to need special treatment because in 'civilisation' the Indians have a thousand years start on them.[50] What he was saying was that the inequality was about entitlement and had to do with the necessity of history—the experiences of cession and indenture on Fijian land had ensured, rather than erased, Fijian paramountcy. In other words, Fiji could never be a democracy where Indo-Fijians and indigenous Fijians developed equally and together to become citizens with equal rights in a nation-state. Indians could never become Fijians nor was it possible for Fijian democracy to allow complete diversity.

The issues of land, nation and identity in Fiji are located fuzzily at the analytical intersection of mercantile forces, British imperialism, the experience of indenture and pre-colonial Fijian political cultures in transition. They cannot be approached as logical outcomes of European commercial penetration, colonisation and assimilation but as historical processes involving complicated European, indigenous and indentured struggles for control over land and resources as well as power, privilege and authority in the aftermath of imperialism. In a sense part of the problem is that both groups are employing different colonisation/conquest paradigms that are part of a zero-sum game.

In Fiji little attempt has been made to address the ever-shifting lines of alliance or confrontation within indigenous and indentured communities and cultures or to create convincing narratives of mutual substance, history or interdependence, or to counter the feeling among a majority of Fijians that encouraging immigrant communities to retain, practice and promote the culture of their homelands squeezes and diminishes the place of Fijian culture in the only possible homeland of Fijian culture. For indigenous Fijians the crucial problem with the 1997 Constitution was that it failed to acknowledge the critical, symbolic, spiritual and practical reality that the Fijian archipelago was the only possible spot on the entire planet where Fijian aspirations of nationhood and cultural pride could be experienced and performed. Once eroded or lost, there was no motherland over the horizon to which pilgrimages could be made to seek rejuvenation or solace (in a clear reference to the Indo-Fijians' heritage in India).

As one indigenous Fijian said to me, 'It is here or nowhere for everything that is Fijian'.[51]

In an article on the Constitutional Review in Fiji, Robert Norton pointed out that the official submission from the governing party, Soqosoqo ni Vakavulewa ni Taukei (SVT). was an exposition of the relationship between *taukei* (indigenous owner), normally at the forefront of decision making, and *vulagi* (guests or foreigners) who are allowed to participate but 'they must not be domineering or forceful ... they need to be reminded time and again of this fact'. This *taukei–vulagi* relationship challenges the universal human rights concepts in which all citizens of a nation are considered equal. The petition went on to say that 'Indians have shown no signs of cultural assimilation or sensitivity'.

Similarly, JN Kamikamica, a past General Manager of the NLTB, considers that one of Fiji's major challenges is to resolve the meaning of *taukei* and *vulagi* so that it accords with the changing nature of Fijian society.[52] He points out that the protection of indigenous ownership of the bulk of land resources and the preservation of their culture and traditions in rural Fiji shields indigenous Fijians from the competitive world of 20th century Fiji. But since Fiji citizenship does not bestow the same rights and privileges on the other communities, when and how, Kamikamica asks, may a non-Fijian aspire to and acquire a position similar to that of a *taukei*?[53]

For some indigenous Fijians, the only way of promoting a sense of a common cultural identity and a shared national purpose is to allow only Fijian nationalism and Fijian national identity. For them, since independence, and indeed during the country's colonial period, the promotion of a collective national identity was discouraged as it was not clear how the Indians would be able to fit in. The result, they claim, has been an unhealthy preoccupation with provincial and ethnic rather than national interests. For them, the new Fiji—its language, symbols, institutions, anthems, history, mythology—must be unequivocally and unmistakably Fijian. Immigrant communities will have no choice other than to embrace this reality and 'once this reality has been accepted into the marrow of all they will finally have earned the right to be called Fijians'.[54] It is interesting that this rhetoric reflects in part the sentiments expressed by fundamentalist Hindu parties in India, such as the Bharatiya Janata Party; for example, their insistence that Muslims and Christians must all become Hindus first, calling themselves 'Muslim Hindus' and 'Christian Hindus'.

In an interview with Vilsoni Hereniko, just before the May 2000 coup, the Indo-Fijian writer Subramani spoke of his vision for Fiji:

> I would like to see a seamless flow of languages. That would be very interesting, something unique. It would make Pacific literature different. In the same way, I think cultures could also flow like that. Then we would have a lot of integration happening and new cultural forms emerging ... If you go to some of our schools now, it's already happening. In the playground students switch from one language to another. They speak a pidgin variety of English that freely incorporates Fijian and Hindi. But it's not reinforced in the classroom, where English is still the dominant language ... The multilingual medium could have a great impact. I think we'll have a situation in which there's great audience participation. At the moment when you watch television, Hindi, Fijian, and English programs appear separately.

There will be a time in the future when programs will not be divided that way; instead there will be a spontaneous flow of multilingual programs.[55]

The archives also have similar stories. They tell us, for example, that when the coolie ship *Syria* was wrecked in 1894, some Fijians looted the ship but many others swam out to save the shipwrecked. They also make clear that, in spite of British laws proscribing such activities, Fijian villages in the 19th century sheltered Indian labourers who fled the plantations. The autobiography of Totaram Sanadhya tells us that there were also some indigenous Fijians who worked in the sugar plantations in spite of Arthur Gordon. When, starving and unable to bear the horrible conditions of plantation life in Fiji, he was about to hang himself, some indigenous Fijians who had previously lived in his coolie line not only prevented him from doing so but also brought him food from their villages.[56]

In the article cited above, Vijay Mishra comments that the present political predicament in Fiji happened partially because the drive for independence was fuelled primarily by Indian desire for change. The Fijian upper classes, protected by patronage and the Great Council of Chiefs, had no interest in an anti-colonial struggle against the British and only came into the picture after the Indian indentured labourers began the struggle. In the process, says Mishra, the *girmitiyas*, or indentured Indians, were gradually reconstructed as symbolic colonisers wishing to alienate the Fijians from their land, while the patrician Fijians were cast as defenders of the charter of the land. The native Fijian, denied the nationalist legacy of anti-colonialism, used the rapidly globalising discourse of land rights as a means of starting a new foundational narrative of the nation-state on the basis of a newly constructed anti-colonial struggle.[57] For many indigenous Fijians, the Indo-Fijians are another migrant race who want 'to step into colonial shoes to control indigenous Fijian development'.[58]

The predicament of Fiji is crucial for postcolonial studies because it foregrounds one of the paradoxes of the post-cold war era and of failed Third Worldism. Late decolonisation in Fiji meant that the government of the newly independent country was not exposed to the discourses of Third World solidarity that emerged from the Bandung era; however, Fijians were able to tap into the rise of movements supporting indigenous rights in the 1970s and 1980s. At the same time, in a postcolonial era overseen by international bodies such as the United Nations, the nation-state was the model imposed by departing imperial powers on their erstwhile colonies. For the Fiji Constitution Review Commmission of 1996, established to draft a new constitution, universal covenants and declarations, often aimed at empowering people in the Third World (such as the Universal Declaration of Human Rights, the Convention on the Elimination of All Forms of Racial Discrimination and those on the Rights of Indigenous People) were not appropriate to a state where the indigenous people consisted of half the population, controlled the majority of the land and were the politically dominant group. According to Kaplan and Kelly:

Unambiguously, Fiji had to be a nation-state. But how the nation-state form, especially in its entitlements, was expected to fit Fiji's situation was utterly ambiguous.[59]

Creating shared narratives that enable communities to co-exist harmoniously demands innovative solutions that may have to extend beyond both the Western model of democracy and the indigenous model of Fijian paramountcy. Thus, the major problem with Joseph Carens' proposition of 'minimal moral standards' is that it privileges the notion of Fijian paramountcy in a way that precludes such possibilities, as does Salman Rushdie's argument in favour of Indo-Fijians:

> migrant peoples do not remain visitors forever. In the end, their new land owns them as once their old land did, and they have a right to own it in their turn.[60]

Stephanie Lawson cautions that the hijacking of the moral discourse of indigenous rights by the Fijian nationalists serves to encourage the notion that indigenous rights must always take precedence over other claims to justice.[61] How do we conceive of 'nativeness' in less absolute terms, constructing articulated, rooted and cosmopolitan practices that register more complex, emergent possibilities? How do we expand our idea of what may be regarded as a 'historical fact' and give credence to 'experience' and its 'truths' that may not always be verifiable by the historian's methods? Perhaps the most effective way to demonstrate that these other claims are not necessarily incompatible with indigenous rights is to approach Fijian history through the lens of colonialism. If, in Dipesh Chakrabarty's words, both Fijian and Indian cultures, knowledges, life-worlds and life-practices were invaded and colonised; if they both experienced what Gayatri Spivak called 'epistemic violence', then this shared predicament of the Indian indentured immigrant and the indigenous Fijian landowner should create the possibility of a dialogue between the two. This conversation is not based only on 'shared histories' (as may be claimed between the settler and native) but on the shared predicament of having been colonised (both politically and intellectually).[62] For, as James Clifford argues, 'an absolutist indigenism, where each distinct "people" strives to occupy an original bit of ground, is a frightening utopia. For it imagines relocation and ethnic cleansing on an unimaginable scale: a denial of all the deep histories of movement, urbanization, habitation, reindigenization, sinking roots, moving on, invading, mixing—the very stuff of human history.'[63]

Notes

[1] D Chakrabarty speaking at a workshop on Subaltern, Multicultural and Indigenous Histories, University of Technology, Sydney, Australia, 20–21 July 2000.

[2] See D Chakrabarty, 'Postcoloniality and the artifice of history: who speaks for Indian pasts', *Representations*, 37, 1992.

[3] M Kaplan & J Kelly, *Represented Communities: Fiji and World Decolonization*, Chicago, IL: University of Chicago Press, 2001, p 199.

[4] P van der Veer (ed), *Nation and Migration: The Politics of Space in the South Asian Diaspora*, Pennsylvania: University of Pennsylvania Press, 1995.

[5] J Carens, 'Democracy and respect for difference: the case of Fiji', *University of Michigan Journal of Law Reform*, 1992.

[6] Carens, *Democracy*, p 576.

[7] *Ibid*, p 594.

[8] *Ibid*, p 595.

[9] *Ibid*, p 628.

116

10 *Ibid*, p 574.
11 P France, *The Charter of the Land: Custom and Colonization in Fiji*, London: Oxford University Press, 1969, passim.
12 HJ Rutz, 'Capitalizing on culture: moral ironies in urban Fiji', *Comparative Studies in Society and History*, 29, 1987, p 557.
13 *Ibid*, p 538.
14 M Jolly, 'Custom and the way of the land: past and present in Vanuatu and Fiji', *Oceania*, 62, 1992.
15 M Kaplan, 'The coups in Fiji: colonial contradictions and the post-colonial crisis', *Critique of Anthropology*, 7 (3), 1988, pp 101–106.
16 *Ibid*, p 106. See also Brij V Lal, *Broken Waves: a History of the Fiji Islands in the Twentieth Century*, Honolulu, HI: University of Hawaii Press, 1992; and Lal, *Crossing the Kala Pani: a Documentary History of Indian Indenture in Fiji*, Canberra: Division of Pacific & Asian History, Research School of Pacific & Asian Studies, Australian National University, 1998.
17 Jolly, 'Custom and the way of the land', p 346.
18 RG Ward, 'Land in Fiji', in BV Lal & Tomasi R Vakatora, *Fiji in Transition: Research Papers of the Fiji Constitution Review Commission*, Vol 1, Suva: University of the South Pacific, 1997, p 248.
19 JN Kamikamica, 'Fiji native land: issues and challenges', in Lal & Vakatora, *Fiji in Transition*, p 259.
20 J Waqanisau, 'Fijians' paramountcy—let's think rationally', undated letter circulated by email by academics at the University of the South Pacific (USP) after the coup in May 2000. I have a hard copy in my possession. This name appears to be a pseudonym and the identity of the writer is unknown to the USP academics who circulated the letter. However, the figures appear to be credible.
21 Letter from a group of unnamed indigenous Fijians circulated on a Fiji email list in June 2000. A hard copy is in my possession.
22 R Robertson, Retreat from exclusion? Identities in post-coup Fiji', in A Haroon Akram-Lodhi (ed), *Confronting Fiji's Futures*, Canberra: Asia Pacific Press, 2000, p 278.
23 United Press International (UPI), 18 September 2000.
24 *Ibid*.
25 Kaplan & Kelly, *Represented Communities*, p 6.
26 K Ganguly, 'Migrant identities: personal memory and the construction of selfhood', *Cultural Studies*, 61, 1992, p 29.
27 *Ibid*, p 30.
28 *Ibid*, p 30.
29 *Ibid*, pp 31–34.
30 Alcoholic drink indigenous to Fiji.
31 J Leckie, 'Women in post-coup Fiji: negotiating work through old and new realities', in Akram-Lodhi, *Confronting Fiji's Futures*, pp 178–201.
32 B Lal, 'From Labasa to Laucola Bay', in Lal, *Mr Tulsi's Store: a Fijian Journey*, Canberra: Pandanus Books, Australian National University, 2001, p 93.
33 See also Leckie, 'Women in post-coup Fiji', p 187.
34 *Balance*, September–October 1997, pp 8–9.
35 Lal, 'Kismet', in Lal, *Mr Tulsi's Store*, p 200.
36 J-F Lyotard, *The Differend: Phrases in Dispute*, trans Georges Van Den Abbeele, Manchester: Manchester University Press, 1988.
37 V Mishra, 'The feudal postcolonial: the Fiji crisis', *Meanjin*, 3, pp 146–165.
38 Mishra, 'The feudal postcolonial', p 147.
39 Jolly, 'Custom and the way of the land', p 346.
40 RC Pillai, 'Labourer's Lament', in Subramani (ed), *The Indo-Fijian Experience*, St Lucia: University of Queensland Press, 1979, p 160.
41 R Norton, 'Reconciling ethnicity and nation: contending discourses in Fiji's constitutional reform', *The Contemporary Pacific*, 12 (1), 2000, p 110.
42 I Boxill, 'Fiji: the limits of ethnic political mobilisation', *Race and Class*, October–December 1997, p 41, n 2.
43 Nii-K Plange, 'The "three Fijis" thesis: a critical examination of a neo-empiricist naturalistic analysis of Fiji's polity', *Journal of Pacific Studies*, 15, 1990, p 21.
44 HJ Rutz, 'Occupying the headwaters of tradition: rhetorical strategies of nation making in Fiji', in RJ Foster (ed), *Nation Making: Emergent Identities in Postcolonial Melanesia*, Ann Arbor, MI: University of Michigan Press, 1995.
45 T Teaiwa, 'Fiji crisis: an analysis', *Sydney Morning Herald*, 22 May 2000.
46 Rutz, 'Occupying the headwaters of tradition'.
47 R Premdas, 'Constitutional challenge: the rise of Fijian nationalism', *Pacific Perspective*, 9, 1980, p 36.
48 Chakrabarty, workshop speech.
49 Subramani, *Altering Imagination*, Suva: Fiji Writers' Association, University of the South Pacific, 1995.
50 Norton, 'reconciling ethnicity and nation', p 106.

[51] These sentiments were expressed in a number of emails and conversations with indigenous Fijians over the latter half of 2000.

[52] Kamikamica, 'Fiji native land', pp 259–260.

[53] *Ibid*, p 289.

[54] Letter cited in footnote 21. Also interviews with interlocutors Suva S2, T3 and Nadi P4 and L7.

[55] An interview with Subramani by V Hereniko, *The Contemporary Pacific*, 13 (1), 2001, p 184.

[56] T Sanadhya, *Bhut Len ki katha: Totaram Sanadhya ka Fiji,* trans and ed Brij V Lal & Yogendra Yadav, New Delhi: Saraswati Press, 1994.

[57] Mishra, 'The feudal postcolonial', pp 150–151.

[58] MT Samisoni, 'Thoughts on Fiji's third coup d'etat', in BV Lal with M Pretes (eds), *Coup: Reflections on the Political Crisis in Fiji*, Canberra: Pandanus Books, 2001, p 44.

[59] Kaplan & Kelly, *Represented Communities*, p 177.

[60] *The Age*, 10 June 2000

[61] S Lawson, 'The state of Fiji's statehood', in R. Rotberg (ed), *State Failure and State Weakness in a Time of Terror*, Washington, DC: Brookings Institution Press, 2002.

[62] Chakrabarty, workshop speech.

[63] J Clifford, 'Indigenous articulations', *The Contemporary Pacific*, 13 (2), 2001, p 468.

Spectres of the Third World: global modernity and the end of the three worlds

ARIF DIRLIK

I would like to begin with a simple question on contemporary usage, and tease out its historical and theoretical implications in the rest of the article: why does the term Third World refuse to go away, when the disappearance of the socialist Second World has rendered the whole three worlds scheme semantically meaningless? There is plentiful evidence (and criticism) to show that, as concepts, the Third World, and its cognates such as 'the three worlds', are no longer relevant, if they ever were. Social science discourse, shifting from modernisation to globalisation, has rendered the idea irrelevant. Postcolonial critics hailing from what used to be the Third World reject it as an analytical or descriptive term. The Third Worldism of erstwhile radicals seems quaint against the emergence to dominance of reactionary forces globally. And yet the Third World continues to pop up regularly in everyday and academic discussion, even in the speech of those, such as the present author, who in theory have consigned to the past the term, the concept, and the realities it purported to describe.[1]

Habit, of course, is one immediate explanation for the persistence of the term, and while it may plausibly explain the persistence of the term in casual speech, it does not explain the persistent engagement with the term that is implied by a volume such as the present one; which may be viewed as one more effort to exorcise a ghost that continues to haunt the ways in which we conceive and map the world, and its politics. Another possibility we might entertain is that we have perhaps gone too far in emhasising the post-World War II constructedness of the concept by social scientists and radicals, rendering it into a representation that is infused and shaped by ideology or utopian wishful-thinking, and ignoring in the process the ways in which the concept has captured certain historical realities that may transcend the moment of its construction. There is possibly a sense, also, that there is no convenient short-hand substitute available in describing the areas of the world covered by the term 'Third World', or one that does so more accurately or efficiently, such as, for instance, the 'South' of 'North–South'. The term 'Third World' would seem to have acquired a life of its own, similar to terms such as colonialism, with implications that go beyond the simply descriptive in a positivistic sense. I would like to suggest, however, that continued use of the term also points to the persistence of the assumptions of modernisation discourse, which first gave birth to the Third World concept, and continues to shape thinking in both the everyday as well as the academic and political realms, even if it is no longer able to contain the forces at work in shaping the contemporary world. Any critique of the Third World concept or the three worlds idea, in other words, needs to be approached within the context of a broader critique of modernisation discourse.

This is what I undertake below through the concept of a 'global modernity', which I will argue points to global realities of power and culture that are quite different from those that informed modernisation discourse, or its more recent reincarnation in globalisation. The idea of a global modernity may suggest additional reasons why the Third World concept refuses to fade away. It also provides important reasons why, if the term continues to bear some relevance to global political economy or cultural geopolitics, it nevertheless points to different realities than it did earlier. These realities are not just postcolonial, as in the wake of decolonisation after 1945 to which the concept was a response, but postcolonial as they have been worked over by the forces of global capitalism over the half century of decolonisation. The transformation of the Third World, the decline and fall of socialism, and the emergence to consciousness of global capitalism have proceeded alongside each other (and in structural entanglement) during this same period, acquiring visibility during the last two decades of the 20th century. It may not be surprising that it was also during these same decades, beginning before the fall of socialism, that objections to the three worlds idea first became audible. I will summarise briefly here important issues in the critique of the three worlds idea, point to some ways in which these critiques ignore the historical realities which the idea addressed and shaped, and discuss global modernity as a way of comprehending recent reconfigurations in the cultural and political economic mapping of the world. These render irrelevant an earlier conceptualisation of the Third World without necessarily eliminating some of its usefulness in compre-hending historical continuities between the present and the past.

The three worlds of social science and radical politics

The three worlds idea, while it had currency, seemed compelling at least in part because it served as both a hegemonic conceptualisation of the world, and of struggles against that hegemony. The idea itself was a by-product of modernisation discourse in Euro-American social science, formulated in the 1950s in response to the entanglement of colonialism and anti-colonial movements in an emergent Cold War that impelled the globe to division between two major power blocs. Modernisation discourse in its political premises sought to ensure continued Euro-American hegemony over the present and the future, as it represented Euro-American social, political and cultural paradigms—the paradigms of capitalist modernity—as the ultimate paradigms of progress. Ironically, once it had appeared, the idea of the Third World was embraced enthusiastically by radical advocates of liberation from Euro-American colonialism and hegemony who saw in it both a mobilising idea to complete the tasks of decolonisation, and a means of reorganising global relationships. It is also noteworthy that these two conflicting understandings of the Third World in modernisation discourse and Third Worldism would be called into question almost simultaneously as the reconfiguration of global relations in ensuing years would call forth a new paradigm, globalisation.

A seminal discussion of the problematics of the three worlds idea is to be found in an article by Carl Pletsch that was published in 1981, when the idea was still very much alive.[2] Pletsch was concerned not so much with the empirical problems of the idea—differences among societies included in those worlds—as with the logic underlying its production. The article made a strong case for the recognition of such differences, of which I will say more below, but its more important contribution lay in arguing that the Third World as a concept was derivative and residual, deriving its meaning not from some intrinsic characteristic of societies encompassed by the term, but from the burgeoning Cold War confrontation between capitalist and communist societies. Pletsch credited a 1952 article by the French demographer Alfred Sauvy, 'Three worlds, one planet', as one of the earliest of an increasing number of writings in the 1950s to use the term 'Third World'. Sauvy wrote in that article that 'we speak readily of two worlds in confrontation, of their possible war, of their coexistence, etc, forgetting all too often that there is a third—the most important and, in fact, the first world in the chronological sense'.[3] The Third World was significant geopolitically, as its conquest was deemed crucial to the outcome of the competition between capitalism and communism, but its significance was matched by its vagueness as a concept. Pletsch's description of the 'deep structure of the Three Worlds concept' is worth quoting at some length for capturing the underlying logic in the production of the Third World:

> One barely has to look beneath [the] surface of supposed realpolitik, however, to see that the division of the planet into three worlds is based on a pair of very abstract and hardly precise binary distinctions. First the world has been divided into its 'traditional' and 'modern' parts. Then the modern portion has been subdivided into its 'communist' (or 'socialist') and 'free' parts. These four terms underlying the idea of three worlds may be thought of as an extremely general social semantics. They are terms which derive their meaning from their mutual opposition rather than from any inherent relationship to the things described ... Making explicit the concept of tradition that underlies these ... terms permits us to tease out all the other implications contained in the idea of the third world and locate them in a structural

relationship with the implications of the other worlds. The third world is the world of tradition, culture, religion, irrationality, underdevelopment, overpopulation, political chaos, and so on. The second world is modern, technologically sophisticated, rational to a degree, but authoritarian (or totalitarian) and repressive, and ultimately inefficient and impoverished by contamination with ideological preconceptions and burdened with an ideologically motivated socialist elite. The first world is purely modern, a haven of science and utilitarian decision making, technological, efficient, democratic, free—in short, a natural society unfettered by religion or ideology.[4]

While there was fierce competition between the first and second worlds over the third, moreover, the modernisation discourse shaped by the three worlds scheme was also informed by a historical teleology that placed the First World at the end of history, showing the others the way to their futures, even though some Third World societies might take a detour through the Second. Pletsch recognised the importance of the Third Worldist embrace of the three worlds concept, which gave the concept substance and sustenance, especially after the Bandung Conference in 1955. The recognition, however, remained marginal to the analysis, possibly because he saw little difference between social science and Third Worldist usages where the relationship of the concept to reality was concerned. He was equally critical of Third Worldist uses of the concept when he wrote that, 'we must ... ask ourselves how the very thought of three worlds on one planet constrained even those who were opponents of the Cold War or partisans of the third world to do work that contributed both to the strategies of containment and to the exploitation of the third world'.[5]

Third Worldism is discussed extensively in the introductory essay to this volume by Mark Berger, and does not call for prolonged discussion here. What is missing from Berger's discussion, I think, is a historical perspective on Third Worldism that explains why the idea of the three worlds might prove attractive under certain circumstances, and why it might have seemed more substantial than it appears in hindsight. About its attractiveness, there is little question, as the Third World was rendered into a utopian concept, countering the paradigms both of capitalism and Soviet-style socialism. As an African American participant in the Bandung Conference of 1955 wrote:

> As I watched the dark-faced delegates work at the conference, I saw a strange thing happen. Before Bandung, most of these men had been strangers, and on the first day they were constrained with one another, bristling with charge and countercharge against America and/or Russia. But, as the days passed, they slowly cooled off, and another and different mood set in ... As they came to know one another better, their fear and distrust evaporated. Living for centuries under Western rule, they had become filled with a deep sense of how greatly they differed from one another. But now, face to face, their ideological defenses dropped. Negative unity, bred by a feeling that they had to stand together against a rapacious West, turned into something that hinted of the positive ... Day after day dun-colored Trotskyites consorted with dark Moslems, yellow Indo-Chinese hobnobbed with brown Indonesians, black Africans mingled with swarthy Arabs, tan Burmese associated with dark brown Hindus, dusty nationalists palled around with yellow Communists, and Socialists talked to Buddhists. But they all had the same background of colonial experience, of subjection, of color consciousness, and they found that ideology was not needed to define their relations.[6]

A utopian moment, to be sure, but one which persisted only so long as the generation that had come of age during the anti-colonial struggles prevailed. When he wrote these lines Richard Wright displayed some scepticism towards the outcome of such utopianism, but for the moment he was caught up in it, as were many others. By 1968, during the world-wide radical ferment, the Third World appeared as a source of inspiration for change in the First World. It was this same longing that underlay the term 'Third World Strike' in ethnic student movements in the USA.

In a study of the problematics of the Third World through the Algerian instance, Robert Malley describes Third Worldism as:

> the belief in the revolutionary aspirations of the Third World masses, in the inevitability of their fulfillment, and in the role of strong, centralized states in this undertaking. Third Worldism was more than political doctrine; it was all-encompassing ideology that permeated fields of intellectual knowledge and militant activism. It was authoritative, not in the sense of ever being the exclusive ideological referent, but in that it provided the instruments by which to legitimate and discredit, to measure success and decree failure. It was pervasive in that not only Third World statesmen but also Third World and Western sociologists, historians, economists, anthropologists, and political scientists drew inspiration from its outlook.[7]

The Third World idea, in other words, not only contained a radical vision which dynamised a politics that spilled over into the other 'worlds' of the Cold War, but also carried considerable plausibility in social science analysis; not only in scholarship of a conservative bent, but in radical scholarship dissatisfied with received modernisation discourse, regardless of whether or not it was capitalist or socialist in its assumptions. The idea may have been an invention, but the invention pointed to certain realities that endowed the concept with substance. We need to ask why. Critiques of the three worlds idea such as those of Pletsch (and, to some extent, Berger's in this volume and elsewhere) focus almost exclusively on the invention of the Third World or Third Worldism within the semantics of the Cold War.[8] They pay less attention to the history that is implicit in the term; a history that predates the invention of the concept, and becomes integral to its message and deployment as soon as it has been invented. Pletsch states explicitly that his approach is 'structural rather than genetic',[9] and while he recognises that the concept serves to bring together in one conceptual space societies that do have something in common, that are distinguishable from other societies (of the capitalist West or the Soviet bloc), he does not pursue the implications of such a recognition.

We may underline here the observation in the statement by Sauvy, cited above, that the Third World was 'in fact, the first world in the chronological sense.' What came to be described as the Third World after World War II, a product of the confrontation of the First and Second Worlds, was the world that was not socialist, but was also a world that was pre-capitalist, the world that had been left behind as some moved out of it through the agencies of capitalism and socialism. This world experienced capitalism as an alien force of colonial or semi-colonial exploitation and oppression, but for that very reason did not yet have the qualifications to move on to socialism. The Third World was a residual category, a dumping ground for all who did not qualify as capitalist or socialist. But the idea had its lineage. This was the world that Marxist radicals had described in the years after World War I as the world of colonialism and semi-colonialism. It was the world that a hegemonic social science emerging in the 19th century alongside capitalism and colonialism had viewed as the world of primitives and of civilisations 'vegetating in the teeth of time'. The renaming of this world as the Third World was equally the product of the emergence of a socialist alternative to capitalism in the aftermath of World War I, and of decolonisation in ensuing years, but especially after World War II. There may thus be little mystery why the new political subject emerging victorious from anti-colonial struggles might find something appealing in a designation that recognised an alternative to capitalist or socialist states, or feel something of a commonality with others engaged in similar struggles.

We may view Third Worldism as an illusion that temporarily disguised the deep differences that divided these societies from one another, which is the image that prevails in historical hindsight. We may view it also as a 'mobilisation myth'.[10] That is, it is a point of departure in an effort to formulate a Third World discourse on revolutionary change that could overcome these differences to create a new world; a discourse that in its origins went back to the earliest struggles against Euro-American hegemony and colonialism around the turn of the 20th century. While the term Third World was coined after World War II, once created, it resonated with longings for alternative development that had been around much longer. As early as the turn of the 20th century Chinese radicals such as Sun Yat-sen, well aware of the rising conflict between capitalism and socialism, were already envisioning an autonomous path, 'a third way', that would provide a national alternative to the other two available paths of development. Examples of a similar consciousness may be found elsewhere, from Turkey to India. Perhaps the most clear expression of a desire for a 'third way' was expressed by Mao Zedong in 1940. He advocated a Chinese version of socialism that would serve in similarly placed societies (colonial or semi-colonial) not as a model for emulation but as a model for inspiration—for people to find their own 'third ways'.[11] It is arguable that the political consciousness that strove for alternative paths of development both underlay and informed the Third World appropriations of the term Third World once it had been coined. Rather than homogenise the societies so described, moreover, 'Third World' in this usage referred to a common experience, while recognising the diversity of the societies so described. The representation of the Third World concept (to be distinguished from the term) merely as a product of a world structured by the conflict between the first and the second worlds overlooks a complex history of the search for potential 'third worlds' as developmental and utopian projects. It also overlooks how these alternatives were marginalised, if not suppressed, by a Cold War conceptualisation of three worlds, which discounted such search for alternatives, reducing them into irrelevancies in societies that had to be headed towards either capitalism or socialism as it existed. Rather than dismiss the Third World concept, we need to consider if, with the fall of socialism, some of these alternatives have indeed made a comeback, albeit in a transformed vocabulary, reduced to nationalist alternatives rather than national liberation alternatives conditioned by a sense of belonging in a Third World.

Where positivist social science sought to render the three worlds into a description of reality, the Third World of Third Worldism was an explicitly political concept. This was most evident in the peculiar twist given to the idea by the Chinese Communist Party in the 1970s, after the break with the USSR had become public. Touted as Mao Zedong's Theory of the Three Worlds, and later elaborated by Deng Xiaoping at the 6th Special Meeting of the United Nations in 1974, the Chinese theory held that: 'The US and USSR are the First World. In the middle Japan, Europe, and Canada belong to the Second World. We are the Third World. The US and the USSR have many atomic bombs and are rich. The Third World has a large population. All Asia, except Japan, belongs to the Third World. All Africa belongs to the Third World. Latin America belongs to the Third World.'[12] Mao's notion of the Third World referred to the same global locations as in modernisation discourse. The Third World remains the same, in this usage; what changes is the composition of the First and Second Worlds, and, consequently, the relationship of these world to the Third World, with transformative consequences for all concerned. It is no longer the structure of the political economy that determines location in the Three Worlds, but political power. Under Deng, the idea would legitimise moving China towards the Second World, but still claiming radical socialist status as the move supposedly contributed to the struggle against the hegemony of the two world powers.

If the invention of the Third World in the aftermath of World War II was entangled in the struggles over hegemony and counter-hegemony for the next three decades, we need to be self-reflexive about the subsequent repudiation of the idea, which is entangled in a different kind of politics. As Pletsch put it perceptively in the conclusion to his article, 'it may be ... appropriate to put ourselves on guard against whatever new conceptual scheme may grow up to replace the three worlds than to congratulate ourselves upon having seen through modernisation theory and the three worlds'.[13] The stakes are not merely academic: they are deeply political.

The decline and fall of socialism in the 1980s on the surface has fulfilled the prediction of the modernisation paradigm where the second world is concerned. Ironically, the much-touted victory of capitalism over communism, rather than confirm the teleology of modernisation, has brought to the surface global conjunctures and disjunctures that have ruptured global spatialisations along systemic boundaries, drawn according to earlier economic and political criteria, and rendered the future even more problematic. Two criticisms of the Third World concept, informed by antithetical readings of the new world situation, are especially noteworthy.

One is that in postcolonial criticism, which has raised questions about all 'foundational' histories. So-called 'post-foundational history', in its repudiation of essence and structure and simultaneous affirmation of heterogeneity, also repudiates any fixing of the Third World subject and, therefore, of the Third World as a category. As one scholar puts it:

The rejection of those modes of thinking which configure the third world in such irreducible essences as religiosity, underdevelopment, poverty, nationhood, [and] non-Westernness ... unsettle[s] the calm presence that the essentialist categories—east and west, first world and third world—inhabit in our thought. This disruption makes it possible to treat the third world as a variety of shifting positions which have been discursively articulated in history. Viewed in this manner, the Orientalist, nationalist, Marxist, and other historiographies become visible as discursive attempts to constitute their objects of knowledge, that is, the third world. As a result, rather than appearing as a fixed and essential object, the third world emerges as a series of historical positions, including those that enunciate essentialisms.[14]

What is rejected here, it seems, is not the concept of Third World, but Third World as a fixed category, which also shifts attention from structures and structured conflicts to a politics of 'location' and 'difference'. The Third World as concept in turn appears as a discursive construct, constructed in different ways according to historical contexts and ideological dispositions.

A second criticism has been offered by Aijaz Ahmad in his critique of some of the seminal literature on the Third World. Ahmad advocates the abolition of the three worlds division on the grounds that:

we live not in three worlds but one; that this world includes the experience of colonialism and imperialism on both sides of ... [the] global divide ... that societies in formations of backward capitalism are as much constituted by the division of classes as societies in the advanced capitalist countries; that socialism is not restricted to something called 'the Second World' but is simply the name of a resistance that saturates the globe today, as capitalism itself does; that the different parts of the capitalist system are to be known not in terms of a binary opposition but as a contradictory unity—with differences, yes, but also with profound overlaps.[15]

Ahmad's repudiation of the Third World stems from a reasoning that is the antithesis of that in postcolonial criticism: the assertion of capitalism as the foundational principle that shapes the globe, uniformly if not homogeneously.

In their range, these criticisms of the Third World concept suffice to illustrate the profound analytical and political problems the concept presents. To summarise:

(a) the concept is a discursive construct that bears no 'inherent' relationship to the reality it represents, but is a product of an ideological structuring of the world into three parts. For Pletsch, primary responsibility for the construct lies with Euro-American social science, with its hegemonic assumptions about the world that are rooted in the teleology of capitalism. In a 1976 essay, Anouar Abdel-Malek had already pointed to the complicity of Third World intellectuals in sustaining such hegemony when he wrote that 'The 'Third Worldists ... the Westernised sector of the intelligentsia and of the political class ... take on, objectively, the role of "compradors" on behalf of the different hegemonic powers ... accepting the vision of themselves as the West's "Third World" '.[16] Recent criticism has been, if anything, even more insistent on questioning the instrumentality of the Third World concept in nationalism and nationalist historiography, in which Third World status privileges the nation and the national struggle as a means to overcome that status.

(b) Represented in terms of a residual category, societies included in the Third World have no autonomous existence of their own, and are placed temporally in one or another available transition from a backward to an advanced status.

(c) The Third World concept erases the heterogeneity of societies so depicted, as well as differences internal to societies. Pletsch's critique was concerned primarily with the former, without any clear specification of where differences are to be located. Postcolonial criticism insists on heterogeneity at both the international and the national levels, bringing a postmodernist sensibility to the question of difference, which ultimately resides in the politics of 'location' or 'identity'. Ahmad's criticism locates the fundamental difference at the level of classes that cut across national boundaries, which, ironically, gives primacy to intranational over international differences.

There is little in these propositions that one could quarrel with, especially in our day when, with the structural constraints of the Cold War removed, the Third World would seem to be at war with itself, boundaries between the three worlds seem to be abolished daily with the globalisation of capital, to be replaced by boundaries within individual societies, and ethnicity has come forward once again to challenge the domination of nation-states. Where class and gender conflicts are concerned, it is more difficult than ever to distinguish the local, the national and the international. Ahmad is certainly right to insist on the primary significance of classes, for with the globalisation of capital, it may be possible for the first time to speak of classes that are not just national but global. On the other hand, judging by the localisation of political struggles, so are the postcolonial critics who insist on the localisation of all categories, and the politics of location. Perhaps most telling is the appearance of 'first worlds' in the capitals of the formerly Second and Third Worlds, and of 'third worlds' in the capitals of the First.

There are serious questions, however, that disturb easy compliance in these propositions as they are stated. Does the recognition of heterogeneity necessitate the repudiation of the existence of structuring forces globally? Conversely, does it suggest a flattening out of global relations that leaves us even less able to account for global phenomena? Second, if the Third World refers to little more than historically conditioned discursive constructs, are all constructs then equally valid? Do we not need to raise the question of the political implications of alternative constructs? The Third World in its radical appropriations may hardly be attributed, as Abdel-Malek does, to a 'comprador' intelligentsia ready to be 'third-worlded' as the West's 'other'. For all its contradictions, Ella Shohat writes, the '"Third World" usefully evokes structural commonalities of struggles. The invocation of the "Third World" implies a belief that the shared history of neocolonialism and internal racism form sufficient common ground for alliances among ... diverse peoples. If one does not believe or envision such commonalities, then indeed the term "Third World" should be discarded.'[17]

The argument based on difference (accompanied by a suspicion of metanarratives and foundational categories) is quite prevalent presently with the popularity of postcolonial criticism. Insistence on heterogeneity is motivated by a critical urge but, unaccompanied by a sense of structural context, it culminates in a radical empiricism that undercuts its own call for critical understanding. Pletsch, for example, criticises the three worlds theory because 'Only if we can remember that "the other" is never defined in intrinsic terms, but always in terms of its difference from the observer, will we have the differentiated understanding of the globe's societies'. His essay does not offer an alternative analysis (or tell us at what level to understand the term 'society'), however, which leaves us with his introductory quotation from de Tocqueville that 'the Deity does not regard the human race collectively' but 'surveys at one glance and severally all the beings of whom mankind is composed; and he discerns in each man the resemblances that assimilate him to all his fellows, and the differences that distinguish him from them'.[18] This is not very helpful, because, in its empiricism, it does not even tell us whether we can compare anything beyond the individual, or why we should even stop at the level of the individual human being. Why should the Deity not survey at one glance all the nations in which humankind is organised, and discern in each resemblances and differences that may place them in larger wholes, which is the question pertinent to the issue at hand?

Pletsch's insistence on 'intrinsic terms', or the postcolonial preoccupation with 'essentialism', on the other hand, focus too exclusively on some approaches to the question of the Third World to the exclusion of others. It is possible to observe that, rather than being inherent in the Third World concept, the association with the concept of some intrinsic or essential quality may have something to do with the scientistic and teleological aspirations of social science, including Marxist social science (in search of immanent qualities for the formulation of laws), or with the obliviousness to history of Orientalist and nationalist historiographies. Those approaches associated with what is described broadly as 'world-system analysis', for example, examine the question not in terms of essences but in terms of historically changing global relationships. While it may not be free of problems in other ways, world-system analysis could hardly be held accountable in this regard; unless, of course, we are prepared to deny capitalism and nationalism as forces structuring global relations, as is the case with some versions of postcolonial criticism.

Ironically, insistence on heterogeneity without reference to structural context leads also to a homogenisation of differences, as if all differences were equally different in terms of either location or the distribution of power. Different heterogeneities (for example, differences between genders versus differences between classes), it is possible to suggest, are qualitatively different from one another, and may not be encompassed within the same 'politics of difference'. Likewise, the recognition of subjectivity to 'the other' does not in fact negate that the self and 'the other' may be placed structurally in very different power positions, which is quite often ignored these days in the application to such situations of the terminology of the market place, chief among them, 'negotiation'.

Let me hasten to add here that the 'flattening' of global relations by the insistence on heterogeneity without structure finds its counterpart in the insistence on structural unity without heterogeneity. This is the case with Ahmad's insistence on a globe under capitalism, differentiated uniformly along class lines, without reference to other differences, be they national, local, ethnic or gender. With regard to the question of the Third World, it is possible to state here that taken in reference to certain structural relationships (rather than essences), and used with due recognition of its historicity, the concept has been enabling of one set among others of important boundary distinctions in global relations, which have been erased in these recent alternatives, however valid they may be in terms of the criticisms they have directed at the concept. To speak of a Third World within the First, with due recognition of context, for instance, is not to equate the Third World in Los Angeles or Eugene, OR, with Somalia, but it does carry certain significance, and is expressive of certain relations within global capitalism.[19]

If I may return here to the question with which I started this article, there may be two major reasons for the refusal of the term to disappear from political or social science discourse. The Third World referred to a condition of life and political activity in some locations of the world, enumerated above in the quotation from Mao. There have been shifts in location and changes in the nature of the political activity, which have transformed not only the spatialisation of the term, but also the relationships of societies so designated with one another and with societies of the other 'worlds'. But the conditions of life described by the term persist in many parts of the area designated as the Third World of an earlier period—the colonial/semi-colonial—and earliest of all, Sauvy's 'first world in the chronological sense'. These conditions of life have worsened in some cases, to the point of marginalising those living them, and also spilling over the geographical boundaries dividing the Three Worlds of an earlier period, reconfiguring those boundaries. The concept becomes even more abstract than earlier in its de-territorialisation from fixed and stable geographical locations, but also acquires a concreteness in its direct association with a condition of life.

The latter is a consideration in what I think is the second reason for the persistence of the term, as an expression of a certain kind of politics, albeit one that is radically different in its goals than a Third Worldism that was directed most importantly against the colonial/capitalist societies of the First World. This politics is directed not only at transforming relations with the one hegemonic power that remains, now unrestrained with the disappearance of socialist opposition, but also with its uneasy allies in Europe, with the Second World of late Maoism and with Third World societies, whose politics seem to be caught between willing participation in a hegemonic neoliberalism and right-wing nativism, increasingly in some combination of the two. Radical liberation ideologies have receded globally with the loss of hope in the promises of socialism that earlier had nourished them. They have left in their wake suspicion of anything that smacks of utopianism—except the utopianism of capital, and atavistic promises of religious salvation, patriarchal order, ethnically pure politics, and the like, which all encourage political parochialism and epistemological nativism, along with compliance in the authoritarianism of leadership that represents or manipulates such values. I would like to elaborate further below on this situation, which I describe as 'global modernity', and on why it might endow Third Worldism with continued political significance under radically different circumstances than those that produced the idea.[20]

Global modernity

Globalisation has an ambivalent relationship to modernisation, which it has displaced from discourses of social science as well as of politics in the past two decades. The discourse of globalisation is, on the one hand, an extension of a hegemonic modernisation discourse and an even older coercive colonialism, now centred on the USA, and in service of US power. It retains a teleology of capitalist modernity patterned after the USA, and seeks now to globalise that pattern by subjecting societies world-wide to US political, military and cultural power. But the spatial extension of this paradigm of modernity, ironically, universalises the contradictions of capitalist modernity, and brings into the interior of modernity contradictions generated by the confrontation between capitalist modernity and past legacies of those societies, including the legacies of socialism. One of the important consequences is the transformation of Eurocentric modernity's temporalisation of difference (modern versus primitive, backward, pre-modern or traditional, etc) into a re-spatialisation of difference, creating different spaces of modernity that generate conflicting cultural claims to modernity. These are expressed in demands to alternative or multiple modernities (or temporalities) against a singular hegemonic modernity of an earlier period in which Euro-America appeared as the vanguard. The latter paradigm has not disappeared, needless to say, and cultural claims on modernity often overlook the important ways in which past legacies have been transformed in their confrontation by a Eurocentric modernity, even if those confrontations also played a major part in the formulation of the latter. But few would deny that there is a new sense of cultural empowerment among societies that have been successful players in the globalisation of capital, which almost inevitably has translated into cultural capital in claims to cultural particularity in the midst of cultural homogenisation. This is the condition that I describe as 'global modernity', in the singular, in which differences represent not alternative or multiple modernities but contradictions within a singular modernity. Nevertheless, these contradictions are powerful enough to disrupt the confident assertion of any dominant teleology, which points not to a multiplicity of modernities but to the loss of any direction to modernity, other than the defence and perpetuation of existing configurations of power. Modernity, like Eurocentrism, lies in ruins at the very moment of its global victory.

Reconceptualising modernity (to the point of renouncing it altogether) has been the goal of much scholarship during this same period: cutting across ideological and methodological divides. The effort to overcome Eurocentrism, and to bring into modernity the voices, experiences and cultural legacies of others has driven discussions of modernity in fields that range from postcolonial studies to more conventional studies of modernisation in sociology and political science. Most revisionist studies of modernity and modernisation project upon the past contemporary perspectives of globality, and argue that modernity has all along been global in scope, plural in form and direction, and hybrid not only across cultural boundaries but also in the relationship of the modern to the traditional. I do not question these conclusions. I nevertheless suggest that there is much to be gained in clarity from viewing 'global modernity' as a period concept, to contrast it with a preceding period, which for all its complexities was indeed marked by Euro/American domination and hegemony. The nearly unchallenged present US domination of the world is a continuation of the power relations of modernity, but in a world that has been transformed significantly in its economic and political configurations. For all the concentration of naked power, this world, when compared with a previous period of modernity dominated by Euro-America, is de-centred ideologically and organisationally, including in the emergent values and organisations of political economy; which makes it possible to speak of 'globalcentrism' against an earlier Eurocentrism.[21]

Modernity has been globalising all along, but the realisation of global modernity was obstructed by two products of capitalist modernity itself: colonialism and socialism. Decolonisation has since World War II restored the voices of the colonised and opened the way for the recognition of the spatial and temporal co-presence of those whom a Eurocentric modernisation discourse had relegated to invisibility and backwardness. Decolonisation owed much to socialism as ideology, and the presence of socialist states. But so long as socialism persisted as a viable alternative to capitalism, the effects of decolonisation were dissolved into the teleologies of Eurocentrically conceived modernity. The decline and fall of socialism in the course of the 1980s opened the way to the globalisation of capital. It also eliminated socialism as a crucial obstacle to cultural appropriations—and, therefore, the proliferation—of modernities, which now finds expression in the fragmentation of a single modernity into multiple and alternative modernities. Questioning Eurocentric teleology in either the capitalist or the socialist guise has revealed modernity in its full historicity, and 'geohistorical' diversity, which is a condition of what I describe here as global modernity.[22]

It was capitalist modernity that produced the societies—as we have them presently—that now make their own claims on modernity against Euro-American domination. The disappearance of the socialist alternative to capitalism may be one important reason for the ascendancy in these claims of arguments based on cultural autonomy or persistence. But so is the globalisation of capital in the emergence of new centres of corporate capital, most importantly in East and Southeast Asia, in the increasingly diverse labour force that staffs transnational corporations, and in the transnationalisation of marketing and advertising; these create new cultural faultlines that call for close management of culture. Culture looms large in contemporary scholarship and politics, as it is deployed in a number of capacities: in opposition to modernity, in explanations of local appropriations of the modern, or in its newfound significance as an instrument of political and corporate management. This new situation is a product of modernity; but it needs to be recognised nevertheless for the new kinds of contradictions it presents, which differentiate it from a period of Eurocentric modernity. Global modernity unifies and divides the globe in new ways. It does not do to emphasise one or the other; as with naive ideas of global unity expressed in slogans of globalisation, or obscurantist notions of conflict that see the world fracturing along 'cultural' divides impervious to all common political and economic activity, as well as to the pervasiveness of class, gender and various spatial divisions that cut across 'cultural' boundaries.

Global modernity gives the kiss of death to the idea of Three Worlds. The temporality that was built into the three worlds idea is no more. While the language of civilisation and primitivism has made a comeback recently, especially in justification of US imperialism in Western Asia, it is no longer convincing to deny 'coevalness' to the many peoples who inhabit the globe.[23] Even more important than the Third World in this regard is the reassertion of indigenous subjectivities in global politics and culture, and the recognition in many quarters of the First itself that these subjectivities may be crucial to human survival in general.

Yet more significant may be the spatialities of global modernity. The spaces implied by Mao Zedong's theory of Three Worlds back in the 1970s have been fragmented and reconfigured. The Second World is no more, except as memory and nostalgia, although traces of socialist legacy continue to disturb complacent assertions of the incorporation of post-socialist societies into global capitalism. Of the tri-continental three worlds that Mao enumerated, only Africa remains as a continental Third World. Asia and Latin America are fractured among those that have made it into incorporation into global capitalism, and those who are increasingly marginalised in the operations of the global economy. Such fracturing applies to divisions between and within individual nations. Third World societies have been at war with one another since the very beginnings of decolonisation, which has done much to discredit Third Worldism from its origins. Even more important in the long run have been the systemic transformations that have been increasingly global in scope. East and Southeast Asian societies in particular have played a crucial part in the emergence of global modernity, and the end of the three worlds. It was the rapid incorporation of these societies (including 'socialist' China) into global capitalism from the late 1970s that gave rise to the ideologies of globalisation, rendered irrelevant a tri-continental Third World idea, and hastened the end of socialism by demonstrating third world capabilities for development under the aegis of capitalism. Equally important are divisions within individual societies in incorporation into global capitalism. Significant sectors in Third World societies have become players in global economy and politics, and are properly located in First World spaces, while the majority in many of these societies continue to survive in an earlier Third World condition or worse. The emergence of a global class participating in common activities, subject to the political, and increasingly cultural, contradictions generated by these activities, is a major reason for speaking of global modernity. Of the three worlds of modernisation discourse, the only one that seemingly remains intact, and has expanded its scope, is the First World. And yet this world, too, is fractured once again, as the recent division between the USA and Europe has demonstrated. Expansion of the scope of the First World also has introduced new contradictions into it, in claims to alternative modernities and 'different cultures of capitalism'.

The reconfiguration of global spaces has been apparent most clearly on the occasion of the recent military adventures of the USA. In the 1991 Gulf war the USA was able to put together a coalition that included representatives from all the three worlds. In the most recent US attack on Iraq, the war divided the USA from powerful members of the former First and Second Worlds, but enabled alliances with a number of Third World societies, which the US administration proudly touted as representing all the continents, all kinds of races and colours, and all manner of political orientations. Last, but not least, cultural fragmentation globally is in the midst of apparent homogenisation. This is apparent in the revival of cultural traditions that modernisation discourse had relegated to being swept aside in the course of the modernisation process. The 'traditions' that were crucial to arguments of modernisation discourse, that were criticised by critics of the discourse, have made a comeback with a vengeance, now promoted not by a hegemonic social science but by those who were the objects of that social science, Third Worlders themselves. The difference is that such cultural revivalism is restricted not only to the Third World, but also to the formerly Second and presently First Worlds. What seems to be emerging globally is a repudiation of the 'Eurocentrism' of universalist Enlightenment ideals of modernity, or the restriction of those ideals to narrow spaces of economy and technology, accompanied by a reassertion of inherited cultural legacies in everyday life, even in the production of social and political knowledge. These developments might appear on the surface to be the kind of corrections demanded by the 'nominalism' advocated by Pletsch against the generalisations of the Three Worlds scheme, or by Abdel-Malek's complaints about Third World intellectuals complicit in their 'third-worlding'. The outcome in practice, however, is hardly in accord with what they might have had in mind, because what has issued from these recent transformations is an epistemological nativism, which postulates in defiance of time and space the existence of an intimate relationship between national and ethnic cultural legacies and the foundations for acceptable systems of knowledge and values. The result at best is a naive relativism, which glosses over global commonalities in the functioning of political economy and power, and asserts against universal ideas parochial values that lend themselves, so it seems, to purposes of social order and control. It is immune to critique from the outside, as a thoroughgoing relativism by definition rules out the outside as a source of significant knowledge. At its worst, epistemological nativism serves as an excuse for suppressing difference, as well as serving as a cover for legacies of oppression and exploitation by rejecting as alien any challenge to those legacies, in some cases by rendering knowledge and ethical values into functions of biological endowment, further contributing to the proliferation of racialised world politics. Judging by available evidence of its spread around the globe, such epistemological nativism is perfectly consistent with—and abets—the globalisation of capital.

Claims for the universality of modern Euro-American values are by no means a thing of the past. And there is some justification for those claims. The values generated by Euro-American capitalist modernity (the bad as well as the good) are now globally diffused, have transformed the perception of inherited legacies, and are internal to the cultural constitution of societies globally. But, while this was widely recognised, and promoted for emulation, by modernisers (including socialist modernisers) in an earlier period of Eurocentric modernity, it has become highly suspect in a period of global modernity, when native values suppressed under the regime of the former have surfaced with great power, especially where they have been empowered by successes in the political and the cultural economy. The past 20 years have witnessed calls for the 'sinicisation' and 'islamicisation' of sociology. There has been a revival in the People's Republic of China of the so-called 'national studies', which advocates a return not only to the epistemologies but to the methodologies of classical studies. The attacks on history and science of thinkers such as Vandana Shiva, Ashis Nandy and Vine Deloria, Jr gain a hearing in the most hallowed organs and institutions of Euro-American learning. While the effect of such criticism is felt most deeply in the humanities and the social sciences, as abstract a field as mathematics is under some pressure to recognise 'ethno-mathematics' as a legitimate area of study. Even US foundations have joined the chorus of criticism against the equation of modernity with Western ways of knowing.[24]

Conclusion: spectres of the Third World

If use of the term Third World under circumstances of global modernity is to make any sense, the term has to differ significantly from the meaning it carried earlier, and in some ways go against the global spaces to which it once referred. The term still refers to those who are 'the first world in the chronological sense', to the billions whose inherited suffering has been compounded by marginalisation in the world economy and their abandonment by transnationalised elites. The global economy may still be dominated by the capitalist First World, but it requires for its successful transnationalisation the participation of elites globally, underlining the emergence of global class interests that bridge ethnic, national, 'religious–civilisational', and other cultural differences, as well as the erstwhile Three Worlds. The majority populations become localised, at the mercy of the vagaries of transnationalisation. These marginal populations are not distributed according to some neat geographical scheme of 'three worlds'; they also cut across any such boundaries, although by far the great majority live in areas designated earlier as Third World—Africa, Asia and Latin America. The term also continues to express faith in the possibility of collective politics, representing the interest and welfare of the populations to which it refers against the evidence of ethnic and national fracturing; a naive faith, perhaps, but at least the source of some hope. If the term is to retain a convincing critical edge, moreover, Third Worldism can no longer be restricted in its politics to struggle against the legacies of colonialism, but must also target the legacies that led to the corruption of earlier leaders of the Third World, and those that are in the process of generating forces of reaction globally. Finally, against epistemological nativism, the term recalls the epistemological polyphony captured eloquently by Wright in his depiction of what he witnessed in Bandung in 1955. This, too, may seem unlikely at the present moment of global predicament, but it is necessary to overcoming confinement between a hegemonic Eurocentrism, and a counter-hegemonic but reactionary epistemological nativism. Odd as it seems, the Third

World may still serve to open up new possibilities of dialogical engagement that may be crucial to realising the promise of a genuinely global modernity.

Notes

1   A Dirlik, 'Three worlds, or one, or many: the reconfiguration of global relations under global capitalism', *Nature, Society and Thought*, 7 (1), 1995, pp 19–42.

2   CE Pletsch, 'The three worlds, or the division of social scientific labour, circa 1950–1975', *Comparative Studies in Society and History*, 23 (4), 1981, pp 565–590.

3   Quoted in *ibid*, p 569.

4   Pletsch, 'The three worlds', pp 571–572

5   *Ibid*, p 572.

6   R Wright, *The Colour Curtain: A Report on the Bandung Conference*, New York: World Publishing Co, 1956, pp 175–176.

7   R Malley, *The Call from Algeria: Third Worldism, Revolution and the Turn to Islam*, Berkeley, CA: University of California Press, 1996, p 2.

8   MT Berger, 'The end of the "Third World"?', *Third World Quarterly*, 15 (2), 1994, pp 257–275.

9   Pletsch, 'The three worlds', p 573.

10 I owe 'mobilisation myth' to A Woodside, 'The Asia–Pacific idea as mobilisation myth', in A Dirlik (ed), *What is in a Rim? Critical Perspectives on the Pacific Region Idea*, Lanham, MD: Rowman and Littlefield, 1997. For a study of interactions between radical Asian intellectuals in the creation of radical discourses around the turn of the 20th century, see RA Karl, *Staging the World: Chinese Nationalism at the Turn of the Twentieth Century*, Durham, SC: Duke University Press, 2002.

11 Mao Zedong, *Selected Works*, Vol 2, *On New Democracy*, Beijing: Foreign Languages Press, 1965, pp 339–394.

12 These were reportedly Mao Zedong's words to President Kaunda of Zambia on the occasion of the latter's state visit to the PRC in February 1974. Cited in B Chen, 'Changes in China's international strategy and goals for the new Millennium', talk at the Institute for the Study of Diplomacy, Georgetown University, May 1998, available at http://ciaonet.org/wps.bog01, p 3.

13 Pletsch, 'The three worlds', p 589.

14 G Prakash, 'Writing post-Orientalist histories of the Third World: perspectives from Indian historiography', *Comparative Studies in Society and History*, 32, 1990, pp 383–408.

15 A Ahmad, *In Theory: Classes, Nations, Literatures*, London: Verso Books, 1992, p 103.

16 A Abdel-Malek, 'The Third World and the Orient', in Abdel-Malek, *Civilisations and Social Theory*, Albany, NY: State University of New York, 1981, pp 130–138.

17 E Shohat, 'Notes on the "post-colonial" ', *Social Text*, 31–32, p 111.

18 Pletsch, 'The three worlds', p 590.

19 For further discussion of this idea, see A Dirlik, 'Global modernity: modernity in an age of global capitalism', *European Journal of Social Theory* (in press).

20 My insistence on the singular is to make sure of a difference between 'global modernity' and 'global modernities'. The latter has not been particularly successful against the fascination with globalisation (which may be the fate of any challenge to that idea presently, given its service to various ideological purposes). See M Featherstone, S Lash & R Robertson, *Global Modernities*, London: Sage, 1995.

21 F Coronil, 'Towards a critique of globalcentrism: speculations on capitalism's nature', *Public Culture*, 12 (2), 2000, pp 351–74.

22 For 'geohistorical', see PJ Taylor, *Modernities: A Geohistorical Interpretation*, Minneapolis, MN: University of Minnesota Press, 1999. Historicity in my usage is not quite the same as 'geohistory', as I denote by it both the spatial and the temporal dimensions of location.

23 J Fabian, *Time and the Other: How Anthropology Makes its Object*, New York: Columbia University Press, 1983, p 41.

24 For the 'sinicisation' of sociology, see Cai Yongmei and Xiao Xinhuang, *Shehuixue Zhongguohua (Sinicization of Sociology)*, Taipei: juliu tushu gongsi, 1985. Islamicisation of sociology is discussed in Nilufer Gule, 'Snapshots of Islamic modernities', *Daedalus*, 129 (1), 2000, pp 112–113. See also Park Myoung-Kyu & Chang Kyung-sup, 'Sociology between Western theory and Korean reality: accommodation, tension, and a search for alternatives', *International Sociology*, 14 (2), 1999, pp 139–156. Shiva, Nandy and Deloria, Jr are the authors of many works. For representative titles, see V Shiva, *Staying Alive: Women, Ecology and Development*, London: Zed Books, 1989; A Nandy, 'History's forgotten doubles', *History and Theory*, 34 (2), 1995, pp 44–67; and V Deloria, Jr, *Red Earth, White Lies: Native Americans and the Myth of Scientific Fact*, Golden, CO: Fulcrum Publishing, 1997. For recent discussions of knowledge systems with reference to Pacific studies, see R Borofsky (ed), *Remembrance of Pacific*

Pasts: An Invitation to Remake History, Honolulu, HI: University of Hawai'i Press, 2000. For ethno-mathematics, see E Greene, 'Ethnomathematics: a step toward peace?', *Dialogue* (Duke University), 15 (9), 20 October 2000. For foundations, see J Heilbrunn, 'The news from everywhere: does global thinking threaten local knowledge? The Social Science Research Council debates the future of area studies', *Lingua Franca*, May–June 1996. Nandy and Deloria, Jr were distinguished speakers at the Duke University Pivotal Ideas series in Spring 2000 and Spring 2001, respectively. For a discussion of these challenges in relation to modernity, see A Dirlik, 'Reading Ashis Nandy: the return of the past or modernity with a vengeance', in Dirlik, *Postmodernity's Histories: The Past as Legacy and Project*, Boulder, CO: Rowman and Littlefield, 2000, pp 119–141.

The empire of capital and the remaking of centre–periphery relations

FOUAD MAKKI

Of all the notions that underpin the idea of the Third World, none is more pervasive and yet more elusive than 'development'. Everyone has some sense of its meaning, but until recently, few had made a serious effort to historicise it.[1] Development was imagined to hold unparalleled opportunities for human advancement, and an evocation of the concept was likely to bring to mind odd snatches and memories of collective endeavours to overcome hunger, disease, poverty and inequality. The captivating desire of its widely diffused meaning was 'human liberation from poverty and want, from oppression, from violence, from the drudgery of monotonous and stultifying work'.[2] Since the 1950s the idea of development has been paired with the concept of a Third World which was itself a portmanteau category encompassing many different societies and cultures. Notwithstanding the evident simplification and homogenisation involved in the concept of a Third World, its juxtaposition to the Second and First Worlds carried questions of global inequality into the international arena. Development thus acquired world-wide significance not as an abstract concept but as a way of making sense of global inequalities in an era marked by cold war rivalry and an interstate system moving towards the formal equality of nation-states. Moreover, unlike the static categories of Third, Second and First Worlds, development was supposed to be the dynamic process of transition from one to the other.

Yet this conventional wisdom about relations of global inequality takes as given the very categories that need to be explained, and is apt to obscure the historical process through which these categories were created. Both logically and historically the 'First World' and 'development' assume the currency of 'Third World' and 'underdevelopment': the condition of the one was largely the creation of the other. It was European overseas expansion between the 16th and 20th centuries that fatefully harnessed separate and distinct worlds into an unequally integrated 'empire of capital'.[3] The resulting world system created the spatial context for the consolidation of capitalism, and the complex social and economic distortions that we now term underdevelopment were themselves provoked by the forces unleashed in these centuries. The new world order, with Europe situated at its centre, was structured by a multi-dimensional polarisation—economic, political and cultural. Its dominant constitutive social relations were always contested, and the modes of rule and hegemonic forms of legitimation varied across space and time. Yet, over the centuries, Europe represented the difference between itself and those it incorporated into its global order through a series of antithetical oppositions: 'noble' and 'savage', 'civilised' and 'primitive', 'coloniser' and 'colonised', 'modern' and 'backward'. The categories of 'First' and 'Third' worlds, and 'developed' and 'underdeveloped' worlds, represented mid-20th century crystallisations of this long-term imperial relationship.

Today, as the distinctions between 'centre' and 'periphery' are once again changing and, as capital becomes increasingly mobile and fluid, processes of uneven development are radically destabilising any composite notion of the Third World. While ruling elites in the Third World become ever more integrated into world-wide circuits of finance and trade, large sections of the populations in the metropolises of the First World are becoming socially marginalised. In this new historical era, in which a whole set of conventional beliefs about the Third World and development have been placed in doubt, a critical examination of the genesis and transformation of development and the Third World has become a necessity. This article is an attempt to examine the historical conjuncture that gave Third World development its particular epochal salience. It argues that, although the concept of development was not new, the infrastructure of development—what I have here called the framework of development—was created on foundations built in the turbulent era between the 1930s and 1950s that culminated with the appearance of the Third World. Its emergence following this period of profound crisis in the world system was an expression of a dramatic alteration in the relationship between metropole and colony. The framework of development and the Third World were articulated and consolidated at the crossroads of three world-historical processes. First, there was the collapse of *laissez-faire* and the idea of a 'self-regulating market' during the Great Depression, and the consolidation of 'national economies' in the wake of the disintegration of the multinational empires in eastern and central Europe and the Near East. Second, there was the crisis and eventual demise of European overseas empires under challenge from anti-colonial movements, and the complex process of decolonisation that ensued. Finally, there was the ascendancy of US global hegemony following the two world wars, and the simultaneous political and ideological bifurcation of the global order around the USSR and the USA. Each process had its own history and dynamic, and the intersection of these distinct but overlapping processes was a matter of historical contingency. The over-determined outcome was nonetheless the creation of a new geopolitical and institutional framework through which global hierarchies could be articulated. Examining the development framework along these lines requires an appreciation of the spatially combined but temporally uneven rhythms of historical processes. Such an approach arguably makes possible a more searching reassessment of the making and unmaking of the development framework, and provides an important historical vantage point from which to survey the current dynamics of centre–periphery relations.[4]

British hegemony and *laissez-faire*

The period from 1815 to 1915 has retroactively been dubbed the age of British hegemony. Within Britain it was born of a pragmatic recognition that England could no longer be agriculturally self-sufficient. It represented a move away from the protectionist position embodied by the 1815 Corn Laws towards an acceptance of an economic and foreign policy based upon manufactures and free trade. Within Europe it was underscored by the settlement of Vienna (1815) following the Napoleonic Wars and the defeat of Britain's main rival, France.[5] From a global perspective Britain's imperial expansion and plunder sealed the supremacy of British industry and navy over its continental European as well as extra-European rivals.

Britain's status as the premier naval power and the 'workshop of the world' inaugurated the era of free-trade imperialism, allowing it to pose as the guardian of 'free trade' for the remainder of the 19th century. The imposition of the gold standard as the pivot of a liberalised world trade subordinated mercantilist policy to currency stability, forcing states to internalise the exigencies of world commerce through budgetary priorities. *Laissez-faire* remained hegemonic for the better part of a century and found conceptual support in the late 18th century writings of Adam Smith as well as the 19th century neoclassical economists. Smith had argued that 'the propensity to truck, barter, and exchange', and the pursuit of rational self-interest, would in the aggregate lead to specialised production for exchange and a general division of labour as individuals sought to make use of their distinctive productive capacities. This would in turn bring about lower-cost production and stimulate an increase in productivity. All this would augment the wealth of nations and lead them through a progression of stages from agriculture to industry to commerce.

The advent of Marginalism, conceived by Alfred Marshall at the end of the 19th century, marked the birth of an economic science ostensibly free from political and sociological variables. Neoclassical equilibrium theory professed to represent a pure logic of the market, and its optimism about economic growth was formulated as a critique of mercantilism and the notion of a national economy. According to Hobsbawm, 'economic theory was thus elaborated uniquely on the basis of individual units of enterprise—persons or firms—rationally maximising their gains and minimising their losses in a market which had no specific spatial extension. At the limit it was, and could not but be, the world market.'[6]

Laissez-faire was only one, albeit dominant, economic doctrine. Alternative protectionist conceptions of the economy were also present, particularly in the so-called late-industrialising countries. In the USA the federalist Alexander Hamilton advocated protectionism and a strong national government. The American debates, in turn, inspired the German nationalist Friedrich List, for whom protectionism was not a goal in itself but a temporary policy that would allow a country to build a strong economy through industrialisation and 'prepare its entry into the universal society of the future'.[7] However, for much of the 19th century these ideas remained in a subordinate position, gaining wider currency during the interwar years following the collapse of *laissez-faire* and the polyglot dynastic empires.

The late 19th century marked the high point of Pax Britannica. Thereafter, transformations in the relative economic strength of the USA and Germany deepened the competitive pressures on British military and industrial supremacy, precipitating a crisis that was manifested politically in World War I and economically in the Great Depression. The political crisis paved the way for the economic crisis. The war had left European nations in deep debt, and to rebuild their economies they borrowed heavily from the USA. Many small businesses and some weak governments were unable to make their debt payments and defaulted on their loans. The consequent collapse of banks and other financial institutions led to panic in the international monetary system. On 24 October 1929 the US stock market collapsed, plunging the global financial and trading system into crisis. The downward spiral of the world economy led to a tightening of commercial policy and the passing of the Hawley–Smoot Tarriff Act by the US Congress, which produced the largest duty increases in international trade history. This in turn provoked a wave of protectionism and a massive contraction of international trade. By the third quarter of 1932 the trade of European countries had fallen to below 40% of its 1929 level.[8]

The crisis revealed that there was no lender of last resort and in 1931, amid competitive devaluations, both Britain and the USA abandoned the gold standard. The world economy fractured into rival currency blocs, and a whole battery of restrictions on trade was initiated to shield domestic economies from external influences. Any prospect of general co-operation to revive international trade ended at the 1933 World Economic Conference, when the USA announced that it was going to ensure the restoration of equilibrium in its domestic economy before worrying about stability in the international order. Unprecedented levels of debt, over-production, and a rapid rise in unemployment followed the abandoning of the gold standard, which was the linchpin of the 'self-regulating' market. The 'snapping of the golden thread', as Polanyi called it, decisively buried the British-led 19th century world economy.[9] Protectionism became rampant, the pursuit of stable currencies was abandoned, and 'world capitalism retreated into the igloos of its nation-state economies and their associated empires'.[10]

The economic crisis, together with the intensification of nationalisms accompanying the dissolution of the Ottoman, Habsburg, Hohenzollern, and Romanov empires, created a new context within which to re-imagine the relationship between state and economy. The depression had convinced many politicians and their economic advisers that the pure logic of the market could no longer be relied on to ensure stability and growth. It was a 'canyon which henceforth made a return to 1913 not merely impossible, but unthinkable. Old-fashioned liberalism was dead or doomed.'[11] As the monetary system fell apart, and the social orders that it underpinned lost their coherence, the notion of the economy as a self-contained and internally dynamic totality, separate from other economies and subject to state intervention, began to crystallise. In his *General Theory of Employment, Interest, and Money*, John Maynard Keynes exposed the fallacies of *laissez-faire* liberalism and argued that the market could not always correct itself, and therefore state intervention was necessary to stimulate the economy, create jobs and manage the money supply. The abstraction of the market, which was the normative construct of pre-Keynesian economics, was here replaced with the 'economic system as a whole', a system whose limits corresponded to specific geopolitical boundaries.[12]

These conceptual shifts found their anchor in a new role for the state, as the parallel development of state planning in its Leninist, Keynesian and fascist forms all represented novel attempts to bound economic processes within specifically circumscribed spheres. As part of an enhanced role in the economy, states were critical in devising various instruments and controls for measuring and representing economic processes. A series of aggregates (production, employment, investment and consumption) and averages (interest rate, price level and real wages) gave the idea of the economy an expressive totality whose unspecified referent was the nation-state. Around the same time, Simon Kuznets systematised a method for estimating national income, while econometrics attempted to create mathematical representations of the 'national economy'. The subsequent elaboration and generalisation of what came to be called the gross national product (GNP) of each economy made it possible to represent the size, structure and growth of this new, self-enclosed entity.[13] These developments provided a set of conceptual categories through which the economy was envisioned as a spatially bounded structure subject to 'national regulation'. Whereas *laissez-faire* had been a mechanism for taking the state cognitively out of the economy, 20th century nationalisms and Keynesian demand management constituted the nation-state as the prime mover of the economy.

The next step was the emergence of growth theory outside the old equilibrium framework, and development economics first emerged within this sub-disciplinary field.[14] In post-depression Latin America, the structuralist economists headed by Raúl Prebisch and housed in the Economic Commission for Latin America (ECLA), were one of the first groups of economists to focus on 'development'. The ECLA thesis, which was also shared by economists from other parts of the world such as the Romanian Mihail Manoilescu and the Polish-born Paul Rosenstein-Rodan, emphasised the unequal nature of trade between an industrial, hegemonic centre and an agrarian, dependent periphery. In order to transform and rectify this structural disadvantage, they advocated import substitution industrialisation.[15] The ECLA theses found political resonance in the new social alliances that were coming to rule parts of Latin America. Although they had managed to stay out of World War I, the Latin American countries could not escape the Great Depression as their economies were caught between the anvil of shrinking markets and the hammer of drastic shortages of credit. The severe economic crisis and contraction of world trade to a third of its pre-crisis level became a forcing-house for a social recomposition of the ruling elites. As neither merchants nor exporting agriculturalists could continue to occupy the privileged position they previously enjoyed, new populist coalitions of nationalists and industrialists came to power.

Once freed from the sanction of the world market, these populist coalitions were able to subsume foreign trade under national political priorities. They looked towards domestic rather than foreign markets as an engine of growth, and promoted a strategy of industrialisation through the production of consumer goods for the home market. This strategy led to 'rapid industrialization, and infant industries demanded protection against primarily Yankee competition'.[16] Outside Latin America, some states in the Middle East pursued similar policies of import substitution industrialisation.[17] But in the rest of the global periphery most countries were still dominated by a handful of imperial powers, and the interstate system was primarily a system of empires. It was the extinction of these empires and the consolidation of an international system of nation-states that eventually furnished the necessary framework for an extension of the idea of 'national development.'

From colonial empires to three worlds of development

Throughout the 19th and early 20th centuries, European colonial expansion had been defended by reference to the superiority of Western civilisation *vis-à-vis* the rest of the world. The ideology of the 'civilising mission' was a late 19th century justification of imperial domination, and it had underpinned colonial rule up to the mid-20th century, when it finally fell into disrepute. A combination of political self-affirmation by the colonised, as well as the experience of two world wars, decisively shattered the self-congratulatory spell of this Eurocentric world order. Nineteenth century moral certainties of imperial mission never recovered from the shell shock they received on the battlefields of Europe and in the urban and rural revolts of the colonies. If Europeans were the most civilised and conscientious beings ever to grace this earth, how then to explain the carnage of the world wars, and the violent conquest, colonisation and destruction of the indigenous cultures and ecology of large numbers of this planet's peoples, by these very same Europeans?

With this fatal blow to the self-serving civilising mission, science and technological know-how became the new 'measure of man', providing the key ingredients for late colonial hegemony.[18] The mastery over nature, which was the essence of the Western scientific ethos, became the new key to the mastery of empire. Because science and technology were viewed as neutral, they could be advanced with confidence, quite unlike the ethnocentric ideologies of cultural chauvinism or racial superiority. Based on Enlightenment ideals of progress, they offered a seemingly more plausible basis for assertions of imperial hege-mony and opened the door to subsequent theories of modernisation. Frederick Cooper and Randall Packard have convincingly argued that, in this new geopolitical configuration, hegemonic knowledge was recast in order to make 'sense' of the new global order. The opposition between 'civilised' and 'primi-tive', which had been intrinsic to justifying colonisation at the height of imperial incorporation, was no longer viable. The formerly colonised had to be brought out of the dialectics of colonial difference into a universalising discourse. 'Development' was in this respect crucial in reconfiguring the global identity of ex-colonies in a way that was incorporative and universalistic yet still hierarchi-cal. It not only defined the terms in which exploitation and relative inequality were understood, but also provided the promise of a future beyond colonialism. Unlike the ideology of the 'civilising mission', development appealed to and was seized by nationalist leaders who saw in it a project that only a society that had rid itself of colonialism could accomplish.[19]

The initial systemic push for the expansion of colonial economies came in the context of a crisis of empire, and had as its aim the alleviation of the metropoles' war debts and the creation of a stable framework for continued imperial rule. The European world had entered the 1930s depression only a decade after relative peace. More than 60 million men were involved in the armed conflict of World War I and, when the armistice was signed in November 1918, Europe had to deal with severe population losses, widespread devastation, financial and political disorganisation, and a serious reduction in civilian output. Analogous circumstances in the British and French empires led to more-or-less similar proposals and commitments of metropolitan funds, culminating in the British Colonial Development and Welfare Act of 1940; and the French *Fonds d'Investissement et Développement Economique et Social des Territoires d'Outre-Mer* of 1946. Colonial administrations were urged to expand commodity production and tie output and trade more directly to metropolitan interests. Large-scale investments in raw materials production were made in the context of an extension of the economic role of the colonial state. As Lord Hailey, the one-time head of the Colonial Research Advisory Committee pointed out, this represented 'the translation into the Colonial sphere of … a new concept which had come to be increasingly accepted in domestic politics, the doctrine, namely, that active state intervention was a necessary lever to the amelioration of social conditions'.[20]

The project of social and economic development in a colonial context nevertheless proved immensely contradictory. Premised on a distorted view of colonial backwardness, and sapped by social conflicts that were fostered by the very projects intended to avert them, colonial development generated expecta-tions it could not meet. Ultimately, most of the projects failed, helping to underscore the anti-colonial contention that only a society that had rid itself of colonialism could complete the project of modernity. According to HS Wilson:

> The disasters of British and French efforts at state-induced colonial development during the late 1940s and early 1950s forced them to reassess their policies. Their prestige as imperial rulers was damaged in the eyes of their own metropolitan publics and their colonial officials ... and, not least, their African subjects for whom the myth of the white man's wisdom was weakened by such crass ineptitude.[21]

The need to find a new material basis for continued colonial rule, which had served as an impetus for a more interventionist colonial state, focused social conflicts directly on the state itself. After a slight economic recovery following the depression years, there was an upsurge of labour mobilisation in the urban centres of the colonies. The continent of Africa alone witnessed general strikes in Mombassa in 1939 and 1947, mine strikes in the copper belt in 1938 and 1940, a general strike in Nigeria in 1945, riots in the Gold Coast in 1948, strike waves in Dakar in 1936–37 and again in 1945–46, and the famous French West African railway strike of 1947–48. These strikes were reverberations of a movement that began in the Caribbean when a series of riots hit the oil fields of Trinidad and the plantations of Jamaica. Ferocious colonial violence in India, Indonesia, Vietnam and Malaysia during the 1930s and 1940s further accentuated the overall crisis of empire.

The strike wave came as a shock to imperial officials, who saw it as a serious threat to the wartime empire. Deepening civil conflict and serious challenges to colonial rule forced them to recognise the need to increase living standards in order to mollify labour and improve productivity. As Frederick Cooper makes clear in his groundbreaking study of the labour question in French and British Africa, the focus on social and economic development legitimated the European standard of living as a reference point for the aspirations of the colonised. Organised workers were well positioned to take advantage of imperial interests in a stable environment for accumulation to push for their own demands. They did so in terms of the conceptual scheme that colonial officials themselves were employing: if workers in the colonies were supposed to behave like industrial workers in the metropole, they should be rewarded as such. As workers made claims for better wages and social benefits that were commensurate with those in the metropole, their demands successfully inverted the universalising discourse of the imperial state back against itself. Politically too, the French attempt to re-imagine empire by promoting a policy of 'assimilation' into the *Union Française* witnessed a similar dialectic of appropriation and subversion. During the 1944 Brazzaville Conference, delegates from the colonies demanded a change in their status from subjects into citizens, with all the social entitlements accruing to the political category of citizenship, thereby laying bare the limitations of imperial claims to inclusivity.[22]

The developmentalist rationale for late colonial rule brought to the fore the underlying contradictions in the entire colonial project. As David Washbrook points out in relation to the 1935 *Government of India Act*, imperial strategy had been designed to:

> extend representation and promote economic growth without, apparently, changing

any of the basic relations of power and wealth constructed under its long period of rule. Democracy and development here were meant to be imprisoned within the structures of the colonial past.[23]

At the same time, the emphasis on applying the universal laws of social science left less and less room for the colonial representatives of European civilisation, whose claim to authority was based on the ethnocentric fantasy that they embodied 'civilisation' in their very being. In the end, under attack from labour and nationalist movements across Africa and Asia, imperial certainty in the function of empire was shaken, and officials retreated and sought ways of disengagement. A pragmatic turn towards designing policies within the framework of particular colonial states was an expression of this retreat. The doctrine of indirect rule was conveniently reasserted, in order 'to break away from making the relevant unit be the empire, and the concept that all workers—and perhaps all citizens or subjects—from Wales to Kiambu, from the Touraine to the Niger Bend, were part of the same polity and had claim on the same basis to imperial resources'.[24]

The combined political and social conflicts of the period decisively challenged the fundamental premise of colonial rule. Across much of Asia, World War II had already unsettled the prewar empires, and once rid of the Japanese occupation, the peoples of liberated Asian territories fought to prevent the restoration of European colonialism. In Africa too, the years after World War II brought increasing pressure for decolonisation, as returning African soldiers swelled the ranks of anti-colonial movements.[25] The inclusionary and exclusionary dynamics of colonial imaginings paradoxically provided nationalist movements with the political and conceptual framework with which to mobilise and eventually bring down the colonial state. Ultimately, it was these contradictory pressures, rather than the awakening of any ethical consciousness, that ended the colonial empires.

Pax Americana, national development and the three worlds

As the catastrophe of World War II was nearing its end, US policy planners had been busy working on a project to shape the postwar system of power. Coming to the rescue of a Europe on the verge of being overrun by fascism and subsequently confronting an ascendant USSR, the USA was in a unique position to impose its vision of the new world order on the old colonial powers. World War I had already revealed the real relationship of forces between the various imperialist powers, and the entente won the war against Germany in part because of the US intervention. A similar pattern was to be repeated following World War II, when the UK again escaped defeat largely thanks to its pact with the USSR and the USA. Economically, too, World War II had enabled the USA to overcome the effects of the depression and to become the dominant creditor of all the other capitalist states. Wartime contracts and expenditures made it possible for the US government to promote scientific and technical research, which in turn became the basis for further growth in productivity through automation and the harnessing of atomic energy.

The demonstration of US power in war together with an industrial capacity that had virtually doubled during the war years signaled the unmistakable emergence of American global hegemony. The postwar US supremacy was codified in the dollar-based monetary order created at Bretton Woods and found expression in an interlocking system of alliances whose instruments were the North Atlantic Treaty Organisation (NATO), the Southeast Asia Treaty Organisation (SEATO), the Organization of American States (OAS), Central Treaty Organization (CENTO), and the US–Japan Security Pact. The postwar reorganisation of political space was henceforth premised on an informal imperial structure. Starting in the war years, but acquiring a new momentum soon after, an international regulatory framework–the United Nations, the World Bank and the International Monetary Fund–replaced the autarchic empires that had dominated the interwar geopolitical landscape. Postwar imperial relations, while respecting the formal equality of sovereign states, could now be concealed behind the façade of these supranational organisations.[26]

The shift in the locus of hegemony from the UK to the USA amounted to a major transformation in the structure of the world-economy itself. America's market liberalism, unlike Britain's commitment to *laissez-faire* liberalism before 1914, was embedded in the state-managed national programmes such as the New Deal. The USA had, moreover, successfully internalised the global division of labour that had once typified the relationship between Europe and its colonial extension, characterised as it was by a vertical division of labour between industry and agriculture. According to Mike Davis, the insertion of the US economy into the world economy was uniquely asymmetrical:

> on the one hand, its absolute contribution to world trade and investment was sufficiently large to produce dynamizing demand and supply effects; on the other, it was relatively autarkic compared to the rest of the OECD economies (until 1970 only 7 per cent of the US GNP circulated in the world market) and, therefore, could flexibly accommodate the increasing shares of Western Europe and Japan in world manufacturing trade.[27]

These features of the US economy proved critical in cementing a shift towards a world economy defined by interacting national systems that were nevertheless unified under the sovereignty of the dollar.[28] The US economy's relatively low level of export specialisation, a gigantic domestic market, as well as the increased postwar autonomy of national financial systems, ensured a relative de-synchronisation of business cycles. This provided national states a degree of autonomy from the fluctuations of the dollar, allowing governments to determine domestic interest rates and fix the exchange rate of their national currencies. National indicative planning could thus be seen as a logical extension of the relative autonomy of national economies.[29]

The restructuring of the world market under US hegemony created a basis for peaceful coexistence between the industrially advanced capitalist countries. This allowed them to concentrate their immense economic and military resources against communist states and revolutionary movements in the Third World. The two superpowers—possessing nuclear weapons, superior armies and a huge industrial might that gave them the power to dominate other nations—vied for influence around the globe. The re-imagining of the global political space into a capitalist first world, a communist second world and a decolonising Third World was in many ways an expression of this conflict. This tripartite division of the world, although it implied different stages of development, was in actuality primarily political. In fact, in the context of the Cold War, the First and Second Worlds projected themselves as alternative paths to modernity, which the newly independent nations of the Third World could emulate. The latter first emerged as a bloc of countries during the Bandung Conference of 1955. Five years later the small nucleus was significantly enlarged as numerous African countries secured their independence. A much-enlarged Non-Aligned Movement was established in 1961 with the stated intention of charting an independent political path. The obstacles to doing so were nonetheless enormous. The distinctly elite-to-elite transfer of power was central to the decolonisation process, and national liberation did little to disrupt Western dominance of the global economic order. This dominance was threatened by the revolutionary eruptions that had already led to communist triumphs in China, Korea, Vietnam and then Cuba. The Soviet role as a counterweight to the USA was crucial in this respect. Despite the bureaucratic tyranny that had turned Soviet society into a virtual dystopia for many in the West, the USSR—and later Chinese and Cuban societies—commanded a certain level of attraction for Third World revolutionary movements. They saw in the USSR's rapid transformation from a backward agrarian society into an industrial superpower the possibility of overcoming their own 'backwardness' in a historically condensed time.[30]

In the face of these mounting social upheavals that could lead to further subtractions from the empire of capital, the USA identified its main strategic objective as containing communism and upholding the integrity of the capitalist world market. The Truman doctrine, formulated in May 1947, made this orientation the central theme of postwar US politics. The promotion of 'modernisation' and development was in this context not just fortuitous: 'The idea of modernisation proved congenial to American policy makers, so much so in fact that "development" and "modernisation" came to be viewed as long-range solutions to the threats of Communism in the Third World'.[31] For some of the proponents of modernisation theory this larger political dimension was always at the forefront. Rostow's 'non-communist manifesto' was the best-known instance of this,[32] but other leading modernisation theorists—Gabriel Almond, Edward Shils, Lucien Pye and Samuel Huntington—were also closely connected to the American state and its geopolitical preoccupation with combating communism.[33] In its classical formulation modernisation theory had two principal components: 'tradition' and 'modernity'. Modernisation implied a linear movement from one to the other, and this idea of a single line of historical progress comprised the deeper temporal framework for much social science writing about the Third World. Modernisation was also a relational process at the level of the world system, in which synchronic comparisons between different kinds of society were ordered diachronically to produce both a temporal and spatial scale of development in which the particular present of some societies was privileged as

147

representing the future of others. History was thus to be understood as an overarching process of societal rationalisation and modernisation, which was propelled by industrialisation and transmitted to 'traditional' societies through the institutions of empire and the mechanisms of the world market.

Harry S Truman signalled the new US stance towards the Third World in his inaugural address, in January 1949, when he declared: 'The old imperialism—exploitation for foreign profit—has no place in our plans. What we envisage is a program of development based on the concepts of democratic fair dealing.'[34] Considering itself the first 'ex-colony', the USA believed that its own history uniquely equipped it to advance the project of global decolonisation and modernisation:

> Just as the decline of Europe's global hegemony opened the way for the emergence of the United States as the premier world power, the Europeans' doubts about their civilizing mission strengthened the Americans' growing conviction that they knew best how to reform 'backward' societies that were racked by poverty, natural calamities, and social unrest.[35]

The Marshall Plan had already secured the vital resources that enabled governing coalitions in Western Europe to recover economically and surmount strong challenges from local communist parties.[36] The perceived success of the Marshall Plan, in turn, became a sort of model for later ideas about 'aid' to the Third World.[37] A range of both international and national apparatuses of development emerged in this period, and the collaboration between academe and centres of power reinforced and institutionalised the new modernisation paradigm. Theoretically, this was a time of expanding horizons, and innovative work inspired research centres and graduate programmes focusing on the sociology, politics and economics of development. By the 1970s 'development studies' had achieved an established position in many universities, and thousands of students from 'developing' countries came to study in these institutions. Within the framework thus established, there were always currents that went against the grain of modernisation theory: the dependency school, world-systems analysis, and modes of production approaches were the most renowned during the 1970s and 1980s. These currents, though having little impact on the formulation and implementation of policy, were intellectually influential and served to create the elements of a counter-tradition that challenged the ruling norms.[38]

Uneven development and the postwar boom

The stable framework provided by Pax Americana enabled a historically unprecedented expansion of the world economy. The downward spiral of the interwar years gave way to a postwar expansionary wave initially founded on the reconstruction of fixed capital and then on the generalisation of neo-Fordism. This was the golden age of affluence in the core capitalist countries. Gross Domestic Product (GDP) and labour productivity grew almost twice as fast as in any previous period since 1820, and there was a rapid acceleration in the rate of growth of the capital stock. The growth in the volume of postwar trade was eight

148

times faster than in the period 1913–50 and twice as great as in the century from 1820. Globally, output of manufactures more than quadrupled between the early 1950s and the 1970s, and world trade in manufactures grew eight-fold.[39] Politically the catastrophe of World War II worked to fire popular mobilisations behind strong ideals of democratic citizenship and social justice, so that with the exception of the Iberian fascist states, the post-1945 period represented the moment of generalised parliamentary democracy in West European history.

In the postcolonial world the first decades after decolonisation witnessed a significant, if uneven, rise in income and enlarged provision of social services and education. Consequently, poverty could be regarded as an effect of policy rather than an inevitable dictate of nature. The most visible effect of these transformations was the rapid rise in urbanisation and concomitant relative reduction of the agrarian population. Similarly, there was an unprecedented expansion of literacy and the presence of an educated middle class as a palpable demographic phenomenon. Before the Second World War, 'three of the largest, most developed and most educated countries—Germany, France and Britain—with a total population of 150 million, then contained no more than 150 000 university students. In the 1980s, Ecuador alone contained more than twice as many.'[40]

For many in the Third World, however, prosperity remained a remote dream, and economic development was much less comprehensive than is sometimes assumed. While the common history of colonial domination and the shared search for a third way provided some basis for mutual action, the Cold War polarised Third World nations, pushing states to choose between the competing superpowers. In the process the USA and the USSR employed coercive pressure against popular movements within their respective spheres of influence, ranging from outright invasions, to sponsorship of military coups, and the provision of support for brutal dictatorships. As a consequence, the cold war era in the North was one of hot wars in the South—including the Korean War, the French wars in Indochina and Algeria, three Middle Eastern wars, the Portuguese wars in Africa, the American war in Vietnam and some 40-odd civil wars in Africa, Asia and Latin America. While national independence had, moreover, opened up a space for mass mobilisations, a closure occurred over time as parasitic military and bureaucratic layers short-circuited the initial phase of democratic effervescence. Newly independent states that were projected to promote democracy and development were now interposed to protect well established privileges and erstwhile relations of dominance.[41]

By the early 1970s the postwar expansionary wave had turned into a recessionary downswing. Overall rates of growth declined as inflation and unemployment mounted. US economic supremacy came under challenge from the Japanese and German economies that had made a remarkable recovery during the boom years. The shift in relative economic position and the attendant trade deficits, combined with the budgetary pressures induced by the Vietnam War, forced the USA in 1971 to abrogate the Bretton Woods system. As stagflation set in, the prices of many of the Third World's primary products plummeted. At the same time, the ruin of primary producers had disastrous effects on the level of employment and manufactured exports in the OECD countries. The international economy sank into a synchronised recession, throwing the development framework into crisis.[42]

The price of crude oil was the one exception in this decline of raw material prices, and the petrodollars from this windfall were re-circulated as loans to Third World states.[43] The loans were used to finance import bills for industrial technology, equipment goods and food. But in the context of longer and deeper recessions in the OECD countries, the market for Third World exports continued to deteriorate. The result was a rapid surge in accumulated Third World debt; Mexico's declaration in 1980 that it could no longer make its debt payments was a sign that the 'development framework' had entered a period of abrupt and terminal decline. It marked the end of the 'development regime' and the establishment, via IMF-imposed structural adjustment programmes, of the 'debt regime'. For the past two decades the Third World has been subjected to a global tributary regime and austerity measures that have crippled social and educational programmes once viewed as emblematic of development. The resultant social dislocation and widespread misery have done much to erode the authority of national states that had once made the promise of 'development' a constitutive element of their legitimacy.

The landslide since the early 1970s was certainly not uniform. Uneven development promoted some regions and demoted others. The spectacular economic performance of the East Asian economies during the long downturn should caution against too generic an image of decline. In contrast to the downturn elsewhere, East Asian economies experienced spectacular growth rates that dwarfed those of the Golden Age in the West. Given the relative demographic weight of this region, this was not a mere marginal phenomenon. Yet, despite this spectacular boom, these countries were not immune to Western pressure, as was demonstrated in the financial crisis of 1997–98. The cumulative upshot of the emergence of this new growth area was nonetheless a re-configuration of regional power dynamics in the world economy as a whole.[44] Although the reasons for East Asia's exceptional economic performance have been much debated, both the Cold War, on whose front lines these states were positioned, and the transformations initiated by Japanese colonialism and sustained by the *dirigiste* postcolonial states, will all have their place in any balanced account. Deliberate policies aimed at fostering pragmatic distortions of the market and the imposition of high but flexible tariffs make it clear, however, that their success had very little to do with neoliberal prescriptions for unregulated markets.[45]

US hegemony, globalisation and the passing of the three worlds

The crisis of the early 1970s marked a watershed between the golden age of sustained growth and the stagnation that followed, altering many of the coordinates within which development was conceived, but outside which it could not survive. Over the debris of the 'development framework', neoliberal globalisation emerged as the reigning orthodoxy. Neoliberalism was born in the aftermath of World War II as a reaction to the expansion of the welfare state, and its guiding spirit was Friedrich von Hayek. In *The Road to Serfdom,* Hayek

150

argued that state intervention represented a mortal threat to the optimal operation of the market and to individual freedom as such. In a spirited declaration that has since become the reigning credo of neoliberalism, Hayek called for a return to the night watchman state.[46] Yet, in the context of the long postwar expansion, when counter-cyclical demand management could simultaneously boost the rate of profit and raise real living standards, neoliberalism could be safely ignored. It was only with the end of the postwar boom and the emergence of conservative regimes across key core states that the disposition to monetarism finally became hegemonic.[47]

By the 1990s the ideology of *laissez-faire* was conjoined with the discourse of 'globalisation'. The immediate context for the latter was the collapse of the Soviet system and the unprecedented geographic expansion of the capitalist market. This coincided with developments in electronics and information technology that accelerated dynamics of time–space compression. According to globalisation theory, the underlying spatio-temporal transformations have reconstituted the globe into a single space, requiring a corresponding transformation in state–market relations. Along with actual processes of transnationalisation— whether in terms of flows of finance and communication or of labor mobility and commodity markets—the rhetoric of globalisation has reversed the postwar conception of the world economy as consisting of autonomous nation-states endowed with powers of economic and political regulation.[48]

A critical consideration of the development framework, with the displacements and reversals of an earlier imperial form of globalisation it represented, enables us to think more clearly about this late-20th century form of neoliberal globalisation. We can begin by dislodging globalisation from certain disarming teleological assumptions. For one thing, the history of 20th century political and economic organisation has not been characterised by a linear process of expansion and integration. In some respects, the world economy at the end of the 1980s was much less integrated than it had been at the beginning of the century.[49] Second, the age of empire was also one of globalisation, in which non-Western societies were subjected to the imperatives of a Europe-centred world market.[50] In this respect, anti-colonial nationalism and the generalisation of the nation-state system constituted a movement against globalisation in the form of this colonial system of integration. By taking at face value the claim that globalisation is a universal process propelled by its own interior logic, we give it a coherence it does not possess. Passive acceptance of the claim that the current form of globalisation is a fate we have to resign ourselves to has become a convenient alibi for governments who willingly or unwillingly subscribe to the dogmas of market purism. To counteract this tendency, we need to highlight globalisation's contingent and contradictory history and identify the forces that regulate its dynamics. Processes of time–space compression—what Marx in the 19th century called the 'annihilation of space through time'—are certainly not a recent novelty.[51] The point here is not that there are no tendencies of actual globalisation, but that attributing to them an ineluctable logic conceals the fact that globalisation is also a project driven by private agencies of capital and transnational institutions such as the IMF and the World Bank.[52]

The political ideal of neoliberalism is a world in which all states share a common normative commitment to a single global market unfettered by social and political obstacles. The radically disempowering and depoliticising nature of this project is evident. As Karl Polanyi has long reminded us, for much of world history the market was a definite place, controlled by specific spatial arrangements that grew out of the organisation of other kinds of social exchange. It was embedded in society. It was only during the 'Great Transformation' of the 19th century that the notion of the market as a placeless, timeless phenomenon coextensive with society itself became widespread. The disembedding of market relations from a wider social practice that had previously contained them, he argued, gave rise to the ideology of a self-regulating market economy.

It was recognition of the devastation wrought by the 'unregulated market' that, more than 50 years ago, impelled the idea of national development into global politics. The conditions that fostered that moment have today all but completely passed away. The present conjuncture is characterised by a radical reversal of each of those forces that initially gave the development framework its wider meaning. The implosion of the USSR put an end to the Cold War and with it, to any countervailing force to US hegemony within the inter-state system. While decolonisation remains a permanent gain, its meaning is increasingly constricted by the power of multinational companies and transnational institutions. The crisis of the past two decades has likewise restructured US capitalism and, as the hegemonic global power, the USA is today at the forefront of a recharged offensive aspiring to nothing less than the universal domination of market liberalism.

Viewed over the 'short twentieth-century', Third World development thus appears as a brief interlude between two transnational ages. The high tide was probably reached in the mid-1970s. Thereafter, changes in the economic and political climate undermined the assumptions upon which it had been built. The current celebration of the unfettered market, together with the renovation of the once exhausted theories of a Milton Friedman or a Hayek, has indeed been a disquieting experience. For many, the hegemony of this model of free-market capitalism appears an immovable horizon. But is this triumphalism likely to be a lasting affair? A world plagued by ecological crisis, staggering social inequality and misery, and a debt burden weighing down on the wretched of the earth, hardly suggests that it is. If anything, such a situation urgently demands globally imaginative alternative social and political projects to the tyranny of the hidden hand. Co-ordination or planning to re-embed the market in society may and, in light of past experience, should take a different form in the future. But all this is a very different matter from simply allowing our lives to be governed by capital unbound.

Conclusion: transforming centre–periphery relations

Through most of the second half of the 20th century, national liberation and the idea of development fired the imagination of millions of people in the Third World. Yet, by the end of the century, the political landscape that had generated that optimism had been transformed beyond recognition. The end of the postwar boom, the rise of a new and more aggressive *laissez-faire* conservatism, and the collapse of the USSR, brought to an end the mid-20th century conjuncture of world politics that had made the idea of Third World development imaginable. At the start of the new millennium the far-reaching social and economic effects of transnational regulatory frameworks and global capital flows, and the discourses of 'globalisation', have gravely undermined democratic accountability and national economic sovereignty. The spontaneous operation of market forces continues to generate wealth at one pole and poverty at the other, further rigidifying economic inequality between the major world zones. A more equitable and sustainable system of growth requires complex international coordination and social arrangements that involve the collective transformation of centre–periphery relations. Developing the forms of politics and analysis adequate to these tasks requires sustained reflection on the circumstances in which the Third World was made and unmade. No alternative to global neoliberalism can hope to be credible if it fails to come to terms with the historical legacy and contemporary agony of this zone of humanity.

Notes

[1] These studies include A Escobar, *Encountering Development: The Making and Unmaking of the Third World*, Princeton, NJ: Princeton University Press, 1995; MT Berger, *Under Northern Eyes: Latin American Studies and US Hegemony in the Americas 1898–1990*, Bloomington, IN: Indiana University Press, 1995; C Leys, *The Rise and Fall of Development Theory*, Bloomington, IN: Indiana University Press, 1996; MP Cowen & RW Shenton, *Doctrines of Development*, New York: Routledge 1996; JL Love, *Crafting the Third World: Theorizing Underdevelopment in Rumania and Brazil*, Stanford, CA: Stanford University Press, 1996; F Cooper & R Packard (eds), *International Development and the Social Sciences: Essays on the History and Politics of Knowledge*, Berkeley, CA: University of California Press, 1997; ME Latham, *Modernization as Ideology: American Social Science and 'Nation Building' in the Kennedy Era*, Chapel Hill, NC: University of North Carolina Press, 2000; KC Pearce, *Rostow, Kennedy, and the Rhetoric of Foreign Aid*, East Lansing, MI: Michigan State University Press, 2001; D Engerman (ed), *Staging Growth: Modernization, Development and the Global Cold War*, Amherst, MA: University of Massachusetts Press, 2003; and MT Berger, *The Battle for Asia: From Decolonization to Globalization*, London: Routledge, 2003. Some of these studies appeared after the completion of this article, and it has not been possible to incorporate their insights here.

[2] M Bienefeld, 'Rescuing the dream of development in the nineties', *Silver Jubilee Paper 10*, Institute of Development Studies, University of Sussex, 1991.

[3] The shorthand use of the term 'empire of capital' should not detract from the structurally different forms of European geopolitical expansion since the later Middle Ages. Justin Rosenberg has pointed out that: 'the early modern empires were reproduced as composite social orders: structured sets of relations which resist attempts to distinguish between "power and plenty" '. The contemporary sovereign states system could not be more different: 'Lines of political jurisdiction halt at fixed national borders, while those of economic activity speed on through a myriad of international exchanges without undermining the ramparts of formal sovereignty above'. J Rosenberg, *The Empire of Civil Society: A Critique of the Realist Theory of International Relations*, London: Verso, 1994. See also E Meiksins Wood, *Empire of Capital*, London: Verso, 2003.

[4] This is a revised version of F Makki, 'The genesis of the development framework: the end of laissez-faire, the eclipse of colonial empires, and the structure of US hegemony', in R Grosfoguel & AM Cervantes-Rodríguez (eds), *The Modern/Colonial/Capitalist World-System in the Twentieth Century*, New York: Praeger, 2002.

[5] According to Perry Anderson: 'The combination of the Industrial Revolution at home and the destruction after Waterloo of any barrier or competition to English global hegemony overseas brought into being a quite new form of world economy, in which British manufacturers possessed overwhelming preponderance amid generalized international free trade'. P Anderson, 'Figures of descent', in Anderson, *English Questions*, London: Verso, 1992, pp 121–192.

[6] E Hobsbawm, *Nations and Nationalism Since 1780: Program, Myth, Reality*, Cambridge: Cambridge University Press, 1990, p 26.

[7] *Ibid*, p 30.

[8] H van der Wee & E Buyst, 'Europe and the world economy during the inter-war period', in C Ludwig Holtfriech (ed), *Interactions in the World Economy: Perspectives from International Economic History*, New York: New York University Press, 1989, pp 239–259.

[9] K Polanyi, *The Great Transformation: The Political and Economic Origins of Our Time*, Boston, MA: Beacon Press, 1944, p 23.

[10] Hobsbawm, *Nations and Nationalism Since 1780*, p 132.

[11] E Hobsbawm, *The Age of Extremes: A History of the World, 1914–1991*, New York: Pantheon, 1994, p 107.

[12] JM Keynes, *The Collected Writings of John Maynard Keynes*, Vol VII, *The General Theory of Employment, Interest and Money*, London: Macmillan, 1973.

[13] T Mitchell, 'Origins and limits of the modern idea of the economy', *Working Papers Series, No 12*, Advanced Study Center, University of Michigan, 1995.

[14] A sense of the expansion of 'development economics' in the USA is imparted by David Landes: 'I compared the volume of publication of articles on growth and development theory in the Index of Economic Journals of the American Economic Association: for the period 1925–1939, a little over one page of citations; of 1940–49, a little over two pages; for 1950–54, over seven pages; and the next quinquennium, sixteen pages ... A new sub discipline had been born.' DS Landes, 'Introduction: technology and growth', in P Higonnet, DS Landes & H Rosovsky (eds), *Favorites of Fortune: Technology, Growth, and Economic Development Since the Industrial Revolution*, Cambridge, MA: Harvard University Press, 1991, p 23.

[15] R Prebisch, 'Five stages in my thinking on development', in G Meir & D Seers (eds), *Pioneers of Development*, Oxford: Oxford University Press, 1984, pp 175–191.

[16] G Kolko, *Confronting the Third World: United States Foreign Policy, 1945–1980*, New York: Pantheon, 1988, p 36.

[17] C Keyder, 'The rise and decline of national economies in the periphery', *Review of Middle East Studies*, 6, 1995, pp 3–14.

[18] M Adas, *Machines as the Measure of Men*, Ithaca, NY: Cornell University Press, 1989. While Michael Adas provides a careful consideration of this shift, he nonetheless locates the rise of scientific rationality as the legitimating ethos of empire earlier than I do here. It is doubtful that racism and cultural essentialism were marginalised until the horrors of fascism brought their consequences into the heart of Europe itself.

[19] F Cooper & R Packard, 'Introduction', in Cooper & Packard, *International Development and the Social Sciences*, pp 1–44.

[20] HS Wilson, *African Decolonization*, London: Edward Arnold, 1994, p 149. For British colonial policies with regard to 'development' see S Constantine, *The Making of British Colonial Development Policy, 1914–1940*, London: Cass, 1984; and M Havinden & D Meredith, *Colonialism and Development: Britain and its Tropical Colonies, 1850–1960*, London: Routledge, 1993. For French policy see JS Canale, 'From colonization to independence in French tropical Africa: the economic background', in P Gifford & WR Louis (eds), *The Transfer of Power in Africa: Decolonization, 1940–1960*, New Haven, CT: Yale University Press, 1982, pp 445–482.

[21] Wilson, *African Decolonization*, p 152.

[22] The dynamics of colonial racism always worked against claims to a wider and inclusive citizenship. With the exception of a handful of tiny islands such as Martinique and Guadeloupe, full citizenship rights were never seriously on offer for the rest of the colonised world. For a discerning discussion of these dynamics in the context of the British and French Empires in Africa, one to which the above summary discussion is indebted, see F Cooper, *Decolonization and African Society*, Cambridge: Cambridge University Press, 1996.

[23] D Washbrook, 'The rhetoric of democracy and development in late colonial India', in S Bose & A Jalal (eds), *Nationalism, Democracy & Development*, New Delhi: Oxford India Paperbacks, 1998, p 37.

[24] Cooper, *Decolonization and African Society*, p 471. African labour movements were also caught in an ideological trap, in this case by the logic of nationalism. It became more difficult for them to assert that the metropolitan standard for wages and benefits should apply to all workers. On the ironies of this contrasting logic, framed in the context of Africa, see F Cooper, 'The dialectics of decolonization: nationalism and labor movements in postwar French Africa', in F Cooper & A Stoler (eds), *Tensions of Empire: Colonial Cultures in a Bourgeois World*, Berkeley, CA: University of California Press, 1997, pp 406–435.

[25] Discussing the impact of the First World War on African colonial conscripts, a French colonial official noted that, 'the 175 000 soldiers enrolled during the years 1914–1918 dug the grave of the old Africa in the trenches of France and Flanders'. Similarly, the French governor-general of Indochina stated that, 'The war which covered Europe with blood has ... awakened in lands far distant from us a feeling of

independence … All has changed in the past few years. Both men and ideas and Asia herself are being transformed.' Quoted in LS Stavrianos, *Global Rift: The Third World Comes of Age*, New York: William Morrow, 1981, p 514. World War II further accentuated these changes.

[26] S Corbridge, N Thrift & R Martin (eds), *Money, Power and Space*, Oxford: Blackwell, 1994.

[27] M Davis, *Prisoners of the American Dream*, London: Verso, 1986, p 190.

[28] In his study of the making of an Atlantic ruling class, Kess van der Pijl has documented the manifold pressure exerted by the US corporate and financial establishment to reconfigure European economic development away from cartelism to auto-centred growth based on consumer durable consumption. K. van der Pilj, *The Making of an Atlantic Ruling Class*, London: Verso, 1985.

[29] G Arrighi, *The Long Twentieth Century*, London: Verso, 1994, pp 280–295; L Mjøset, 'The turn of two centuries: a comparison of British and US hegemonies', in DP Rapkin (ed), *World Leadership and Hegemony*, Boulder, CO: Lynne Rienner, 1990, pp 21–48; and M Aglietta, 'World capitalism in the eighties', *New Left Review*, 136, 1982, pp 5–41.

[30] This eventually led to the promotion of a Soviet version of the modernisation paradigm not surprisingly privileging the USSR itself as a model of a 'non-capitalist road' to modernity. For some perceptive reflections on 'modernisation' in the context of the Soviet empire's own periphery, see D Kandiyoti, 'Modernization without the market? The case of the "Soviet East" ', *Economy and Society*, 25 (4), 1996, pp 529–542. For the articulation of a theory of 'a non-capitalist road' to development, see P Bellis, 'The non-capitalist road and Soviet development theory today: a critique of some recent accounts', *Journal of Communist Studies*, 4 (3), 1988, pp 258–281.

[31] DC Tipps, 'Modernization theory and the comparative studies of societies: a critical perspective', *Comparative Studies in Society and History*, 15, 1973, p 210.

[32] WW Rostow, *The Stages of Growth: A Non-Communist Manifesto*, Cambridge: Cambridge University Press, 1960.

[33] I Gendzier, *Managing Political Change: Social Scientists and the Third World*, Boulder, CO: Westview Press, 1985.

[34] P McMichael, *Development and Social Change: A Global Perspective*, Thousand Oaks, CA: Pine Forge Press, 1996, p 30. Gustavo Esteva, commenting on Truman's declaration, notes: 'Underdevelopment began, then, on January 20, 1949. On that day, two billion people became underdeveloped. In a real sense, from that time on, they ceased being what they were, in all their diversity, and were transmogrified into an inverted mirror of other's reality … a mirror that defines their identity … simply in terms of a homogenizing and narrow minority.' G Esteva, 'Development', in W Sachs (ed), *The Development Dictionary*, London: Zed Books, 1992, p 7.

[35] Adas, *Machines as the Measure of Men*, p 402.

[36] Between 1948 and 1952 the USA transferred $13 billion—an estimated 4.5% of its gross national product—to Western Europe. The Marshall Plan was viewed as critical to the project of constructing 'a prosperous and stable European community secure against the dangers of Communist subversion and able to join the United States in a multilateral system of world trade'. MJ Hogan, *The Marshall Plan: America, Britain, and the Reconstruction of Western Europe, 1947–1952*, Cambridge: Cambridge University Press, 1987, p 427.

[37] R. Packenham, *Liberal America and the Third World: Political Development Ideas in Foreign Aid and Social Science*, Princeton: Princeton University Press, 1973.

[38] H Alavi & T Shanin (eds), *Introduction to the Sociology of 'Developing Societies'*, New York: Monthly Review Press, 1980; B Hettne, *Development Theory and the Three Worlds*, London: Methuen, 1990; and Leys, *The Rise and Fall of Development Theory*. Discourses of development often presented themselves as detached centres of objectivity and rationality, and tended to conceal relations of power and inequality both at the local and the international level. For two illuminating critiques of development discourse, see J Ferguson, *The Anti-Politics Machine: 'Development,' Depoliticization and Bureaucratic Power in Lesotho*, Cambridge: Cambridge University Press, 1990; and T Mitchell, 'The object of development', in Mitchell, *Rule of Experts: Egypt, Techno-Politics, Modernity*, Berkeley, CA: University of California Press, 2002.

[39] A Glynn, A Hughes, A Lipietz & A Singh, 'The rise and fall of the Golden Age', in SA Marglin & JB Schor (eds), *The Golden Age of Capitalism: Reinterpreting the Postwar Experience*, Oxford: Oxford University Press, 1991, pp 41–42. Immanuel Wallerstein points out that 'the absolute expansion of the world-economy—in population, in value produced, in accumulated wealth—has probably been as great as the entire period of 1500–1945'. I Wallerstein, *Unthinking Social Science: The Limits of Nineteenth Century Paradigms*, Cambridge: Polity Press, 1991, p 113.

[40] E Hobsbawm, 'Today's crises of ideologies', *New Left Review*, 192, 1992, p 56. Especially dramatic cases of urbanisation are Colombia, where between 1951 and 1973 the rural population fell from 64% to 36.4% while the metropolitan population rose from 6.2% to 27.6%; and Paraguay, where the corresponding figures for 1950–1972 were 65% and 22.9%, and from 0% to 24%, respectively. Commenting on the bewildering pace of social transformation during this period, Eric Hobsbawm notes, 'Never before in history has

ordinary human life, and the societies in which it takes place, been so radically transformed in so short a time: not merely within a single life time, but within part of a lifetime'. *Ibid*, pp 55–64.

[41] M Mamdani, *Citizen and Subject: Contemporary Africa and the Legacy of Late-Colonialism*, Princeton, NJ: Princeton University Press, 1996; and J-F Bayart, *The State in Africa: The Politics of the Belly*, London: Longman, 1993.

[42] Numerous studies from different theoretical perspectives attempt to explain the end of the postwar expansion and the subsequent long downturn. For representative approaches, see Arrighi, *The Long Twentieth Century*; R Brenner, 'The economics of global turbulence', *New Left Review*, 229 (special issue), 1998, pp 1–265; D Harvey, *The Condition of Postmodernity*, London: Blackwell, 1989; E Mandel, *Late Capitalism*, London: New Left Books, 1975; and Marglin & Schor, *The Golden Age of Capitalism*.

[43] The growth of Third World debt occurred in the context of a phenomenal expansion of public and private credit in the world economy. From 1964 until 1987 net international bank loans rose 11 times faster than world trade, 20 times faster than world-wide fixed capital formation and 21 times faster than the global gross national product. *Trade and Development Report*, New York: UN Conference on Trade and Development, 1990, p 110 (table 28).

[44] G Arrighi, S Ikeda & A Irwan, 'The rise of East Asia: one miracle or many?', in RA Palat (ed), *Pacific–Asia and the future of the World-System*, Westport, CT: Greenwood Press, 1993, pp 41–65.

[45] A Amsden, 'Third World industrialization: "global Fordism" or a new model?', *New Left Review*, 182, 1990, pp 5–31. For the attempt by the Japanese government to convince the World Bank to consider East Asia's actually existing economic models, and for the way in which the US view prevailed when the World Bank finally produced the report entitled The East Asian Miracle, see R Wade, 'Japan, the World Bank, and the art of paradigm maintenance: the East Asian miracle in political perspective', *New Left Review*, 217, 1996, pp 3–37. For the long-term structural causes of East Asian ascendancy see Arrighi *et al*, 'The rise of East Asia', pp 41–65.

[46] F von Hayek, *The Road to Serfdom*, Chicago, IL: University of Chicago Press, 1944.

[47] P Anderson, 'Histoire et leçons du néo-liberalisme: la construction d'une voie unique', *La Pensée*, 320, 1999, pp 47–59.

[48] Philip McMichael notes that: 'The world is on the threshold of a major transition in the political regulation of economic activity: from a primarily national to a primarily global form of regulation. The current restructuring of states proceeds via limitation of democratic politics, declining economic sovereignty, and the enlistment of state administrations in the service of global circuits.' P McMichael, 'The new colonialism: global regulation and the restructuring of the inter-state system', in DA Smith & J Böröcz (eds), *A New World Order? Global Transformations in the Late Twentieth Century*, Westport, CT: Greenwood Press, 1995, pp 37–38.

[49] A Glynn & B Sutcliff, 'Global but leaderless? The new capitalist world order', *Socialist Register*, 1992, pp 76–95.

[50] The case of India is perhaps the most instructive: from the status of one of the early modern world's leading manufacturing and merchandising economies, according to Bairoch, South Asia had shrunk to possessing barely 1% of world industrial output and trade by the middle of the 20th century. P Bairoch, 'International industrialization levels from 1750 to 1980', *Journal of European Economic History*, 11 (2), 1982, pp 269–334.

[51] Writing in the *Grundrisse* (1857), Marx noted: 'While capital … must strive to tear down every barrier … to exchange and conquer the whole earth for its markets, it strives on the other side to annihilate this space with time'. Karl Marx, *The Grundrisse: Foundations of the critique of Political Economy*, London: Penguin, 1973, pp 538–539.

[52] P Cammack, 'Attacking the global poor', *New Left Review*, 13, 2002, pp 125–134.

From national bourgeoisie to rogues, failures and bullies: 21st century imperialism and the unravelling of the Third World

RADHIKA DESAI

The related concepts of the Third World, development and non-alignment have been as nebulous as they have been programmatically persistent in the global politics of the 20th—the American—century. All the ink that has been spilled in describing and analysing, not to mention attempting to resolve, this paradox has, however, for all the local insights and general erudition, only succeeded in perpetuating it. This article argues that, if there is a single referent to which these vague concepts relate, and from which they derive programmatic longevity, it was the idea (and the reality, such as it was) of the progressive potential of nationalism within capitalist imperialism, and in particular the idea of 'national bourgeoisies'. This is also known as the idea of bourgeois economic nationalism.

The idea originated in Vladimir Ilych Lenin's theory and practice of global politics, and that coincided with the early elaboration of US hegemony at the beginning of the American century in the First World War and the Wilsonian diplomacy that attended its aftermath. The idea of the progressive potential of nationalism and national bourgeoisies had been a keystone of Lenin's adaptation of the resources of Marxist theory, with class as its core concept of historical and political agency, to a real world in which the relevance of class was being challenged by another idea and reality: the nation. Nations and nationalism had tragically trumped European social democracy on the eve of the imperialist First World War but seemed, to Lenin, to hold a rather different set of possibilities elsewhere. In his March 1916 'Theses on the Socialist Revolution and the Right of Nations to Self-determination', Lenin divided the countries of the world into three groups depending on how class and nation were combined in each. This is, to my knowledge, the first clear adumbration of the idea of 'three worlds'. In this form it was central to the theory and practice of communism well before its use became current in various streams of political opinion and practice in the US-dominated world after the Second World War. In this original formula the 'three worlds' were conceived thus:

> First, the advanced countries of Western Europe and the United States ... [where] the bourgeois progressive national movements came to an end long ago ... Second, Eastern Europe: Here it was the twentieth century that particularly developed the bourgeois–democratic national movements and intensified the national struggle. The tasks of the proletariat in these countries—in regard to the consummation of their bourgeois–democratic reformation, as well as in regard to assisting the socialist revolution in other countries–cannot be achieved unless it champions the right of nations to self-determination. In this connection, the most difficult but most important task is to merge the class struggle of the workers in the oppressing nations with the class struggle of the workers in the oppressed nations. Thirdly, the semi-colonial countries ... and all the colonies ... [where] the bourgeois–democratic movements have either hardly begun, or are far from having been completed. Socialists must not only demand the unconditional and immediate liberation of the colonies ... but must render the most determined support to the more revolutionary elements in the bourgeois–democratic movements for national liberation in these countries and assist their rebellion—and if need be their revolutionary war— AGAINST the imperialist powers that oppress them.[1]

Beginning with Lenin, the accommodation between the Left's internationalism and at least some of the world's proliferating nationalisms has been based on the evaluation of the latter's class character and, where they were bourgeois nationalisms, on the anti-imperialist potential of the nationalism and the national bourgeoisie in question. It was argued that the international class struggle would be advanced by supporting certain bourgeois national struggles in less developed parts of the world, for they too were anti-imperialist. Popular, usually communist, national struggles were, of course, quite unproblematically anti-imperialist, but others too, led by a 'national bourgeoisie' whose interests were opposed to those of metropolitan capital, and could therefore be expected to be anti-imperialist, were to be supported. In addition to seeking autonomy internationally, such nationalisms were expected to be conducive to greater equality—civic and economic—and productivity domestically than could be expected in the shadow of imperialism.

Although it originated in Lenin's reflections during the Great War, this idea of nationalism's progressive potential really came into its own only in the second half of the 20th century, by which time it enjoyed a currency in far wider political circles than those of the Left. Political independence and the finalisation of the nation-state system in the 20th century was the result of communist and national anti-colonial struggles, on the one hand, and US sponsorship of decolonisation and national self-determination as the final act in the 20th century drama of European decline and American ascent, on the other. The popular hopes raised by the bourgeois national movements were re-articulated, largely via US intellectual and ideological sponsorship, as different national projects of 'development', ie for translating political independence into 'genuine' economic independence. In this more nebulous form, the idea of 'development' was to be something more than just exploitative and crisis prone capitalism. It was assumed that these states would pursue national capitalist development that was both productive and egalitarian, in the social democratic temper of the times, and autonomous, although the nature of this autonomy was rarely specified. Furthermore, it was also rarely specified that this 'development' was capitalist development; not specifying this was part of the nebulousness of this and related ideas. It was ideologically very inconvenient to do so in those now lost and lamented times. 'Development' *sans phrase* was not only to be less exploitative or crisis-prone and more autonomous, it was also supposed, in the related conceptual universe of non-alignment and Third Worldism, to be a 'third way'. All this could appear realistic only on the basis of one assumption: that (capitalist) development would be different in these nations because they were, or would soon be, graced by the presence of *national* bourgeoisies who would be able and willing to use their influence over the national government to fashion an autonomous capitalist development. The postwar order, under US direction, had, after all, created a panoply of institutions at Bretton Woods which placed a number of apparently powerful economic decisions, particularly control over flows of capital, in the hands of national governments. This seemed designed to permit these governments to manage their economies to promote growth and employment largely independently of external considerations.

If the concept of the Third World that became current at this stage was to mean anything, it referred to regimes of this type—regimes that were expected to be more benign, egalitarian, anti-imperialist, but nevertheless in some never stated manner *capitalist*. Otherwise they would have been socialist. Development referred to *capitalist* development. Non-alignment, at its best, meant a *relatively* independent sort of capitalist regime, which the presence of the USSR made possible. Of course, very few of the regimes so designated ever came close to these hopes. However, given certain historical conditions, and certain theoretical assumptions (or presumptions), the idea that at least some of them would live up to these hopes, setting an example to the rest, lived on.

This article reviews the historical realities and conceptual distinctions that successively articulated these possibilities through three decades of development (1950s–1970s), one 'lost decade' (1980s) and even through almost a decade of 'globalisation' (1990s). After globalisation ran aground in the financial crisis of East and Southeast Asia, however, and even more since the launching of the war on terrorism, new realities have come starkly into view, and new light has been shed upon old realities in such a way that these hopes can no longer be sustained. This means, effectively, that the era when the concept of the Third World made sense, either as a nascent reality or a relatively realistic hope, is now past. The new world, and world (dis)order, in the new phase of US (unstable) hegemony which has succeeded that era, cannot be fully elaborated here for reasons of space. Suffice it to say that in this new world, national bourgeoisies and the hopes of national, autonomous, egalitarian capitalist development which they sustained, have given way to a new cast of characters in what used to be the Third World. There are, first, 'bully' states, allying with and emulating the increasingly brazen US imperialism regionally. Second, there are 'rogue' states, with no prospects of such alliance and emulation but a substantial capacity for violence. Finally, 'failed' states are in financial and political receiverships to the US or one or another of its local, bully, allies. In this world questions of Third World solidarity, autonomy from imperialism, 'third way' development or non-alignment simply do not arise.

Capitalist development and the national bourgeoisie in development and development theory

At an earlier stage in the long death of development and development theory Colin Leys argued with forceful clarity that the key factor in the tragedy of development was development theory's politically driven decoupling from the kind of world-historical understanding of capitalism that was actually indispensable to development. This understanding, the origins of which lay in Hegel and Marx (to which we might add Lenin), had been made both possible and necessary by 'the sudden acceleration in the rate of change that the establishment of capitalist production and bourgeois society had generated'.[2]

> The theories of Hegel or Marx ... are not incoherent, but just very large scale and necessarily full of selective simplifications, speculative elements, debatable assumptions and middle-level problems of all kinds. What is really incoherent is a 'development theory' that does not rest explicitly on as clear a general theory of world history, and of world capitalism in particular, as it is possible to have.[3]

Just as, in sufficiently denatured and politically defused forms Lenin's idea of the 'three worlds' was later appropriated by mainstream social science and journalism, so the kind of Marxist world-historical understanding of (capitalist) development which Leys refers to formed the largely unacknowledged source of the more Americanised idea of 'development' after the Second World War. The closely intertwined trajectories of this development theory and the actual processes of development thus provide the best vantage point from which to trace the changing fortunes of the idea of the national bourgeoisie and its associated concepts of development, the Third World and non-alignment. Indeed, the development of development theory is, seen from one point of view, a story of the gravitational pull which Marxist theories have exerted on mainstream development theory as history successively unravelled its assumptions.

Early development theory, actually 'development economics', was most innocent of the Marxist historical understanding. It was the work of economists 'strongly influenced by Keynes, and the wartime and post-war practices of state intervention in the economy, including the perceived success of the Marshall Plan'. These economists shared the 'conviction that economic problems would yield to the actions of benevolent states endowed with sufficient supplies of capital and armed with good economic analysis'.[4] But such theoretical innocence was soon robbed by history. The state itself, the key agent of this management, it was soon found, was unable to behave in the manner required by neoclassical economics. It 'seemed to lack the capacity to live up to the social democratic ideal of a rational, firmly benevolent enforcer of the national interest and impose the necessary discipline on everyone from businessmen and landlords to small peasants'. For, as Leys points out, the assumptions about the state made in development economics glossed over its political character: 'Marx had long ago grasped that states were, as he put it, but the "official resumes" of civil society. In the first phase of development economics this had been forgotten.'[5]

Modernisation theory succeeded development economics, with its Parsonian structural functional analysis, far more openly Eurocentric assumptions, and cold war political proclivities. For all that, modernisation theory focused on society, rather than on the state itself, and it was not until the emergence of underdevelopment theory (UDT), that the centrality of the idea of autonomous national capitalist development to the theory and practice of development became really clear. UDT arose originally to show up the hypocrisy of the idea of national autonomous development in the context of the powerful and varied structures and practices of imperialism. Indeed, it revived the concept of imperialism or, as it was also called, neocolonialism, to theorise the reality of the now nominally independent nation-states of the Third World, still struggling, in many cases after two decades of independence, to foster 'development. It is not surprising, of course, that UDT had its origins in Latin America, the one region of the Third World where the independence of the vast majority of nation-states was actually more than a century old.

UDT was inspired by Marxism and played a crucial role in exposing the obstacles to national capitalist development in the context of imperialism in a way that effectively inverted the propositions of modernisation theory. Politically UDT theorists ranged from '"organic intellectuals" of their own national bourgeoisies (Brazil's former president, Fernando Henrique Cardoso, comes to mind here), chafing at their subordination to the interests of foreign companies and the influence of the US state in domestic politics',[6] to those who clearly sided with the working class and other radical currents. They all shared, however, the idea that there was an alternative autonomous national development path, thus rescuing the core of 'development theory'. It was, in other words, so centrally a critique of the idea of national autonomy that, ironically, it kept alive the idea of such autonomy as the goal of 'development'. 'Underdevelopment' was a critique of 'development' and 'comprador bourgeoisie' of 'national bourgeoisie'. In practice, the former terms kept the aspirations and hopes embodied in the latter terms alive.[7]

The effect of the rise of the Asian 'miracle' economies—South Korea, Taiwan, Singapore and Hong Kong—and the general acknowledgement of substantial industrialisation in the Third World, if in pockets, forced on UDT, in particular by Bill Warren, was complex.[8] It constituted an episode in the development of development theory that was crucial. Not since the rise of Japan in the early 20th century had non-European nations industrialised to the degree and with the speed that was now being witnessed, and not only in the East Asian countries. Originally seen as a refutation of UDT, these experiences, particularly those of South Korea and Taiwan, which were very closely examined, actually corroborated UDT: they were not examples of industrialisation through blanket integration in the world market, they had involved heavy state intervention and direction, and they were specially placed in the larger politics of the Cold War in East Asia, which gave them access to imperial markets and capital on a scale no other Third World country could reasonably expect.[9] They were, at best, instances of 'dependent development' under the umbrella of imperialism and the Cold War. But, for all that, these experiences continued to be regarded as exemplary cases of autonomous national capitalist development, particularly by proponents of the 'developmental state', and until the East Asian financial crisis, this notion still retained a wide currency.

The crisis, however, exposed the economic vulnerability of some of the strongest developmentalist states to metropolitan capital, particularly international financial capital. But it did more: it exposed, particularly in the measures taken to 'resolve' it by the US government and its agencies, these states' *political* vulnerability to imperialist design. For the IMF and the US government clearly aimed not only to restructure the political economy of developmentalism radically in a neoliberal direction, but also to ensure that vast agglomerations of Korean capital, as well as that of other affected countries, became available for US capital to acquire at crisis-deflated prices. The ideological attack on 'crony capitalism' indicated clearly, furthermore, that what was once fostered and tolerated for cold war purposes—the 'developmentalism' of these states—was now not only dispensable but constituted an obstacle to the interests and intentions of metropolitan capital which could and would be removed.

Critical scholars read this crisis in two slightly, but importantly, different ways. One reading, exemplified by Prabhat Patnaik, saw in it the end of the hopes for national capitalist development. In his view the crisis exposed the dynamics of a new phase of capitalism, characterised by stagnation in the metropolitan countries, increasing inequality and asset transfer from across the world into the hands of metropolitan financial capital and, of course, increasing poverty in the Third World. Crucially, 'This new phase also entails the end of bourgeois economic nationalism as a practical project in the Third World, ie of the attempt of the Third World bourgeoisie to carve out a space for itself and build a capitalism that is relatively autonomous of imperialism'.[10] Mitchell Bernard, however, reminded us in his assessment of the same events that, however spectacular, East Asian development had always been dependent development, even at the height of its developmentalism and that the ideal of autonomous state-sponsored national capitalist development had always been hollow. The real difference was merely this: whereas there was once dependent capitalist development led by the big bourgeoisie and the *chaebol*, which was driven by fairly extensive state intervention of a recognizably developmentalist sort, by the 1980s a 'rising stratum of middle-class managers, professionals and technicians with its anti-*chaebol* attitudes underpinned a new more neo-liberal economic strategy which eventually led to the crisis of 1997/8'. He warned in particular against thinking of 'state-centred dependent capitalism as a desirable alternative to the re-imposition of neo-liberalism', as some middle classes and capitalists adversely affected by the recent events, trade unions, and certain sorts of development theorists, votaries of developmental states, were already doing in the affected Asian economies.[11]

While Patniak appeared to believe that there was something qualitatively new in the present phase of capitalism, as he identified it, which has put an end to the possibility of what he calls a national capitalism 'relatively autonomous of imperialism', Bernard saw South Korea and other developmental states as having been dependent rather than even 'relatively autonomous' all along. Whereas both agreed that such development is now impossible, what remained at issue was whether autonomy in some meaningful measure had been possible in the past, particularly in the second half of the 20th century when most Third World and Asian states embarked on political independence and 'development'.

Imperialism, national bourgeoisies and national autonomy

This issue can only be resolved by looking back over the history of the 'combined and uneven development' of capitalism and imperialism particularly in the 20th century. Whatever the shape and force of the imperial system, in addition to political independence, there are two internal political conditions which have to be satisfied before capitalist development can take place in any country. First, a bourgeoisie must exist, and therefore a degree of penetration of capitalist relations of production, or another social force, an elite of some kind, must be committed to fostering capitalist development. Second, either social force must be able to employ its control over the state (usually in alliance with pre-capitalist elites) to foster and sustain capitalist accumulation. For this, it must be able to impose the costs of such development, in a controlled manner, on powerful constituencies if necessary, and devise and implement a strategy to maintain levels of export competitiveness within a world capitalist system which suffices to finance import needs. Most Latin American states, the poorer European nations and the few Asian and African states which were nominally independent by the 19th century are evidence that, unless these conditions were fulfilled, autonomous national capitalist development was not possible. The external context faced by a nation that fulfils these conditions in its quest for autonomous national capitalist development is, however, surely the real issue.

Before the Great War the few countries where the above conditions obtained also benefited from a certain configuration of power in the world system: neither the technological lead, including, crucially, that in military technology, nor the economic and financial control, of the most advanced nation of the time, or of any stable alliance of such nations, over other such actual or would-be competitors was great enough to make relatively autonomous national capitalist development for some of them impossible. Indeed, after about 1870 the premier capitalist manufacturing nation, Great Britain, lost competitiveness in world markets, precisely because of the rise of other such capitalist powers—Germany, Japan and the USA in particular, the three most notable 'late developers'. The reason why Britain's relative economic decline continued throughout the 20th century is instructive: being the first industrial capitalist nation, it had not needed for its rise, nor did it subsequently acquire, an institutional capacity to systematically gear up for competition against other *capitalist* manufacturers. Rather it had merely undermined pre-capitalist production in one part of the world after another on the basis of the supremacy of manufacturing itself over other forms of production.[12]

Britain's competitors, on the other hand, were geared precisely to compete with other *capitalist* manufacturers.[13] In this they fulfilled the second, and harder, of the two conditions required for industrialisation in an already capitalist and imperialist world system: their capitalists and elites were able to employ state power to create, and sustain against competitive challenges, capitalist accumulation. In order to compete at all in a world economy already dominated by a capitalist manufacturing nation, they had to fashion the requisite institutional structures, economic, financial and technological in particular, indeed an entire political economy, able to counter and pre-empt foreign competition. And they were conscious of precisely this necessity: Friedrich List had theorised his National Economy against 'free trading' English Political Economy (which would only benefit the most competitive nation, and prevent the emergence of competitive challenges) as early as 1841. There is, however, a crucial factor missing in this account. The conflicts between these powers were not just over market share within each other's economies. They were, mainly, over external economic territories—colonies.

From its very beginnings, imperial exploitation of colonies was necessary (but not sufficient—witness Spain or Portugal) for autonomous national capitalist development. The 'late developers' realised this. The articulation of goals and policies in the last, most frenzied, phase of the competition for colonies, the 'Scramble for Africa' in the final decade of the 19th century, clearly shows this. A central feature of the world capitalist system before the First World War was that there still remained until then significant areas of the non-capitalist world to colonise.

Colonies served many purposes. Profits generated through economic activities in them, and outright colonial tribute, provided investment funds for the early as well as continuing development of capitalism in the imperial countries. In addition, however, was what Prabhat Patniak has more recently identified as the crux of imperial domination: the colonies, and today the Third World, constitute vast regions of the world whose labour forces can be exploited by metropolitan capitalists in a way quite different from the exploitation of labour on their own soil. The labour of the colonies was exploited, as it continues to be, by being employed 'indirectly, via the use of commodities produced by this section'. This kind of employment has 'the distinguishing characteristic that its *ex ante* wage claims relative to productivity (even in terms of expected prices) are compressible'.[14] What, in addition to political domination, made, and still makes, these wage claims compressible is precisely that their products are oversupplied, substitutable, dispensable or simply dated. This applies to the proverbial primary commodity as it also does, today, to the now vast industrial output of the former colonies. Where this is not the case, as with oil, the confrontation between the imperialised and imperial powers takes both economic and military forms. As a *policy*, imperialism was and is about maintaining the structure of relations which allows this system to continue.

A central feature of the rise of the initial 'late developers' against British hegemony and manufacturing supremacy was, then, competition for colonies. The Great War was the culmination of this inter-imperialist competition. The consequences of this war were, if possible, even more fateful for the colonies: for it crucially changed the imperial configuration of power. The First World War was the climax of a pattern of world capitalist development, which had permitted some autonomous national capitalist development. Its end saw the removal of *both* of the necessary *external* conditions for relatively autonomous national capitalist development: first, the absence of any imperial power with overwhelming economic and military superiority in the world system and second, the absence of any more territories for colonisation by any emerging power. The absence of an overwhelmingly superior imperial power may have encouraged head-on conflicts between established and emerging capitalist nations, but it also enabled the exploitation of conflicts between imperial powers by emerging ones. What now emerged out of the war was a single country, the USA, which (and this is surely a historical contingency of the highest order in the recent history of the world) was now an economic, military and, as a result of the war, financial giant far surpassing not only Great Britain, the paramount imperial power hitherto, but also, all other autonomously developed national capitalisms put together.[15] Having abandoned its isolation from Europe at a historically ripe moment, it now wielded this status to the fullest and began to reconstruct the world economic and political order to the requirements of its own imperium, an imperium that was markedly different from the earlier *Pax Britannica*.

The unity of the entire period of US hegemony since the Great War is often not clearly registered, because the focus is usually on one or another of its eventful phases—the interwar decades, the post-Second World War/Cold War era, the post-1989–1992 period and now, post-2001. It is, however, possible to see that *Pax Americana* had begun to take a clearly recognisable shape at the end of the Great War. Its chief features, and its differences from British hegemony, under which some autonomous national capitalist development had taken place, are central to any discussion of development, the Third World or the progressive potential of national bourgeoisies in the 20th century. Perhaps the most obvious, but also the least discussed, is the operation of the US-centred imperial system, not through formal empire, but in and through a system of politically independent states.[16] Formal colonialism had reached its peak in the Great War. There was no significant territory left for any aspiring Great Power to colonise. Nor could any emerging nation seize such territory from other imperial nations. This was not merely because of the already formidable military might of the USA and other countries of advanced capitalism. Rather, the USA changed the very form of imperial control by refusing to rest its imperium on formal political control. Instead, it set about breaking up the already existing system of formal empires and reconstituting them as politically independent states. Thus the former imperial powers were weakened within the world system, and the imperialised world became areas for the operation of US capital. The USA was already habituated to this mode of imperialism in its own Western 'sphere of influence', where its empire had been established over states which had gained their political independence from European colonial powers within the first half-century of the USA's own independence from Great Britain.

Of course, this did not mean anything so simple as *Pax Americana* operating through a system of 'economic' rather than 'political' control. Economics and politics had never been quite as separate as is often implied in 'pure' and neoclassical theories of capitalism. And what is true of capitalism is also true of imperialism. The period leading up to the First World War itself saw the emergence of finance capital—great concentrations of productive and financial capital aided by their respective nation-states. That this generated inter-imperialist rivalries, and ultimately the Great War itself, is well known. However, as Michael Hudson argues in *Super Imperialism* (an important but neglected study from 1972 that has recently been republished), the end of the Great War introduced a change that was even more far-reaching in its effects on the shape and operation of imperialism, and that now meant US imperialism. While the period before the war had already seen a great concentration of finance capital—a phenomenon which was then extensively analysed on the left and identified as the chief cause of the war—by the end of the war, in place of the concentration of finance in private hands, this concentration was now in the hands of governments, in particular the US government. The war's vast unproductive consumption had created a mountain of debt owed by governments to each other in a complex web of indebtedness. The ultimate creditor in this web was the US government. This change, notes Hudson, was 'not only unforeseen but unforeseeable in the evolving economic and international relations of the period'. Analysed by none of the great writers on imperialism of the time—Hobson, Lenin or Kautsky—it was 'as revolutionary as the Bolshevik revolution itself'. And it raised questions quite different from the ones they had examined: 'The real question which called for examination by scholars, and was not examined, was what it portended for the world that a leading capitalist government would subordinate the interests of its national bourgeoisies to the autonomous interests of a national government'.[17] Indeed, in an interesting further argument, Hudson contended that:

> [The US government] subordinated the individual interests of its separate capitalist groupings to a national political purpose without injuring these interests but subjecting them to more or less effective regulation depending upon the character of the regime. Precisely this but in a far more benign fashion, was implicit in the assumption of the role of the nation and the world's main credit functions by the government of the United States. There was no resistance to this usurpation of power by even the most formidable of domestic or international finance capital

aggregations. On the contrary, the world financial order grew to rest upon the dominant part in world finance not only able to be played but actually played by the government of the United States.[18]

As the sun set on European and Japanese imperialism after the Second World War, the USA undoubtedly maintained an overwhelming military capacity in its favour and has not shied away from using it, or threatening to use it, in its world-wide exercise of power. But the US imperialism that emerged out of the momentous destruction of the two world wars was formatively constituted by a great, and far more complex, intermeshing of the political and the economic, the financial and the military. The historically unprecedented magnitude of unproductive consumption on the part of governments in the wars radically changed the nature of state–economy relations within capitalism, nationally and internationally, and therefore also the characteristic modes and channels through which imperial power worked the system. The US state exercised imperial control not only over territory and population, the necessary substratum of capitalist accumulation, but more than that, it also exercised control over capital itself and its flows.

As mentioned earlier, this financial power of the US government was originally built during the Great War, when the USA, as an initially neutral economic power, made loans to its warring European allies. In the interwar period, the USA built on this original financial superiority further, by insisting, in a departure from the normal practice of financial aid to allies during wars, on the full repayment of the loans that it had made to its allies. These loans, which the allies, in particular Great Britain, the chief target of this policy, had originally been led to believe were on the softest of terms, bordering on grants, now had to be repaid, whether or not defeated Germany was able to pay reparations to its erstwhile enemies. The clear-eyed intent of the USA was to ensure the economic and financial diminution of its chief imperialist rivals in relation to its own power, even at the fateful cost of re-invigorating Germany's productive infrastructure. Only in this way was it able to emerge as 'unquestioned creditor vis-à-vis the world'.[19] The chaotic financial merry-go-around eventually collapsed, and the transmission of its effects to the USA through the repayments mechanism produced the greatest depression in that country, by far the biggest economy of the time. In its turn, by radiating out to the rest of the world economy, this also became the greatest collapse of economic activity seen before or since. It was also the most proximate general cause of the Second World War.[20]

In that conflict, ironically with the help of the USSR, the USA and its allies defeated fascism, the only (reckless) challenge to its overwhelming imperial power ever to have emerged. After its defeat, the requirements of the Cold War meant that various historically differently configured national capitalisms, such as Germany's or Japan's, had to be tolerated,[21] and even new ones, such as South Korea's, fostered. But the end of the Cold War, and particularly the end of financial globalisation in the East Asian Financial crisis of 1998 and the stock market collapse of 2001, showed that such tolerance, whether for a Japan, a Korea or a Germany, now had definite limits. In retrospect it is clear that the dynamics of US imperialism during the Cold War had required tolerance of developmental states among allies. The end of the Cold War, and the opening of a new more volatile and unstable phase of US imperialism, puts an end to such tolerance, and therefore to any realistic aspiration to autonomous national capitalist development.

The dynamics of unstable US hegemony and the end of the Third World

The chief lineaments of this new phase of US imperialism may be briefly summarised. Whereas until 1980 the metropolitan core of the world economy registered the relative advance of Europe and East Asia at the expense of the USA, since then the US economy has grown, initially at the expense of Europe and, starting in the mid-1990s, at the expense of East Asia as well. US growth in this period has been financed by its competitors' trade surpluses with it. The US-dominated world financial system is the mechanism through which the rest of the world, chiefly East Asia and the Third World, has lent the US funds to purchase their exports, thus fuelling investment in the US economy and by US corporations abroad.[22]

The neoliberal 'counter-revolution' in economic policy, launched by the USA and the UK in the early 1980s, and the financial globalisation that went with it, were meanwhile clearly designed to increase the power of US private financial institutions. While critical attention has tended to focus on the depredations of financial dominance in a largely secular sense, its effects on reordering the control of world productive power have been less noticed. Its deflationary effect on the rest of the world economy served to increase the relative productive position of the USA. At the same time, US-dominated world financial markets served to siphon capital from around the world into its decade-long investment boom, a move which further increased the USA's relative productive dominance among the metropolitan economies, and in the world in general. However, the success of this strategy, even for the USA, remains open to question. On the one hand it is still unclear that the core sector identified by the USA—information and communications technology—is able to yield productivity increases, which would make investment in general synonymous with investment in this technology.[23] On the other, potentially more decisive, hand, the economic architecture of this phase of US expansion may be self-contradictory: 'to the extent that the US successfully diverts capital to its own expansion, it brings down the world market into which it must sell ... [while] ... to the extent that other advanced countries set in place effective counter-measures, the US is unable to finance its expansion.'[24] An accompanying countervailing strategy has been:

> the drive to open up the jurisdictions of the East and South East Asian political economies in ways that will enable core capitals to capture economic assets within them and thus ensure that streams of value generated in these societies become the property of the possessing classes of the United states and other OECD states ... this drive is not simply one sided plunder by the dominant states but has real appeal to the propertied classes of the dominated states. They can take advantage of the free movement of capital enforced by the US and its allies to

transfer their assets into metropolitan financial centers and live as rentiers rather than risking their capital in hazardous development strategies locally.[25]

The attempt by the USA to recover its dominance—financial and, if possible, productive—from its low point 30 years ago has been accompanied by a vast military build-up, entailing a third of world expenditure on arms—larger than that of the next nine largest spenders combined—and giving the USA 'unchallengeable military predominance over any combination of hostile states for the foreseeable future'.[26] Any political or military challenge to this US-dominated order, which its allies serve to entrench locally, would have to be an economic one as well and would have to involve an alliance of subordinate powers, something which seems rather remote today either in Europe or in Asia. Nevertheless the USA must today pursue its goals on the basis of a much-reduced relative economic dominance (today it accounts for about a quarter of world GNP, as opposed to almost half at the end of the Second World War). The recent exercise of US global policy has achieved 'unstable expansion', distinct from the 'hegemonic expansion' which preceded it: 'in a hegemonic expansion, the expansion of the leading nation is a condition for the expansion of the other advanced nations. In an unstable expansion, the expansion of the leading nation is an obstacle to the expansion of the other nations.'[27] Like that other declining hegemon, Britain in the late 19th century, the USA today can be expected to pursue two objectives: '1) harnessing and subordinating the labour and wealth of these territories to the expansion of its own capital, effectively providing a privileged zone in which to locate its capital; 2) excluding its otherwise more productive rivals from these advantages.'[28]

The political independence of the Third World was realised at a time when political independence itself became the basis upon which (US) imperium was built. The new modes of imperial control rendered these nominally independent countries incapable of translating political into economic independence in a capitalist world economy. Because the potential for autonomous capitalist development of politically independent states was a reality only in a world where military and imperial conflict between various nations was feasible. *Pax Americana* altered the relations between advanced capitalist states into a fundamentally different one: that of economic competition—a competition supervised and policed by the vastly superior economic and military might of the USA. During the Cold War this reality tended to be concealed and the discourse of development seemed meaningful. The USSR compelled US management of the world order to be focused on defeating communism. As long as the Cold War lasted, its requirements included not only permitting various already advanced and historically distinctive national capitalisms, mainly European and Japanese, to pursue their respective and distinctive paths, but also the development of high levels of capitalist industrialisation in countries which formed crucial fronts in the Cold War, South Korea and Taiwan in particular, even though they competed with US manufactures. The resultant over-capacity created in the world has been seen as the chief cause of the long-term slowdown in capitalist growth that began in the 1960s.[29]

The end of the Cold War has allowed the USA to withdraw its tolerance of

169

this over-capacity and, in the same process, to extend further control over what remains. This was the US– IMF strategy in South Korea, for example, after the 1998 crises. But while this is easier to see now, it is surely not a 'new' reality. The necessary conditions for the autonomous national capitalist development of countries of the Third World had ceased to exist long before. While they lasted, the USSR and the communist bloc generally (China until 1972) were the weak fire which sustained the smoke of the notion of autonomous anti-imperialist national development. And to be sure, it was not an unimportant fire, sustaining small states—such as Cuba and Yugoslavia—in their anti-imperialist stance and extending the room for manoeuvre of some of the more ambitious of the bourgeois states. But it was ultimately simply economically too weak and politically and militarily too hedged in, 'contained', for there to be much more reality to the possibility of a wider 'national bourgeois' and anti-imperialist capitalist, let alone socialist, development. Rather than aiding in a national capitalist anti-imperialism, Soviet support for the various capitalist regimes which emerged in the Third World actually helped to perpetuate the hegemony of the bourgeoisie over the national anti-imperialist struggle.[30] This situation made the possibility of anti-imperialist struggle even more remote, contrary to the idea of a 'national bourgeoisie' which has been so central to the progressive conception of nationalism.

Classes, the nation-state and the Third World

Not only had changes in the configuration of the world order more-or-less extinguished the necessary conditions for autonomous national development at the end of the Great War, the history of capitalist development in the Third World over the past 50 years also demonstrates the lack of the sufficient internal conditions relating to class structure and the nature of the dominant classes for it to take place. This renders questionable either the desire or the imperative for autonomous national development generally imputed to the 'national bour-geoisie'. In an article of 1985 Prabhat Patnaik dwelled on the fate of regimes which had attempted one or another kind of autonomous capitalist development in the second half of the 20th century, regimes like those in India, Egypt, Indonesia and Brazil.[31] He focused on the general reasons why they all eventually succumbed to economic liberalisation, which also meant more open and, indeed, enthusiastic subordination to metropolitan capital. The interest of the article lies in its recognition that imperialist pressures on such regimes, from a flat opposition to industrialisation to later opposition to autonomous industrial-isation, do not in themselves explain liberalisation without an internal context for the same. It is only this context in backward capitalist states that explains why it is that the very 'national bourgeoisie' that had seemed to support, and to have an interest in, autonomous capitalist accumulation began, in one peripheral state after another, to succumb to the lures of economic liberalisation and globalisa-tion. It also helps us to understand why the transition from attempting some sort of statist and autonomous path of development to liberalisation and globalisa-tion, that is, from 'national bourgeoisie' to 'comprador bourgeoisie', has actually been eerily pacific, almost stealthy.

Patnaik provides an insightful structural explanation for this. He argues that the class character of these regimes usually ensures that political independence does not result in significant changes in asset distribution. In backward economies this means, most importantly, that agricultural productivity remains low. In turn, low agricultural productivity limits domestic industrial growth, both through demand constraints and through the further constraint of inequality as the rich save and demand expensive imports while the poor have no excess income beyond spending on the cheaper agricultural wage goods. In such a situation both agriculture and industry become dependent on state expenditure for growth. However, and here lies the crux of the argument, the state is a coalition of the bourgeoisie and landed interests, and with both unwilling to pay taxes in requisite amounts, the state has no recourse but deficit financing. This is not only unjust and exploitative, but precisely because it is so, further exacerbates the constraints on growth. It is, moreover, inflationary, constituting an indirect tax on the poor even as it concentrates income-earning assets among the rich. It is, therefore, a form of revenue raising which constitutes 'a rise in the rate of surplus value', a form of revenue raising preferred in a given class configuration to 'appropriation by the state of part of the surplus value accruing to private propertied classes'.[32] The squeeze on working class consumption further reduces demand for industrial wage goods in a way that the pattern of demand and the 'developmental' efforts of the state, even before any significant liberalisation, create top-heavy industrialisation in capital and luxury goods. The development of such state-aided means of private appropriation and consumption hardly alleviates the revenue problems and this pattern of capitalist development inevitably runs into a fiscal crisis of the state. Despite rising savings, the state cannot generate the revenues to power growth. This is the crisis that leads to liberalisation. As the state ceases to be able to function as an engine of growth, that is sought elsewhere. It is a crisis of capitalist development that is caused by the alliance of the bourgeoisie with the landed classes. Now this bourgeoisie seeks to resolve it by allying with the metropolitan bourgeoisie. Thus the increasing desire of the bourgeoisie for technological links with metropolitan capital, for investment abroad and for investment in luxury goods, not to mention the generalised import mania for elite consumption.

One may add here that the record since Patnaik wrote also shows that the alliance with the landed classes is not necessarily broken, but undergoes complex changes. Differentiation of the peasantry accompanied by the penetration of capitalist production in the countryside may make many among the landed classes themselves capitalist producers, and not just in agriculture but in other sectors as well. These now become just another section of the bourgeoisie, which may compete for state largesse and support in the same way as any other fraction thereof. Indeed, given close ties between the state and the more established fractions of the big industrial bourgeoisie, the rise of this new capitalist fraction usually takes place under anti-statist and neoliberal banners. While some fractions of the capitalist class may actually be hard hit by liberalisation and globalisation and may express their opposition in various ways, such opposition can also be ambiguous or limited given that capitalist development remains the goal and imperative even among these sections. The developmental state having sunk into a fiscal dead end, some form of subordination to metropolitan capital is the only option open to these fractions.

Conclusion: from national bourgeoisie to rogues, failures and bullies

Thus, as it turns out, the 'national' bourgeoisie was not so national in the first place and has become even less so. But it *was* the chief referent of the idea of 'development', the 'Third World' and 'non-alignment'. During the Cold War phase of US imperialism the idea of a national bourgeoisie seemed to be plausible, even though it was not warranted by historical reality. Indeed, given the dynamics of US imperialism, it could not have any basis in reality. We must conclude that what has laid the ideas, such as development and the Third World, to rest is the *implausibility* of the idea of 'national bourgeoisie' in the current phase of US imperialism, not its objective difficulty, which is of much longer standing.

Notes

[1] Cited in A Mayer, *Wilson vs Lenin: The Political Origin of the New Diplomacy*, New York: Meridian Brooks, 1963, p 229.

[2] C Leys, *The Rise and Fall of Development Theory*, Nairobi: James Currey, Indiana University Press and East African Educational Publishers, 1996, p 4.

[3] *Ibid*, p 44.

[4] *Ibid*, p 8.

[5] *Ibid*, p 9.

[6] *Ibid*, p 12.

[7] Colin Leys' critique of UDT is, to my mind, the most thorough and clear headed. See particularly the title essay, 'Underdevelopment and dependency: critical notes', in *ibid*. It rests on transcending the vexed issues of autonomy under imperialism and the 'national bourgeoisie' by conceptualising the problems and prospects of human welfare in the developing world in general, and Africa in particular, and focusing on the prospects of the development of reasonably stable, equal and productive relations of production—either capitalist or socialist. Never, however, shy of the requisite 'pessimism of the intellect' he does not disagree that in contemporary world economic conditions and the configuration of world power, both may be impossible in sub-Saharan Africa. On this see his assessment of the African predicament in the same book.

[8] B Warren, *Imperialism: Pioneer of Capitalism*, London: Verso, 1980.

[9] For example, see B Cumings, 'The North East Asian political economy', in F Deyo (ed), *The Political Economy of the New Asian Industrialism*, Ithaca, NY: Cornell University Press, 1989. See also S Haggard, *Pathways from the Periphery*, Ithaca, NY: Cornell University Press, 1990; and MT Berger, *The Battle for Asia: From Decolonization to Globalization*, London: RoutledgeCurzon, 2003.

[10] P Patnaik, 'Capitalism in Asia at the end of the Millennium', *Monthly Review*, 51 (3), 1999, p 67.

[11] M. Bernard, 'East Asia's tumbling dominoes: financial crises and the myth of the regional model', in L Panitch & C Leys (eds), *Socialist Register*, London: Merlin Press, 1999, pp 196, 203.

[12] The clearest, most succinct discussion of the nature and political implications of this relative decline for the UK itself is C Leys, *Politics in Britain*, London: Verso, 1990.

[13] The literature on 'late development' and its institutional requirements is also extensive. Its beginnings are usually located in Friedrich List's 1841 writings on National Economy as against the Manchesterian 'Free Trade' orthodoxy. Alexander Gerschenkron, *Economic Backwardness in Historical Perspective*, Cambridge, Belknap Press, 1962, is another milestone.

[14] P Patnaik, *Accumulation and Stability under Capitalism*, Oxford: Oxford University Press, 1997, p 9. He clarifies that this is not a mere restatement of underdevelopment theory, mainly because what keeps the periphery in this role of 'stabiliser of the metropolis', even though it is home to substantial manufacturing,

is not imperial political control *per se* but the nature of class relations within the periphery. But there is a radical inconsistency here, for the nature of class relations in the periphery is also importantly determined by imperialism, as his own account betrays. When he argues that 'even if the periphery embarks on the production of what today are "frontier goods", by the time it has mastered this production, product innovation in the metropolis shifts the concept of "frontier goods" ... The relative prices in this situation are not very consequential for reversing the absolute preference ... for the goods of the metropolis. The periphery's ... capacity to undertake a conscious development effort on a scale that would release it from the status of being a stabiliser of the metropolis remains forever impaired ... because the periphery is incapable of being an innovator. It is incapable not because it lacks innovativeness per se but because tastes, including within it, and the definition of what constitutes innovation, are defined by the metropolis. The mere institution of import-substituting industrialisation cannot alter this predicament.' If the 'tastes' of the imperial and imperialised world are constituted in a certain way, what but the structures of imperial cultural control account for this?

[15] 'By 1913 the USA had already become the largest economy in the world, producing over one third of its industrial output—just under the combined total for Germany, Great Britain and France. In 1929 it produced over 42 per cent of the total world output, as against just under 28 per cent for the three European Industrial powers ... In short, after the end of the first World War the USA was in many ways as internationally dominant an economy as it once again became after the Second World War. It was the Great Slump which temporarily interrupted this ascendancy.' E Hobsbawm, *The Age of Extremes: The History of the World 1914–1991*, New York: Pantheon, 1994, p 97. The *World Development Report* puts the GNP of the USA in 1998 at $7921.4 billion, with that of Japan at $4089.4 billion and Germany at $2122.7 billion. The fourth and the fifth largest economies were France ($1466.2 billion) and the UK ($1263.8 billion).

[16] For elaboration of the relationship between the universalisation of the nation-state system and US hegemony, see P Gowan, 'The American campaign for global sovereignty', in L Panitch & C Leys (eds), *Fighting Identities: Race, Religion and Ethno-Nationalism*, London: Merlin Press, 2003; and Berger, *The Battle for Asia*.

[17] M Hudson, *Super Imperialism: The Economic Strategy of American Empire*, New York: Holt Reinhart Winston, 1972, p 6. See also M Hudson, *Super Imperialism: The Origin and Fundamentals of US World Dominance*, London: Pluto Press, 2003.

[18] Hudson, *Super Imperialism* (1972), pp 6–7.

[19] *Ibid*, p 5.

[20] 'It would be false to say that the United States provoked World War II ... It is true, however, that no act, by whatever nation, contributed more to the genesis of World War II than the intolerable and insupportable burdens which the United States deliberately imposed upon its allies of World War I and, through them, upon Germany. In essence, every American Administration, from 1917 through the Roosevelt era, employed a strategy of compelling repayment of the war debts, specifically by England, to so splinter Europe that, politically, the whole of Europe was laid open as a possible province of the United States.' *Ibid*, p 34.

[21] The literature on the historically different national capitalisms is also extensive. Perry Anderson's discussion of these capitalisms in Western Europe, aimed at highlighting the historical lack of anything like this in England, is particularly incisive. See P Anderson, 'The light of Europe', in Anderson, *English Questions*, London: Verso, 1992. On Japan see WK Tabb, *The Postwar Japanese System*, Oxford: Oxford University Press, 1995.

[22] A Freeman, 'Europe, the UK and the global economy', paper presented at the Fifth International Conference in Economics organised by the Economic Research Centre of the Middle East Technical University, Ankara, 11–13 September 2001, mimeo; and R Brenner, *The Boom and the Bubble*, London: Verso, 2002.

[23] Freeman, 'Europe, the UK and the global economy', p 19

[24] *Ibid*. The same contradiction is noted by Brenner, *The Boom and the Bubble*.

[25] P Gowan, 'After America?', *New Left Review*, 13, 2002, pp 139–140.

[26] *Ibid*, p 136.

[27] Freeman, 'Europe, the UK and the global economy', p 18.

[28] Freeman, 'Europe, the UK and the global economy', p 18.

[29] This is the chief argument of Robert Brenner in his, 'The economics of global turbulence', *New Left Review*, 229, 1998.

[30] I owe this point to Prabhat Patnaik.

[31] P Patnaik, 'Political economy of economic liberalisation', *Social Scientist*, July–August, 1985, pp 3–17.

[32] *Ibid*, pp 9, 11.

Reconstituting the 'Third World'? Poverty reduction and territoriality in the global politics of development

HELOISE WEBER

To think about 'development' in global politics has generally meant to think about 'international' development.[1] More specifically, one would think about developing states and, in particular, states of the 'Third World'. In this sense, the

Third World has signified ideas about, and practices of, international development politics and policy. However, in an era of globalisation—distinguished from internationalisation—one might assume that it would be fairly reasonable no longer to find the concept of the Third World an analytically useful category for at least two reasons. First, the Third World—despite its diversity—was associated primarily with postcolonial states as well as states of the global South. Constitutively, the Third World in this sense was *territorially* delineated.[2] Since globalisation implies the decreasing significance of territoriality (at least with reference to the way governance is formed and structured) in global politics, it then also implies that states (conceptualised as sovereign territorially defined polities) and governments associated with the modern state form can no longer be conceived as the central sites of political authority.[3] David Held and Anthony McGrew argue that it is 'clearer than ever that the fortunes of political communities and peoples can no longer be simply understood in exclusively national or territorial terms'.[4] Thus, to use the concept of the Third World (or Third World states) as an *analytical* category, which in its classic form relied on the territorial-sovereignty-authority link, is, it would seem, to continue to invoke a way of thinking that no longer offers a meaningful reference point for contemporary global politics. Moreover, as Mark Berger notes in his introduction to this special issue, the Third World also expressed, or at least implied, a political (ideological) commitment to non-alignment during the Cold War. Therefore, with the end of the Cold War and with it the passing of the notion of the Second World, the category of the Third World has lost much, if not all, of its political significance.[5]

But, because the Third World was first and foremost a concept that signified (and continues to signify) a point of reference for development in global politics, it has retained a political utility that has survived the end of the Cold War. This political utility derived primarily from the conception that the idea of underdevelopment was central to the territorially grounded notion of the Third World, and to the ideological connotations expressed by it during the Cold War: there was a direct and immediate conceptual association of the Third World with underdevelopment.[6] From this perspective, as Marc Williams argues, if the Third World is 'anything', it 'is a political and ideological concept', and it is as such that it continues to be utilised in political analyses of global inequality.[7] Its usage in the latter sense is new, in that it generally transcends the association of the term with territoriality (ie with particular states) and, as such, attempts to capture and express, if not the idea of underdevelopment, then certainly increased risk and vulnerabilities and new forms of social stratification in a global context. For example, Caroline Thomas has stated that as 'we enter the millennium, the Third World, far from disappearing, is becoming global'.[8] In a similar mode William Robinson has stated that globalisation 'involves restructuring in both centre and periphery, which is resulting in what some have called the "Latinamericanization" of the United States or the "Third-Worldization" of the First World'.[9] Berger, on the other hand, in a critical overview of both the uses of the term and its analytical limitations, has observed that the 'idea of a Third World now serves an important function in terms of the management of the

175

global political economy and allows for the homogenisation of the history of diverse parts of the world'. To both capture the political significance of the term and overcome the problems associated with its use, he proposed, as an alternative, an approach that 'locates the politics of development in both historically particular and global processes'.[10] This is a useful point of departure for thinking about the social and political organisation of global inequality. Political analyses conducted from this vantage point explicate the way in which ideology is intrinsic in emancipatory discourses that seek to legitimate the reproduction of the conditions which enable continuing practices of inequality. The perspective shifts from engaging ideas about development as an apolitical 'issue' to a concept that is ideological and hence political. It is precisely the extent of what constitutes the political—the ideas and processes that delimit and define the boundaries of the political—that is at stake when one explores the global organisation of inequality through a critical evaluation of the politics of (international) development.

My primary objective in this article is to explore the relationship between the politics of international development and the reproduction of global inequality. Thus, while I consider the social and political impact of the emerging 'architecture for development' by engaging the strategy on its own terms, a core objective is to elucidate the political (ideological) underpinnings of *international* development by locating this idea and practice within a broader structural framework of *global* politics, in the context of the organisation of capitalism. In other words, I want to show how the politics of (international) development[11] is implicated in both a discourse and the practices that legitimate and reproduce certain core assumptions of global politics, which themselves render the conditions for the reproduction of specific constitutional features conducive to the organisation of capitalism on a global scale. This refers to the way in which the politics of development both relies on and at the same time reproduces assumptions about state sovereignty and territoriality. These assumptions form key operating premises of both International Relations (IR) and Development Studies (DS), and the two disciplines converge in framing the politics of development in accordance with them. If it can be argued that the politics of development has been implicated in the organisation of global capitalism and the management of social and political contradictions of inequality and poverty, the idea of the *international* has served as a necessary politically disciplining boundary. The notion of the international circumscribes political boundaries because it can only define itself by reference to state sovereignty and territoriality that have been (and are) central to the operating assumptions of DS and are also at the foundation of the theory and practice of most IR.[12] That these assumptions function as powerful ideological tools can be discerned by focusing on the way in which they preclude analyses of how unequal global social relations are *socially* (and *politically*) constituted.

To explicate this point, my analysis of the governance—in particular the disciplinary—aspects of the form and content of the emerging architecture for development relies to some extent on understanding the history of the political uses of the Third World, and the way in which this has shaped the contemporary development agenda. I limit my analysis to the politics of development as it emerged through DS in the post-1945 era, an era which was also ostensibly of the project of 'national development'. In this context, I revisit key methodological premises that shaped the study of the Third World and Third Worldism during the Cold War. These are the primacy of the territorial (a privileging of spatial ordering) and the overall presence (and acceptance) of modernisation through capitalism in conceptualisations of (and approaches to) development.[13] The politics of development functioned against the backdrop of these assumptions; this dynamic, played out in the inside/outside logic, can be seen to inform the political utility of the Third World.

Why ought this to be a problem, both in and of itself, and especially in an era of globalisation? As Berger has argued the 'idea and practice of national development as it was consolidated and universalised after 1945 was profoundly flawed', while the shape of the globalisation project since the 1970s 'compounded the failures of national development and introduced new problems'.[14] Julian Saurin has similarly unpacked the ideological content of the discourse of 'national development' in relation to the organisation of global inequality.[15] One might then perhaps expect—in an era of globalisation, and especially 'contested globalisation' under which social and political solidarities are emerging in a more pronounced way to challenge the incremental trend towards the consolidation of a 'constitution for global capitalism'[16]—there to be a decline in efforts which draw on foundational assumptions about the political form rendered in terms of International Politics. At one level, such a tendency is clearly evident, for instance with reference to globalisation theory[17] and analyses of emerging forms of regional integration,[18] and is even implied by the proponents of development.[19] Yet how and why, one might then ask, is the project of 'national development' at the same time being revived so rigorously through the politics of development? Even a cursory inquiry into the emerging architecture for development clearly shows that it continues to be framed in terms of the methodological premises that informed analyses of the Third World. This poses several questions, particularly if one were to take the analysis of globalisation theorists as cited above seriously, whose stance would entail that such a framework for development is no longer appropriate.[20] Additionally, one could also argue that it is no longer tenable—even in the form of a social democratic model—given the way the global political economy has evolved especially since the 1970s.[21]

If questions of inequality inform the overall analyses, one could take this critique further and problematise the meta-theoretical assumptions which framed, and still frame, the project of national development itself, independently of its functional capacity under globalisation. From such a perspective the constitutive rules that define global politics in terms of the inside/outside logic—reflected in terms of the domestic/international divide—themselves become the focus of critical scrutiny. As Saurin has argued, applications of methods of enquiry into poverty and development, which do not start by questioning the very 'constitutive rules' (territorialism and state sovereignty), have:

> Typically involved the disaggregation of global development into a parallel series of national narratives of separate and discrete development, which only come

together in some contrived domain known as the international. The corollary of this focus is the displacement of analyses of the *global reconfiguration of social authority* which is not territorially based and which, indeed, transcends any spatial division of the world.[22]

To understand the implications of this blind spot (ie the obscuring of the social dimension) reinforced through the ideology of national development, it is necessary to step beyond state-centric assumptions and the way in which these inform understandings about political community. In the realm of social and political struggle today it is possible to identify both direct engagement of this problem of the form and manifestations of political tension which reflect a crisis of legitimacy *vis à vis* the two assumptions cited above.[23] This indicates a potential to transcend established ideas about the political limits of (national) territorial boundaries and hence places at stake precisely the constitutive rules of political discipline. It is at this particular historical juncture that the politics of international development returns in the form of the project of national development; the necessary existence of developing states also makes possible the ideas and practices which revolve around the notion of the international (together with the associated political consequences). In this context I make my case about the reconstitution of the political utility of the Third World, through a renewed global focus on international development.

I proceed in three stages. First, I expand on what I mean by the political utility of the Third World and outline the significance of this for the consolidation of the core elements of the post-1945 structures of governance. Second, I provide a brief overview of the contemporary global political context in which the emerging architecture for development is situated. Here I engage the ideological content of the politics of 'contested globalisation' by reading the globalisation/anti-globalisation dynamic in terms of struggles between efforts to further entrench the legislative framework of global capitalism and social and political struggles for alternatives. I critically explore the methodological premises underpinning the emerging architecture for development and relate these to that which framed the political utility of the Third World. Third, I focus on the recasting of the IMF and World Bank's conditional lending strategy in terms of the Poverty Reduction Strategy Papers (PRSP) to illustrate the emerging form and content of the architecture for development. The PRSP approach is represented, by its sponsors, as a means to enhance democratic participation in governance, implying opportunities to shape policy in context-sensitive situations. I identify the PRSP approach as instrumental to efforts to constitutionalise a particular form of governance (for developing countries) conducive to capitalist restructuring. This form frames the content of the PRSPs in a way that aligns it with the objectives of the World Trade Organization (WTO). Through this example I demonstrate the way the particular form of (state) sovereign territoriality and a liberal property rights regime is reproduced, expanded (and consolidated) globally through the politics of international development. I conclude on the issue of the politics of methodological choices and the advancement of critical scholarship (and progressive politics).[24]

The Third World and world order

Political utility, underdevelopment and the Third World

The political utility of the Third World derived to a significant degree from its close connection to the concept of underdevelopment; in particular by reference to the way in which this was conceptualised (ie in relational terms to other states and, for example, by reference to various economic indicators of development). Approaches that informed the methods of inquiry into the Third World and its problematique (ie underdevelopment) were based on the two key assumptions outlined above (territoriality and modernisation via capitalism). The story about the Third World, as told in general terms as well as self-referentially by officials of Third World states, partakes unambiguously in the first assumption, and proffers the conceptual undercarriage for the second through the notion (and narratives) of underdevelopment.[25] This narrative informed the way in which the solution was then defined (ie the national development project). By recourse to the two methodological premises Third World state representatives sought to be the 'third force' during the Cold War through a form of 'self-identification' which entailed notions of social marginalisation, deprivation and political power-lessness.[26] The political utility of the 'third force' was constructed through these very sentiments, which were actively appropriated in order to call either for 'special needs' in the new world order or for a reform of that order to meet those special needs. The strategy was to seek a context-sensitive position that would create a more reasonable playing field for partaking in the organising of global capitalism. At no time did the coalition of Third World states seek to transcend either, or both, of the two assumptions outlined above. Rather, the two assumptions were constitutive to the political project for which they actively utilised their 'Third Worldness' and their need to move from underdevelopment to development to advance their wider political goals.[27]

The political utility of the Third World then rested with reference to the political space (and opportunities) its (ideological) appropriation enabled for strategies of governance in global politics. There is no doubt, as many have argued, that the complexities of the Cold War made it near impossible for Third World states to consolidate their social divisions internally (many of which were the legacies of colonialism) in order to be able speak and think in solidarity about development alternatives to capitalism-cum-territoriality.[28] It is nevertheless also the case that some agents within these states actively pursued the modernisation project through capitalism. Third Worldism (however unwittingly) legitimated and contributed to the reinforcing of the constitutive rules enabling the political reproduction of global inequality. It is at this juncture that complementary workings of the ideology of a dominant theory of international relations in the discipline of IR (realism) and the remit of DS of providing the means to address the Third World problem in world order become discernible.

International Relations theory, global inequality and the Third World

The two methodological assumptions outlined above sit neatly between a realist theory of IR and the imperatives of global capitalism. With the first the point of reference of development is the 'state', understood in a reified sense, and read in accordance with the structuring of its relations 'outside' premised upon Sovereignty. With the second, the focus is on the reified state as well, but from 'within', enabling the comparative measurement of state performance with reference to 'development indicators' such as Gross National Product (GNP) 'within' the bounded territory. Such an approach takes as its point of departure the territorial and reads—within its confines—the story of development through particular indicators, such as gross national product (GNP). Yet its indicators say nothing in and of themselves about the distribution of the GNP, or how this GNP came about (labour input, wages in relation to purchasing power parity, labour standards, environmental impacts, etc). These indicators of 'development' must be seen as 'important abstractions' that 'are unable to record the insecurities which characterise capitalist development, nor to reflect the permanent revolt against development'.[29] Fundamentally, because the *social* does not constitute the analytical point of reference, the approach cannot capture these conditions in terms of social experiences or explain them as consequences of global social relations. Because the state is perceived in terms of both a natural and reified form, one cannot see, from this angle, world order as constituted in terms of global social relations.

Part of the relevance of this story for the politics of development, framed as it was by the notion of underdevelopment of the states of the Third World, was about the social experiences (development/equality) of the developed states of the 'First World'. Assumptions about development as modernisation (through capitalism) which informed a Third World political project were partly constructed on the Third World's own self-image and partly in relation to images and assumptions of and about the First World. The latter have been precisely just that; images and assumptions of near perfect development.[30] This myth has been part of the problem, an important part that has contributed to the human tragedy encountering 'development' as a planned process of modernisation through capitalism.[31] For instance, the labour struggles in the post-1945 era are testimony to the class differentiation and inequality of the development model aspired to by the majority of the states of the Third World. These social experiences were often not made explicitly visible during the Cold War; in this period they could be displaced as a problem in, and for, the Third World. In this sense the political utility of the Third World can be seen to have had a disciplinary function in that it legitimated inequality within through stories about the external Other. While the dominant approach in IR provides the normative and associated legal theory of sovereignty and the territorially constituted (nation) state, DS gives further legitimacy to these structures by drawing on their very premises to make the enabling environment for capitalism from 'within', so to speak.

Development Studies, the political utility of the Third World and global capitalism

The relationship between DS and the organisation of global capitalism has occurred very much against the backdrop of the political utility of the Third World. For instance, although DS is ostensibly responding to underdevelopment as an (apolitical) issue, the ideology and practice of DS is grounded in the norms and values of liberal politics. It is with reference to the ideological struggles of the Cold War that DS emerged in a clearly defined way in the post-1945 world. 'Development practice' through the politics of the aid regime is one example of the way in which DS contributed to the organisation of global capitalism.[32] For example, through the World Bank and the United States Agency for International Development (USAID) considerable effort was made to entrench the ideology of liberal political economy (through notions of freedom and discourses of entrepreneurial success).[33] These 'ideas' underpinned the appropriate changes to national and local legislation. By the 1970s the 'basic needs' approach provided an added impetus to what was already in the making. As Third World states called for a New International Economic Order (NIEO) to address their development concerns, the World Bank stepped in to provide for the 'poor' who, they claimed, were being hard done by, by their states. The global political restructuring since the 1970s (especially of the advanced capitalists states) was significantly facilitated by the political utility of the Third World: it legitimated the implementation of legal rules and cultural norms on to which more enhanced forms of 'structural adjustment' came to be grafted in a way so as to accommodate the shifts of the 1970s.[34] By the 1980s structural adjustment was well underway together with 'emergency social funds' and other targeted poverty reduction strategies to give adjustment a 'human face'. It has been demonstrated how these very targeted poverty reduction policies were consciously designed primarily to further liberalisation and privatisation strategies, and in particular financial sector liberalisation.[35]

Importantly, this does not mean that political restructuring advanced through DS (although it emerged in the USA) was carried out in ways that suggested ideological incompatibility between those liberal values and those proposed by certain factions or groups or people within the states of the Third World itself.[36] It is precisely this social and political dynamic that cannot be captured in terms of a state-centric perspective. Here we can reconnect again to the political utility of the Third World: the association of problems of underdevelopment and inequality with territorially delineated Third World (nation)-states obscured the realm of social relations—and more precisely their global constitution—in political (ideological) struggles. It deflected from the need for explanations about inequality 'within', and distracted from focussing on the way in which the foundations of world order were already of global character, at least with reference to political economy (the establishment, for instance, of the WTO is already 'anticipated' in the way in which the Bretton Woods system was conceived). By reinforcing the methodological premises of the politics of development, DS can be seen to function instrumentally in global politics, giving legitimacy to the territorially bounded consolidation of global capitalism.

Globalisation, the WTO and developing states

Many of the political-economy aspects of globalisation can be directly related to the crisis of the 1970s. Thus, 'the restructuring arising in the late 1970s, and continuing through the 1980s and 1990s, has entailed a reorganisation *via global* regulation'.[37] One key example of the latter is reflected in the legal framework of the WTO.[38] It is important to recognise that these processes were facilitated via the state form itself. The rise of the 'new economy' since has entailed an increase in perceptions of risk as well as actual practices of risk enhancement.[39] As social and political movements from within the Third World posed sustained challenges to the representatives of their states for their role in the instituting of ever-more 'market'-based policies, there was at least a symbolic rejection of the politics of the New Right in the advanced capitalist states. It is precisely the normative shift in governance since the 1970s which advanced transnationally, ushered in the challenges in an equally transnational fashion. This has set new political challenges for the project of consolidating global capitalism and especially the framework of the 'new economy' as it has emerged since the 1970s.[40]

The 'clash of globalisations', the new terrain of ideological struggle and the political utility of the Third World

The many emerging sites of resistance to neoliberal hegemony expressed through social movements protests or organised groupings are no longer confined—if they ever really were—within the nation-state system as it was universalised during the second half of the 20th century. Given the way in which these struggles are circumscribed, they can be conceptualised heuristically, in terms of a double movement (the struggle between attempts to further entrench 'marketisation' and efforts to resist and direct this trend towards 'social purposes' or needs).[41] Issues of poverty conceptualised as immiseration, notions of development, inequality and social risk are central to the debates engendered by this constellation.

Even though some of these contestations are local in context, their political ontology, at least with reference to 'strategy' is not necessarily framed in terms of—or by—the national territorial form. This differentiates these struggles from the dominant state-centric expression of ideological struggles during the Cold War. For example, one of the most visibly global movements *qua* organisation is evident in the politics of the World Social Forum (WSF). The WSF has now been meeting annually in Porto Allegre, Brazil to coincide with the annual World Economic Forum (WEF) normally held at Davos, Switzerland.[42] What is interesting about something like the WSF and the self-consciously political forces reflected in such gatherings is that these forces are not taking underdevelopment as their point of reference, nor the Third World as traditionally conceptualised. Rather, they reflect an awareness of the way in which the proponents of neoliberal politics are organising globally in ways that heighten risk and attempt to de-politicise these very practices globally. Even on a sparse reading of the political potential of these emerging social forces one could not but acknowledge the rejection of trends to further entrench 'market society'. In this sense, the metaphor of the 'clash of globalisations'[43] can be seen to circumscribe the social and political struggle that ensues globally over the global (re)production of social risk and immiseration. This crisis of legitimacy of global politics is also a crisis of legitimacy of *international* politics in so far as the constitutive rules are—consciously or unconsciously—bypassed because of a growing implicit understanding that the discipline of the territorial state form is part of the problem rather than the solution.

Recent political (public policy) responses to the legitimacy problems immanent to these political struggles suggest a turning-point in the 'policies' advancing 'marketisation', which is reflected in an intense and forceful new global discourse about poverty reduction and development. Yet these shifts and accompanying sets of 'development strategies' are not constructed so as to respond to either the target of the criticisms (ie neoliberal ideology), nor do they speak to the *global* dimension of social and political struggle. Instead, the focal point is the construction of the architecture for development that is to be targeted at developing countries.

In the course of the making of this architecture, references to poverty reduction and empowerment of the 'poor in poor countries' and 'developing countries' have recently taken centre stage at key global conventions. Commitments to the millennium development goals—targeted toward the developing countries—are often invoked in these contexts. More recently the WTO's Doha ministerial meeting was declared a 'development round', the success of which would enable poor countries to 'trade themselves out of poverty'.[44] Such a narrative has now acquired a powerful momentum that has contributed to a veritable frenzy about development and poverty reduction. While the contemporary context is very different, this return to the question of poverty reduction is still suggestive of the earlier post-1945 context (of decolonisation, Cold War and the universalisation of the nation-state system) out of which development studies emerged. Thus, here we have once again the revival of the national development project; international development becomes an important moral purpose in the context of the crisis of international politics.

The formal story about the emergence of this 'new' development focus, however, makes no reference to this crisis of legitimacy, rather it tells us that in 1999 key policy decisions taken at the level of global institutions paved the way for the architecture for development.[45] An important aspect of this was outlined in the World Bank's Comprehensive Development Framework (CDF)[46]. This was rapidly followed by the decision to enhance the link between international debt relief and poverty reduction, which resulted in the Heavily Indebted Poor Country initiative (HIPC2).[47] The CDF principles are supposed to create an enabling environment to help the HIPCs (and other developing states) meet the international development targets and generally facilitate the conditions conducive to investment. The latter is viewed as a precondition for growth, which in turn is anticipated to result in poverty reduction. In this context it has been emphasised that for both globalisation and development:

> 1999 could well have been a turning point, from three angles: implementation of poverty reduction strategies; promoting real and operational partnership, based on shared responsibilities; and a systematic focus on the principles of policy coherence and governance.[48]

As to what exactly the above might entail, this has been explained by the Development Assistance Committee of the OECD in the following terms:

> The success of the strategy of partnership and integration into the global economy will depend also on the attention that is paid, concretely and systematically to policy

coherence ... Here, coherence means coherence between policies in the North and South alike, and of all within the multilateral organization.[49]

This emerging dynamic was also reflected in the Ministerial Declaration at the WTO meeting in Doha in 1999, which stated that:

> The challenges Members face in a rapidly changing international environment cannot be addressed through measures taken in the trade field alone. We shall continue to work with the Bretton Woods institutions for greater coherence in global economic policy-making.[50]

The global organisation of the project of poverty reduction entails in particular policy co-ordination between the WTO, the IMF and the World Bank.[51] This dynamic constitutes a core aspect in the making of the architecture for development and can be seen to frame private commercial law as 'public policy' for poverty reduction. The *form* this co-operation facilitates comprises aspects of constitutional/quasi-constitutional norms and rules, which define in legal terms the limits of what is politically possible. Its *content* prescribes the range, scope and depth of policies accommodated either within the constraints of the form, or in ways that contribute to advancing its constitutional force.[52] The PRSP initiative—as an approach to national development—advances this dynamic to a considerable degree.

The Poverty Reduction Strategy Papers and world order

International development and the PRSPS

The IMF and the World Bank, in a recent review, described the PRSP initiative in the following terms:

> In December 1999, the Boards of the World Bank and the IMF approved a new approach to the challenge of reducing poverty in low-income countries based on country-owned poverty reduction strategies. These strategies were expected to be country-driven, results oriented, comprehensive and long-term in perspective, and foster domestic and external partnership in line with the principles that underpin the Comprehensive Development Framework (CDF). They were to be embodied within a Poverty Reduction Strategy Paper (PRSP), which was expected to serve as a framework for development assistance *beyond* the operations of the Fund and the Bank.[53]

The PRSPS are single policy documents—which are supposed to be written by respective state officials in close consultation with the IMF, the World Bank and other multilateral donors, where applicable. The content of a country's PRSP and its respective Country Assistance Strategy (CAS) of the World Bank and Poverty Reduction and Growth Facility (PRGF) of the IMF ought to be in alignment. In other words, the *content* of a PRSP has to be substantially compatible with the framing prescriptions of the CAS and the PRGF.[54]

Since July 2002 PRSPS have formally replaced the Policy Framework Papers (PFPS). The PFPS were 'tripartite' documents between a low-income country, the IMF and World Bank. Unlike the former PFPS, the PRSPS are extensive in their reach and objectives. They apply to *all* Part II member countries of the Bretton Woods institutions that wish to access funds on a concessional basis, not just those that fall within the HIPC2 initiative. For countries that fall within the latter the PRSP framework is mandatory. Bilateral and multilateral donor assistance, as well as the operational policies of regional development banks, will be streamlined in accordance with a country's respective PRSP.[55] The European Union has already decided to 'base its assistance to the Africa, Caribbean, and the Pacific region on the PRSP framework'.[56]

All PRSPs whether written by a country's own national, regional or even local level policy-making teams must have the endorsement of the Boards of the IMF and the Word Bank. A PRSP for a particular government/country:

> will be considered by the Fund and Bank Boards and, if deemed adequate, endorsed in so far as it relates to policies and programs supported by each institution in its area of responsibility.[57]

This implies that their policy content should be compatible with prescriptions of the key institutions underwriting the process. To this effect, the IMF and World Bank are explicit on the fact that the 'PRSPs will be applied in accordance with Board-approved operational policies'.[58] A key criterion of the PRSP initiative is that the government concerned must, at least to some degree, have already implemented IMF and World Bank-supported structural adjustment programmes (SAPS). In the absence of such implementation, Interim-PRSPs are deployed to set the 'enabling environment' for the implementation of the full PRSP process. Moreover, the set of strategies proposed in an Interim-PRSP or a full PRSP are to build on existing policies, particularly the poverty reduction strategies that may have been in place already (subject to these being endorsed as appropriate by the Boards of the IMF and World Bank).[59] This ensures the continuity of the SAPS process and the policy (political) framework this entails, which, as stated above, is one of the preconditions for moving on to the full PRSP process.

The PRSP initiative is said to have direct implications for the World Bank's forthcoming Operational Policy (OP 1.00) on Poverty Reduction.[60] OP 1.00 is set to frame overall operations of the World Bank and is based on the recognition that the World Bank's foremost task is 'poverty reduction'. This makes clear the relevance of the World Bank's Operational Policies for the formulation of their content. The way in which the World Bank's Operational Policies are being defined with reference to the harmonisation drives that are ensuing as a result of 'inter-agency co-operation' between itself, the IMF and the WTO, must, as a consequence, also pre-frame the policy framework of the PRSPs.[61]

The World Trade Organization and the PRSPs

There are also examples of PRSPs written to meet the objectives of the General Agreement on Tariffs and Trade (GATT). This is gradually being expanded to include the re-regulation of other sectors, a focus that can be seen to coincide with various WTO Agreements.[62] The World Bank has stated that through the PRSPs it 'seeks to link external support to domestically developed, results-based poverty strategies'. The aim of the approach, said to be based on 'broad participatory dialogue with representatives of civil society and the private sector' is to:

- help national authorities develop a better understanding of the obstacles to poverty reduction and growth and devise good indicators of progress in poverty reduction;
- deepen a shared vision of desired poverty reduction goals across society;
- lead to formulation of *priorities for public actions* to achieve the desired poverty reduction outcomes;
- encourage the development of participatory processes for setting poverty reduction goals and monitoring implementation and progress.[63]

A comprehensive review of the PRSP approach stated that closer attention ought to be paid to the programme's emerging content,[64] and goes on to identify priority public actions for the coming years. These comprise the inclusion of sector-based policies in PRSPs: the sectoral focus is explained in terms of enhancing market access for poverty reduction.[65] These initiatives are closely associated with the WTO and the General Agreement on Trade in Services (GATS) and with GATS-type policies, which are core concerns of the Doha round. The PRSP framework is uniquely suited to catalyse the implementation of the Doha round objectives by facilitating the stages of implementation for the final 'lock in' at the level of the WTO. This can be achieved either by writing in commitments made with reference to the WTO or independently through the Interim-PRSP or full PRSPs.[66] With reference to efforts to co-ordinate the imperatives of the 'new economy', it can come as no surprise that the World Bank's 2003 *World Development Report* is to focus on *services* for development. A recent analysis of the post-Doha development agenda by Bernard Hoekman suggested that the implementation of development-'friendly' WTO rules,[67] as well as any problems of implementation, ought to be considered in 'the context of a nation's overall development strategy'.[68] He also suggested that such assessments could be informed by 'national development frameworks' such as the PRSPs.[69] This idea parallels those already proposed in key reports on coherence between the WTO, IMF and World Bank.

Reproducing inequality

The PRSP approach—as a core determinant of the emerging architecture of development—is firmly grounded in the two methodological premises that also informed the political project of the Third World. These give legitimacy to the constitutive rules of global politics and the inequality they entail. Thus this methodological problem alone, or indeed, the politics that inform the choice of this methodology, should, in the light of the above analysis, be sufficient to challenge the 'development'-orientated discourses that frame the PRSP approach. This point can be made with reference to both the form and content it projects in global politics. Through its form the very contested normative framework of global capitalism—private commercial law—is being extended and consolidated as public policy.[70] What of the arguments that point to the status of PRSPs as 'conditionalities', and hence suggest that they are an imposition on 'developing states' and are undermining their 'sovereignty', thus also implying opportunities to develop alternative 'development' policies? It must be noted here that, although the PRSPs are to be endorsed by the boards of the IMF and Word Bank, this is not a requirement in the formal sense; yet without this endorsement they are void.[71] The logic of the predefined framework for PRSPs stands. As a descriptive point then, one would need to concede this observation about the 'conditional' status of the PRSPs.

If, for a moment, we were to consider international criticisms of the kind suggested above, we could fall sympathetically on the side of Brazil and India (developing states) with reference to their continued rejection of, say, GATS and GATS-type policies and argue that through the PRSPs they become imposed.[72] This overlooks the reality of the promises of 'development' for the landless movement in Brazil and the communities in the *favelas*, the risk and misery that engulf many a human being who stares you in face in the streets of Calcutta or New Delhi. This poverty lives alongside much affluence. One must surely question why the *modus operandi* that has produced this as the past is very much a part of the present. What is clear is that regulation of the conditions of poverty (past and existing) and the continued restructuring from Bolivia to New Zealand to Bangladesh to Mexico to Canada in the ongoing logic of commodification has been imposed insofar as social groups within these states opposed its implementation. Its implementation (through legislature), however, has been facilitated by those who subscribe to these very ideals globally and they have been rejected by those with alternative political visions also globally. What is clear is that alternative policies, particularly those that fall outside the framework of private commercial law, may not be regarded as representative of equally valid forms of knowledge to be incorporated in political practice.[73] Again, on the supreme 'authority' of the state will the decision to exclude and include acts of compliance and resistance rest. One need only look at the latest Ministerial Declarations of the Group of 77 to appreciate their formal commitment to international development in the logic of this emerging 'architecture for development'.[74]

Going back to the issue of the PRSPs and sovereignty: the simple point here is that to invoke the critique of conditionality as the limitation of national autonomy vis-à-vis inequality and poverty is to reinforce the very conditions upon which the organisation of global inequality is premised. I do not wish to be misunderstood here. I do not make claims that abject poverty is always experienced in the same way by all peoples, rather that, to address the problem and understand the way it is organised on a global scale, we need to look beyond the given framework of analysis. In this context we need to become aware of the role of the constitutive principle(s) in the ordering of social and political discipline (not only, but also, through the politics of development) which enable the reproduction of these practices.[75]

Conclusion

I have shown how since 1945 the global politics of international development has been complicit in the making of a particular world order both conceptually and through appropriately structured forms of governance. This world order is premised on narrow conceptions of the political. Certain ontological premises have been crucial to legitimating the given framework of analysis within which the stories about national development through the practices of *international* development are said to occur. These ontological premises aid a reified conception of the structure of the world in ways that have obliterated the realm of the social. The ideological dimension of these ontological premises, however, become visible once we ask what international development has to do with the development of global constitutional features such as the WTO.

International development, as I have argued, has played a constitutive role in the ordering of this global trend by disguising the way in which modern inequality and immiseration are a product of global social relations. In particular, I have discussed the return of 'international' development at this particular historical juncture when 'anything could happen'[76] in an era of 'contested globalisation'. The idea of the Third World of developing countries functions similarly to legitimate practices of governance in a way that relies on the framing of poverty and inequality in terms conducive to the constitutive rules which frame global politics: as territory/state together with a liberal political economy. Through the example of the PRSP approach I have also demonstrated that the territorial state form is clearly far more significant to the ordering of capitalism than is commonly assumed under the aegis of de-territorialised global social relations.

The continued global organisation of the politics of international development can be seen then as an attempt to reconstitute the political utility of the Third World. At this particular historical juncture it is an attempt to firmly ground the 'constitutive rules' of global politics, at least for the present. The project of comprehensively consolidating a global constitution such as the WTO is still very much in the making; it needs the disciplinary capacity of the state to frame the rules and rule over the global territory. Many of the Southern states (and surely others as well), have still to make the appropriate binding legal commitments central to the new economy (and which are also at the centre of the Doha 'development' round).[77] Through the PRSP initiative a framework is established with predefined sets of 'policies' by which the state makes commitments to amend the constitution or legislation in a way that will guarantee the property rights regimes as instituted, for example, in the WTO.

Thus, through the way in which the discourses about development replay the co-ordinates of inequality/equality, underdeveloped/developed through a spatial cartography, they can be seen to function as a counter-discourse to displace what is generally also implicit in the dynamic of the 'clash of globalisations': the problematisation of territoriality as a political principle. The politics of international development also displaces the point of reference of the critics—global capitalism—while consolidating forms of 'new constitutionalism' which aim to discipline global social struggle through the undemocratic practice of the legal foreclosure of the democratic provision for political alternatives. It is in this sense that the architecture for (international) development functions as a crucial marker both discursively and practically in the organisation and reproduction of global inequality.

188

One may ask here, which way forward? How could the spirit of social solidarity be reinforced as a counter-measure to the ever more de-solidarising implications of neoliberal governance? We could start by reflecting on the assumptions about disciplinary boundaries that are reinforced by, and grounded in, the (nation)-state system. This is important, not least because analysis of the political reproduction of immiseration and social discipline in world order has to acknowledge the way in which 'the problem of inequality is already deeply inscribed in our modern accounts of the international, and thus of modern politics'. For Walker this ought to be seen as preceding 'any consideration of the dynamics associated with modern capitalism as a specific form of economic life that thrives on the production of inequality as a condition of its own dynamic'.[78] These premises nevertheless play a foundational role in the organisation and management of global capitalism and the global social struggles it engenders.[79] Subscribing to them as meta-theoretical assumptions constitutes a political act in so for as they are implicated in legitimating the structures of inequality *before* their practical consolidation. The continued framing of the 'development problematique' in terms of the methodological territorialist approach through which the normative ideal of freedom through capitalism is to be realised is to reinforce the conditions that enable the reproduction of inequality and poverty.

The critique advanced in this argument does not imply that, what could be seen as the corollary approach—methodological cosmopolitanism—necessarily resolves the 'development problematique' in contemporary world politics. Rather, it implies that to meaningfully address the specificities of *social* and *political* experiences in the context of a changing global order it is necessary to develop an approach sensitive to the various sites of social struggle in the context of their 'locales' as well as their connectivity in global space. Such an approach offers the potential to identify and build upon the 'spaces of hope' for social (and political) transformation. On this reading, 'development' can no longer be conceived of as an 'issue in world politics', but rather as a central integral element of the political (and ideology) as such.[80] Reflecting on the implications of the form (which can be seen as a means to safeguard the content) in the making of disciplinary boundaries of political community might be a step in the right direction. To grasp this moment in the movement of history is to reflect on the form and the way in which it is socially and politically constituted. This means that the moment is ever present; to lose sight of this would indeed be a tragedy.

Notes

1. The use of international rather than inter-national is intended to capture conceptual problems and political implications of some fundamental assumptions about the territorial and spatial framing of global politics; these will become evident as I develop my critique of the politics of development.
2. See for example, Marc Williams, *International Economic Organisation and the Third World*, Hemel Hempstead: Harvester Wheatsheaf, 1994, p 4. See also Caroline Thomas, *In Search of Security: The Third World in International Relations*, Brighton: Wheatsheaf Books, 1987, pp 1–4.

[3] I use the term 'state' rather than 'nation-state' at this point in the argument in order to address the problem of Westphalian assumptions about the idea of the permanence of sovereignty and territoriality. See, for instance, RBJ Walker, 'Claims about history are also usually indispensable to claims about nation. By contrast, claims about state sovereignty suggest permanence; relatively unchanging territorial space to be occupied by a state characterised by temporal change; or a spatial-cum-institutional container to be filled by the cultural or ethnic aspirations of a people. Governments and regimes may come and go, sovereign states, these claims suggest, go on forever.' Walker, *Inside/Outside: International Relations and Political Theory*, Cambridge: Cambridge University Press, 1995, p 166. For interesting discussions of the state and nation-state see the collection of essays in Joseph A Camilleri, Anthony P Jarvis & Albert J Paolini (eds), *The State in Transition—Reimagining Political Space*, London: Lynne Rienner, 1995.

[4] David Held & Anthony McGrew (eds), *Governing Globalization—Power, Authority and Global Governance*, London: Polity, 2002, p 7. Pursuing a similar analytical approach, Mathias Albert and Tanja Kopp-Malek observe 'the way in which both academic and political discourses express a substantial shift in the way in which the political is unbound from the structures of the modern state/system of states'. M Albert & T Kopp-Malek, 'The pragmatism of global and European governance: emerging forms of the political "beyond Westphalia" ', *Millennium: Journal of International Studies*, 31 (3), 2002, p 469.

[5] Of course (and as Berger has argued in this special issue), in practice non-alignment really meant a diverse set of political alignments and an ideological mix of political development strategies.

[6] For example, both Williams and Thomas take this association as a given with (among other things) reference to development indicators, both internally and in relation to 'developed' states. Williams, *International Economic Organisation*, p 7; and Thomas, *In Search of Security*, pp 2–3. That these two concepts have sometimes been conflated and/or informed each other for political goals is critically addressed in MT Berger, 'The end of the "Third World"?', *Third World Quarterly*, 15 (2), 1994, pp 257–274.

[7] Williams, *International Economic Organisation*, p 4.

[8] Caroline Thomas, 'Where is the Third World now?', *Review of International Studies*, 25 (5), 2000, p 225.

[9] William I Robinson, *Promoting Polyarchy: Globalization, US Intervention and Hegemony*, Cambridge: Cambridge University Press, 1998, pp 341–342.

[10] Berger, 'The end of the 'Third World"?', p 270.

[11] In the remainder of this article the term 'politics of development' will simply be used to imply the politics of international development.

[12] For excellent critiques of these foundational assumptions see Walker, *Inside/Outside*, 1995; RBJ Walker, 'The territorial state and theme of Gulliver', *International Journal*, 3, 1984, pp 529–552; Richard K Ashley, 'Untying the sovereign state: a double reading of the anarchy problematique', *Millennium*, 17 (2), 1988, pp 227–262; John Maclean, 'Marxism and International Relations: a strange case of mutual neglect', *Millennium*, 17 (2), 1988, pp 295–320; Steve Smith, 'Singing our world into existence: International Relations theory and September 11', *International Studies Quarterly*, June 2004 (forthcoming); Richard Devetak, 'Incomplete states: theories and practices of statecraft', in John Macmillan & Andrew Linklater (eds), *Boundaries in Question*, London: Pinter, 1995, pp 19–39; Julian Saurin, 'The end of International Relations? The state and international theory in the age of globalization', in Macmillan & Linklater, *Boundaries in Question*, pp 244–261; and A Claire Cutler, 'Critical reflections on the Westphalian assumptions of international law and organization', *Review of International Studies*, 27 (2), 2001, pp 133–150.

[13] There were of course some efforts directed at what seemed like alternative approaches—even if premised on the territorial form—such as Julius Nyerere's experiment of the *ujamaa* system. This too, however, was contingent on the modernisation approach. See Thomas, *In Search of Security*, 1987, p 30.

[14] Mark T Berger, 'The rise and demise of national development and the origins of post-cold war capitalism', *Millennium*, 30 (2), 2001, p 211.

[15] Saurin, 'The end of International Relations?'.

[16] See Stephen Gill, 'Constitutionalising inequality & the clash of globalizations', paper presented at the International Studies Association Annual Convention, Chicago, IL, 21–24 February 2001, p 2.

[17] Roland Robertson, 'mapping the global condition: globalization as the central concept', in Mike Featherstone (ed), *Global Culture, Nationalism, Globalisation and Modernity*, London: Sage, 1990, pp 15–30. See also M Albert, L Brock & KD Wolf, *Civilizing World Politics—Society and Community beyond the State*, Oxford: Rowman & Littlefield, 2000.

[18] See Albert & Kopp-Malek, 'The pragmatism of global and European governance'.

[19] For example the UK government's recent White Paper on International Development is entitled, *Eliminating World Poverty: Making Globalisation Work for the Poor*, Norwich: Stationary Office, 2000.

[20] For a critique of globalisation theory, see Justin Rosenberg, *The Follies of Globalisation Theory*, London: Verso, 2000.

[21] See for example, William I Robinson, 'Remapping development in light of globalisation: from a territorial to a social cartography', *Third World Quarterly*, 23 (6), 2002, pp 1047–1071, esp pp 1062–1065.

190

[22] See Saurin, 'The end of International Relations?', p 246 [original emphasis].

[23] See for example, Teivo Teivainen, 'The World Social Forum and global democratisation: learning from Porto Alegre', *Third World Quarterly*, 3 (4), 2002, pp 621–632; Emir Sader, 'Beyond civil society—the left after Porto Alegre', *New left Review*, 17, 2002, pp 87–99; Michael Hardt, 'Today's Bandung?', *New left Review*, 14, 2002, pp 112–118; Tom Mertes, 'Grass-roots globalism—reply to Michael Hardt', *New left Review*, 17, 2002, pp 101–110; François Houtart & François Polet, *The Other Davos—The Globalization of Resistance to the World Economic System*, London: Zed, 2001.

[24] A brief word is due here on the premises of my own argument. First, I do not see the territorial state as a progressive form of global politics. Second, I reject a state-centric approach because it is analytically limited for understanding social relations in the ordering of global politics. Third, modern deprivation and immiseration is not external to capitalism but integral to its reproduction. For a good explication of the latter, see Julian Saurin, 'Globalisation, poverty and the promises of modernity', *Millennium*, 25 (3), 1996, pp 657–680, esp p 675.

[25] See A Ahmad, *In Theory: Classes, Nations, Literatures*, London: Verso, 1992, pp 292–293.

[26] See Peter Worsley, 'How many worlds?', *Third World Quarterly*, 1 (2), 1979, pp 100–107; Shu-Yun Ma, 'Third World studies, development studies and post-communist studies: definitions, distance and dynamism', *Third World Quarterly*, 19 (3), 1998, pp 339–348, p 340.

[27] See Berger, 'The end of the "Third World"?', pp 268–269.

[28] This is based on the recognition of the complexity of sovereignty-cum-territoriality in the context of decolonisation. It does not, however, negate the point made by Walker (see note 78) and Ahmed (see note 25).

[29] See Saurin, 'Globalisation, poverty and the promises of modernity', pp 656–657.

[30] See also Berger, 'The end of the "Third World"?', p 269.

[31] See, for example, Sandra Halperin, *In the Mirror of the Third World: Capitalist Development in Modern Europe*, Ithaca, NY: Cornell University Press, 1997.

[32] There have been many studies on this; one is Teresa Hayter, *Aid as Imperialism*, London: Penguin Books, 1971. For excellent analyses of 'development theory' see Colin Leys, *The Rise & Fall of Development Theory*, Oxford: James Curry, 1996; Bjorn Hettne, *Development Theory and the Three Worlds*, Essex: Longman, 1990.

[33] See for instance Robert L Ayres, *Banking on the Poor—The World Bank and World Poverty*, London: MIT, 1984.

[34] Many of the contested policies which underpin the WTO Doha development round evolved through elite lobby groups during the crisis of the 1970s in the advanced capitalist states. The 1980s and 1990s did much to 'hard sell' re-regulation within these states by relating these trends to the issue of cheap labour and production potential to be exploited in developing states.

[35] H Weber, 'The imposition of a global development architecture: the example of microcredit', *Review of International Studies*, 28, 2001, pp 537–555.

[36] One example that illustrates this and also shows its relevance to the contemporary context is the case of the Bangladesh and the way in which the ideological struggles that ensued internally were shaped through the politics of aid. For instance, the origins of the now much flaunted example of the Grameen Bank in Bangladesh can be located in this context. Indeed, its founding director refers to the approach as 'grassroots' capitalism. For more on this, see Heloise Weber, 'Global governance and poverty reduction: the case of microcredit' in Rorden Wilkinson & Steve Hughes (eds), *Global Governance—Critical Perspectives*, London: Routledge, 2002.

[37] Saurin, 'Globalisation, poverty and the promises of modernity', p 671.

[38] See Sol Picciotto, 'Private rights versus public standards in the WTO', *Review of International Political Economy* (forthcoming); Markus Krajewski, 'Democratic legitimacy and constitutional perspectives of WTO law', *Journal of World Trade*, 35 (1), 2001, pp 167–186; and Robert Howse & Kalypso Nicolaidis, 'Enhancing WTO legitimacy: constitutionalization or global subsidiarity?', *Governance: An International Journal of Policy, Administration, and Institutions*, 16 (1), 2003, pp 73–94.

[39] By 'new economy' is meant the rise of the so-called 'services sector' which includes, for instance, financial markets. On the politics of risk production and implications for governance, see Timothy J Sinclair, 'Synchronic global governance and the international political economy of the commonplace', in Martin Hewson & Timothy J Sinclair (eds), *Approaches to Global Governance Theory*, New York: State University of New York, 1999.

[40] For a discussion of the way in which microcredit (and microfinance) facilitate the imperatives of the new economy, though presented in terms of a poverty reduction strategy, see Heloise Weber, 'The new economy and social risk: banking on the poor?', *Review of International Political Economy* (forthcoming, 2004).

[41] See, for example, RW Cox et al (eds) *International Political Economy: Understanding Global Disorder*, London: Zed, 1995.

[42] For more on the WEF, see www.weforum.org.

[43] Stephen Gill, 'Constitutionalizing inequality and the clash of globalizations'.

[44] See WTO, Doha Ministerial Conference, Fourth Session Doha, 'Ministerial Declaration', 14 November 2001, paragraphs 2 and 38 respectively, at www.wto.org; and WTO, 'Changes in the multilateral trading system: challenges for the WTO', WTO News, 5 July 2001, at www.wto.org/english/news_e/spmm_e/spmm66_e.htm.

[45] For a detailed account of these initiatives see Development Assistance Committee, OECD, 'Development co-operation 1999 report', DAC Journal, 1 (1), 2000.

[46] World Bank, A Proposal For A Comprehensive Development Framework, Washington, DC: World Bank, 1999.

[47] IMF–World Bank, 'Heavily Indebted Poor Countries (HIPC) initiative—strengthening the link between debt relief and poverty reduction', Washington, DC: IMF and World Bank, 1999.

[48] OECD, 'Development co-operation 2000 report', DAC Journal—International Development, 2 (1), 2001, p 11.

[49] OECD, 'Development co-operation 1999 report', p 3.

[50] WTO, 'Ministerial Declaration', 2001.

[51] Formal agreements of co-operation have been signed between the WTO and the IMF and the WTO and the World Bank. These agreements fulfil the mandate of the WTO Marrakesh Declaration on Greater Coherence in Global Economic Policy Making. See Christian Tietje, 'Global governance and inter-agency co-operation in international economic law', Journal of World Trade, 36 (3), 2002, pp 501–515. For an indication of how these inform policy co-ordination, see WTO, 'Coherence in global economic policy-making: WTO cooperation with the IMF and the World Bank', WT/TF/COH/S/3, 1999, at www.wto.org.

[52] I use the terms 'form' and 'content' here to capture a similar logic in the way it is employed by Claus Offe and Volker Ronge to explain the way governance is constructed in the course of managing the contradictions of the capitalist state. See Offe & Ronge, 'Theses on the theory of the state', in Robert E Goodin & Philip Pettit (eds), Contemporary Political Philosophy: an Anthology, Blackwell, 2001.

[53] International Development Association (IDA) (World Bank) and IMF, 'Review of the poverty reduction strategy paper (PRSP) approach: main findings', 15 March 2002, p 3 (emphasis added), at www.worldbank.org/prsp/PRSP_Policy_Papers/prsp-papres.html.

[54] For decisions taken early on about this issue, see IMF and IDA, 'Poverty Reduction Strategy Papers—progress in implementation', Washington, DC: World Bank and IMF, 7 September 2000, pp 19–21, 32. A follow-up review has reiterated this premise and reinforced the strategy of alignment by linking this also to implementation. See IMF and World Bank Development Committee, 'Poverty Reduction Strategy Papers (PRSP)—progress in implementation', Washington, DC: World Bank and IMF, 13 September 2002, sections on Donor Alignment and Collaboration under the PRSP and Harmonization and Donor Coordination Efforts, pp 28–34.

[55] Nearly all donors have agreed in principle to align their programmes with the contents of respective PRSPS. The recent review stipulates the following: 'There is considerable scope for alignment with PRSPS even without programmatic lending'. See IDA and IMF, 'Review of the Poverty Reduction Strategy Paper (PRSP) approach, p 22, emphasis added. See also IDA and IMF, 'Review of the Poverty Reduction Strategy Paper (PRSP) approach: early experience with Interim PRSPS and Full PRSPS', 26 March 2002, pp 75–79, at www.worldbank.org/prsp/PRSP_Policy_Papers/prsp_policy_papers.html.

[56] See World Bank and IMF, 'Update on the HIPC initiative and the PRSP program', Washington, DC: IMF and World Bank, 6 February 2001, pp 3–4.

[57] World Bank Group, Operations Policy and Strategy, 'Poverty Reduction Strategy Papers—internal guidance note', 21 January 2000, p 6, at www.worldbank.org/poverty/strategies/intguid.pdf.

[58] Ibid, p 15.

[59] See the Joint Note to World Bank and IMF staff (approved by the Joint Implementation Committee), 'Interim Poverty Reduction Strategy Papers (I-PRSPS): guidance on I-PRSPS and joint staff assessments of I-PRSPS', 7 September 2000, Washington, DC: World Bank, pp 1–6. In this context, those countries eligible for the HIPC initiative were given an extension of two years of the 'sunset clause' in order to allow them to adopt World Bank and IMF-supported adjustment programmes. See World Bank Goup and IMF, 'Memorandum: Heavily Indebted Poor Countries initiative and Poverty Reduction Strategy Papers—progress reports', Washington, DC: IMF and World Bank, 7 September 2000, pp 1–7, p 3.

[60] World Bank Group, Operations Policy and Strategy, 'Poverty Reduction Strategy Papers—internal guidance note', p 15.

[61] The Integrated Framework (IF) of the WTO is being developed as a key mechanism by which this process could be co-ordinated, which would (also) then be consolidated, and implemented, through the PRSPS. See World Bank and IMF, 'Review of the PRSPS: early experience', p 72; WTO (Sub-Committee on Least-Developed Countries), 'Report on the seminar by the IF core agencies', WT/LDC/SWG/IF/15/Rev.1, 17 April 2001, pp 3–4, at www.itd.org/ldc_iii/ldciii_e.htm; and WTO, 'Progress report on the integrated framework for trade-related technical assistance to least-developed countries', WT/LDC/SWG/IF/17/Rev.1, 17 April 2001, p 5, at www.itd.org/ldc_iii/ldciii_e.htm.

[62] See World Bank and IMF, 'Review of the Poverty Reduction Strategy Paper (PRSP) approach', pp 72–75.

[63] World Bank, *World Development Report 2000/2001*, Oxford: Oxford University Press, 2000, p 195 (emphasis added).

[64] See World Bank and IMF, 'Review of the Poverty Reduction Strategy Paper (PRSP) approach', p 8. For the decision to accord primacy to the content of the PRSPs see also World Bank and IMF, 'Review of the Poverty Reduction Strategy Paper (PRSP) approach: main findings', p 7.

[65] See World Bank and IMF, 'Review of the Poverty Reduction Strategy Paper (PRSP) approach', pp 62–63.

[66] For an idea of the status of I-PRSPs and full PRSPs (it is expected that the full will reach over 40 by late 2004), see World Bank and IMF, 'Poverty Reduction Strategy Papers (PRSP).

[67] Bernard Hoekman, 'Strengthening the global trade architecture for development: the post Doha agenda', *World Trade Review*,1 (1), 2002, p 24.

[68] *Ibid*, p 35.

[69] *Ibid*, p 35.

[70] For an excellent study on the political making of private commercial law, see A Claire Cutler, *Private Power and Global Authority—Transnational Merchant Law in the Global Political Economy*, Cambridge: Cambridge University Press, 2003.

[71] See World Bank and IMF, 'Progress report on Poverty Reduction Strategy Papers', 13 April 2000, n 1, available at www.imf.org/external/np/pdr/prsp/2000/041400.htm.

[72] See Pierre Sauve, 'Developing countries and the GATS 2000 round', *Journal of World Trade*, 34 (2), 2000. 'As was often the case in those days, Brazil and India led the resistance, arguing that services were primarily a matter of domestic regulatory conduct' (p 85).

[73] In this context it must come as no surprise that those advocating alternatives to the given policies have in some instances been excluded from the PRSP process. See, for example, Malawi Economic Justice Network, 'The status of civil society involvement in the Malawi PRSP', *World Bank Watch* (South Africa), 3, 2001, p 9, at see www.aidc.org.za. For more criticisms of this process see also, Focus on the global South, 2002. 'Structural Adjustment in the Name of the Poor: The PRSP experience in the Lao PDR, Cambodia and Vietnam', at www.focusweb.org.

[74] Ministerial Declaration of the Group of 77, New York, 15 November 2001, at www.nam.gov.za/documentation/mindec177.htm.

[75] See an interesting study by Siba N Grovogui, 'Regimes of sovereignty: international morality and the African condition', *European Journal of International Relations*, 8 (3), 2002, pp 315–338. See also H Radice, 'Responses to Globalisation: A Critique of Progressive Nationalism', *New Political Economy*, 5 (1), 2000, pp 5–19.

[76] Immanuel Wallerstein, 'Entering global anarchy', New Left Review, 22, 2003, pp 27–35. Wallerstein qualifies this point with reference to certain tendencies he highlights, which include the possibility of the political potential of the WSF (or the political resistance it has come to symbolise in global politics) becoming stronger or becoming co-opted.

[77] See, for instance, Christopher Arup, *The New World Trade Organization Agreements—Globalizing Law Through Services and Intellectual Property*, Cambridge: Cambridge University Press, 2001.

[78] RBJ Walker, 'International/inequality', *International Studies Review*, 4 (2), 2002, pp 21-22.

[79] See, for example, the study by Kurt Burch, *'Property' and the Making of the International System*, London: Lynne Rienner, 1998.

[80] See for example David Harvey, *Spaces of Hope*, Edinburgh: Edinburgh University Press, 2000; Hannes Lacher, 'State centrism and its limits', *Review of International Studies*, 29 (4), 2003, pp 521–542; Neil Brenner, 'Beyond state-centrism? Space, territoriality, and geographical scale in globalization studies', *Theory and Society*, 28, 1999, pp 39–78.

Beyond the Third World: imperial globality, global coloniality and anti-globalisation social movements

ARTURO ESCOBAR

'After the Third World' signals both the end of an era and way of thinking and the birth of new challenges, dreams and real possibilities; both observations, however, can be hotly contested. On the one hand, what has really ended? Assuming that the historical horizon that has finally come to a close is that of anti-colonial nationalist struggles in the Third World, how about the other, perhaps less intractable, aspects of the spirit of Bandung and Third Worldism? For instance, how about the tremendous international solidarity that this spirit elicited among exploited peoples? How about its passionate call for justice, or its eloquent demand for a new international economic order? And is the centrality of the political on which that spirit was based also a thing of the past? Are all of these features ineluctably left behind by the steamroller of modern capitalist history? I believe the articles in this special issue of *Third World Quarterly* demonstrate that they are not, even if they are in dire need of rearticulation. To begin with, many of the conditions that gave rise to Third Worldism have by no means disappeared. Today the world is confronted with a capitalist system—a global empire led by the USA—that seems more inhumane than ever; the power of this empire makes the ardent clamouring for justice of the Bandung leaders appear timid to us today. Even more, the inhumanity of the US-led empire continues to be most patently visible in what until recently was called the Third World. So it can be argued that the need for international solidarity is greater than ever before, albeit in new ways. Equally great is the indubitable necessity of resisting a now global market-determined economy that commands, in more irrefutable tone than in the past, the world to be organised for exploitation and that nothing else will do.

On the other hand, if the end the Third World signals something new, there is little agreement about this newness and the theoretical and political needs that it demands. For some an entirely new paradigm is not only needed but already on the rise. Others speak of the need for a new horizon of meaning for political struggle after the ebbing of the dream of national sovereignty through popular revolution. Still others caution that, since most alternative visions of the recent past—from national liberation to socialism—operated within a modernist frame-work, then the paradigms of the future have to steer carefully away from modern concepts. As the saying goes, easier said than done. The fact is that there are many good analyses of, and ideas about, the contemporary impasse, but they do not seem to coalesce or converge into shared proposals or neat formulations, let alone clear courses of political action that might capture the collective imagin-ation. In this regard our Bandung forefathers fared much better—their wide appeal being of course a problem in itself for many, given the questionable practices that sustained it. David Scott put it bluntly, and constructively, by saying that today's global situation ushers in a new problem-space to which neither Third Worldism nor the ensuing (1980s–90s) postcolonial criticism provide good answers. What is needed, he says, is 'a new conceptualisation of postcolonial politics' that is able to imagine 'joining the radical political tradition of Bandung ... to an ethos of agonistic respect for pluralizations of subaltern difference'.[1]

Scott's conclusion finds resonance, to a greater or lesser extent, in a number of recent theoretical–political proposals, such as Boaventura de Sousa Santos' 'oppositional postmodernism',[2] the calls for new anti-capitalist imaginaries by long-time critics of capitalism such as Aníbal Quijano[3] and Samir Amin,[4] and the emphasis on non-Eurocentric perspectives on globality by the Latin Ameri-can modernity/coloniality research group, to be discussed at some length in this paper. The notion of subaltern difference as an important source for new paradigms also resonates constructively with those who call for place-based epistemologies, economies and ecologies,[5] and those who see in anti-globalisation or global justice movements a new theoretical and political logic on the rise. A number of observers, finally, find in the World Social Forum movement, despite the many criticisms, an expression and enactment of this new paradigm, political vision, anti-capitalist imaginary, or what have you, even if their contours are still barely discernible at present.[6]

This article weaves some of these insights into an argument that focuses on the limits of imagining 'after the Third World' within the order of knowledge and politics that gave us the third world notion and its associated social

195

formations in the first place. Mark Berger (this issue) is right in saying that the conditions that saw the emergence of anti-colonial nationalisms at the dawn of Third Worldism have been superseded, and that their favoured tropes (romantic views of pre-colonial traditions, Marxist utopianism, and Western notions of modernisation and development) thus have to be discarded. The question then becomes: what languages and visions will be appropriate to today's problem-space of capitalist hegemony and counter-hegemonic struggles? What might be the role, if any, of what used to be called 'traditions' in this regard? Can new forms of utopianism be invented? What should be the contribution of Western modernity to this endeavour? Conversely, at what point should we attempt to move beyond it? I shall attempt to demonstrate that in the languages of subaltern difference, critical utopianism and a re-intrepreted modernity (one in which modernity is not only 'reduced to size' but re-contextualised to allow for other cultural formations to become visible) we might be able to find a novel theoretical framework for imagining 'after the Third World' in ways that at least re-work some of the modernist traps of the past.

The argument to be made in this regard has three parts, developed in subsequent parts of the article.

First, modernity's ability to provide solutions to modern problems has been increasingly compromised. In fact, it can be argued that there are no modern solutions to many of today's problems.[7] This is clearly the case, for instance, with massive displacement and ecological destruction, but also with develop-ment's inability to fulfil its promise of a minimum of well-being for the world's people. At the basis of this modern incapacity lie both a hyper-technification of rationality and a hyper-marketisation of social life—what Santos refers to as the increasing incongruence of the functions of social emancipation and social regulation.[8] The result is an oppressive globality in which manifold forms of violence increasingly take on the function of regulation of peoples and econom-ies. This feature has become central to the neoliberal approach of the American empire (even more so after the March 2003 US-led invasion of Iraq). This modernist attempt at combating the symptoms but not the cause of the social, political and ecological crises of the times results in multiple 'cruel little wars' in which the control of territories, people and resources is at stake.[9] Regimes of selective inclusion and hyper-exclusion—of heightened poverty for the many and skyrocketing wealth for the few—operating through spatial–military logics, create a situation of widespread social fascism. The ever widening territories and peoples subjected to precarious living conditions under social fascism suggest the continued validity of a certain notion of a Third World, although not reducible to strict geographical parameters. In short, the modern crisis is a crisis in models of thought; modern solutions, at least under neoliberal globalisation (NLG), only deepen the problems. Moving beyond or outside modernity thus becomes a *sine qua non* for imagining after the Third World.

Second, if we accept that what is at stake is the recognition that there are no modern solutions to many of today's modern problems, where are we to look for new insights? At this level it becomes crucial to question the widely held idea that modernity is now a universal and inescapable force, that globalisation entails the radicalisation of modernity, and that from now on it is modernity all the way down. One fruitful way to think past this commonly held idea is to question the interpretation of modernity as an intra-European phenomenon. This re-interpretation makes visible modernity's underside, that is, those subaltern knowledges and cultural practices world-wide that modernity itself shunned, suppressed made invisible and disqualified. Understood as 'coloniality', this other side has existed side by side with modernity since the conquest of America; it is this same coloniality of being, knowledge and power that today's US-led empire attempts to silence and contain; the same coloniality that asserts itself at the borders of the modern/colonial world system, and from which subaltern groups attempt to reconstitute place-based imaginaries and local worlds. From this perspective, coloniality is constitutive of modernity, and the 'Third World' is part of its classificatory logic. Today, a new global articulation of coloniality is rendering the Third World obsolete, and new classifications are bound to emerge in a world no longer predicated on the existence of three worlds.

Third, this analysis suggests the need to move from the sociology of absences of subaltern knowledges to a politics of emergence of social movements; this requires examining contemporary social movements from the perspective of colonial difference. At their best, today's movements, particularly anti-globalisation and global justice movements, enact a novel logic of the social, based on self-organising meshworks and largely non-hierarchical structures. They tend to show emergent properties and complex adaptive behaviour that movements of the past, with their penchant for centralisation and hierarchy, were never able to manifest. This logic is partly strengthened by the self-organising dynamics of the new information and communication technologies (ICTs), resulting in what could be called 'subaltern intelligent communities'. Situated on the oppositional side of the modern/colonial border zones, these communities enact practices of social, economic and ecological difference that are useful for thinking about alternative local and regional worlds, and so for imagining after the Third World.

The failures of modernity and the rise of imperial globality

What I am trying to argue is that to imagine beyond the Third World we also need to imagine beyond modernity in some fashion. I will begin by discussing the dominant tendencies in the study of modernity from what we can call 'intra-modern perspectives' before moving on to provide the building blocks of an alternative framework. I am very much aware that the view of modernity presented below is terribly partial and contestable. I present it only in order to highlight the stark difference entailed by the few frameworks that seek to go beyond it. In the last instance, the goal of this brief excursus is political. If, as most intra-modern discussions suggest, globalisation entails the universalisation and radicalisation of modernity, then what are we left with? Does radical alterity become impossible? More generally, what is happening to development and modernity in times of globalisation? Is modernity finally becoming univer-salised, or is it being left behind? The question is the more poignant because it can be argued that the present is a moment of transition: between a world defined in terms of modernity and its corollaries, development and modernisation, and the certainty they instilled—a world that has operated largely under European hegemony over the past 200 years if not more; and a new (global) reality which is still difficult to ascertain but which, at opposite ends, can be seen either as a deepening of modernity the world over or, on the contrary, as a deeply negotiated reality that encompasses many heterogeneous cultural formations—and, of course, the many shades in between. This sense of a transition is well captured by the question: is globalisation the last stage of capitalist modernity, or the beginning of something new? As we shall see, intra-European and non-Eurocentric perspectives give a very different answer to this set of questions.

Globalisation as the radicalisation of modernity: an intra-modern view of modernity

The idea of a relatively single globalisation process emanating out of a few dominant centres remains prevalent. The root of this idea lies in a view of modernity as essentially an European phenomenon. From this perspective, modernity is characterised as follows. Historically, modernity has identifiable temporal and spatial origins: 17th century northern Europe, around the processes of Reformation, the Enlightenment, and the French Revolution. These processes crystallised at the end of the 18th century and became consolidated with the Industrial Revolution. Sociologically, modernity is characterised by certain institutions, particularly the nation-state, and by some basic features, such as self-reflexivity, the disembedding of social life from local context, and space/time distantiation, since relations between 'absent others' become more important than face-to-face interaction.[10] Culturally, modernity is characterised in terms of the increasing appropriation of previously taken-for-granted cultural backgrounds by forms of expert knowledge linked to capital and state administrative apparatuses—what Habermas describes as the increasing rationalisation of the life-world.[11] Philosophically, modernity entailed the emergence of the notion of 'Man' as the foundation of all knowledge about the world, separate from the natural and the divine.[12] Modernity is also seen in terms of the triumph of metaphysics, understood as a tendency—extending from Plato and some of the pre-Socratics to Descartes and the modern thinkers, and criticised by Nietzsche and Heidegger among others—that finds in logical truth the foundation for a rational theory of the world as made up of knowable and controllable things and beings. Vattimo emphasises the logic of development—the belief in perpetual betterment and overcoming—as crucial to the philosophical foundations of the modern order.[13]

Is there a logical necessity to believe that the order so sketchily characterised above is the only one capable of becoming global? For most theorists, on all sides of the political spectrum, this is exactly the case. Giddens has made the argument most forcefully: globalisation entails the radicalisation and universalisation of modernity. No longer purely an affair of the West, however, since modernity is everywhere, the triumph of the modern lies precisely in its having become universal. This may be called 'the Giddens effect': *from now on, it is modernity all the way down, everywhere, until the end of time.* Not only is radical alterity expelled forever from the realm of possibilities, all world cultures and societies are reduced to being a manifestation of European culture. No matter how variously qualified, a 'global modernity' is here to stay.[14] Recent anthropological investigations of 'modernity at large'[15] have shown modernity to be de-territorialised, hybridised, contested, uneven, heterogeneous, even multiple, or in terms of conversing with, engaging, playing with, or processing modernity. Nevertheless, in the last instance these modernities end up being a reflection of a Eurocentred social order, even if under the assumption that modernity is now everywhere, a ubiquitous and ineluctable social fact.[16] This inability to go beyond modernity is puzzling and needs to be questioned as part of any effort to imagine beyond the Third World.

Beyond modernity: oppositional postmodernism

Boaventura de Sousa Santos has forcefully made the argument that we are moving beyond the paradigm of modernity in two senses: epistemologically, and socio-politically. Epistemologically this move entails a transition from the dominance of modern science to a plural landscape of knowledge forms. Socially, the transition is between global capitalism and emergent forms of which we only have glimpses in today's social movements and in events such as the World Social Forum. The crux of this transition, in Santos' rigorous conceptualisation, is an untenable tension between modernity's core functions of social regulation and social emancipation, in turn related to the growing imbalance between expectations and experience. Intended to guarantee order in society, social regulation is the set of norms, institutions and practices through which expectations are stabilised; it is based on the principles of state, market and community. Social emancipation challenges the order created by regulation in the name of a different ordering; to this end, it has recourse to aesthetic, cognitive–scientific and ethical rationalities. These two tendencies have become increasingly contradictory, resulting in ever more noticeable excesses and deficits, particularly with neoliberal globalisation. The management of these contradictions—chiefly at the hands of science and law—is itself in crisis. The result has been the hyper-scientificisation of emancipation (all claims to a better society have to be filtered through the rationality of science), and the hyper-marketisation of regulation (modern regulation is ceded to the market; to be free is to accept market regulation) and, indeed, a collapse of emancipation into regulation. Hence the need for a paradigmatic transition that enables us to think anew about the problematic of regulation and social emancipation, with the ultimate goal of de-Westernising social emancipation. To this end, a new approach to social theory, 'oppositional postmodernism', is called for:

> The conditions that brought about the crisis of modernity have not yet become the conditions to overcome the crisis beyond modernity. Hence the complexity of our transitional period portrayed by oppositional postmodern theory: we are facing modern problems for which there are no modern solutions. The search for a postmodern solution is what I call oppositional postmodernism ... What is necessary is to start from the disjunction between the modernity of the problems and the

postmodernity of the possible solutions, and to turn such disjunction into the urge to ground theories and practices capable of reinventing social emancipation out of the wrecked emancipatory promises of modernity.[17]

Santos thus points at another paradigm, distinct from modernity, even if still not fully visible, that makes imagining beyond modernity plausible. His reading of modernity builds on various readings of capitalism, distinguishing between those that posit an end to capitalism, even if in the very long run,[18] and which thus advocate transformative practices, and those that conceive of the future as so many metamorphoses of capitalism, and which favour adaptive strategies within capitalism.[19] For this latter group one may say that globalisation is the last stage of capitalist modernity; for the former, globalisation is the beginning of something new. As we shall see shortly, the Latin American modernity/coloniality perspective would suggest that transformative practices are taking place now, and need to be socially amplified.

The new face of global empire and the growth of social fascism

One of the main consequences, for Santos, of the collapse of emancipation into regulation is the structural predominance of exclusion over inclusion. Either because of the exclusion of many of those formerly included, or because those who in the past were candidates for inclusion are now prevented from being so, the problematic of exclusion has become terribly accentuated, with ever growing numbers of people thrown into a veritable 'state of nature'. The size of the excluded class varies of course with the centrality of the country in the world system, but it is particularly staggering in Asia, Africa and Latin America. The result is a new type of social fascism as 'a social and civilizational regime'.[20] This regime, paradoxically, coexists with democratic societies, hence its novelty. This fascism may operate in various modes: in terms of spatial exclusion; territories struggled over by armed actors; the fascism of insecurity; and of course the deadly financial fascism, which at times dictates the marginalisation of entire regions and countries that do not fulfil the conditions needed for capital, according to the IMF and its faithful management consultants.[21] To the former Third World correspond the highest levels of social fascism of these kinds. This is, in sum, the world that is being created by globalisation from above, or hegemonic globalisation.

Before moving on, it is important to complete this rough representation of today's global capitalist modernity by looking at the US-led invasion of Iraq in early 2003. Among other things, this episode has at last made two things particularly clear: first, the willingness to use unprecedented levels of violence to enforce dominance on a global scale; second, the unipolarity of the current empire. In ascension since the Thatcher–Reagan years, this unipolarity reached its climax with the post-11 September regime, based on a new convergence of military, economic, political and religious interests in the USA. In Alain Joxe's compelling vision of imperial globality, what we have been witnessing since the first Gulf war is the rise of an empire that increasingly operates through the management of asymmetrical and spatialised violence, territorial control, sub-

200

contracted massacres, and 'cruel little wars', all of which are aimed at imposing the neoliberal capitalist project. At stake is a type of regulation that operates through the creation of a new horizon of global violence. This empire regulates disorder through financial and military means, pushing chaos to the extent possible to the outskirts of empire, creating a 'predatory' peace to the benefit of a global noble caste and leaving untold poverty and suffering in its path. It is an empire that does not take responsibility for the well-being of those over whom it rules. As Joxe puts it:

> The world today is united by a new form of chaos, an imperial chaos, dominated by the *imperium* of the United States, though not controlled by it. We lack the words to describe this new system, while being surrounded by its images ... World leadership through chaos, a doctrine that a rational European school would have difficulty imagining, necessarily leads to weakening states—even in the United States—through the emerging *sovereignty* of corporations and markets.[22]

The new empire thus operates not so much through conquest, but through the imposition of norms (free-markets, US-style democracy and cultural notions of consumption, and so forth). The former Third World is, above all, the theatre of a multiplicity of cruel little wars which, rather than being barbaric throwbacks, are linked to the current global logic. From Colombia and Central America to Algeria, sub-Saharan Africa and the Middle East these wars take place within states or regions, without threatening empire but fostering conditions favourable to it. For much of the former Third World (and of course for the Third World within the core) is reserved 'the World-chaos', free-market slavery, and selective genocide.[23] In some cases this amounts to a sort of 'paleo-micro-colonialism' within regions,[24] in others to balkanisation, in yet others to brutal internal wars and massive displacement to free up entire regions for transnational capital (particularly in the case of oil, but also diamonds, timber, water, genetic resources, and agricultural lands). Often these cruel little wars are fuelled by mafia networks, and intended for macroeconomic globalisation. It is clear that this new Global Empire ('the New World Order of the American imperial monarchy')[25] articulates the 'peaceful expansion' of the free-market economy with omnipresent violence in a novel regime of economic and military global-ity—in other words, the global economy comes to be supported by a global organisation of violence and vice versa.[26] On the subjective side, what one increasingly finds in the Souths (including the South within the North) are 'diced identities' and the transformation of cultures of solidarity into cultures of destruction.

The Colombian case: modernity, development and the logic of displacement

Colombia exemplifies Joxe's vision, and in this way I believe Colombia prefigures situations that could become more common world-wide. Despite the complexity of the situation, it is possible to make a few general observations: First, this country represents patterns of historical exclusion found in many parts of Latin America but rarely with such depth. Colombia today has the second most skewed income distribution, after Brazil. While this has been aggravated over the past 20 years by successive neoliberal regimes, it has a long historical base, particularly in the structure of land tenure. Today, 1.1% of landowners control over 55% of all arable land (and as much as one-third of this may well be linked to drug money). Over 60% of the Colombian population live on incomes below the poverty line; 25% live in absolute poverty, that is, they earn less than one dollar a day. Rural poverty is 80%, and urban poverty has also reached high levels, with at least two consequences of particular relevance here: the creation of vast neighbourhoods of absolute poverty, with very limited or no state presence, which are largely ruled by local laws, including pervasive violence; and the emergence of a new group of people, locally known as *desechables*, or disposable ones, who are often the target of 'social cleansing' by death squads linked to the right. Since the 1980s in particular drug mafias have achieved tremendous presence at all levels of society, encouraged by a very lucrative international business. The armed conflict that presently affects Colombia is well known. It brings together a disparate set of actors—chiefly left-wing guerrillas, the army and right-wing paramilitary groups—into a complex military, territorial and political conflict, which I do not intend to analyse here.[27] Suffice it to say that, from the perspective of imperial globality, these can all be seen as war machines more interested in their own survival and sphere of influence than in peaceful solutions to the conflict. Massacres and human rights abuses are the order of the day, primarily by paramilitaries but also by guerrillas, and the civilian population is most often brought into the conflict as unwilling participants or sacrificial victims. Increasingly, guerrillas have been unwilling to recognise and respect the autonomous needs and strategies of other struggles, such as those of black and indigenous peoples and environmentalists.

The sub-national dynamics of imperial globality is pathetically illustrated by the experience of Colombia's Pacific region. This rainforest area, rich in natural resources, has been home to about one million people, 95% of them Afro-Colombian, with about 50 000 indigenous peoples of various ethnicities. In 1991 a new Constitution granted collective territorial rights to the black communities. Since the mid-1990s, however, guerrillas and paramilitaries have been steadily moving into the region, in order to gain control of territories that are either rich in natural resources or the site of planned large-scale development projects. In many river communities both guerrillas and paramilitaries have pushed people to plant coca or move out. Displacement has reached staggering levels, with several hundred thousand people displaced from this region alone. In the southernmost area this displacement has been caused in large part by paramilitaries paid by rich African oil palm growers, intent on expanding their holdings and increasing their production for world markets. This is being done in the name of development, with resources provided by Plan Colombia.[28]

It is little known that Colombia today has about three million internally displaced people, constituting one of the largest refugee crisis in the world. Over 400 000 people were internally displaced in 2002 alone. A disproportionate percentage of the displaced are Afro-Colombians and indigenous people, which makes patently clear a little discussed aspect of imperial globality, namely, its racial and ethnic dimension. One aspect of this is of course that, as in the case of the Pacific, ethnic minorities often inhabit territories rich in natural resources that are now coveted by national and transnational capital. Beyond this more empirical observation, however, lies the fact that imperial globality is also about the defence of white privilege world-wide. By white privilege here I mean, not so much phenotypically white, but a Eurocentric way of life that has historically privileged white people at the expense of non-European and coloured peoples world-wide—and particularly since the 1950s those around the world who abide by this outlook. As we will see, this dimension of imperial globality is better drawn out through the concept of global coloniality.

The case of Colombia and of its Pacific region thus reflects key tendencies of imperial globality and global coloniality. The first tendency is the link between the economy and armed violence, particularly the still prominent role of national and sub-national wars over territory, peoples and resources. These wars contribute to the spread of social fascism, defined as a combination of social and political exclusion whereby increasingly large segments of the population live under terrible material conditions and often under the threat of displacement and even death. In Colombia the government response has been to step up military repression, surveillance and paramilitarisation within a conception of 'democratic security' that mirrors the US global strategy as seen in the Iraqi case: democracy by force, and without the right to dissent—a deterrence against the people. Social fascism and political fascism (networks of paid informers, suppression of rights) are joined in this strategy to maintain a pattern of capital accumulation that benefits an increasingly narrow segment of the world population.

Second, Colombia also shows that, despite what could be seen as excellent conditions for a peaceful society and capitalist democracy (eg very rich natural endowments and a large and highly trained professional class), what has happened is the opposite. This has been so in part because the local war is, at least partially, a surrogate for global (especially US) interests, in part because of a particularly rapacious national elite that refuses to entertain a more significant democracy, and in part also because of war orientations (including drug mafias) that have taken on a self-perpetuating dynamic. Finally, and more importantly for our argument, the Colombian case makes patently clear the exhaustion of modern models. Development and modernity, to be sure, were always inherently displacement-creating processes. Yet what has become evident with the excesses of imperial globality is that the gap between modernity's displacement-producing tendencies and displacement-averting mechanisms is not only growing but becoming untenable—that is, unmanageable within a modern framework.[29] In short, while there are socioeconomic and political features that could still make talking about a third world legitimate (poverty, exclusion, oppression, uneven development, of course imperialism, and so forth), they have to be rearticulated in ways that make not talking about a third world, but imagining after the Third World, more appropriate. This articulation must preserve those social conditions that made talk of the Third World necessary in an earlier period. But they have to be brought up to date through concepts that are more attuned to the problem-space of today. So far we have discussed some of these concepts, particularly imperial globality and social fascism. We also started the discussion of what thinking beyond modernity might mean. It is time to develop this idea more fully by introducing the Latin American modernity/coloniality research programme.

Beyond modernity: subalternity and the problematic of coloniality

The seeming triumph of Eurocentred modernity can be seen as the imposition of a global design by a particular local history, in such a way that it has subalternised other local histories and designs. If this is the case, could one posit the hypothesis that radical alternatives to modernity are not a historically foreclosed possibility? If so, how can we articulate a project around this notion? Could it be that it is possible to think about, and to think differently from, an 'exteriority' to the modern world system? That one may envision alternatives to the totality imputed to modernity, and adumbrate not a different totality leading to different global designs, but networks of local/global histories constructed from the perspective of a politically enriched alterity? This is precisely the possibility that may be gleaned from the work of a group of Latin American theorists who, in refracting modernity through the lens of coloniality, engage in a questioning of the character of modernity, thus unfreezing the potential for thinking from difference and towards the constitution of alternative worlds. In what follows, I present succinctly some of the main arguments of these works.[30]

The conceptualisation of modernity/coloniality is grounded in a series of operations that distinguish it from established theories. These include: 1) locating the origins of modernity with the conquest of America and the control of the Atlantic after 1492, rather than in the most commonly accepted landmarks such as the Enlightenment or the end of the 18th century; 2) attention to colonialism, postcolonialism and imperialism as constitutive of modernity; 3) the adoption of a world perspective in the explanation of modernity, in lieu of a view of modernity as an intra-European phenomenon; 4) the identification of the domination of others outside the European core as a necessary dimension of modernity; 5) a conception of eurocentrism as the knowledge form of modernity/coloniality—a hegemonic representation and mode of knowing that claims universality for itself, 'derived from Europe's position as center'.[31] In sum, there is a re-reading of the 'myth of modernity' in terms of modernity's 'underside' and a new denunciation of the assumption that Europe's development must be followed unilaterally by every other culture, by force if necessary—what Dussel terms 'the developmentalist fallacy'.[32] The main conclusions are, first, that the proper analytical unit of analysis is modernity/coloniality—in sum, there is no modernity without coloniality, with the latter being constitutive of the former. Second, the fact that 'the colonial difference' is a privileged epistemological and political space. In other words, what emerges from this alternative framework is the need to take seriously the epistemic force of local histories and to think theory through the political praxis of subaltern groups.

Some of the key notions that make up the conceptual corpus of this research programme include:

- the modern colonial world system as a structurally heterogeneous ensemble of processes and social formations that encompass modern colonialism and colonial modernities;

- coloniality of power (Quijano), a global hegemonic model of power in place since the conquest that articulates race and labour, space and peoples, according to the needs of capital and to the benefit of white European peoples;
- colonial difference and global coloniality (Mignolo) which refer to the knowledge and cultural dimensions of the subalternisation processes effected by the coloniality of power: the colonial difference brings to the fore persistent cultural differences, which today exist within global power structures;
- coloniality of being (more recently suggested by Nelson Maldonado-Torres[33]) as the ontological dimension of colonialty, on both sides of the encounter; it points to the 'ontological excess' that occurs when particular beings impose on others and also critically addresses the effectiveness of the discourses with which the other responds to the suppression as a result of the encounter.
- Eurocentrism, as the knowledge model of the European historical experience which has become globally hegemonic since the 17th century (Dussel, Quijano), hence the possibility of non-Eurocentric thinking and epistemologies.

Here is a further, and enlightening, characterisation of coloniality by Walter Mignolo:

> Since modernity is a project, the triumphal project of the Christian and secular west, coloniality is—on the one hand—what the project of modernity needs to rule out and roll over, in order to implant itself as modernity and—on the other hand—the site of enunciation where the blindness of the modern project is revealed, and concomitantly also the site where new projects begin to unfold. In other words, coloniality is the site of enunciation that reveals and denounces the blindness of the narrative of modernity from the perspective of modernity itself, and it is at the same time the platform of pluri-versality, of diverse projects coming from the experience of local histories touched by western expansion (as the Word Social Forum demonstrates); thus coloniality is not a new abstract universal (Marxism is imbedded in modernity, good but shortsighted), but the place where diversality as a universal project can be thought out; where the question of languages and knoweldges becomes crucial (Arabic, Chinese, Aymara, Bengali, etc) as the site of the pluriversal—that is, the 'traditional' that the 'modern' is rolling over and ruling out.[34]

The question of whether there is an 'exteriority' to the modern/colonial world system is somewhat peculiar to this group, and easily misunderstood. It was originally proposed by Dussel in his classic work on liberation philosophy,[35] and reworked in recent years. In no way should this exteriority be thought about as a pure outside, untouched by the modern; it refers to an outside that is precisely constituted as difference by hegemonic discourse. By appealing from the exteriority in which s/he is located, the Other becomes the original source of an ethical discourse *vis à vis* a hegemonic totality. This interpellation of the Other comes from beyond the system's institutional and normative frame, as an ethical challenge. This is precisely what most European and Euro-American theorists seem unwilling to consider; both Mignolo and Dussel see here a strict limit to deconstruction and to the various Eurocentered critiques of Eurocentrism.

Dussel's notion of 'transmodernity' signals this possibility of a non-Eurocentric dialogue with alterity, one that fully enables 'the negation of the negation' to which the subaltern others have been subjected. Mignolo's notions of 'border thinking' and 'pluritopic hermeneutics' are important in this regard. They point to the need 'for a kind of thinking that moves along the diversity of historical processes',[36] and which 'engages the colonialism of Western episte-mology (from the left and from the right) from the perspective of epistemic forces that have been turned into subaltern (traditional, folkloric, religious, emotional, etc) forms of knowledge'.[37] While Mignolo acknowledges the contin-ued importance of the monotopic critique of modernity by Western critical discourse (critique from a single, unified space), he suggests that this has to be placed in a dialogue with critique(s) arising from the colonial difference. The result is a 'pluritopic hermeneutics', a possibility of thinking from different spaces which finally breaks away from Eurocentrism as sole epistemological perspective.[38] Let it be clear, however, that border thinking entails both 'dis-placement and departure',[39] double critique (critique of both the West and other traditions from which the critique is launched), and the positive affirmation of an alternative ordering of the real.

The corollary is the need to build narratives from the perspective of modernity/coloniality 'geared towards the search for a different logic'.[40] This project has to do with the rearticulation of global designs from local histories; with the articulation between subaltern and hegemonic knowledge from the perspective of the subaltern; and with the remapping of colonial difference towards a worldly culture—such as in the Zapatista project, that remaps Marxism, Third Worldism and indigenism, without being either of them, in an excellent example of border thinking. Thus, it becomes possible to think of 'other local histories producing either alternative totalities or an alternative to totality'.[41] These alternatives would not play on the 'globalisation/civilisation' couplet inherent to modernity/coloniality; they would rather build on a '*mundi-alización*/culture' (MC) relation centred on the local histories in which colonial global designs are necessarily transformed. The diversity of *mundialización* is contrasted with the homogeneity of globalisation, aiming at multiple and diverse social orders—in sum, pluriversality. One may say, with Mignolo, that this approach 'is certainly a theory *from/of* the Third World, *but not only for the Third World* ... Third World theorizing is also *for* the First World in the sense that critical theory is subsumed and incorporated in a new geocultural and epistemological location.'[42]

Some partial conclusions: coloniality incorporates colonialism and imperial-ism but goes beyond them; this is why coloniality did not end with the end of colonialism (formal independence of nation states), but was rearticulated in terms of the post-World War II imaginary of three worlds (which in turn replaced the previous articulations in terms of Occidentalism and Orientalism). Similarly, the 'end of the Third World' entails a rearticulation of the coloniality of power and knowledge. As we have seen, this rearticulation takes the form of both imperial globality (new global link between economic and military power) and global coloniality (the emergent classificatory orders and forms of alterisation that are replacing the cold war order). The new coloniality regime is still difficult to discern. Race, class and ethnicity will continue to be important, but new, or newly prominent, areas of articulation come into existence, such as religion (and gender linked to it, especially in the case of Islamic societies, as we saw in the war on Afghanistan). However, the single most prominent vehicle of coloniality today seems to be the ambiguously drawn figure of the 'terrorist'. Linked most forcefully to the Middle East, and thus to the immediate US oil and strategic interests in the region (*vis à vis* the European Union and Russia, on the one hand, and China and India in particular on the other, as the most formidable potential challengers), the imaginary of the terrorist can have a wide field of application (it has already been applied to Basque militants and Colombian guerrillas, for instance). Indeed, after 11 September, we are all potential terrorists, unless we are American, white, conservative Christian, and Republican—in actuality or epistemically (that is, in mindset).

This means that, in seeking to overcome the myth of modernity, it is necessary to abandon the notion of the Third World as a particular articulation of that myth. Similarly, the problematic of social emancipation needs to be refracted through the lens of coloniality. Emancipation, as mentioned, needs to be de-Westernised (as does the economy). If social fascism has become a permanent condition of imperial globality, emancipation has to deal with global coloniality. This means conceiving it from the perspective of the colonial difference. What does emancipation—or liberation, the preferred language of some of the MC authors—mean when seen through the lens of coloniality, that is, beyond exclusion defined in social, economic and political terms? Finally, if not the Third World, what? 'Worlds and knowledges otherwise', based on the politics of difference from the perspective of the coloniality of power, as we shall see in the final section.[43]

Other worlds are possible: social movements, place-based politics, and global coloniality

'World and knowledges otherwise' brings to the fore the double aspect of the effort at stake: to build on the politics of the colonial difference, particularly at the level of knowledge and culture, and to imagine and construct actual different worlds. As the slogan of the Porto Alegre World Social Forum puts it, 'another world is possible'. At stake in thinking beyond the Third World is the ability to imagine both 'other worlds' and 'worlds otherwise'—that is, worlds that are more just and sustainable and, at the same time, worlds that are defined through principles other than those of Eurocentric modernity. To do this, at least two considerations are crucial: what are the sites where ideas for these alternative and dissenting imaginations will come from? Second, how are the dissenting imaginations to be set into motion? I suggest that one possible, and perhaps privileged, way in which these two questions can be answered is by focusing on the politics of difference enacted by many contemporary social movements, particularly those that more directly and simultaneously engage with imperial globality and global colonialty.

The reasons for this belief are relatively simple. First, as understood here, 'difference' is not an essentialist trait of cultures not yet conquered by modernity, but rather the very articulation of global forms of power with place-based worlds. In other words, there are practices of difference that remain in the exteriority (again, not outside) of the modern/colonial world system, incompletely conquered and transformed, if you wish, and also produced partly through long-standing place-based logics that are irreducible to capital and imperial globality. I suggest that we think of this difference in terms of practices of cultural, economic and ecological difference, corresponding to the process of cultural, economic and ecological conquest by imperial globality (as we saw for the case of the Colombian Pacific). Second, many of today's social movements not only build on these practices of difference, they also enact a different logic of politics and collective mobilisation. This logic has two related dimensions; first, these movements often entail the production of self-organising, non-hierarchical networks. Second, in many cases they enact a politics of place that contrasts with the grandiose politics of 'the Revolution' and with conceptions of anti-imperial politics that require that empire be confronted in its totality.[44] In other words, I would like to think that these movements suggest novelty at two levels: at the level of the organising logic itself (self-organisation and complexity); and at the level of the social basis of mobilisation (place-based yet engaging with transnational networks). Let me explain briefly these two dimensions before making some concluding remarks about the concept of the Third World.

The novel logic of anti-globalisation social movements

When confronted with new social phenomena, such as these recent movements, social theorists do well to ask themselves whether we have the appropriate tools for analysing them. In the case of anti-globalisation movements (AGMs), it has become increasingly clear that existing theories of social movements are at pains to explain the global mobilisations of recent years.[45] The search for new theories and metaphors, however, has begun in earnest. In beginning the arduous task of understanding today's AGMs, I have found particularly useful theories of complexity in the natural sciences (and, to a lesser extent, theories of cyberspace). I will introduce here only the bare minimum elements necessary to make the point about why these movements—provisionally interpreted through the theoretical lens of self-organisation—offer perhaps our best hope of imagining 'worlds and knowledges otherwise'. In examining the recent wave of global protest in terms of Polanyi's double movement of economic transformation and social protection, McMichael suggests that, because they oppose both the modernist project and its market epistemology, they also go beyond the Polanyian classical counter-movement. In other words, 'a protective movement is emerging', but not one that would simply regulate markets: instead it is 'one that questions the epistemology of the market in the name of alternatives deriving from within and beyond the market system'.[46] For this reason, these movements can be properly called 'anti-globalisation'; that is, they entail the negation of the globalisation project in terms of the universalisation of capitalist modernity—at least in its neoliberal form (even if of course other labels also make sense).

At the metaphorical level at least, I believe it is possible to find inspiration for interpreting the logic of these movements in two domains: cyberspatial practices and theories of complexity in the biological and physical sciences. Over the past few hundred years modernity and capitalism have organised economic and social life largely around the logic of order, centralisation and hierarchy building (this also applies to really existing socialisms for the most part). In recent decades cyberspace (as the universe of digital networks, interactions and interfaces) and the sciences of complexity have made visible a different model for the organis-ation of social life.[47] In terms of complexity in particular, ants, swarming moulds, cities, certain markets, for instance, exhibit what scientists call 'complex adaptive behaviour'. (Thousands of invisible single-celled mould units occasion-ally coalesce into a swarm and create a visible large mould. Ant colonies have developed over a long timespan with no central pacemaker. Medieval markets linked efficiently myriad producers and consumers with prices setting themselves in a way that was understood locally.) In this type of situation, simple beginnings lead to complex entities, without the existence of a master plan or central intelligence planning it. They are bottom-up processes, where agents working at one (local) scale produce behaviour and forms at higher scales (eg the great anti-globalisation demonstrations of the last few years). Simple rules at one level give rise to sophistication and complexity at another level through what is called emergence: the fact that the actions of multiple agents interacting dynamically and following local rules rather than top-down commands result in visible macro-behaviour or structures. Sometimes these systems are 'adaptive'; they learn over time, responding more effectively to the changing needs of their environment.

A useful distinction between different types of network structures is that between hierarchies and meshworks.[48] Hierarchies entail a high degree of centralised control, ranks, overt planning, homogenisation and goals and rules of behaviour conducive to those goals. Meshworks, on the contrary, are based on decentralised decision making, non-hierarchical structures, self-organisation, and heterogeneity and diversity—two very different life philosophies. It should be made clear, however, that these two principles are found mixed in operation in most real life examples, and may give rise to one another. The logic of hierarchy and control, however, has tended to predominate in capitalism and militarism as a whole. The model of self-organisation, non-hierarchy (or heterarchy) and complex adaptive behaviour is closer in spirit to philosophical anarchism and anarcho-socialism and may provide general guidelines for internationalist net-working. It could be said, again provisionally, that this model also confronts the left with a novel politics of emergence that should be taken into account.[49]

Politics of place as a novel logic of the political

The goal of many (not all) of the anti-globalisation struggles can be seen as the defence of particular, place-based historical conceptions of the world and practices of world-making—more precisely, as a defence of particular constructions of place, including the reorganisations of place that might be deemed necessary according to the power struggles within place. These struggles are place-based, yet transnationalised.[50] The politics of place is an emergent form of politics, a novel political imaginary in that it asserts a logic of difference and possibility that builds on the multiplicity of actors and actions operating at the level of everyday life. In this view, places are the site of live cultures, economies and environments rather than nodes in a global and all-embracing capitalist system. In Gibson-Graham's conceptualisation, this politics of place—often favoured by women, environmentalist and those struggling for alternative forms of livelihood—is a lucid response to the type of 'politics of empire' which is also common on the Left and which requires that empire be confronted at the same level of totality, thereby devaluing all forms of localised action, reducing it to accommodation or reformism. As Gibson-Graham does not cease to remind us, 'places always fail to be fully capitalist, and herein lie their potential to become something other'.[51] Or, in the language of the MC project, there is an exteriority to imperial globality—a result of both global coloniality and place-based cultural dynamics, which are irreducible to the terms of capitalist modernity.

As I have analysed elsewhere,[52] the struggle of the social movements of black communities of the Colombian Pacific illustrates the politics of place in the context of imperial globality. This movement, which emerged in the early 1990s as a result of the deepening of the neoliberal model and in the wake of the new 1991 Constitution that granted cultural and territorial rights to ethnic minorities such as the black communities of the Pacific, was from the very outset conceived as a struggle for the defence of cultural difference and of territories. The movement has since emphasised four rights: to their identity (hence, the right to be different), to their territory (as the space for exercising identity), to a measure of local autonomy, and to their own vision of development. In the encounter with state agents, experts, NGOs, international biodiversity networks, etc, the movement has developed a unique political-ecology framework that articulates the life project of the river communities—embedded in place-based notions of territory, production systems, and the environment—with the political vision of the social movement, incarnated in a view of the Pacific as a 'region–territory of ethnic groups'. In this way the movement can legitimately be interpreted in terms of the defence of practices of cultural, economic and ecological difference. Emerging from the exteriority of the modern/colonial world system—within which blacks of marginal regions have always been among the most excluded and 'forgotten'—this group of activists can also be seen as practising a kind of border thinking from which they engage with both their communities, on the one hand, and the agents of modernity, on the other. In connecting with other continental or global movements (eg Afro-Latin American and anti-globalisation movements), they also become part of the transnational movement meshworks analysed in this section.

Two more aspects of movement meshworks before ending: first, when confronting neoliberal globalisation and imperial globality, local, national and transnational movements—often making up networks and meshworks—may be seen as constituting a form of counter-hegemonic globalisation.[53] They not only challenge the rationality of NLG at many levels, they propose new horizons of meaning (clearly, in cases such as the Zapatista, with their emphasis on humanity, dignity and respect for difference) and alternative conceptions of the economy, nature, development, and the like (as in the case of the social movement of black communities of the Colombian Pacific and many others). Counter-hegemonic globalisation is a tremendously diverse movement, and this is not the place to analyse it. Suffice it to say that counter-hegemonic movements often seek to advance the goals of equality (and social justice in general) and difference at the same time. This struggle for difference-in-equality and equality-in-difference is a feature of many contemporary movements, in contradistinction to those of the most recent past.

But this also means that there is a dire need for what Santos has called a theory of translation—one that propitiates mutual understanding and intelligibility among movements brought together into networks but with worldviews, life worlds and conceptions that are often different and at odds with each other, if not plainly incommensurable.[54] How can mutual learning and transformation among subaltern practices be promoted? This is increasingly recognised as an important element for advancing counter-hegemonic globalisation (for instance, by the world network of social movements that emerged from the World Social Forum process). If it is true that many of the subaltern movements of today are movements of knowledges that have been marginalised and excluded, does this not amount in some fashion to a situation of 'transnational third worlds of peoples and knowledges',[55] whose articulation might usher in new types of counter-hegemonic agency? No longer conceived as a classificatory feature within the modern epistemic order, these 'third worlds of peoples and knowledges' could function as the basis for a theory of translation that, while respecting the diversity and multiplicity of movements (albeit questioning their particular identities), would enable increasing intelligibility of experiences among existing worlds and knowledges, thus making possible a higher level of articulation of 'worlds and knowledges otherwise'. As Santos put it:

> such a process includes articulating struggles and resistances, as well as promoting ever more comprehensive and consistent alternatives ... an enormous effort of mutual recognition, dialogue, and debate will be required to carry out the task ... Such a task entails a wide exercise in translation to enlarge reciprocal intelligibility without destroying the identity of what is translated. The point is to create, in every movement or NGO, in every practice or strategy, in every discourse or knowledge, a contact zone that may render it porous and hence permeable to other NGOs, practices, strategies, discourses and knowledges. The exercise of translation aims to identify and potentiate what is common in the diversity of the counter-hegemonic drive.[56]

Conclusion: beyond the Third World

Imagining beyond the Third World has many contexts and meanings. I have highlighted some of them, such as the following:

1. In terms of context, the need to move beyond the paradigm of modernity within which the Third World has functioned as a key element in the

classificatory hierarchy of the modern/colonial world system. If we accept either the need for moving beyond modernity, or the argument that we are indeed in a period of paradigmatic transition, this means that the concept of the Third World is already something of a bygone past. Let it rest in peace, and with more sadness than glory, Third Worldism notwithstanding. At this level we need to be puzzled by what seems to be a tremendous inability on the part of Eurocentric thinkers to imagine a world without and beyond modernity, and they need to be made aware of that. Modernity can no longer be treated as the Great Singularity, the giant attractor towards which all tendencies ineluctably gravitate, the path to be trodden by all trajectories leading to an inevitable steady state. Rather, 'modernity and its exteriorities', if one wishes, should be treated as a true multiplicity, where trajectories are multiple and can lead to multiple states.

2. It is important to start thinking in earnest about the new mechanisms introduced by the new round of coloniality of power and knowledge. So far, this rearticulation of globality and coloniality is chiefly effected through discourses and practices of terrorism. These are not completely new, of course; in some ways, they build (still!) on the regime of classification that took place at the dawn of modernity, when Spain expelled Moors and Jews from the peninsula and established the distinction between Christians in Europe and Moors in North Africa and elsewhere. 'After the Third World' thus implies that new classifications are emerging, which are not based on a division of the world into three. Imagining beyond the Third World may contribute to this process from a critical position.

3. The analysis above also suggests that the politics of place should be an important ingredient of imaging after the Third World (fears of 'localisms' notwithstanding, but of course taking all the risks into account). Politics of place is a discourse of desire and possibility that builds on subaltern practices of difference for the (re)construction of alternative socio-natural worlds. Politics of place is an apt imaginary for thinking about the 'problem-space' defined by imperial globality and global coloniality. Politics of place may also articulate with those social movement meshworks and networks that confront NLG. In this articulation lies one of the best hopes of re-imagining and re-making local and regional worlds—in short, of 'worlds and knowledges otherwise'. Politics of place could also give new meaning to concepts of counter-hegemonic globalisation, alternative globalisations, transmodernity, or what have you.

4. A number of persistent social conditions continues to suggest that a concept of a third world could still be useful. The concept of social fascism is a useful notion for thinking about this issue. In this case it would be necessary to speak of 'third worlds', which would be made up of vast archipelagos of zones reduced to precarious living conditions, often (not always) marked by violence, and so forth. If this scenario is correct, it will be crucial to find really unprecedented ways of thinking about these 'third worlds' and the people inhabiting them that go beyond the prevailing pathologised idioms (underclass, ghettos, warlords, potential criminals and terrorists, *desechables*, the absolute poor, etc, all of which are almost always thoroughly racialised). They could well be the majority

of the world, and thus will have to be central to any attempt at making the world a better place. What kinds of logics are coming out of such worlds? These need to be understood in their own terms, not as they are constructed by modernity.[57]

There are of course many important aspects of imagining 'after the Third World' that have been left out, from the role of the state to national economic and development policy. I believe, however, that the framework presented above has implications for how we think about these as well. I would like, in ending, to suggest a few measures that would make sense in this regard, for instance:

1. At the level of imperial globality, novel types of coalitions, either regionally based (eg the Andean countries, West Africa) or networked according to other criteria (eg size, existence of a large technocratic elite and economic and technological basis. For instance, a coalition of some of the larger countries in the former Third World, even at the level of reformist elites *vis à vis* the excesses of imperial globality.) By novel, I mean complicating the nation-state and regional economies, for instance. Is it unthinkable to imagine, say, a pan-Andean confederation of autonomous regions drawn on cultural–ecological considerations, rather than traditional geopolitical concerns? This would be a confederation without nation-states, of course. Given the current role of many states within imperial globality, it is not unthinkable that the former Third World might be better off in a world without states, with the proviso that both local/regional and meta-national forms of structuring and governance be created to avoid the most dreadful traps of the nation-state while creating new forms of protection and negotiation.

2. It is clear by now that the Argentinean crisis was caused not by insufficient integration into the global economy but rather because of an excess of it. Even dutifully following the neoliberal advice of the IMF or home-grown economists did not save this important country from a profound crisis. Why can't we dare to imagine the unimaginable, that Argentina could have a better chance by stepping somewhat outside and beyond imperial globality, rather than staying fully within it? Can partial delinking—selective delinking and selective re-engagement—offer an alternative path, perhaps at the level of world regions (eg Southern Cone), or network of world regions? This means that it would be possible to rethink the proposal of de-linking introduced by Samir Amin in the 1970s to fit the new conditions.[58] Needless to say, everything seems to militate against this possibility. The proposal for a Free Trade Area of the Americas (ALCA, as it is known in Latin America and FTAA as it is known in North America) is being pushed with considerable force by the USA and most Latin American leaders. And, of course, any country or region that dares to attempt a path of autonomy is bound to incur the ire of empire, risking military action. This is why opposition to ALCA is today indelibly linked to opposition to militarism by most activist organisations.

These are just two examples of the kind of 'macro' thinking that, while not radical, could create better conditions for the struggle against imperial globality and global coloniality. If approached from this vantage point, they are likely to contribute to advance the idea that other worlds are possible. The social movements of the past decade are, in effect, a sign that this struggle is already under way. Imagining 'after the Third World' could become a more integral part of the imaginary of these movements. This would involve, as we saw, imagining beyond modernity and beyond the regimes of economy, war, coloniality, the exploitation of people and nature, and social fascism that it has brought about in its imperial global incarnation.

Notes

1 D Scott, *Refashioning Futures: Criticism After Postcoloniality*, Princeton, NJ: Princeton University Press, 1999.

2 B de S Santos, 'The World Social Forum: toward a counter-hegemonic globalization', paper presented to the XXIV International Congress, Latin American Studies Association (LASA), Dallas, TX, March 2003. Also available at http://www.ces.fe.uc.pt/bss/fsm.php.

3 A Quijano, *El Nuevo Imaginario Anti-capitalista*, at http://www.forumsocialmundial.org.br/dinamic/es/tbib_Anibal_Quijano.asp.

4 S Amin, 'For struggles, global and national', *Frontline*, 20 (2), pp 1–10. Also available at http://www.flonnet.com/fl2002/stories/20030131008201200.htm.

5 W Harcourt & A Escobar, 'Women and the politics of place', *Development*, 45 (1), pp 7–14; JK Gibson-Graham, 'Politics of empire, politics of place', unpublished manuscript, Department of Geography, University of Massachusetss, and Department of Geography, Australian National University, 2003; and P McMichael, 'Can we interpret anti-globalisation movements in Polanyian terms?', unpublished manuscript, Cornell University, 2001. See also Patel & McMichael in this issue.

6 Santos, 'The World Social Forum'; J Sen, 'The World Social Forum as logo', unpublished manuscript, Delhi, 2003; W Fischer & T Ponniah (eds), *Another World Is Possible: Popular Alternatives to Globalization at the World Social Forum*, London: Zed Books, 2003; and A Anand, J Sen, P Waterman & A Escobar, *Are Other Worlds Possible? The Past, Present, and Possible Futures of the World Social Forum*, Delhi: Viveka, in press.

7 B de S Santos, *Towards a New Legal Common Sense*, London: Butterworth, 2002; E Leff, *Saber Ambiental*, Mexico: Siglo XXI, 1998; and A Escobar, 'Other worlds are (already) possible: cyber-internationalism and post-capitalist cultures', paper presented to the Cyberspace Panel, Life After Capitalism Programme, World Social Forum, Porto Alegre, January 2003. Also available at http://www.zmag.org/lac.htm.

8 Santos, *Towards a New Legal Common Sense*.

9 A Joxe, *Empire of Disorder*, New York: Semiotext(e), 2002.

10 A Giddens, *The Consequences of Modernity*, Stanford, CA: Stanford University Press, 1990.

11 J Habermas, *Legitimation Crisis*, Boston, MA: Beacon Press, 1973; and Habermas, *The Philosophical Discourse of Modernity*, Cambridge, MA: MIT Press, 1987.

12 M Foucault, *The Order of Things*, New York: Vintage Books, 1973; and M Heidegger, 'The age of the world picture', in Heidegger, *The Question Concerning Technology*, New York: Harper and Row, 1977, pp 115–154.

13 G Vattimo, *The End of Modernity*, Baltimore, MD: Johns Hopkins University Press, 1991. See Escobar, 'Worlds and Knowledges Otherwise: the Latin American modernity/coloniality Research Program', *European Review of Latin American and Caribbean Studies*, in press, for further discussion.

14 Giddens, *The Consequences of Modernity*.

15 A Appadurai, *Modernity At Large*, Minneapolis, MN: University of Minnesota Press, 1996.

16 I believe a Eurocentred view of modernity is present in most conceptualisations of modernity and globalisation in most fields and on all sides of the political spectrum, including in those works that contribute novel elements for rethinking modernity. See M Hardt & A Negri, *Empire*, Cambridge, MA: Harvard University Press, 2000. In this latter case, Eurocentrism surfaces in the authors' identification of the potential sources for radical action, and in their belief that there is no outside to modernity (again, *à la* Giddens). In other cases Eurocentric notions of modernity are implicit in otherwise enlightening views of globalisation. See I Wallerstein, 'Globalization, or the Age of Transition? A long-term view of the trajectory of the world system', *International Sociology*, 15 (2), 2000, pp 249–265.

17 Santos, *Towards a New Legal Common Sense*, pp 1–20. Santos distinguishes his position from those who

think that there are modern solutions to modern problems (Habermas, Giddens) and from those 'celebratory postmoderns' (Baudrillard, Lyotard, Derrida), for whom the lack of modern solutions to modern problems is not itself a problem, but rather a solution of sorts.

18 See Wallerstein's analysis of Kondratieff cycles, in Wallerstein, 'Globalization, or the Age of Transition?'.

19 See M Castells, *The Rise of the Network Society*, Oxford, Blackwell, 1996; and Santos, *Towards A New Legal Common Sense*, pp 165–193.

20 Santos, *Towards A New Legal Common Sense*, p 453.

21 *Ibid*, pp 447–458.

22 A Joxe, *Empire of Disorder*, pp 78, 213.

23 *Ibid*, p 107.

24 *Ibid*, p 157.

25 *Ibid*, p 171.

26 *Ibid*, p 200.

27 For recent treatments of the current situation in Colombia, see JL Garay (ed), *Colombia: Entre la Exclusión y el Desarrollo*, Bogotá: Contraloría General de la República, 2002; C Ahumada *et al*, *¿Qué Está Pasando en Colombia?*, Bogotá: El Ancora Editores, 2000; F Leal, (ed), *Los Laberintos de la Guerra: Utopías e Incertidumbres sobre la Paz*, Bogotá: Tercer Mundo, 1999; and the special issue of *Revista Foro* on 'Colombia's New Right', 46, January 2003.

28 Plan Colombia is a US-based multibillion dollar strategy intended to control both drug production and trafficking and guerrilla activity. Spearheaded by the Colombian and US governments, Plan Colombia actually constitutes a strategy of militarisation and control of the Andean region as a whole (including the Amazon region linked to the Andean countries). Its first installment of $1.3 billion (2000–02) was largely spent on military aid. Even the small percentage of the funds allocated to social development was largely captured by NGOs set up by capitalist groups to extend their control over valuable territories and resources, as in the case of the palm growers in the Southern Pacific region. Among the aspects most criticised of Plan Colombia by Colombian and international organisations are the indiscriminate programme of fumigation, the increased militarisation it has fostered, and the overall escalation of the armed conflict it has brought about, particularly in Colombia. It is a centrepiece of the Uribe administration (2002–06).

29 Local social movements in the Pacific seem to be clear about this. For them, displacement is part of a concerted counter-attack on the territorial gains of ethnic communities throughout the continent, from the Zapatista to the Mapuche. This happens because the socioeconomic projects of the armed actors do not coincide with those of the ethnic communities. This is why local social movements emphasise a principle of return as a general policy for the displaced groups of the Pacific, and the declaration of the region as a territory of peace, happiness and freedom, free of all forms of armed violence. See A Escobar, 'Displacement and development in the Colombian Pacific', *International Social Science Journal*, 175, pp 157–167 for an extended discussion of these issues.

30 This is a very sketchy presentation of this group's ideas in the best of cases. See Escobar in press for an extended discussion, including its genealogy, tendencies, relation to other theoretical movements, and current tensions. This group is associated with the work a few central figures, chiefly the Argentinean/ Mexican philosopher Enrique Dussel, the Peruvian sociologist Aníbal Quijano, and the Argentinean/US semiotician and cultural theorist Walter Mignolo. There is, however, a growing number of scholars associated with the group, particularly in the Andean countries and the USA. In recent years the group has gathered around several projects and places in Quito, Bogotá, México City, and in Chapel Hill/Durham and Berkeley in the USA. For the main ideas presented here, see E Dussel, 'Europe, modernity, and Eurocentrism', *Nepantla*, 1 (3), 2000, pp 465–478; Dussel, *The Underside of Modernity*, Atlantic Highlands, NJ: Humanities Press, 1996; Dussel, 'Eurocentrism and modernity', in J Beverly & J Oviedo (eds), *The Postmodernism Debate in Latin America*, Durham, SC: Duke University Press, 1993, pp 65–76; Dussel, *1492. El Encubrimiento del Otro*, Bogotá: Antropos, 1992; Dussel, *Introducción a la Filosofía de la Liberación*, Bogotá: Editorial Nueva América, 1983; Dussel, *Filosofía de la Liberación*, Mexico: Editorial Edicol, 1976; A Quijano, 'Coloniality of power, ethnocentrism, and Latin America', *Nepantla*, 1 (3), 2000, pp 533–580; Quijano, 'Modernity, identity, and utopia in Latin America', in Beverly & Oviedo, *The Postmodernism Debate in Latin America*, pp 140–155; W Mignolo, 'Local histories and global designs: an interview with Walter Mignolo', *Discourse*, 22 (3), 2001, pp 7–33; Mignolo, *Local Histories/ Global Designs*, Princeton, NJ: Princeton University Press, 2000; Mignolo (ed), *Capitalismo y Geopolítica del Conocimiento*, Buenos Aires: Ediciones del Signo, 2001; E Lander (ed), *La Colonialidad del Saber: Eurocentrismo y Ciencias Sociales*, Buenos Aires: CLASCO, 2000; S Castro-Gómez, *Crítica de la Razón Latinoamericana*, Barcelona: Puvill Libros, 1996; S Castro-Gómez (ed), *La Reestructuración de las Ciencias Sociales en América Latina*, Bogotá: Universidad Javeriana, 2000; S Castro-Gómez & E Mendieta (eds), *Teorías sin Disciplina, Latinoamericanismo, Poscolonialidad y Globalización en Debate*, Mexico, DF: Miguel Angel Porrúa–University of San Francisco, 1998; and C Walsh, F Schiwy & S Castro-Gómez (eds), *Interdisciplinar las Ciencias Sociales*, Quito: Universidad Andina-Abya Yala, 2002. Little of these debates has been translated into English. See Beverly & Oviedo (eds), *The Postmodernism Debate in*

Latin America, for some of these authors' works in English. A volume in this language has been recently devoted to Dussel's work. See L Alcoff & E Mendieta (eds), *Thinking from the Underside of History. Enrique Dussel's Philosophy of Liberation*, Lanham, MD: Rowman and Littlefield, 2000. The journal *Nepantla. Views from South* has featured the works of this group. See especially Vol 1, No 3, 2000. Another volume in English, by Grosfogel and Saldívar, is in preparation. A feminist critique of Dussel is found in E Vuola, 'Thinking *other*wise: Dussel, liberation theology, and feminism', in Alcoff & Mendieta (eds), *Thinking from the Underside of History*, pp 149–180.

[31] Dussel, 'Europe, modernity, and Eurocentrism'; and Quijano, 'Coloniality of power, ethnocentrism, and Latin America'.

[32] See Dussel, 'Europe, modernity, and Eurocentrism; and Dussel, 'Eurocentrism and modernity'.

[33] N Maldonado-Torres, 'Imperio y colonialidad del ser', paper presented to the XXIV International Congress, LASA, Dallas, TX, March 2003.

[34] Email correspondence, 31 May 2003.

[35] Dussel, *Filosofía de la Liberación*.

[36] Mignolo, 'Local histories and global designs', p 9.

[37] *Ibid*, p 11.

[38] On the application of the notion of diatopic hermeneutics to incommensurable cultural traditions, see also Santos, *Towards a New Legal Common Sense*, pp 268–274.

[39] Mignolo, *Local Histories/Global Designs*, p 308.

[40] *Ibid*, p 22.

[41] *Ibid*, p 329.

[42] *Ibid*, p 309 [original emphasis].

[43] 'Worlds and knowledges otherwise' is the new subtitle of the journal *Nepantla*, published at Duke University. I am highly indebted to Walter Mignolo for the points in these concluding paragraphs (email correspondence, May 2003).

[44] Gibson-Graham, 'Politics of empire, politics of place'.

[45] M Osterweil, '"Non ci capiamo questo movimento!" Towards theoretical and methodological approaches based in an ethnographic epistemology', unpublished MA thesis, Department of Anthropology, University of North Carolina, 2003; and Escobar, 'Notes on networks and anti-globalization social movements', Presented at the American Anthropological Association Annual Meeting, Washington, DC, November 2000. Available from: www.unc.edu/ ~ aescobar/.

[46] McMichael, 'Can we interpret anti-globalisation movements in Polanyian terms?', p 3.

[47] See Escobar, *Notes on Networks and Anti-Globalization Social Movements*; and Escobar, 'Other worlds are (already) possible' for further explanation of this model and additional references. See L Peltonen, 'Fluids without a cause? Tracing the emergence of a local green movement', in Y Haila & C Dyke (eds), *How Does Nature Speak? The Dynamics of the Human Ecological Condition*, unpublished book manuscript, University of Helsinki, 2003 for an application of complexity to a particular social movement in Finland.

[48] M de Landa, 'Meshworks, hierarchies and interfaces', at http://www.t0.or.at/delanda/; and de Landa, *A Thousand Years of Nonlinear History*, New York: Zone Books, 1997.

[49] A caveat should be kept in mind: often ethnic minorities, women and the poor are the most marginalised from some of these trends, especially at the level of ICTs. Nevertheless, these same agents are often at the forefront of struggles over ICTs. See, for instance, Maria Suárez's work with the FIRE radio and internet network in Costa Rica, 2003; and W Harcourt (ed), *Women@Internet. Creating New Cultures in Cyberspace*, London: Zed Books, 1999 for empowering uses of ICTs by women's groups. See also GL Ribeiro, 'Cybercultual politics: political activism at a distance in a transnational world', in SE Alvarez, E Dagnino & A Escobar (eds), *Cultures of Politics/Politics of Culture: Revisioning Latin American Social Movements*, Boulder, CO: Westview Press, 1998, pp 325–352; and P Waterman, 'Some propositions on cyberspace after capitalism', paper presented to the Cyberspace Panel, Life after Capitalism Programme, World Social Forum, Porto Alegre, January, 2003. Also available at http://www.zmag.org/lacsite.htm.

[50] Harcourt & Escobar 'Women and the politics of place'; and Escobar, 'Culture sits in places: reflections on globalism and subaltern strategies of localization', *Political Geography* 20, 2001, pp 139–174.

[51] Gibson-Graham, 'Politics of empire, politics of place', p 15.

[52] See Escobar, *Culture Sits in Places*.

[53] Santos, *Towards a New Legal Common Sense*, p 459ff.

[54] Santos, 'The World Social Forum'.

[55] Santos, *Towards a New Legal Common Sense*, p 234.

[56] Santos, 'The World Social Forum', p 25.

[57] Charles Price is attempting a hopeful reconceptualisation of the concept of 'lumpenproletariat' to explain the so-called 'garrisons' in the outskirts of Kingston; these are neighborhoods ruled by local bosses through a political, armed regime that combines particularistic provision of welfare, regulated forms of violence, and little or no state presence. Garrisons become, in this way, relatively self-ruling, self-organising urban enclaves. C Price, 'What the Zeeks Rebellion reveals: issues of development, moral economy, and the

lumpenproletariat in Jamaica', paper presented at the Department of Anthropology Colloquium, Chapel Hill, NC, 21 October 2002.

[58] The idea of rethinking Professor Amin's original proposal in terms of 'selective de-linking and selective re-engagement' emerged in a conversation with Ahmad Samattar and Amparo Menéndez-Carrión at Macalaster College in Minnesota, April 2002.

Third Worldism and the lineages of global fascism: the regrouping of the global South in the neoliberal era

RAJEEV PATEL & PHILIP McMICHAEL

> The despised, the insulted, the hurt, the dispossessed—in short, the underdogs of the human race were meeting [in Bandung]. Here were class and racial and religious consciousness on a global scale. Who had thought of organizing such a meeting? And what had these nations in common? Nothing, it seemed to me, but what their past relationship to the Western world had made them feel. This meeting of the rejected was in itself a kind of judgment upon the Western world![1]

> Even in the horrors of the Nazi regime, then, it is possible to see some resemblances to the trajectories of other countries.[2]

Historians can only see the past through the lens of the present. Our enterprise explicitly views the rise and demise of the Third Worldism launched at Bandung through contemporary offensives and resistances to capital.[3] Today, at the World Social Forums, at the protests against the World Bank, the IMF, the WTO, NATO and G8, we see phenomena strikingly similar to Richard Wright's observation in

Bandung, quoted above: a variety of different causes allied in their opposition to, now, variants of a single kind of capitalism. There is, however, a key difference. While Bandung trumpeted the possibility of national–statist politics as a vehicle of resistance to the inequalities both of the world capitalist order and of the Soviet alternative, few parliamentarians have taken seriously the demands of the contemporary resistances to neoliberal capitalism. The demise of Third Worldism coincides with the capture of Third World elites by capital, and by its ideology.

We contend that the seeds of the takeover were already in place at the time of Bandung, and germinating in the greenhouse of developmentalist politics. In order to demonstrate this, we trace the history of development as colonial project and show that, at its inception, it instituted a particular politics of biopower necessary for state-led capitalist accumulation. Crises of capitalist accumulation in the early 20th century reveal these tropes most clearly, but they are present, and dynamic, throughout the colonial process. Importantly, they are left substantially untouched either by national liberation politics or by changes in subsequent regimes.[4] Indeed, the process of postcolonial nation-building deployed disciplinary colonial technologies to create, through coercion and consent, a national hegemony that operated through the state. This was an outcome predicted, albeit in different language, by Fanon. At the very same time as the Non-Aligned Movement (NAM) matured, deploying the UN Conference on Trade and Development (UNCTAD) as a seat of Third World power in inter-state politics, states and rulers were internalising the disciplines, self-definitions and elitism of developmentalism.

The development illusion is a persistent but ever-changing one. There are continuities, however. It is striking, for instance, that the Declaration adopted by the UN General Assembly at its 18th Session in 1963 calls for trade arrangements and concessions fundamentally similar to those currently, and equally unsuccessfully, being demanded by developing countries at the World Trade Organization. More recently, the bubble of development rhetoric has been resoundingly punctured by a variety of commentators.[5] While some groups (the South Centre, Third World Network) are keen to participate in the modification of development institutions, many are vociferous about the limits of the developmental state. We highlight the global justice movements (such as the *Vía Campesina*—the international peasant farmers' movement) as organisational attempts to transcend developmentalism. We argue that their projects, grounded in a firm scepticism of the state, and wedded to a robust internationalism that maintains an uneasy and increasingly critical relation to the 'nation', come not as a continuation of the Third Worldist project, but have risen, phoenix-like, from its ashes. The intentionally provocative component to our argument is to link contemporary and historical phenomena in world history, Third Worldism included, to fascism. We explain, in the following section, exactly why we choose to do this.

Two conversations about fascism

In the political-economy literature 'fascism' has a fairly specific and historicised definition.[6] It refers to that period of politics in Germany, Italy and, arguably, Japan incipient in the two decades before the beginning of World War II,

219

In the political-economy literature fascism has a fairly specific and historicised definition.[6] It refers to that period of politics in Germany, Italy and, arguably, Japan incipient in the two decades before the beginning of World War II, concluding with the defeat of Nazi Germany in 1945. The fascism of these regimes lies in the following characteristics:

1. Fascism was a response by capital to a direct threat to its hegemony. At the time, this threat was that of communism.
2. It offered itself as a solution to the woes of the Great Depression, through a pseudo-corporatism that brought the needs of workers, capital and the state together.
3. Fascism was, however, profoundly anti-worker. There was, in other words, a contradiction between the state's mobilisation against unions and autonomous worker organisation on the one hand, and its self-proclaimed interest in workers' welfare on the other. To resolve this, elites within the (dominant) hegemonic bloc deployed state apparatus to banish working-class demands with the surrogate of nationalism. Cultural technologies that elided state with nation, and demanded fealty to the unified nation-state, were deployed in the service of quelling class discontent. These included, but were not limited to, notions of national purity—extended, famously in the Nazi case, to environmental, bodily and geographical purity.
4. Culture was strictly controlled and non-state-sanctioned thinking was suppressed. *Weltanschauungskrieg* (world-view war) was systematically and scientifically propounded, with rigorous justification by elites for particular suppressions and celebrations, accompanied by a strict policing of cultural interactions in order to root out deviance.
5. A hetero-normative sexual division of labour was strenuously enforced. Reproductive labour was vigorously policed, through cultural celebrations of female domesticity, through strict monitoring of women's entry into the formal economy, and through the extermination of homosexuals.
6. Technologies of coercion and consent, particularly military authoritarianism, were used by the state in order to secure hegemony over dissidents.

We modify the term 'fascism' with 'global'. This we do for a number of reasons. We do not claim that the tendencies we see at work from the early days of the development project to contemporary developmentalism replicate exactly the features of mid-1930s and –1940s Germany, Italy and Japan. Although, as Gourevitch notes, important features of Nazi Germany were present in the policies of other states at the time, we readily acknowledge the historic specificity of this period.[7] What we attempt to do, however, is to broker a conversation between two different kinds of heterodox approaches to development in which the idea of facism plays a key role. The first lies in the tradition of Marx and, specifically, Karl Polanyi. The latter's *The Great Transformation* (1944/1957) is usually read as an argument about the dislocation of social relations through the instantiation of 'fictitious commodities', and the markets that trade in them. We note that Polanyi's contribution to an essentially Marxist corpus of ideas lies not in his re-presentation of *Capital*, but in his application of these ideas to the rise of fascism.[8]

220

The literature to which we connect Polanyi stems from the British Cultural Studies tradition. We borrow the term 'global fascism' from Paul Gilroy, who uses it extensively in *Against Race*, in which he situates the continuities of contemporary capitalism, in North and South, in biopolitics (the deployment of disciplinary technologies at the level of the individual). Gilroy's definition of fascism: 'anticonservative, antiliberal, populist, fraternalist, and revolutionary', assigns a central role to the state in orchestrating the production and reproduction of its citizens.[9] Caution and history are important here. Following Tariq Ali, we do not want to suggest that the presence or absence of certain criteria exclude or include a particular regime or time within the ambit of fascism. Ours is not a 'checklist' approach to the study of fascism. We want, through the addition of the adjective 'global', to render the term 'fascism' more porous. We do this not to scandalise, but to recast the present. Fascism does not arise *ex nihilo* but as a result of a particular configuration of social forces—it is the subtle dynamics of these forces to which we want to direct our attention, and it is a lesson we willingly learn from the cultural studies tradition. As Gilroy suggests, the 'threat of fascism'

> should not be an open license to indulge in paranoia. It loses none of its force when we appreciate that the trains are not necessarily being loaded right now in our own neighbourhoods. Fascism is not permanently on the brink of assuming terroristic governmental power ... If we wish to live a good life and enjoy just relations with our fellows, our conduct must be closely guided not just by this terrible history, but by the knowledge that these awful possibilities are always much closer than we like to imagine.[10]

Second, we emphasise that global fascism, as a form of ruthless (for want of a better qualifier) biopolitics, has always been a world-historical phenomenon. This is not to say that fascism *qua* fascism is, and always has been, smeared across the world. We do, however, suggest that its component forces, in coming together under colonialism, have informed the project of development, albeit in attenuated form. We have only to think of the colonial project—beginning with the cultural genocide in Iberian America, through slavery to forced/contract labour in the late colonial period, and perhaps including the forced expropriation and starvation of Indians, Chinese and Brazilians, among others, documented in *Late Victorian Holocausts*: *El Niño Famines and The Making of the Third World* by Mike Davis.[11] Indeed, we see our project as allied to Davis. He extends the notion of 'holocausts', which had previously been applied to a European phenomenon, into the colonial past.[12] We go one step further, pushing the historical boundaries of global fascism back into colonial time and space, and then drawing it forward, into the colonised present.

We conjecture that fascist relations are immanent in global capitalism, intensify state biopolitics at moments of crisis, and may be sustained post-crisis for hegemonic purposes. Consider the 1930s, when a rogue state (Germany) was forced to structurally adjust by the League of Nations powers as a consequence of the collapse of the gold–sterling regime. The result was what has come to be known as fascism: a manoeuvring of elites and a populist appeal by the Nazi party to regenerate an idealised national culture through selective mobilisation based on ethnic and racial intolerance, and dedicated to reconstructing modernity via state technologies of control. Culture is, of course, always part of capitalism. Stuart Hall's work informs our use of culture as synonymous with 'ideology'. The relation between culture and capital that informs our use of 'global fascism' is one that invokes particular relations of control between the state, media, the military, and tropes such as 'family', 'homeland', 'nation', 'God' and the market.[13]

Our use of 'global fascism' is also an attempt to represent today's *transformed* international conjuncture, where the crisis of market rule is premised on the defeat of Third World utopianism, and on a definitive 'globalisation' of the commodity form: the combined assault on organised labour (global labour market casualisation), on peasant cultures, and public goods. As early 20th century fascism was premised on the defeat of anti-capitalist forces, so global fascism now targets forces with collective claims that stand in the way of commodification. The increasingly unaccountable institutions of market rule (including the 'market state') provide a mechanism for one of the key forces of 'global fascism' and, while this is a universal process, it is so contingently, because it continues the racist project begun under colonialism. In this sense we submit that fascism has foundational roots in European-centred development. The capitalist cultural technologies, with their origins in Europe, have now, under a US aegis, been extended under multilateral developmental institutions. This is very much in keeping with the idea of development—an idea with distinct cultural roots and heritage, but an idea that must, of necessity disavow these roots if it is successfully to claim its goal of disinterested and normalised universality.

The project of development

Colonialism and development

Development was integral to colonialism. While 19th century Europeans may have experienced development as a specifically European phenomenon, colonialism nevertheless represented it as a universal necessity. Development praxis involved managing the social transformation attending the rise of capitalism and industrial technologies.[14] Development matched the apparent inevitability of technological change with social intervention—represented ideologically as improving human society, but pursued as a method of control of citizen subjects subordinated to wrenching social transformation.

This social engineering impulse framed European colonisation of the non-European world. The always-contested relationship of plunder between Europe and its colonies necessitated new forms of social control of subject populations in metropolitan as well as colonial regions. In the latter development served a legitimacy function, since, compared with Europeans, native peoples were cast as 'backward'.[15] Subject populations were exposed to a variety of new disciplines, including forced labour schemes, schooling, and segregation in native quarters. Forms of colonial subordination differed across time and space, but the overriding object was either to adapt and/or marginalise colonial subjects to the European presence.

Adaptation included the use of the popular factory model of schooling, where knowledge was subdivided into specialties, and pupils submitted to continuous monitoring by supervisors. Punctuality, task specialisation and regularity were the hallmarks of this new discipline, breaking down social customs and producing individual subjects who confronted a new, rational order, which they both resisted and reproduced. In 1843, for example, the Egyptian state (under the suzerainty of the declining Ottoman, and rising British, empire) introduced the English 'Lancaster school' factory model to the city of Cairo, in order to consolidate the authority of its emerging civil service. Egyptian students learned the new disciplines required of a developing society that was busy displacing peasant culture with plantations of cotton for export to English textile mills, and managing an army of migrant labour building an infrastructure of roads, canals, railways, telegraphs and ports.[16] Across the colonial divide industrial capital transformed English and Egyptian society in lock-step, producing new forms of social discipline among labouring populations and middle-class citizen-subjects. Given the world-historical relations of industrial capitalism, the new class inequalities within each society were premised on a racist international inequality produced by colonialism. It was this inequality, and its 'local face' in the colonies, that fuelled anti-colonial resistances.

As Europeans were 'civilising' their colonies, colonial subjects explored the paradox of European colonialism—the juxtaposition of the European discourse of rights and sovereignty against their own subjugation.[17] The decolonisation movement peaked as European colonialism collapsed in the mid-20th century, when World War II sapped the power of the colonial empires to withstand anti-colonial struggles. After millions of colonial subjects were deployed in the Allied war effort for self-determination against fascist expansionism from Europe to Southeast Asia, the returning colonial soldiers turned this rhetoric and sometimes violence on their colonial masters in a bid for independence.

Sovereignty was linked to overcoming the deprivations of colonialism, through an expression of state-centred autonomy from the colonial metropole. The idea of sovereignty demands more treatment than we can afford here. In its classical sense it is a call for autonomy, delimited by geography, and accompanied by a unitary sovereign, an agent with a monopoly on force within prescribed boundaries. Equally traditionally, this agent has been the state, and its boundaries have been those of the state. Yet, in this context, it is also a technology of disavowal, of amnesia—for it projects Third World elites *exclusively* as victims, as a class absolutely sinned against and unsinning, demonising—correctly—the imperial apparatuses of control without implicating themselves in its functioning. It also permits a platform not only for cultural nation building, but also cultural *state* building. As we shall see, contemporary understandings of sovereignty come shorn of the state apparatus, with conflicting and complex geographies of claims to autonomy.[18]

Fascism and development

It is important to recall that, from the outset, both sociology and development were responses to European class tension. Auguste Comte, the founding father of sociology, published his *Plan des travaux scientifiques nécessaires pour réorganiser la société* in 1822, when the social dislocations of industrial capitalism were beginning to be felt. Comte could hardly have failed to be aware of the nascent working class's conditions in Paris, London and Manchester. The spreading phenomenon of urban unemployment (against the backdrop of empire) taxed the theories of human progress advanced by the Scottish enlightenment.[19] Under these material and historical circumstances, Comte, building on Saint Simon, completed the positivist project.

Applying positivist methods to the historical record, Comte claimed to derive a three-stage model of human progress. This model came with none of the caveats that accompany many of today's more defensive applications of positivist methods. Comte's work was as much a bold manifesto for a new science—sociology—as a revisionist history. He argued that the laws he claimed to discover were not convenient simplifying assumptions, but actually existed 'in society'.

Comte's observation, produced as it was in a period of high colonialism, was not, however, an explicitly imperial one. It stemmed purely from the logic of domestic considerations—in order for Comte to understand Europe as he did, he cast other parts of the world in particular relationship to Europe, and cast their peoples as populations whose manifest destiny was to become as enlightened as the French. This is the violent consequence of humanism; in imputing universal characteristics to all people, contingency, diversity and specificity are homogenised in the name of a specious and often violent attempt to create human unity. This, in itself, lends legitimacy to cultural and biopolitical colonisation.

For Comte this interpretation involved an explicit set of policy responses *vis-à-vis* the state. His three stages of increasing human order began with savagery, progressed through a belief in God, to a final stage where humans, through their mental faculties, transformed their natural tendencies for self-love into a pan-human altruism. Comte located himself and his followers firmly at the point of transition from the stage of 'love of God' to 'love of humanity'.[20] This is an important Occidental cultural technology. The violence of the French Revolution, argued the positivists, had been necessary to sweep away the vestiges of old (second-stage) thinking. But the *laissez-faire* economic policies that followed in the wake of the revolution had, paradoxically, retarded progress. In particular, the slavish pursuit of markets in property and labour encouraged underdevelopment; the most pressing manifestation of this lay in the new phenomenon of widespread urban unemployment.

The forces of natural development could, however, be shifted to a faster track by removing a key blockage—private property. It is in retrospect striking that the positivists should have focused on property as a problem of development. Perhaps even more striking was their solution, which involved not the dismantling of private property, but its trusteeship, in the hands of those most able to manage it with required technical skill. For Comte and the positivists, the remedy for unemployment, and the most effective means to expedite the social transition to altruism, lay in the hands of bankers. Banks would hold property in trust for the community, managing it wisely for the common good. Of course, these bankers would need to be instructed about their 'social function', to be 'moralised' in suitable ways.[21] Banks have remained central to the development project, either as trustees of communal property, sources of finance for national industrial expansion, or indeed as sources of micro-finance for village women.[22]

From this summary history of development we make three observations. First, development was, among other central features, a capitalist project. From its very inception, Comte saw development (and sociology writ large) as the ordering of society for progress, through the regulation of private property. In order to render more public the corrupting influence of private property, Comte's solution was to have bankers (not legislators) administer the public good. These administrators would be guided by positivist rationality. Central to this vision, then, is a conception of *progress*, managed through a system of class relations, not by capitalists *per se*, but by an elite cadre of gurus of order and science. Second, the state was a central locus of the ordering of society. The project of colonial development required the construction in essence, and in effigy, of the apparatus of the modern European state. This 'gift'[23] was an integral part of the development enterprise. The mechanisms of control and domination, the bio-politics of development, were created specifically to pacify, monitor, police and conscript to labour, the rural communities of the Third World, just as they did in Europe. These politics were predicated on an exclusive state sovereignty, and much effort was spent securing this sovereignty. Third, biopolitics and capitalism are mutually constitutive within the development project. The limit case of development, we argue, is fascism. We take Polanyi's analysis to be indicative of incipient trends not only at the emergence of Third Worldism, but also in contemporary global political economy.

Biopolitics and development

At the heart of the development project, then, are core ideas of managerialism and, less explicitly, of sovereignty. Managerialism is instituted through a process of 'civilising' people as a nation, a class, a race and a gender, specifically through control of individually coded bodies—where they work, how they reproduce, even the language they dream in. This is what we mean when we refer to biopolitics. Gilroy states that biopolitics 'specifies that the person is identified only in terms of the body'.[24] The idea of biopolitical discipline is Foucault's: 'For the first time in history, no doubt, biological existence was reflected in political existence'—the fact of living was no longer an inaccessible substrate that only emerged from time to time, amid the randomness of death and its fatality; part of it passed into knowledge's field of control and power's sphere of intervention.[25] For the successful coupling of biological and political existence, competing conceptions of the biological, and the political, had to be tamed. This process required the extension, and exclusive and absolute maintenance, of state sovereignty. We see the twin facets, of management and sovereignty, in the various businesses of the development project: including the regulation of education, sexuality, criminality and gender.[26]

A biopolitical approach to understanding colonial development praxis broadens our conventional understanding of what the state does and does not do.

There are few areas of life that the state does not seek to regulate. Gender regulation practices exemplify how the state's engagement was at once bio-political, orientated through capitalism and ideas of progress. In southern Africa, for example, the decreeing of pass laws in 1892 served to create, institute and discipline a labour market, and to monitor tax payments. These passes served a variety of other unstated purposes. They aimed to identify, to surveille and to push into wage labour the black men required to mine gold, and to work on the farms expropriated and alienated by the settlers. The passes soon became ways of tracking and limiting the movements of male black bodies in and around the colonised terrain. They provided a mark of recognition of colonised subjects by the state, geographically policing the division between colonial citizens and subjects. Mamdani's helpful categories of citizen and subject and his investigation of technologies of governance used to discipline colonies points to the spatial character of juridical control.[27]

Critical to these operations of power, however, was the creation of exclusive sovereignty by colonial regimes. Indeed, the exercise of biopower and sovereignty were co-eval.[28] This should come as no surprise—the existence of competing sovereignties was anathema to the universal and exclusive character of development; given that development was both inevitable and unilinear, competing sovereignties could be permitted neither in theory nor practice.

The case for global fascism

Having outlined our understanding of development, and its biopolitical basis, it is now time to make the case for 'global fascism'. One of the most striking accounts of the rise of fascism lies in Polanyi's *Great Transformation*. Polanyi views fascism as a solution to the '*impasse* reached by liberal capitalism'—the untenability of the illusion of the self-regulating market. The liberal market can only ever be a fiction. Despite economic liberalism's rhetorical and ideological separation of the market and the state, and of the separation of economics and politics more widely, the market is an inescapably political construct. The process of its institution undermines the very conditions of its existence.

Fascism, argued Polanyi, explicitly recognises the social bases of productive activity and seeks to reorganise society to rectify the crisis of the self-regulating market. Fascism follows market liberalism inevitably, because the very liberalism that called for global freedom of capital falls victim to the shocks to international capital markets. Through these shocks, paradoxically, the nation becomes a more, not less, important site of political engagement. The logic of fascism is a panicked response 'to protect society from the market by sacrificing human freedom'.[29] The logic is flawed, relying as it does on totalitarianism (nationalist, religious, patriarchal) and an emphasis on state support for capital. But the problem is real. The implication that freedom and the market are incompatible opposes Polanyi to Hayek and Schumpeter in his time, and to contemporary neoliberal ideologues in ours.

The importance of deploying the term 'fascism' lies in its ability to help us interpret the present. For Polanyi, the key puzzle was the abrupt transition from decades of relative peace to the Great War and then to fascism in Europe.

226

Polanyi argued that the self-regulating market, despite the counter-movement to mitigate and prevent it, irretrievably weakened the social mechanisms forestalling the sacrifice of freedom on the altar of the market. Similar processes operate today, in a world of neoliberal economics, with concomitant political disavowal. This political–economic understanding of fascism, we feel, can be profitably combined with a cultural studies perspective, such as that of Gilroy, who argues that the genealogy of fascism extends to the present. Traces are found in the obsessions with 'leaders', with the increasing policing of boundaries and nation, with the racialisation of criminality in North and South, and in the troubling rise of nationhood as a mooring for identity on both the left and the right.[30]

The convergence of biopolitical technologies of control and neoliberal forms operates through the trope of individuality. That the 'individual' is both the simultaneous object of control of biopolitics, and the explicit creation of neoliberalism is no accident. When Margaret Thatcher famously asserted that society didn't exist, she attempted, among other things, to instantiate, and to celebrate, a model of biopolitical control *pur*. The subject of neoliberalism as a disembodied *homo economicus* is precisely the subject which biopolitics seeks to create, individuate and control. This is exemplified through the current commodification of public services, where the substantive criteria for consumption of such market services is distinctly biopolitical, compared with a public welfare arrangement where the state might provide healthcare to all comers, without eligibility criteria—in which case access to such service would only be formal and not subject to an economic calculus and individual monitoring.

In the current global trajectory of privatisation of services, access to healthcare, for example, heightens the policing of bodies—payment systems demand an accounting system at the level of individual bodies, and with that accounting system a prior history of health and of access to cash (and hence paid labour) for the patient. It invokes an entire system of state monitoring, evaluation by capital and control of individuals, individuating bodies as repositories of asymmetrical and delimited (market) rights. The healthcare example is useful because it is also a transnational phenomenon, one increasingly under the scrutiny of supranational organisations, through the General Agreement on Trade in Services (GATS) 2000. The GATS, an agreement within the WTO currently under negotiation, offers (though does not guarantee) providers of healthcare and other (formerly public) services the chance to enter new markets.

Another, different example of the transnational capitalist recognition of the body is through crime. That certain activities are criminalised under liberal capitalism does not stop their occurrence. Although the state is a prime locus of biopolitical activity, its sovereignty is far from absolute. Biopolitics doesn't need the state—the recognition of the body by capital does not require state sanction to occur. For example, it is estimated that 700 000 to two million women and children are trafficked annually, and that there are about 10 million trafficked people working at risk. After drug smuggling and gun running, human trafficking is the third largest illegal trade (annual profit of about $6 billion). Child trafficking already dwarfs the transatlantic slave trade at its peak, by a magnitude of 10. Destinations include farming, restaurant labour, domestic servitude, fishing, mail-order brides, market stall labour, shop work, and the sex trade.[31]

These are the tropes associated with biopolitics. We contend that Third Worldism failed to uproot the biopolitics instituted by colonialism and, in the following section, we attempt to demonstrate why, despite the clear differences between colonised and coloniser, Third World colonised elites (to different degrees) operated within a similar set of assumptions as their erstwhile masters about power and the role of statism and nationalism for the masses as loci of development.

Rise of Third Worldism

Third Worldism, situated between the empires of capitalism and communism, embodied the contradictions of the age: the universal institutionalisation of national sovereignty as the representation of independence of decolonised peoples, political confrontation with European racism, and a movement of quasi-nationalist elites whose legitimacy depended on negotiating their economic and political dependence.

Decolonisation was rooted in a liberatory upsurge, expressed in mass political movements of resistance—some dedicated to driving out the colonists, and others to forming an alternative colonial government to assume power as decolonisation occurred. In this context development was used by retreating colonisers as a pragmatic effort to preserve the colonies by improving their material conditions—and there was no doubt that colonial subjects understood this and turned the ideology of development back on the colonisers, viewing development as an entitlement.[32]

From 1945 to 1981, 105 new states joined the United Nations as the colonial empires crumbled, ushering in the development era via the extension of political sovereignty to millions of non-Europeans. But political sovereignty was the formal attribute of a new world order substantively rooted in the political economy of imperialism. Fanon understood well the historical shortcomings of African postcolonial elites in these terms, characterising them as a lumpen-bourgeoisie.[33]

Just as colonised subjects appropriated the democratic discourse of the colonisers in fuelling their independence movements, leaders of the new nation-states appropriated the legitimating ideals of the development era. Part of the development promise was the proclamation of equality as a domestic and international goal, informed by the Universal Declaration of Human Rights (1948). The UN Declaration included *individual* citizens' rights in the social contract: every body 'is entitled to realization, through national effort, and international co-operation and in accordance with the organization and resources of each State, of the economic, social and cultural rights indispensable for his dignity and the free development of his personality'.[34] We note that this declaration names states as the exclusive guardians of rights, specifically via the social contract, sanctioning a form of biopolitics and sovereignty originating under colonialism.[35]

Development legitimised rulers' disciplining of their subject-citizens. In

Africa forms of discipline included 'tribalisation'—a legacy of European colonialism, combining forms of urban power directly excluding natives from civil freedoms on racial grounds with forms of indirect rule of natives in the countryside via a reconstruction of tribal authority. Independence abolished racial discrimination and affirmed civil freedoms, nevertheless dividing power within new nations according to the inherited artificial tribal constructs along ethnic, religious and regional lines.[36]

Fanon's sociology of the postcolonial African state identifies the roots of neocolonial biopolitics:

> Powerless economically, unable to bring about the existence of coherent social relations ... the bourgeoisie chooses the solution that seems to it the easiest, that of the single party ... It does not create a state that reassures the ordinary citizen, but rather one that rouses his anxiety ... It makes a display, it jostles people and bullies them, thus intimating to the citizen that he is in continual danger. The single party is the modern form of the dictatorship of the bourgeoisie ... In the same way that the national bourgeoisie conjures away its phase of construction in order to throw itself into the enjoyment of its wealth, in parallel fashion in the institutional sphere it jumps the parliamentary phase and chooses a dictatorship of the national–socialist type. We know that this fascism at high interest, which has triumphed for half a century in Latin America, is the dialectic result of states, which were semi-colonial during the period of independence.[37]

As a bloc the Third World was incorporated into a hegemonic project of ordering international power relations, where states adopted a universal standard of national accounting (GNP), and foreign aid disbursements subsidised state apparatuses and elite rule. In postcolonial India, 'Instead of the state being used as an instrument of development, development became an instrument of the state's legitimacy'.[38] Internally the reification of the state as the source of order and progress perpetuated a capitalist biopolitics of subjugation introduced via the colonial project. Externally Third Worldism depended on state mediation of a politics of opposition to capitalist dependencies and an unequal world order.

The harmonisation of internal and external demands was not, however, always favourably achieved—US imperial imperatives often trumped the fragile domestic hegemony won by Third World elites. We illustrate this through an account of the changing fortunes of Third World sovereignty. On balance the conscription of Third Worldism to neoliberalism, across four decades, was achieved with a great deal of continuity. Its culmination in the 'lost decade' of the 1980s, during which capital's capture of the state was secured by the debt regime and the elaboration of financial technologies of control, demonstrates this point. These technologies dovetailed with, and intensified, a domestic biopolitics now reconstituted as 'privatisation'—the explicit shifting of the intensified control of bodies and the economic organisations that serve them to the sphere of capital, beyond the illusion of 'public', governmental control.

First World counter-attack

Third Worldism demands to be interpreted within a world-historical context. The 1955 Bandung conference did not, after all, happen in a vacuum, but within a fraught and tense international context, at one of the nadirs of the Cold War. The process of postwar reconstruction and decolonisation had stretched the pre-war lines of colonial control between the two poles of the USA and the USSR. The liquidation of European economies had both provided an exogenous shock to the colonies, but also permitted degrees of economic and political freedom that had previously been unthinkable, for those in a position to exercise it.[39]

Just as the Third World was born as an elite political entity, so it died, expressing the dialectic of economic nationalism in the development project. Proclaimed as the objective of the developmental state, economic nationalism nevertheless was at odds with US hegemonic objectives. Early indicators of this dialectic were the 1953 CIA-sponsored coup against Iranian Prime Minister Mossadegh's nationalisation of British oil holdings, and the 1954 overthrow of Guatemalan President Arbenz, whose land reforms threatened United Fruit interests.[40]

A decade later a geopolitically strategic coup in Indonesia opened a door for corporate transnationalism, presaging a two-decade reversal of economic nationalism. By the time of Indian Prime Minister Jawaharlal Nehru's death in 1964, the non-alignment strategy of Third Worldism was weakening. A key figure in the NAM, Indonesian President Sukarno (as outlined in the introduction to this special issue), nurtured a state- and military-sponsored form of national development, supported by a complex coalition of nationalist, Muslim and communist parties, forming what he called a 'Guided Democracy'. Sukarno's regime had mobilised more than 15 million citizens to join parties and mass organisations encouraged to challenge Western influence in the region.[41]

In 1965 President Sukarno was overthrown in a bloody CIA-supported coup, which included a pogrom claiming between 500 000 and a million lives—mostly of members of Indonesia's huge and popular communist party (PKI)—'one of the most barbaric acts of inhumanity', 'the "final solution" to the Communist problem in Indonesia'. Recently declassified documents reveal that a British Foreign Office file called in 1964 for defence of Western interests in Southeast Asia which was 'a major producer of essential commodities. The region produces nearly 85 percent of the world's natural rubber, over 45 percent of the tin, 65 percent of the copra and 23 percent of the chromium ore.'[42]

Following the regime change, Time Inc sponsored a 1967 meeting in Geneva between General Suharto, his economic advisors, and corporate leaders representing 'the major oil companies and banks, General Motors, Imperial Chemical Industries, British Leyland, British–American Tobacco, American Express, Siemens, Goodyear, the International Paper Corporation, and US Steel.' With Ford Foundation help, General Suharto reformulated a development partnership with foreign investment. Billed 'To Aid in the Rebuilding of a Nation', the conference nevertheless invited corporations to identify the terms of their involvement in the Indonesian economy. James Linen, president of Time Inc, expressed the birth of this new global order, observing: 'We are here to create a new climate in which private enterprise and developing countries work together ... for the greater profit of the free world. This world of international enterprise is more than governments ... It is the seamless web of enterprise, which has been shaping the global environment at revolutionary speed.'[43]

The coup marked a turning point in the trajectory of Third World nationalism, introducing new forms of state developmentalism, partnering with global corporations in market expansion (anticipating liberalisation 1980s-style). The war waged in Vietnam by a US-led coalition over the next one-and-a-half decades confirmed this policy, and it was followed up with strategic interventions in Chile (1973) and, in the 1980s, in El Salvador, Nicaragua, Grenada and Iraq, as well as with disbursements of military and economic aid to secure the perimeter of the 'free world' and its resource empire. Military power was critical to the securing and prising open of the Third World as part of an emerging project of global development orchestrated by the USA as the dominant power. Through the biopolitical expedient of 'officer training schemes' and strategic support, the USA incited 'military modernisation' and dictatorship as the rule rather than the exception, sanctioning predatory Third World states as the alternative to 'conservative civilian elites with strong nationalist bents'.[44]

The Vietnam War (early 1960s to 1975) came to symbolise global inequality. Just as terrorism of the 21st century is often identified as a product of poverty, so communism and/or national liberation struggles were identified with underdevelopment. (It is instructive to note that, in both cases, structural issues about capitalism itself were never understood as causal factors.) Between 1974 and 1980 national liberation forces came to power in 14 different Third World states, perhaps inspired by the Vietnamese resistance. The possibility of a united South presented itself in two forms in this decade: first, through the formation of the Organization of Petroleum Exporting Countries (OPEC), representing the possibility of Third World control over strategic commodities like oil. Second, with the 1974 proposal to the UN General Assembly by the G-77 for a New International Economic Order (NIEO).[45] The NIEO proposal demanded reform of the world economic system to improve the position of Third World states in international trade and their access to technological and financial resources. It operationalised the dependency perspective, namely, that First–Third World structural relations compromised the Third World's path of development.

Perceived as 'the revolt of the Third World', the NIEO was indeed the culmination of collectivist politics growing out of the Non-Aligned Movement. But it was arguably a movement for reform at best and, at worst, an intensification of the development project insofar as it called for Northern concessions, geared to increasing external revenues available to Third World elites, strengthening the sovereignty of the rentier state. Its initiates were the presidents of Algeria, Iran, Mexico and Venezuela—all oil-producing nations distinguished by their recently acquired huge oil rents.[46] Although much of the wealth was oil money, recycled through bank lending to the Third World, it nevertheless met the demands of Third World elites for development financing, including conspicuous construction and consumption (in addition to financing costly fuel imports and military hardware, accounting for about one-fifth of Third World borrowing). Much of this money concentrated in the middle-income states, undercutting Third World political unity, and subsidising military subjugation of citizens. In the short term Third World unity fragmented as the prospering OPEC states and the newly industrialising countries (NICs) pursued upward mobility in the international order. In the long term the redistributive goals of the NIEO (which were never implemented) were overtaken by the new doctrine of monetarism that ushered in the 1980s debt crisis through drastic restrictions on credit and, therefore, on social spending by governments.[47]

Managing the debt crisis: co-ordinating the technologies of financial discipline

The management of the debt crisis introduced what is euphemistically called 'global governance', which subjects individual debtor state policies to co-ordinated, rule-based procedures strengthening the grip of the international financial institutions (IMF and World Bank). Structural adjustment policies evolved, requiring a comprehensive restructuring of economic priorities and government programmes in order to qualify for new lines of credit. Opening economies, imposing austerity and mandating privatisation became a common formula applied (with some variation, and considerable resistance) across the indebted Third World. The debt managers drew on the Chilean model of the 1970s, where a military junta experimented with monetarist policies (backed up by military force), slashing social expenditures in order to reduce debt. Alluding to the particular biopolitical consequences of the debt regime, in 1989 the Executive Director of UNICEF, James P Grant, observed:

> Today, the heaviest burden of a decade of frenzied borrowing is falling not on the military or on those with foreign bank accounts or on those who conceived the years of waste, but on the poor who are having to do without necessities, on the unemployed who are seeing the erosion of all that they have worked for, on the women who do not have enough food to maintain their health, on the infants whose minds and bodies are not growing properly because of untreated illnesses and malnutrition, and on the children who are being denied their only opportunity to go to school ... it is hardly too brutal an oversimplification to say that the rich got the loans and the poor got the debts.[48]

The debt regime divided and ruled the Third World through an impoverishing reversal of development policy, while it also built a new discipline into states. States were brought under direct financial surveillance by the international financial institutions, and given little room to manoeuvre in formulating policies basically geared to ensuring debt collection. Within states, reduction of currency values, wages and development subsidies undermined living standards, and privatisation compromised state capacity to honour the developmentalist social contract. Third World Network director Martin Khor characterised structural adjustment as 'a mechanism to shift the burden of economic mismanagement and financial mismanagement from the North to the South, and from the Southern elites to the Southern communities and people. Structural adjustment is also a policy to continue colonial trade and economic patterns developed during the colonial period, but which the Northern powers want to continue in the post-colonial period.'[49] Arguably economic and financial mismanagement is the phenomenal form of periodic, *market-induced* financial crises visited upon the global South (most recently East Asia and Argentina), externalising the problem of overproduction of fictitious capital via financial markets that victimise states low in the global currency hierarchy.[50]

What is today termed 'globalisation' is in fact a form of hegemonic crisis management. It stems from the collapse of the Bretton Woods regime of capital controls and fixed currency exchanges and includes the subsequent rupture of the social contract. An unregulated global money market (facilitating arbitrage and raising the opportunity cost of fixed capital) accompanied by currency floats, encouraged 'financialisation': an investor preference for liquid rather than fixed capital. Bank deregulation and a proliferation of financial instruments, creating new money out of expected future income, encouraged securitisation and tradeable debt. With the financial liberalisation required by evolving conditions of debt management, destabilising money flows associated with currency specu-lation characterise the global financial landscape. Currency stability under these conditions depends on speculators' ongoing evaluation of national economic policies, effectively subordinating all states' policies to market rationality (in-cluding liberalisation) to stabilise national currencies.[51] As crisis management, then, 'globalisation' involves a structural (financial) imperative to conform to market relations, and to the political project of market rule (via the IMF, WTO), which, through financial liberalisation, allows the USA to extract financial capital from the rest of the world, *and* transmits/exports financial crises to states with weaker currencies.[52]

The politics of debt

At the turn of the 21st century, the politics of debt has assumed a new form. As IMF conditionality has evolved, stripping away social protections, so have the forms of resistance. During the 1980s 'IMF riots' swept across the Third World, focusing on the withdrawal of public subsidies, and blaming IMF-enforced conditionalities. Urban populations in Latin America, Eastern Europe and Africa targeted policies that eroded social supports, with food subsidies as the charac-teristic flashpoint. The politics of a diminishing social contract governed this action. As the 1990s proceeded privatisation came to define the IMF's 'second-generation structural adjustment' (linking credit to 'good governance'), as loan repayment conditions deepened their hold on debtor states. In Indonesia, where living standards plummeted with the loss of three-quarters of the value of the rupiah, resulting from the Asian financial crisis of 1997 (and exacerbated by the IMF response), 80% of privatisation contracts went to President Suharto's cronies. The political response here was a mass movement for democracy, replacing Suharto's military regime with a parliamentary regime, but not essentially disturbing the course of privatisation.[53]

Several thresholds have come to define periods of world ordering. The Indonesian coup in 1965 underlined, geopolitically, the principle of the freedom of corporate enterprise within the US cold war empire. This was followed by the 1973 coup in Chile that implemented, with force, drastic social reversals via economic liberalisation before it became a global strategy. Covert intervention in Nicaragua throughout the 1980s suppressed resistance to imperial policies in Central and South America. Implementation of NAFTA was accompanied, in 1994, by militarisation of Chiapas to neutralise opposition to implementation of new rules of a global property regime (anticipating the WTO regime). And rolling market-induced financial crises, from Mexico to Asia, to Russia and on to Brazil and Argentina, exerted financial discipline over various forms of 'fast-track capitalism' at the expense of the working poor and their activist representatives.[54]

Sovereignty crises, with growing public incapacity in the global South, lead inevitably to the forceful centralisation of power, and the tightening of bio-political controls, pushing the development project to its limit. Arundhati Roy observes this process at work in India, and calls it by name:

> Fascism is about the slow, steady infiltration of all the instruments of state power. It's about the slow erosion of civil liberties, about unspectacular, day-to-day injustices ... Fascism has come to India after the dreams that fueled the freedom struggle have been frittered away like so much loose change ... Over the past fifty years ordinary citizens' modest hopes for lives of dignity, security and relief from abject poverty have been systematically snuffed out. Every 'democratic' institution in this country has shown itself to be unaccountable, inaccessible to the ordinary citizen and either unwilling or incapable of acting in the interests of genuine social justice. And now corporate globalization is being relentlessly and arbitrarily imposed on India, ripping it apart culturally and economically ... There is very real grievance here. The fascists didn't create it. But they have seized upon it, upturned it and forged from it a hideous, bogus sense of pride. They have mobilized human beings using the lowest common denominator—religion. People who have lost control over their lives, people who have been uprooted from their homes and communities, who lave lost their culture and their language, are being made to feel proud of something.[55]

We could never have put it so well. But what we lack in concise eloquence, we can make up for in plodding explanation. This fascist political resolution lies low, prowling, as a real practice in the very idea of development, in the very idea of capitalism, particularly that kind of capitalism nurtured by the state, indeed premised on the state's sovereignty. Yet it is neither inevitable, nor invincible. We turn now to examine trends in the resistance to this kind of developmental state, and to this kind of sovereignty.

Resistance today: global justice movements

A defining feature of contemporary global justice movements is the reformulation of 'sovereignty'. Movements attempt to appropriate sovereignty where it has been debased in the state—expressing the dialectic of modernity, which at once celebrated the progressive Enlightenment principle of self-organisation but contained it through the device of state sovereignty.[56] Historically political sovereignty was constructed as a relationship of power, channelling citizen and subject sovereignties through the state. The bankrupting of political sovereignty, through development and its intensified complicity with capital via neoliberal mechanisms, amplifies movements for alternative sovereignties.

Countering the centralising thrust of development and/or authoritarian politics, global justice movements promote decentralised conceptions of politics governed by locality (place) and/or situated identity (where relations of class, gender, race, ethnicity, environmental stewardship are specified world-historically—in networks, diasporas and movements). Contrary to the universalist conception of sovereignty governing the modern states system, these alternative forms of sovereignty express the particulars of locality/class/identity-based relations. They transcend corporate globalisation, which reveals, through its capture of the state, the world market to be a political construction—an 'empire of civil society'.[57]

The unclothing of the 'empire of civil society' marks the transition from the citizen-state to the market-state, as national sovereignty yields to the sovereignty of monetary relations, beginning with the debt regime. The devastating devaluation of southern economies and societies, imposed by the multilateral agencies on behalf of finance capital, exposed not only the growing 'autonomy' of global economic relations, but also the structural and institutionalised *necessity* of state sponsorship of these relations, thereby exposing the complicity of the state with capital.[58]

The legitimacy problem is underlined by, among other trends, a growing rebellion against neoliberalism across Latin America (significant regime shifts in Brazil, Venezuela, Ecuador, for example), as well as the emergence, in 2001, of the World Social Forum (WSF), as a counter-summit, in Porto Alegre, stronghold of the Brazilian Workers' Party. While the WSF slogan is 'another world is possible', it celebrates difference, viewing itself as a process, not an organisation. Its Charter of Principles declares that it is a body 'representing world civil society', and that it is not a 'locus of power' as such, rather it is a plural, diversified *context* that 'in a decentralized fashion, interrelates organizations and movements engaged in concrete action at levels from the local to the international to build another world ... [and] encourages its participant organizations and movements to situate their actions as issues of planetary citizenship.'[59]

The global justice movement is so called because of its characteristic cosmopolitan activism, located in its constituents' 'focus on virtually identical opponents: the agencies and representatives of neoliberal capitalism—global, regional, national and local'. The *Zapatista* resistance to the Mexican state's complicity in NAFTA articulated such world-historical conditions of a regional struggle, notably in the 1994 communiqué: 'When we rose up against a national government, we found that it did not exist. In reality we were up against great financial capital, against speculation and investment, which makes all decisions in Mexico, as well as in Europe, Asia, Africa, Oceania, the Americas—everywhere.' *Zapatista* politics are not about civic inclusion of a marginalised people *per se*, but about redefining citizenship, expressed in the call for 'A political dynamic not interested in taking political power but in building a democracy where those who govern, govern by obeying'.[60]

Contemporary resistances to the international food order exemplify the new politics of justice—countering globalist conceptions of food security, which are premised on managed dumping of Northern agricultural surpluses that undermine peasant farming, and where free markets exclude and/or starve populations dispossessed by their implementation.[61] Vía Campesina organises around an alternative conception of food sovereignty. This means not just protecting local farming, but revitalising democratic–collective, cultural and ecological processes at the sub-national level. The several-million strong Vía Campesina, formed in

1992, unites local and regional chapters of landless peasants, family farmers, agricultural workers, rural women and indigenous communities across Africa, Europe, Asia and North, Central and South America. It claims that: 'biodiversity has as a fundamental base the recognition of human diversity, the acceptance that we are different and that every people and each individual has the freedom to think and to be. Seen in this way, biodiversity is not only flora, fauna, earth, water and ecosystems; it is also cultures, systems of production, human and economic relations, forms of government; in essence it is freedom.'

Food sovereignty, in this vision, is 'the right of peoples, communities and countries to define their own agricultural, labour, fishing, food and land policies which are ecologically, socially, economically and culturally appropriate to their unique circumstances'.[62] Central to this conception of rights is the understanding of a right as something whose content is not necessarily preordained by the state. In fact, Vía Campesina's conception of a right here is one that is explicitly without content—the right is a right to self-determination, for communities to redefine for themselves the substance of the food relations appropriate to their geographies. This is a contradictory understanding of rights—where the state remains a guarantor of the rights, but where it plays no role in the authorship of these rights. In fact, the Vía Campesina call for policy formulation runs explicitly counter to the state: since the state has been captured by capital, the rights of small farmers, and the ability of small farmers to influence state policy (despite their numerical superiority *vis-à-vis* large farmers) has been abrogated. This violation of rights has resulted simultaneously both in a disillusionment with the state's ability to represent its constituents to international capital, and in a recognition of the power of the state to impose dicta from international capital. Also important is the 'queering' of the attribution of rights. Rights here are not ascribed exclusively to humans, but to 'peoples, communities, and countries'. This challenges deeply the notion that rights are only justiciable for individual bodies and, therefore, challenges the forms of biopolitics based on this individuating assumption.

Perhaps the most significant chapter of Vía Campesina is the Brazilian landless workers' movement, the Movimento dos Trabalhadores Rurais Sem Terra (MST). In the past 17 years, the MST has settled over 400 000 families on 15 million acres of land seized from unproductive use. The stimulus has been a Brazilian development model of structural adjustment, in a context where 1% of landowners own (but do not necessarily cultivate) 50% of the land, leaving 4.8 million families landless. Between 1985 and 1996 rural unemployment rose by five-and-a-half million, and between 1995 and 1999 a rural exodus of four million Brazilians occurred.[63]

The landless workers' movement draws legitimacy for its land occupations from the Brazilian constitution's sanctioning of the confiscation of uncultivated private property: 'It is incumbent upon the Republic to expropriate for social interest, for purposes of agrarian reform, rural property, which is not performing its social function'.[64] Land seizures, under the slogan of 'Occupy! Resist! Produce!' lead to the formation of co-operatives, which involve social mobilisation 'transforming the economic struggle into a political and ideological struggle'.[65] Democratic decision making is practised to develop co-operative relations among workers, and alternative patterns of land use, financed by socialising a portion of settlement income, used for participatory budgeting to cover social and technical needs. The MST has pioneered the production of staple foodstuffs for the Brazilian population at large (with a formal outlet through the national Zero Hunger programme), filling a significant gap left by agro-export priorities. Most recently, the MST has ranged itself against corporate sovereignty. In a declaration (19 May 2003) the MST declared that fields planted with transgenic crops by large farmers would be burned.

On a global scale perhaps the distinguishing mark of this emergent global justice movement is its commitment to building solidarity out of a respect for diversity. The WSF is a springboard for constructing enduring networks of relationships among diverse civic and cultural initiatives, to forge an alternative organisational and discursive space to that occupied by corporate globalisation. Previous anti-systemic social movements worked to reform or institutionalise countervailing power within institutions or societies. While this has been an indispensable part of giving substance to modernity, it has privileged the universalist themes of modernity—which of course crystallised in the statist project of development, and which are now the target of a new sensibility that challenges this singular, reductionist vision of development. This is not to say that the global justice movement should not work to reform or transform existing institutions, but it has the historic opportunity to do this by drawing on, and supporting, alternative models that are not paralysed by the logic of economic reductionism and proto-fascist rationality.[66]

Conclusion: Third Worldism and the lineages of global fascism

At the World Trade Organization talks in Cancun in 2003, a new political grouping in the Global South, the G20 + , was made. As with its predecessors, the G20 is a group dependent on the support of large Third World governments (Brazil, India, China). It emerged in a political space created by tense EU–US relations over trade in agriculture. It is, as with its predecessors, a tentative expression of the dialectics of power in the state system. The targeting and erosion of the G20 by the USA in the weeks since its birth confirm the arguments in this paper. The state sovereignty upon which Third Worldism was founded was always fragile and fractured by international capital. We have offered an explanation of why this has been so, and why contemporary social movements find alternative forms of sovereignty so attractive. The biopolitical proto-fascism of development has always been immanent. Extreme hegemonic crises bring these tendencies in capitalism to the surface. We suggest that they were just as 'fascist' in their 19th and 20th century instantiations in the Third World as they were in their more recognisable early-to-mid 20th century European forms. Moreover, we see similar trends arising today in the configuration of state forces, not only in the USA but also in the global South. Fascism deserves to be unmoored from its historical European home; its technologies of control, its ideology, its body count, and even its concentration camps precede its orthodox recognition in European fascism. And, as Guantanamo Bay suggests to us today, the fascist threat is alive and well, for all people, citizens of the USA no less than those in the global South, especially insofar as empire is accomplished through the mobilisation of ever-decreasing rights for domestic citizens.

Global justice movements have responded to the crises of development and an array of neoliberal projects by detaching ideas of sovereignty from the state and from its attempted (nationalist) monopoly on biopolitics. Through an explicit encouragement of alternative forms of anti-colonial sovereignty, these movements, we have argued, inherit the promise of Third Worldism, a genuine alternative, now, to a form of imperialism spearheaded by the USA and mimicked with alarming precision by nation-states across the globe. Fanon called for the Third World to 'not want to catch up with anyone. What we want to do is to go forward all the time, night and day in the company of Man, in the company of all Men ... It is a question of the Third World starting a new history of Man.'[67] Today, to paraphrase Richard Wright, where citizens are despised, insulted, hurt, and dispossessed by Third World states, social movements are fostering resistance to capital as a nexus of social relations on a global scale, not through specious ideas about the nation, but through far more complex, and uncertain, ideas of local sovereignty. These initiatives practice 'politics without guarantees'.[68] In world-historical terms, there is no paradox in such initiatives, in that they are a genuine and hopeful alternative to the contemporary totalitarianism surrounding us again.

Notes

[1]   Richard Wright, *The Color Curtain: a Report on the Banding Conference*, New York: World Publishing Company, 1956, p 12.
[2]   PA Gourevitch, *Politics in Hard Times: Comparative Responses to International Economic Crises*, Ithaca, NY: Cornell University Press, 1986, p 25.
[3]   We should say at the outset that our critique is directed at a particular vision of state nationalism and national statism that, while clear and vehement in its rejection of US- and Soviet-sponsored visions of development, was grounded in a variety of programmes of national development co-ordinated and managed by elites. Clearly, we do not seek to indict anti-colonial struggle—rather, we suggest that it continues to be necessary.
[4]   We note that, while Third Worldism came to be elite managed, its origins were in historic, spontaneous mass movements. The historiography of this phenomenon demands abstraction and an observation of continuities across time. These continuities are not, however, intended to provide any sort of claim about the ultimate permanence or inevitability of any phenomenon, but rather an orthogonal and reorientating framework through which to recast our current understanding of, in this case, Third Worldism. We note, in passing, that the state, though a central feature of our analysis, is not the only locus of power in international political economy. The power of corporations, the media (both domestic and international/imperial), local 'traditional structures of power', the family, prisons, schools and the military is also important.
[5]   See, for example, S George, *A Fate Worse than Debt*, New York: Grove Press, 1988; G Arrighi, 'The developmentalist illusion: a reconceptualization of the semiperiphery', in WG Martin (ed), *Semiperipheral States in the World Economy*, Westport, CT: Greenwood, 1990, pp 11–42; and A Escobar, *Encountering Development: The Making and Unmaking of the Third World*, Princeton, NJ: Princeton University Press, 1995.
[6]   See WL Adamson, 'Gramsci's interpretation of fascism', *Journal of the History of Ideas*, 41 (4), 1980, pp 615–633; RO Paxton, 'The five stages of fascism', *Journal of Modern History*, 70 (1), 1998, pp 1–23; and D Renton, *Fascism: Theory and Practice*, London: Pluto Press, 1999.
[7]   Gourevitch, *Politics in Hard Times*, p 25.

[8] K McRobbie & K Polanyi-Levitt (eds), *Karl Polanyi in Vienna: The Contemporary Significance of The Great Transformation*, Montreal: Black Rose, 2000.

[9] P Gilroy, *Against Race: Imagining Political Culture Beyond the Color Line*, Cambridge, MA: Harvard University Press, 2000.

[10] 'Liberal definitions of fascism adopt the approach of ticking off items from an already printed menu and seeing if they match. But many social-democratic and most Marxist definitions grew out of the actual experience ... deriving from the overall dynamics of capitalist societies. Fascism was a weapon of last resort, used by a ruling class faced simultaneously with an economic crisis and the threat of a revolutionary labour movement.' T Ali, *The Clash of Fundamentalisms. Crusades, Jihads and Modernity*, London: Verso, 2002; and Gilroy, *Against Race,* p 86.

[11] Mike Davis, *Late Victorian Holocausts: El Niño Famines and The Making of the Third World*, London: Verso, 2001.

[12] Davis was not the first to unmoor ideas normally associated with the Shoah. See, for example, DE Stannard, *American Holocaust: The Conquest of the New World*, New York: Oxford University Press, 1992.

[13] Robert Kaplan, writing on technologies of control in the American Empire, demonstrates these relations well through the following approving quotation: 'RULE NO 9 FIGHT ON EVERY FRONT'. R Kaplan, 'Supremacy by stealth', *Atlantic Monthly*, July–August 2003, p 65. In their recent article 'An emerging synthesis for a new way of war', published in the *Georgetown Journal of International Affairs*, Air Force Colonels James Callard and Peter Faber describe what they call 'combination warfare'—a concept derived from a 1999 Chinese text by two colonels in the People's Liberation Army, Qiao Liang and Wang Xiangsui. In the 21st century a single conflict may include not only traditional military activity but also financial warfare, trade warfare, resource warfare, legal warfare, and so on. The authors explain that it may eventually involve even ecological warfare (the manipulation of the heretofore 'natural' world, altering the climate). Because combination warfare draws on all spheres of human activity, it is the ultimate in total war. It 'seeks to overwhelm others by assaulting them in as many domains ... as possible', Callard and Faber write. 'It creates sustained, and possibly shifting, pressure that is hard to anticipate ... Combination warfare has already begun, though it has yet to be codified in military doctrine. The most important front, in a way, may be the media. Like the priests of ancient Egypt, the rhetoricians of ancient Greece and Rome, and the theologians of medieval Europe, the media constitute a burgeoning class of bright and ambitious people whose social and economic stature can have the effect of undermining political authority.'

[14] MP Cowen & RW Shenton, *Doctrines of Development*, London: Routledge, 1996.

[15] This is a linguistic and biopolitical tactic that is alive and well, for example in the Indian government's Ministry of Scheduled Castes and Backward Classes.

[16] T Mitchell, *Colonising Egypt*, New York: Cambridge University Press, 1988, pp 68–75, 96.

[17] See, for example, CLR James, *The Black Jacobins. Toussaint L'Ouverture and the San Domingo Revolution*, New York: Vintage Books, 1963.

[18] P Chatterjee, *The Nation and its Fragments: Colonial and Postcolonial Histories*, Princeton, NJ: Princeton University Press, 1993. We are grateful to Dia Mohan for pointing out the ambiguous role of Third World elites.

[19] RL Heilbroner, *Behind the Veil of Economics: Essays in the Worldly Philosophy*, New York: Norton, 1988; and MP Cowan & RW Shenton, *The Invention of Development. The Power of Development*, London: Routledge, 1995, ch 1.

[20] Indeed, a great deal of Comte's energy was directed towards reducing the influence of Catholicism in French society, in order that French society eventually arrive at the end of history. Gronemeyer reminds us that 'every epoch pervaded with a belief in progress has needed ... the tendency [to] conceive [of the present] as the penultimate stage in history, to fancy itself as a kind of positive final time in which only the last breakthrough remains before the harvest of history can be gathered into humanity's granary.' M Gronemeyer, 'Helping', in W Sachs (ed), *The Development Dictionary: A Guide to Knowledge and Power*, London: Zed Books, 1990, pp 53–69. This is no less true of post-revolutionary France as of millennial Europe and North America, as Francis Fukuyama's current popularity attests.

[21] Cowan & Shenton, *Doctrines of Development*, p 40.

[22] F List, *National System of Political Economy*, Philadelphia, PA: JB Lippincott & Co, 1856; A Gershenkron, *Economic Backwardness in Historical Perspective*, New York: Frederick Praeger, 1965; R Hilferding, *Finance Capital: A Study of the Latest Phase of Capitalist Development*, London: Routledge & Kegan Paul, 1985; and CL Dokmo & L Reed, 'Development and poverty in a global age—building blocks— microfinance and entrepreneurship in the developing world', *Harvard International Review*, 21 (1), 1998, pp 66–68.

[23] N Karagiannis, 'Giving development. responsibility and efficiency in the European development discourse towards the ACP countries (1970s–1990s)', unpublished PhD thesis, Political Science, European University, Florence, 2002.

[24] P Gilroy, *Against Race*, p 196.

[25] M Foucault, *The History of Sexuality*, New York: Vintage Books, 1980, p 142.

[26] EP Thompson, 'Time, work-discipline, and industrial capitalism', in Thompson, *Customs in Common*, London: Merlin, 1991, pp 352–403; AL Stoler, *Race and the Education of Desire: Foucault's History of Sexuality and the Colonial Order of Things*, Durham, SC: Duke University Press, 1995; and P McFadden, 'Women workers in South Africa', *Journal of African Marxists*, 4, 1983, pp 54–62.

[27] M Mamdani, *Citizen and Subject: Contemporary Africa and the Legacy of Late Colonialism*, Princeton, NJ: Princeton University Press, 1996.

[28] G Agamben, *Homo Sacer: Sovereign Power and Bare Life*, Stanford, CA: Stanford University Press, 1998.

[29] F Block, 'Introduction', in K Polanyi, *The Great Transformation*, Boston, MA: Beacon Press, 2001, p 5.

[30] *Ibid*; AM Smith, *New Right Discourse on Race and Sexuality: Britain, 1968–1990*, Cambridge: Cambridge University Press, 1994; JC Torpey, *The Invention of the Passport: Surveillance, Citizenship, and the State*, Cambridge: Cambridge University Press, 2000; S Abramsky, *Hard Time Blues*, New York: Thomas Dunne Books, 2002; F Fanon & CL Markmann, *Black Skin, White Masks*, New York: Grove Press, 1968; J Mander & E Goldsmith, *The Case Against the Global Economy: And For a Turn Toward the Local*, San Francisco: Sierra Club Books, 1996; and SP Huntington, *The Clash of Civilizations and the Remaking of World Order*, New York: Simon & Schuster, 1996.

[31] 'Slavery in the 21st century', *New Internationalist*, July–August, 2001, p 18.

[32] See F Cooper & AL Stoler, *Tensions of Empire: Colonial Cultures in a Bourgeois World*, Berkeley, CA: University of California Press, 1997.

[33] LS Stavrianos, *Global Rift. The Third World Comes of Age*, New York: William Morrow, 1981, p 624; and F Fanon, *The Wretched of the Earth*, London: Penguin, 1967, p 120.

[34] Quoted in T Clarke & M Barlow, MAI. *The Multilateral Agreement on Investment and the Threat to Canadian Sovereignty*, Toronto: Stoddart, 1977, p 9.

[35] M Hardt & A Negri, *Empire*, Cambridge, MA: Harvard University Press, 2000; and R Patel, 'Rights to food: a critical perspective', *Feminist Economics*, forthcoming 2004.

[36] M Mamdani, 'Making sense of political violence in post-colonial Africa', in L Panitch & C Leys (eds), *Socialist Register. Fighting Identities: Race, Religion and Ethno-Nationalism*, London: Merlin Press, 2003, pp 132–151.

[37] Fanon, *The Wretched of the Earth*, pp 132, 133, 138, 146.

[38] S Bose, 'Instruments and idioms of colonial and national development: India's historical experience in comparative perspective', in F Cooper & R Packard (eds), *International Development and the Social Sciences*, Berkeley, CA: University of California Press, 1997, p 153.

[39] For the effects of this in Africa, see G Arrighi, 'The African crisis: world-systemic and regional aspects', *New Left Review*, 15, 2002, pp 5–36.

[40] G Kolko, *Confronting the Third World. United States Foreign Policy 1945–80*, New York: Pantheon, 1988, pp 102–103.

[41] J Pilger, *The New Rulers of the World*, London: Verso, 2002, p 29.

[42] Kolko, *Confronting the Third World*, p 181; and Pilger, *The New Rulers of the World*, pp 25, 28.

[43] Pilger, *The New Rulers of the World*, p 28.

[44] Kolko, *Confronting the Third World*, pp 134, 148, 184.

[45] George, *A Fate Worse than Debt*, p 6.

[46] G Rist, *History of Development: From Western Origins to Global Faith*, London: Zed Books, 1997, pp 152–153.

[47] A Hoogvelt, *The Third World in Global Development*, London: Macmillan, 1987, pp 87–95.

[48] Quoted in DM Roodman, *Still Waiting for the Jubilee. Pragmatic Solutions for the Third World*, Washington, DC: Worldwatch Paper 155, 2001, p 30.

[49] Quoted in K Danaher & M Yunus (eds), *50 Years is Enough. The Case Against the World Bank and the International Monetary Fund*, Boston, MA: South End Press, 1994, p 112.

[50] Cf B Cohen, *The Geography of Money*, Ithaca, NY: Cornell University Press, 1988.

[51] G Arrighi, *The Long Twentieth Century. Money, Power and the Origins of Our Times*, London: Verso, 1994; and A Hoogvelt, *Globalization and the Postcolonial World. The New Political Economy of Development*, London: Macmillan, 1997, p 82.

[52] G Arrighi, 'The social and political economy of global turbulence', *New Left Review*, 20, 2003, pp 5–71; and E Helleiner, *States and the Reemergence of Global Finance. From Bretton Woods to the 1990s*, Ithaca, NY: Cornell University Press, 1996, p 112.

[53] J Walton & D Seddon, *Free Markets & Food Riots: The Politics of Global Adjustment*, Oxford: Blackwell, 1994; and S Erlanger, 'Suharto fostered rapid economic growth, and staggering graft', *New York Times*, 22 May 1998, p A9.

[54] W Bello, *Addicted to Capital: The Ten-year High and Present-day Withdrawal Trauma of Southeast Asia's Economies. Focus on the Global South*, Bangkok: Chulalonkorn University, 1998.

[55] A Roy, 'Fascism's firm footprint in India', *The Nation*, 30 September 2002, p 18.

[56] Hardt & Negri, *Empire*, p 74.

[57] J Rosenberg, *The Empire of Civil Society: A Critique of the Realist Theory of International Relations*, London: Verso, 1994.

[58] P McMichael, 'Globalization', in T Janoski, R Alford, AM Hicks & MA Schwartz (eds), *A Handbook of Political Sociology: States, Civil Societies and Globalization*, New York: Cambridge University Press, 2004.

[59] World Social Forum, 2001. There are, even within movements, critics of Porto Alegre. See, for instance, Peter Waterman's *Second Reflections on the Third World Social Forum*, available at http://www. voiceoftheturtle.org/show_article.php?aid = 342.

[60] P Bond, 'Radical rhetoric and the working class during Zimbabwean nationalism's dying days', *Journal of World-Systems Research*, VII (1), 2001, p 7. Zapatista quotes from A Starr, *Naming the Enemy. Anti-Corporate Movements confront Globalization*, London: Zed Books, 2000, p 14; and N Harvey, *The Chiapas Rebellion. The Struggle for Land and Democracy*, Durham, SC: Duke University Press, 1999, p 210.

[61] R Patel & A Delwiche, 'The profits of famine: southern Africa's long decade of hunger', *Food First*, 8 (4), 2002, pp 1–8; P McMichael, 'Food security and social reproduction: issues and contradictions', in I Bakker & S Gill (eds), *Power, Production and Social Reproduction*, Basingstoke: Palgrave Macmillan, 2003, p 178; R Patel, 'Rights to food: a critical perspective', *Feminist Economics*, forthcoming; and W Bello, 'The crisis of the globalist project & the new economics of George W Bush. Focus on the global South', 10 July 2003, at http://www.tni.org/archives/bello/globalistproject.htm.

[62] www.ns.rds.org.hn/via/. Via Campesina is a movement we find particularly interesting because of the centrality of autonomy and sovereignty in its history. The history of Latin American peasant movements had, until the advent of structural adjustment, been overwhelmingly tied to urban political parties. Corporatist structures of political patronage had been used by urban political elites to pacify and, at election time, mobilise peasant constituencies to vote for their political patrons. Peasantries were, however, at the tail of a political system wagged by urban dogs. Structural adjustment changed this dramatically. With a reduction in the surpluses controlled by the state came a concomitant reduction in the capital available to pacify rural communities. This staunching of patronage led to a radicalisation and separation of peasant constituencies from their erstwhile urban masters. Politically, this was given expression through 'autonomous peasant organisation', where the term 'autonomous' denoted autonomy from urban and state-embroiled political parties (and non-governmental organisations). Via Campesina emerged through a political process in Central America of precisely these autonomous peasant organisations. Personal communication with Peter Rosset, Food First.

[63] www.mstbrazil.org/EconomicModel.html (accessed 23 July 2001).

[64] Article 184, quoted in FM Lappé & A Lappé, *Hope's Edge: The Next Diet for a Small Planet*, New York: Jeremy P Tarcher/Putnam, 2002, p 70.

[65] L Flavio de Almeida & F Ruiz Sanchez, 'The landless workers' movement and social struggles against neoliberalism', *Latin American Perspectives*, 22 (5), 2000, pp 11–32.

[66] See, for example, J Brecher, T Costello *et al*, *Globalization from Below: The Power of Solidarity*, Cambridge, MA, South End Press, 2000; Starr, *Naming the Enemy. Anti-Corporate Movements confront Globalization*; and P Waterman, *Globalization, Social Movements and the New Internationalisms*, London: Continuum, 2001.

[67] Fanon, *The Wretched of the Earth*, pp 254–255.

[68] S Hall, 'The problem of ideology: Marxism without guarantees', in D Morley & K-H Chen (eds), *Stuart Hall: Critical Dialogues in Cultural Studies*, London: Routledge, 1996.

Globalising the Zapatistas: from Third World solidarity to global solidarity?

THOMAS OLESEN

When indigenous peasants in the remote and impoverished Mexican state of Chiapas rebelled 10 years ago, solidarity activists from around the world soon rushed to their aid, first through the use of different media and later in the form of a physical presence. The rebels, popularly known as the Zapatistas, emerged in a context in which the repercussions of the end of the Cold War were still widely felt.[1] Their rebellion called the interpretative framework of an entire generation into question.[2] For more than five decades, the cold war conflict had permeated social relations and political action from East to West and from North to South. The widespread use of arms as a way to achieve social change and political ends was a defining characteristic of this period. This method fell into disrepute with the closing of the cold war era. The dissolution of the cold war imperative opened the door to a situation in which the idea and practice of democracy has become the main source of social and political legitimacy. At first, the armed Zapatista uprising therefore appeared to be an anachronism, a relic from the Cold War and a time when Latin America was the home of numerous armed groups inspired by socialist ideas. Early Zapatista communiqués seemed only to confirm this impression. But the Zapatistas soon started moving in a different direction, inspiring Carlos Fuentes to label the rebels as the first post-communist rebellion in Latin America.[3] The armed element acquired an increasingly symbolic role, while concepts such as democracy and civil society replaced the socialist rhetoric usually associated with armed groups. In transforming themselves into armed democrats, the Zapatistas have become an oxymoron embodying the major differences between the time before and after the ending of the Cold War.[4]

The Zapatistas retain many of the emancipatory ideals of earlier progressive groups, but they formulate their social critique in a manner which is more profoundly democratic and global than that of most groups during the cold war period. As a consequence, their interpretation of contemporary social and political problems does not build on the distinction between first, second and third worlds that has inspired so many analyses in the preceding decades. This is perhaps most evident in the way solidarity is understood by the Zapatistas and the transnational activists who have been engaged in solidarity efforts from the early days of the uprising until the present. The solidarity relationship between the Zapatistas and transnational activists is highly globalised in the sense that it is based on mutuality. In contrast, solidarity relationships in the cold war period, including Third World solidarity, tended to have more of a one-way character in which there was a clear distinction between providers and beneficiaries of solidarity.[5] These changes to a large extent result from social innovations on the part of the Zapatistas, that is, their ability to mediate constantly between the particular and the universal. On the other hand, they cannot be fully analysed without accounting for the conjunctural shifts of the 1990s. The argument presented in this essay attempts to establish such a theoretical and historical link between the specific case of Zapatista solidarity and the more structural level.

The first part of the essay, sections one and two, thus lays out a theoretical framework. Under discussion here is a typology of solidarity forms in a historical perspective, with an emphasis on the contemporary relationship between globalisation and solidarity. The second part of the essay, sections three and four, then demonstrates how the Zapatistas and the solidarity network surrounding them exemplify a new conception of solidarity that involves a reconfiguration of the relationship between the local, the national and the global. The third part of the essay, section five, points to conditions that may limit the further development of this form of solidarity.

The origins and rise of solidarity

Solidarity relationships between individuals and groups separated by physical, social and cultural distances have been present at least since the middle of the 19th century.[6] Today solidarity activities are beginning to take place on a much wider horizon and the incipient international community is becoming increasingly important as an audience for political and solidarity activists.[7] What is at play, in other words, is an intensified globalisation of social and cultural relations. This development does not appear out of nowhere, but is a continuation of ideas associated with modernity. At the centre of modern thinking stands the theory of democracy. In theory, if not always in practice, democracy builds on a high degree of global consciousness and the idea of a shared humanity with inalienable individual rights.[8] A global consciousness, in short, entails the ability and aspiration to see the world as a single place.[9] Despite the obvious lack of global consciousness in the numerous wars and xenophobic outbursts of the past two centuries, this current of thought has nevertheless continued to inform human interaction; perhaps most clearly in the large number of civil society organisations involved in transnational solidarity activities.[10]

But solidarity can mean many things and it makes sense, therefore, to propose a tentative and ideal-typical distinction between different forms of solidarity: political solidarity, rights solidarity and material solidarity. Political solidarity has its roots in the traditions of Marxism and socialism. Left-wing internationalism was prevalent especially in the first decades of the 20th century. In its early form it presented a cosmopolitan alternative to global capitalism, expressed in slogans such as 'workers of the world unite.'[11] Left-wing internationalism built on a degree of global consciousness that assumed that the working classes all over the world faced similar conditions and similar prospects of social change, but it was also characterised by strife and struggles over the definition of socialist strategy. In general, left-wing internationalism and solidarity was not conceived of as the voluntary actions of individuals and civil society organisations, but was structured from above through national parties and states with socialist governments. Despite its elements of global consciousness, this old internationalism consequently had an explicitly national dimension.[12] since the end of the Cold War this form of solidarity has virtually disappeared.[13] Third World solidarity is another form of political solidarity that had its highpoint in the 1970s. Its activists were mainly located in the rich parts of the world, especially Europe and the USA. Third World solidarity in many ways grew out of the student movement of the 1960s and was concerned with the consequences of structural inequalities between the rich and poor parts of the world.[14] Although Third World solidarity activists worked within a framework that divided the world into first, second and third worlds, it still reflected a growing global consciousness in which the world was analysed as one structure. In the 1970s Third World solidarity activism was highly politicised and it typically considered the gross inequalities in poor countries to be fertile soil for the development of revolutionary movements. When solidarity work consisted in aiding these movements it also often reflected the bipolar conflict between East and West.

Rights solidarity is a form of solidarity concerned with human rights abuses and other forms of human oppression that is a result of the actions of states or extra-legal forces. Rights solidarity work generally aims at putting pressure on human rights abusers. This may be done directly by lobbying the governments of the countries in which the violations take place, but often pressure is exerted through other governments or intergovernmental organisations expected to have a certain influence on the state in which the violations occur.[15] Rights solidarity primarily works on issues involving bodily harm to vulnerable individuals or inequalities in legal opportunity. This means that rights solidarity work is most common in relation to cases where the violation of rights is the result of intentional acts on the part of specific individuals or states, and consequently less common in cases where violations have more structural causes.[16] Rights solidarity is therefore often less politicised than political solidarity. The theory of rights solidarity has deep historical roots in ideas and thoughts associated with Christianity and the Enlightenment.[17] These ideational currents both see human beings as endowed with certain universal rights and thus rest on a high degree of global consciousness. The main difference between historical and contemporary transnational rights solidarity lies in the institutional references available to rights solidarity activists in present times, as well as in the increasing interdependence of states. This interdependence, which is often a result of trade and economic agreements, makes it difficult to commit human rights violations without being subjected to criticism from other states and civil society organisations.[18]

Material solidarity is directed mainly towards victims of disasters and to different forms of underdevelopment. These problems may have natural as well as human causes. Natural disasters include a variety of phenomena such as droughts, earthquakes and floods. Manmade disasters mainly include wars and other forms of violent conflict that turn large numbers of people into refugees either inside or outside their own country. Material solidarity reflects a global consciousness in that it constructs a world in which the fate of distant people can no longer be ignored. Obviously, this form of solidarity, as is the case with other forms, is greatly enhanced and aided by the availability of images and information from faraway places. Historically, this form of solidarity goes back at least to the foundation of the International Committee of the Red Cross following the Battle of Solferino in 1859. The period following the end of World War II in particular witnessed the birth of a large number of organisations whose objective was to deliver aid to populations suffering from the consequences of the war. Like rights solidarity, material solidarity is often carried out by organisations that take a neutral position in specific conflicts.[19]

The coming of global solidarity

The forms of solidarity described so far all display elements of inequality. The discussion is ideal-typical and used to set apart the primary characteristics of a more global and mutual form of solidarity that is currently emerging. These forms all denote a one-way relationship between those who offer solidarity and those who benefit from it.[20] As a consequence, they often reflect a situation where the provider of solidarity is supposed to be stronger than the beneficiary. This element is visible in most instances of rights and material solidarity and in solidarity relationships between people and groups in the rich and poor countries.[21] This type of solidarity usually involves the transfer of different forms of resources. It is the result of initiatives by activists in the rich world, but may also be inspired by calls from aggrieved groups and populations in the poor parts of the world. In general, rights and material solidarity are rather non-political and do not fundamentally challenge the underlying causes of the grievances that inspire the solidarity effort.

In contrast to rights and material solidarity, global solidarity involves a more reciprocal relationship between providers and beneficiaries. Or, put differently, global solidarity blurs the distinction between providers and beneficiaries. While all forms of transnational solidarity build on a degree of global consciousness, global solidarity is an expression of a more extensive global consciousness that constructs the grievances of physically, socially and culturally distant people as deeply intertwined. This perception is partly inspired by environmental thinking and the increasing awareness that environmental problems and risks cannot be contained within borders. Such a world risk society is therefore a self-critical society capable of analysing events in a global rather than local or national perspective.[22] The world risk society is a planetary society where it becomes more and more difficult to project social conflicts into the future or an external space.[23]

Political and solidarity activists navigate in this type of society in an increasingly conscious fashion. Global solidarity is often rather politicised, as distant social struggles and problems are analysed with a point of departure in a common framework centred on the concept of neoliberalism. It was argued above that rights solidarity and material solidarity are often characterised by relatively low levels of politicisation. If we accept the claim that global solidarity rests on a more politicised relationship (with the exception of some of the highly politicised forms of material solidarity between the 1960s and the 1980s) between providers and beneficiaries, it may appear that it shares more with the political and Third World solidarity described earlier. This form of solidarity, however, entails an often binary analysis of the world and in a historical perspective it therefore reflects some of the limitations and dichotomies imposed by the Cold War on political action. Those people and groups worthy of solidarity were, accordingly, those committed to the same set of strategies and goals as the provider of solidarity.

Just like rights and material solidarity, political and Third World solidarity has an in-built notion of distance between providers and beneficiaries in the solidarity exchange. The providers are in one place, mainly Europe and the USA, where there is a generally high degree of stability, while the beneficiaries are located in a distant place with severe problems. Global solidarity, in contrast, is a form of solidarity that emphasises similarities between physically, socially and culturally distant people, while at the same time respecting and acknowledging local and national differences. Seen in this light, global solidarity constantly mediates between the particular and the universal and through a democratic matrix. The Zapatistas and the network that has been spun around them are perhaps the most obvious contemporary examples of this form of solidarity.

The politics of overflowing

The transnational solidarity work surrounding the Zapatistas has not come out of the blue. It builds on earlier solidarity work, especially that directed to political groups in Nicaragua, El Salvador and Guatemala in the 1980s. But, as indicated already, transnational Zapatista solidarity has a number of characteristics that diverges significantly from the solidarity work of previous decades: 'The main difference is, at least for most of the younger or newer solidarity activists

246

focusing on Chiapas, that the "solidarity" is less material, and in other ways less explicit. The new solidarity activist is looking here, to the community, to the "belly of the beast," for the site of action.' The Zapatistas thus serve as a source of inspiration and not mainly as an object of solidarity: 'When people come back from a delegation to Chiapas, or an extended stay there, typically they want to figure out ways to apply what they've learned in Chiapas to community organising here. And when they go down to visit Chiapas in the first place, they aren't going as teachers, but as students'.[24]

This way of approaching solidarity work takes it beyond the methods and theories applied in the solidarity forms described earlier and outlines the central ideas in global solidarity. To be in solidarity with the Zapatistas, in other words, does not mean to 'simply write letters to your congressperson. It means to fight everywhere against what the EZLN is fighting against: racism, sexism, homophobia, and a global economic order that guarantees the rights of capital while it takes away the rights, identities, and cultures of people.'[25] The global and extended conception of solidarity evident in these quotes has to a large extent been inspired and promoted by the Zapatistas, who in turn mirror many of the major changes since the end of the Cold War. The Zapatistas acknowledge and accept solidarity in the form of material aid and the presence of human rights observers, but at the same time they have made it explicit that solidarity with the Zapatistas also involves struggling 'at home' against what is considered a neoliberal development model with global reach. One of the objectives of the 'First Intercontinental Encounter for Humanity and Against Neoliberalism' convened by the Zapatistas in Chiapas in 1996 was precisely to extend their political analysis of neoliberalism beyond Mexico and Chiapas.[26] But the resonance generated by the Zapatistas is not only the result of the ability to present a globally relevant analysis of neoliberalism, it is also very much a reflection of the way the Zapatistas define their own contribution to the formulation of this critique. In particular, the Zapatistas refused to play the role of vanguard in the struggle against neoliberalism. Instead, they ceaselessly emphasise the power of diversity and networked forms of interaction and resistance. The anti-vanguardist position entails a radical departure from previous and contemporary armed movements in Latin America, as well as a rather ambiguous relationship with the armed element of the Zapatistas: 'Our army is a very different army because it is proposing to cease being an army ... If the EZLN persists as an army, it is destined for failure ... What would have been a success for a political–military organisation in the 1960s and 1970s ... would be a failure for us.'[27]

Social change through armed struggle is portrayed by the Zapatistas as inevitably leading to an authoritarian situation and benefiting only a minority of the population. This partly explains the constant emphasis on civil society as the main force in creating social change. The abandonment of the armed path to social change was partly a result of the encounter between the Zapatistas and foreign and domestic solidarity activists: 'The EZLN prepared for January 1, but not for January 2 ... The EZLN appears on January 1, starts the war and realises that the world is not what it was thought to be, but something else. Anyway, since then the virtue of the EZLN, if we can call it that, has been the ability to listen.'[28] Before the uprising on 1 January 1994 the Zapatistas had worked with two scenarios. They expected that the uprising would be met with either indifference and apathy or that it would ignite a general uprising in the Mexican population, but neither of these scenarios materialised. The people did not want to join the armed struggle, but neither were they indifferent to the fate and message of the Zapatistas. What emerged instead was a demand that the Zapatistas and the Mexican government enter into negotiations, which they did after 12 days of fighting in January 1994. The decision to respond to these calls from civil society to some extent echoes the experiences surrounding the formation of the Zapatistas in the 1980s. The Zapatistas were formed through an encounter between, on the one hand, a small group of urban intellectuals with a revolutionary vision and, on the other hand, the indigenous communities of Chiapas.[29] This handful of non-indigenous revolutionaries came to Chiapas with a baggage of Marxist–Leninist orthodoxy that was soon challenged by the world-view and traditions of the indigenous communities. Initially, this group looked at the indigenous people as exploited peasants who needed to be shown the way to liberation.[30] But this perception was gradually broken down, and in the end the indigenous communities turned out to be the teachers rather than the students: 'The original EZLN, the one that is formed in 1983, is a political organisation in the sense that it speaks and what it says has to be done. The indigenous communities teach it to listen, and that is what we learn.'[31]

The focus on listening rather than giving orders and proposing solutions is captured in the Zapatista phrase 'asking we walk'. This principle defines a process and a method rather than an end goal. As already indicated, this approach to social change differs widely from the one promoted by revolutionary movements of the 20th century, which in the majority of cases proceeded with a well defined recipe for how to obtain their objectives. The principle of 'asking we walk' clearly reflects the essentially democratic character of the Zapatistas. Democracy is seen not only as an end, but also as an integral part of the process of social change and it is a perspective that makes it impossible to predefine the path of social struggle or revolution and to think of a defined point of arrival.[32] What is argued is not that the Zapatistas do not have long-term strategies and concrete goals, as demonstrated for example in the struggle for constitutional reform in the area of indigenous rights. This definition, however, constantly 'overflows, thematically and politically. The definition of indigenous rights is seen not as an end-point, but as a start, as a basis for moving on into other areas of change, but also as a basis for taking the movement forward, a basis for breaking out.'[33] Had the Zapatistas limited themselves to the quest for indigenous autonomy, the transnational resonance would have been much less significant. The fundamental vision of the Zapatistas is, in other words, not to create a new identity or affirm an old identity in a negative manner by establishing a 'them' and 'us' dichotomy.[34] The indigenous people and the Zapatistas are instead transformed into a universal symbol of exclusion and oppression. This is done in a way that invokes a global consciousness and opens the way to a solidarity allowing a variety of social struggles to articulate their particularity in a manner that simultaneously asserts and transcends identity.[35]

'A world in which many worlds fit'

The concept of dignity, which is a recurring theme in the Zapatista discourse, is the key to understanding this process. The power of the concept of dignity has not come from the urban intellectual element of the Zapatistas, but from the indigenous communities and their century-long tradition of resistance. While dignity is the right to define and defend one's own identity, it is also much more than this. During their March for Indigenous Dignity in February/March 2001, the Zapatistas gave a number of speeches en route to Mexico City. In a message delivered in Puebla, the Zapatistas presented this definition of dignity, which clearly transcends the question of indigenous identity: 'Dignity is a bridge. It needs two sides that, being different, special, and distant, are united in the bridge without ceasing to be different and special, but ceasing to be distant ... Dignity demands that we are us. But dignity is not that we are only us. In order for dignity to exist, the other is necessary ... Dignity should be a world, a world in which many worlds fit.'[36] This latter expression is one of the Zapatistas' most well known. Through the establishment of a linkage between the notion of indigenous dignity and the desire for 'a world in which many worlds fit', the Zapatistas constantly transcends the particularity of the indigenous people and project their struggle into a universal and global arena. Only by turning the particular into something universal, and by envisioning an alternative form of globalisation rather than rejecting it altogether, have the Zapatistas succeeded in opening their movement to the outside and to many different currents on the Left and in the solidarity sector. Transnational support and solidarity for the Zapatistas would have been inconceivable, or at least much less conspicuous, had they opted for a predominantly defensive and nationalistic answer to the challenge of neoliberalism. This is not to suggest that the transnational attention has moved the Zapatistas away from the national and indigenous topics that sparked the movement. On the contrary, the main concern for the Zapatistas remains the question of indigenous rights and the critique of neoliberalism in Mexico. This critique is, moreover, often rooted in somewhat nationalistic terminology.[37] What is called for, then, is not some kind of global coalition of resistance dissolving national and cultural differences. The Zapatistas, instead, emphasise the value of national, local and cultural differences.

At the same time, however, the Zapatistas define a number of common global trends that are threatening the survival of these values. This threat, as discussed earlier, is often condensed in the concept of neoliberalism. Neoliberalism is considered to be anti-democratic because of its marginalising and excluding effects.[38] This also implies a critique of the liberal or electoral democratic model that characterises most of the world today.[39] The Zapatistas do not reject liberal democracy, but propose a radicalisation of liberal democracy that includes questions of socioeconomic inequalities and narrows the distance between people and decision-making structures. This critique is directed to the national level as well as to the democratic problems associated with the increasing number of decisions made by intergovernmental and largely unaccountable organisations such as the IMF, the World Trade Organization (WTO) and the World Bank. By formulating their critique of neoliberalism and democracy in democratic terms the Zapatistas have demonstrated awareness of the changed global political situation after the end of the Cold War, which means that social critiques not formulated in a democratic language have little resonance and legitimacy.

The democratic element, and its integration with a profound socioeconomic critique, is central to the Zapatistas and the solidarity network around them. In many ways this is also what marks the main difference between global solidarity and Third World solidarity. The latter form of solidarity, shaped as it was by the Cold War confrontation, tended to subsume democracy in other concerns and generally did not see democratic ideas as having a contentious potential. More than anything the Zapatistas are the proponents of a vision in which democracy and civil society are the main engines of a radical social change that fundamentally challenges contemporary economic and political arrangements and which takes place from below rather than from above, as envisioned by most radical and revolutionary groups during the Cold War.

While a democratic world-view does not necessarily rest on a global consciousness, this is indeed the case with the Zapatistas and the transnational solidarity network. The spacious, open and networked character of the Zapatistas and Zapatista solidarity is essentially global, not in the sense of erasing local and national differences, but in constructing the world as a whole. This is a world in which social problems in the rich and poor parts of the world, despite obvious and significant variations in their appearance and severity, are seen as part of the same processes and where solutions are consequently proposed from within the same radical democratic framework. The distinction between first, second and third worlds that was central to the theory and practice of solidarity with the Third World also rested on a global consciousness, but the conception of solidarity brought forward by the Zapatistas and by solidarity activists who support them and work with them suggests a new phase of transnational solidarity that is more genuinely global. This emerging global solidarity is a form of solidarity for which the distinction between first, second and third worlds is increasingly irrelevant.

The limits of global solidarity

The focus on global solidarity in this essay does not mean to suggest that forms of rights and material solidarity are not present within the solidarity network. Indeed, the Zapatistas are very much aware of the potential benefits of more traditional solidarity forms like rights and material solidarity, reflected for example in the numerous projects to improve infrastructure and educational facilities in Chiapas. Moreover, their concerns are visible in the more-or-less constant presence of human rights observers in Chiapas, as well as in the occasional visits by human rights observation delegations and their subsequent lobbying work directed at the Mexican government and the US and European governments. This indicates that the solidarity network displays a simultaneous presence of global and rights and material solidarity. This does not necessarily present a problem, and in many cases the different types of solidarity are in fact practised by the same activists. Nevertheless, the distinction does point to important fault lines within the solidarity network.[40]

While these differences should not be exaggerated, there are clearly internal limitations in relation to the development and future of global solidarity. But attention also need to be devoted to problems that have to do with the way global structural inequalities limit the potential of global solidarity. Up until this point, the concept of global solidarity has been presented as describing a situation in which distance becomes increasingly irrelevant and where globalisation has no obvious direction. Distance, however, should not be measured only in physical terms, but also in social and cultural terms. By including these parameters for measuring distance, we are also forced to realise a number of obstacles and limitations to global solidarity that in some ways contradict the arguments made so far and, at the same time, perhaps point to a continued relevance of the notion of the Third World. The world today, in other words, is not a level playing field where global citizens are free to enter and exchange ideas and solidarities. Those who take part in solidarity activities around the Zapatistas thus 'continue to be divided by cultural barriers, linguistic gaps, tactical differences, and radically different lifeworlds'.[41] Despite a strong presence of solidarity activists from other Latin American countries, the large majority of activists are based in the USA and Europe, while Africa and Asia are underrepresented, partly because of a lack of the communicative resources that are vital to all forms of transnational solidarity. A different angle on this situation is the fact that the dialogue between the Zapatistas and solidarity activists takes place almost exclusively through the educated leadership of the Zapatistas, most notable Subcomandante Marcos, and to a lesser extent between activists and 'ordinary' people in the Zapatista base communities.

These points also indicate some problems for current and future groups addressing issues of social change. The case of Zapatista solidarity demonstrates that it is becoming increasingly important for such groups to interpret and present their particular problems and issues in a way that gives them trans-national resonance. Often, the attraction of support and resources hinges on this ability. For groups operating under repressive local and national conditions, the ability to generate transnational support may be crucial for their survival. But obtaining this is no easy task, especially for those who have few resources in terms of technology and education. The Zapatistas have benefited significantly from the communication skills of Subcomandante Marcos, who has a cosmo-politan and well educated background that makes it easier to connect to a non-Mexican audience than it would have been, for example, for an indigenous peasant leader with little education and experience outside Mexico and Chiapas. Put differently, groups without a skilled communicator risk their messages never reaching beyond the local and national level. At the same time, there is a growing competition for transnational attention and support, as local and national groups increasingly attempt to give their struggles a transnational dimension.

On an even larger scale, events in the first years of the new millennium appear inhospitable for the further development of global solidarity. The 11 September terrorist attacks have given rise to a new world order where terrorism and the fight against it is the main priority. The major combatants in this confrontation both represent world-views that are fundamentally at odds with those of global solidarity activists. In many ways this situation has recreated the binary analysis that characterised the cold war period, limiting the room for manoeuvre for political action and subsuming democracy and human rights in security concerns. In this kind of world, however, the challenge for, and responsibility of, solidarity activists promoting the globalisation of democracy and the globalisation of dignity is more pertinent than ever.

Conclusion: globalizing the Zapatistas

Using the Zapatista case the common thread of this essay has been a sketch of an emerging, albeit fragile, global solidarity and the way it departs from earlier forms of solidarity. The resonance of the Zapatistas beyond their local and national origins is thus in large part explained by their ability to interpret their particular problems through a global framework that enables them to establish links, physical and mediated, to a wide variety of movements and struggles around the globe. This process, in turn, has been facilitated by a number of structural changes related to the end of the Cold War, but may also be constrained by the new world political situation created in the wake of 11 September.

But the idea of global solidarity may appear somewhat abstract and detached from the physical spaces in which human activity is mostly situated. Critics might even suggest that it expresses a normative ideal rather than an analytical concept, an example of the global thinking so typical of academics rooted in a cosmopolitan and Western Enlightenment tradition.[42] In anticipation of such critiques it is important to make it clear that the global solidarity concept does not intend, normatively or analytically, to paint a portrait of a world where states, cultures and identities are gradually dissolving. Global solidarity activities in fact often originate at the local and national level and revolve around cultural and identity characteristics tied to these spaces. What is argued, though, is that we are witnessing a growing imbrication of local, national and global spaces in a way that does not erase difference but leads to new social and political forms and expressions. From an academic point of view, overlooking this fact results, at best, in analyses of limited scope and, at worst, in flawed conclusions. From a political and normative point of view, the reification of the boundaries between local, national and global spaces, at best, overlook new transformative potentials and, at worst, involve social closures whose expressions are only too well known. What makes global solidarity global is consequently not a one-sided focus on the global as opposed to the local and national, but rather the attempt to mediate constantly between the local, the national and the global, although the emphasis obviously differs from time to time and from place to place.

Notes

[1]   The official name of the Zapatistas is *Ejército Zapatista de Liberación Nacional*, or EZLN (Zapatista Army of National Liberation).

[2] See T Olesen, *International Zapatismo: The Construction of Solidarity in the Age of Globalization*, London: Zed Books, forthcoming 2004.

[3] C Fuentes, 'Chiapas: Latin America's first post-communist rebellion', *New Perspectives Quarterly*, 11 (2), 1994.

[4] The description of the Zapatistas as armed democrats is inspired by A Touraine, 'Marcos, el demócrata armado', *La Jornada Semanal*, 22 December 1996.

[5] Of course, there are some partial exceptions to this, such as the way in which radical Third Worldism in the 1960s and 1970s had some impact on New Left thinking with regard to North American and Western European politics. See, for example, V Gosse, *Where the Boys Are: Cuba, Cold War America and the Making of a New Left*, London: Verso, 1993; and M. Elbaum, *Revolution in the Air: Sixties Radicals turn to Lenin, Mao and Che*, London: Verso, 2002.

[6] For an account of historical precursors to transnational activism, see ME Keck & K Sikkink, *Activists Beyond Borders: Advocacy Networks in International Politics*, Ithaca, NY: Cornell University Press, 1998; and Keck & Sikkink, 'Historical precursors to modern transnational social movements and networks', in JA Guidry, MD Kennedy & MN Zald (eds), *Globalizations and Social Movements: Culture, Power, and the Transnational Public Sphere*, Ann Arbor, MI: University of Michigan Press, 2000.

[7] GW Seidman, 'Adjusting the lens: what do globalizations, transnationalism, and the anti-apartheid movement mean for social movement theory?', in Guidry *et al*, *Globalizations and Social Movements*, p 344.

[8] For a more detailed discussion, see T Olesen, 'The struggle inside democracy: towards a global solidarity?', paper presented at the European Sociological Association conference, Murcia, Spain, 23–26 September 2003.

[9] R Robertson, *Globalization: Social Theory and Global Culture*, London: Sage, 1992, p 183; and R Cohen & P Kennedy, *Global Sociology*, Basingstoke: Macmillan, 2000, p 35.

[10] One of the most striking examples of this thinking is the adoption of the Universal Declaration of Human Rights in 1948. For a description and analysis of international non-governmental organizations (INGOs) in the latter half of the 20th century, see K Sikkink & J Smith, 'Infrastructures for change: transnational organizations, 1953–93', in S Khagram, JV Riker & K Sikkink (eds), *Restructuring World Politics: Transnational Social Movements, Networks, and Norms*, Minneapolis, MN: University of Minnesota Press, 2002.

[11] AC Drainville, 'The fetishism of global civil society: global governance, transnational urbanism and sustainable capitalism in the world economy', in MP Smith & LE Guarnizo (eds), *Transnationalism from Below*, New Brunswick: Transaction Publishers, 1998, p 47; P Waterman, *Globalization, Social Movements and the New Internationalisms*, London: Mansell, 1998, p 236; and P Cheah, 'The cosmopolitical—today', in Pheng Cheah & Bruce Robbins (eds), *Cosmopolitcs: Thinking and Feeling beyond the Nation*, Minneapolis, MN: University of Minnesota Press, 1998.

[12] M De Angelis, 'Globalization, new internationalism and the Zapatistas', *Capital & Class*, 70, 2000, p 11.

[13] Drainville, 'The fetishism of global civil society', p 47.

[14] D Rucht, 'Distant issue movements in Germany: empirical description and theoretical reflections', in Guidry *et al*, *Globalizations and Social Movements*, p 81.

[15] Seen from the perspective of activists in the country where rights violations are taking place, the ability to mobilise other governments as well as intergovernmental organisations to exert pressure on their national governments is described by Keck & Sikkink, *Activists Beyond Borders*, as a boomerang pattern.

[16] *Ibid*, p 27.

[17] F Passy, 'Political altruism and the solidarity movement', in M Giugni & F Passy (eds), *Political Altruism? Solidarity Movements in International Perspective*, Lanham, MD: Rowman and Littlefield, 2001, p 8.

[18] T Risse & K Sikkink, 'The socialization of international human rights norms into domestic practices: introduction', in Risse & Sikkink (eds), *The Power of Human Rights: International Norms and Domestic Change*, Cambridge: Cambridge University Press, 1999.

[19] What is interesting about solidarity work is that, to some extent, it breaks down rational choice-inspired explanations of why people participate in collective action. In other words, engaging in solidarity activities cannot be expected to lead to personal benefits in a more narrow sense. This challenge is especially evident with regard to transnational variants of solidarity work, where distances between those who offer solidarity and those who benefit from it are considerable in physical as well as in social and cultural terms. Rucht, 'Distant issue movements in Germany', p 79.

[20] I Eterovic & J Smith, 'From altruism to a new transnationalism? A look at transnational social movements', in Guigny & Passy, *Political Altruism?*, p 198.

[21] Waterman, *Globalization, Social Movements and the New Internationalisms*, p 235; and Eterovic & Smith, 'From altruism to a new transnationalism?', p 198.

[22] U Beck, *What Is Globalization?*, Cambridge: Polity Press, 2000.

[23] A Melucci, 'Third World or planetary conflicts?', in SE Alvarez, E Dagnino & A Escobar (eds), *Cultures of Politics, Politics of Culture: Revisioning Latin American Social Movements*, Boulder, CO: Westview Press, 1998.

[24] Brian Dominick, interview, e-mail received November 2000.

[25] Justin Paulson, interview, e-mail received October 2001.

[26] As a result of the coincidence between the uprising and the coming into force of the North American Free Trade Agreement (NAFTA) such an analysis was, however, already indirectly present from the first days of the uprising and served to create an immediate link between the Zapatistas and struggles against NAFTA in Canada and the USA. HM Cleaver, 'Introduction', in Cleaver, *Zapatistas: Documents of the New Mexican Revolution (December 31, 1993–June 12, 1994)*, New York: Autonomedia, 1994, p 21; and C Bob, 'Marketing rebellion: insurgent groups, international media, and NGO support', *International Politics* 38 (1), 2001.

[27] G Garcia Márquez & R Pombo, 'Habla Marcos', *Revista Cambio*, 28 March 2001, available at www.cambio.com.co/web/interior.php?idp = 21&ids = 1&ida = 898. The article is an interview with Sub-comandante Marcos, the primary spokesman for the Zapatistas.

[28] C Monsivaïs & H Bellinghausen, 'Marcos a Fox: Queremos garantías; no nos tragamos eso de que todo cambió', *La Jornada*, 8 January 2001. Interview with Subcomandante Marcos.

[29] Y Le Bot, *El sueño zapatista*, Barcelona: Plaza y Janés, 1997, p 142. The book is mainly an interview with Zapatista commanders, including Subcomandante Marcos.

[30] N Higgins, 'The Zapatista uprising and the poetics of cultural resistance', *Alternatives*, 25 (3), 2000, p 364.

[31] Subcomandante Marcos, quoted in J Holloway, 'Dignity's revolt', in J Holloway & E Peláez (eds), *Zapatista! Reinventing Revolution in Mexico*, London: Pluto Press, 1998, p 163.

[32] Holloway, 'Dignity's revolt', 1998, p 165.

[33] *Ibid*, p 173.

[34] J Holloway, 'La resonancia del zapatismo', *Revista Chiapas*, 3, 1996.

[35] This is perhaps most evident in the now famous response from Subcomandante Marcos to a question concerning his sexuality: 'Marcos is a gay in San Francisco, a black in South Africa, an Asian in Europe, a Chicano in San Isidro, a Palestinian in Israel, an indigenous person in the streets of San Cristóbal ... In other words, Marcos is a human being in this world. Marcos is every untolerated, oppressed, exploited minority that is resisting and saying "Enough!" ' Quoted in J Holloway & E Peláez, 'Introduction: reinventing revolution', in Holloway & Peláez, *Zapatista!*, p 10.

[36] EZLN, 'Palabras del EZLN el 27 de febrero del 2001 en Puebla, Puebla', 2001, available at www.ezln.org/marcha/20010227b.es.htm.

[37] J Johnston & G Laxer, 'Solidarity in the age of globalisation: lessons from the anti- MAI and Zapatista struggles', *Theory and Society*, 32 (1), 2003, p 70.

[38] EZLN, 'Primera declaración de la realidad', 1996, available at www.ezln.org/ documentos/1996/19960130.es.htm.

[39] EZLN, 'Communiqué', 2000, available at www.ezln.org/documentos/2000/ 20000619.es.htm.

[40] Differences persist for example between those working from an anarchistic and highly politicised perspective and those based in more traditional rights solidarity: 'Day by day the European network is becoming an ever more bureaucratically organised humanitarian aid organisation, that will do *anything* in the aid of the good cause ... The main focus of the European solidarity network has become putting pressure on the European Union and Parliament not to accept the preferential treatment treaty between the European Union and the Mexican government. The other focus is to pressure the United Nations to intervene in Chiapas (as either a mediator or human rights observer). Both the European Union and the United Nations are instruments of the governments of the world, and we see no reason to ask them favours. Asking them for favours is to passively accept their authority and existence. We do not accept that and never will.' J ten Dam, 'Solidarity at all cost? On the lack of criticism in the solidarity movement with the Zapatistas', 1999, available at www.noticias.nl/prensa/zapata/dissolve.htm.

[41] J Johnston, 'We are all Marcos? Zapatismo, solidarity and the politics of scale', in G Laxer & S Halperin (eds), *Global Civil Society and Its Limits*, Basingstoke: Palgrave, 2003, pp 97–98.

[42] For an argument along these lines, see G Esteva & MS Prakash, *Grassroots Post-Modernism: Remaking the Soil of Cultures*, London: Zed Books, 1998.

Index

Page references to Endnotes will have the letter 'n' following the number

For Product Safety Concerns and Information please contact our EU
representative GPSR@taylorandfrancis.com Taylor & Francis Verlag GmbH,
Kaufingerstraße 24, 80331 München, Germany

Batch number: 08153807

Printed by Printforce, the Netherlands